A Documentary
History of
AMERICAN
INTERIORS

From the Colonial Era to 1915

A Documentary History of
AMERICAN INTERIORS

From the Colonial Era to 1915

Edgar de N. Mayhew & Minor Myers, jr.

CHARLES SCRIBNER'S SONS · NEW YORK

Copyright © 1980 Edgar de Noailles Mayhew and Minor Myers, jr.

Library of Congress Cataloging in Publication Data

Mayhew, Edgar de Noailles, 1913–
   A documentary history of American interiors.

   Bibliography: p.
   Includes index.
   1. Interior decoration—United States—History.
2. Decoration and ornament—United States. I. Myers,
Minor, 1942–   joint author. II. Title.
NK2002.M39   747.213   80–11744
ISBN 0–684–16293–8

1 3 5 7 9 11 13 15 17 19   Q/C   20 18 16 14 12 10 8 6 4 2

Printed in the United States of America

Acknowledgments

Obviously, many people have been involved in the completion of this volume, but we would like to take note of several whose contributions and help have been especially valuable. We would like to mention the late Mr. William P. Campbell of the National Gallery in Washington; Mrs. Nina Fletcher Little of Brookline, Massachusetts; Mr. Richard Nylander of the Society for the Preservation of New England Antiquities in Boston and his wife, Mrs. Jane Nylander of Old Sturbridge Village. Much of the information on the Southwest was provided by Mrs. Mary F. Ward, historian of the City of San Diego Parks and Recreation Department, and Mr. John M. Cahoon, archivist of the Natural History Museum, Los Angeles County.

Mention should also be made of Mrs. Marion R. Shepard of the Lyman Allyn Museum, New London, who has typed hundreds of inquiries, letters, and requests for information; Mr. Louis S. Martel of the Lyman Allyn Museum staff, who has made innumerable photographs; Miss Helen Aitner of the Connecticut College Library, who has located many rare and elusive volumes; Mr. John P. Burnham, curator of coins at Yale University, for answers to numismatic questions; Mrs. Ellen A. Myers, who helped with the manuscript; and research assistants Miss Jean Ann Maxwell, Miss Alison Holland, and Miss Elizabeth S. Pictor. Special thanks are due also to Mrs. Patricia Gallagher, our editor at Charles Scribner's Sons.

Edgar deN. Mayhew
Minor Myers, jr.

Contents

Foreword

A T the center of American life from the beginning to the present has been the
family in that orderly, secure, and private place called home. "The true
character of Americans is mirrored in their homes," commented Moreau de Saint-
Méry in his *American Journey* in the 1790s.

During the past decade, the social history of the American family has emerged
as a field of research and writing for scholars from a variety of disciplines; yet,
somewhat inexplicably, the cultural history of the home and its interior arrangements has languished, in part, by the intractability of the materials. To understand
the massive transformations in family history is to appreciate the dramatic
changes in the home, as it became less a center of economic production with the
decline of family farms and handcrafts of the cottage industry and more a place
of cultural transmission and family community.

In Victorian society there was a weakening of paternal authority as the
mother became the guardian of manners and morals when the father left home
to work in the factory. Here in the home the woman was recognized as the high
priestess of moral, religious, and other cultural values; here children were in-
doctrinated with the proper values before being sent forth to make their way in
a rapidly changing, and sometimes terrifying and intimidating world. Victorians
acknowledged this with their "cult of domesticity," replacing the "cult of in-
feriority" in preindustrial society.

With versatile and prolific illustrations, and with lucid and readable quotations, Edgar Mayhew and Minor Myers have provided a useful panoramic over-
view in their evocative book of the interior arrangements of the American home.
Historians who have traditionally viewed the decorative arts with condescension
would do well to examine this model combination of history and the decorative
arts. This freshly researched, elegantly written, and finely argued book should
become a classic; by its sharp focus on the American home, this calmly reasonable
book makes a tremendous impression in its reconstruction of the past.

Wendell Garrett

Preface

WHY another heavily illustrated book on American interiors? Already in print are Harold L. Peterson's *Americans at Home*, covering the years before 1870, and William Seale's *The Tasteful Interlude*, offering many Victorian interiors. Also available are such handy guides as Helen Comstock's *American Furniture* and her *Concise Encyclopedia of American Antiques*. But none of these volumes has done what we attempt to do here.

We portray the American interior as it appears from the days of the first European settlements in the early seventeenth century to 1915. Drawing from research conducted in the last fifty years, we describe the contents and arrangement of American rooms as they evolve through a diversity of historic styles. In addition to recent books and articles (especially those in *The Magazine Antiques*, which we have surveyed in its entirety), we have relied on pattern books, household guides, diaries, letters, estate inventories, period advertisements, and surviving artifacts to provide solid documentation on the contents of period interiors.

We have depended on paintings, prints, and drawings to determine the manner in which the furnishings were actually arranged. On the Continent it was customary for people with attractive homes to have water colors or drawings made to record their interiors visually; unfortunately, this tradition was not as common in the United States. Thanks to a generous grant from the American Philosophical Society of Philadelphia in 1966, an archive began to be assembled of whatever illustrations of American interiors might be found. Over 700 possible sources were contacted by letter or personal visit, including museums, historical societies, galleries, and private collectors, in hopes of unearthing visual material that had not previously been well known. The total number of photographs amassed is about 1,500, and this archival record is now permanently housed at the Lyman Allyn Museum in New London, Connecticut.

In this volume we present 241 black-and-white pictures and 32 color plates, supplemented by cuts representing each style. Illustrations are difficult to find for the early periods, but after the mid-nineteenth century hundreds of pictures can be found for each style. We have tried to select those pictures that illustrate the most important points of each. Many have been published before; others have not. In the text and notes we have often referred to other illustrations as an aid to those seeking further details on specific periods. The Bibliography likewise provides basic books offering particulars of styles and decorative arts. Research on regional styles continues apace, and those interested in authentic local materials and fashions are advised to consult nearby museums or historical societies.

In analyzing pictures and data, we have tried to provide comprehensive answers to questions that have vexed restorationists since the turn of the century. Consider the illustration of Mount Vernon as it appeared about 1900 (Fig. 140). Presumably the curators wanted to present the house as it appeared in General Washington's time, but as they later found out, they made many mistakes. Not only are the furniture and the mirrors too late for the general's time, but the furnishings are arranged in a Victorian, and not a Federal manner. The late nineteenth century displayed pictures on the floor; the eighteenth century did not. Similarly, the rooms were painted with nineteenth- and not eighteenth-century colors.

But does simply installing Chippendale or Federal furniture of the best quality in a Chippendale or Federal house achieve a more accurate restoration? It depends upon whose house is being restored and where.

In his book *Early American Furniture*, John T. Kirk differentiated among high style, country, primitive, and rustic furniture. We think similar distinctions can be applied to American interiors.

According to Kirk, high style pieces were inspired directly by European design and sometimes made by European immigrants. Country furniture displayed fine cabinet work that was modeled after high style domestic pieces rather than European originals. Primitive pieces drew on both high style and country models, but combined elements of several styles with a free, less disciplined eclecticism. High style was usually found in the major cities, country pieces in the towns, and primitive examples everywhere. Rustic furniture was "simply joined together in the most rudimentary fashion," and reflected necessity more than any discernible style.

Virtually every period has what could be called high style interiors. Numerous advertisements reveal that many immigrant craftsmen announced they worked in London styles, and orders show that Americans were eager to follow British fashions as closely as they could, often without even knowing what they were. From the mid-seventeenth century on, there developed a hunger for fashionable furnishings among wealthy Americans, and it never stopped.

High style rooms in turn were emulated in smaller towns or rural settings where the details of the style were less reflective of the originals. One might find, too, comparable primitive interiors in which elements of various periods were mixed with unrestrained enthusiasm. Rustic interiors were common on the frontier and became fashionable only toward the end of the nineteenth century.

In the countryside, furniture and decoration modes survived for decades after fashionable urbanites had rejected them. The Pennsylvania Germans continued to make Chippendale bride chests until the 1840s, and the German settlers in Missouri produced late Empire and Victorian Classical designs well into the 1860s.

One focus we have tried to keep constantly before the reader is the economic status of householders. A poor resident of Newport or a farmer of small means in nearby Tiverton would not own the most elaborate secretary John Goddard produced, yet occasionally one finds such anomalies in restorations. We try to indicate where possible not only the choices available to the wealthy of a city and outlying town, but also what was attainable by moderate- and low-income families in each area. All too often, books on antiques and decoration have been written as though every house in America were furnished by Thomas Affleck or Duncan Phyfe. Such clearly was not the case. But it is the poor who are hardest to document. Artists painted few pictures of them in their rooms, and their heirlooms are of intrinsically less value to collectors, and less worth keeping to their families.

In studying each style, we have looked at a diversity of decorative elements. For each period we have examined the furniture, floor coverings, pictures and mirrors, textiles, wall treatment, architectural details and ceilings, lighting, color schemes, and accessories. We have used the term "accessories" to refer to brass, ceramics, glass, iron, pewter, silver, tin, and wooden ware, whether used for decorative or for more utilitarian purposes.

In many ways the furniture determines the general appearance of a style, but the other elements of a room do much to reinforce the basic characteristics found in the furniture. Thus, Gothic furniture was accompanied by Gothic wallpaper, architecture, and fabrics with Gothic designs. But Figure 79, for example, depicts a room that is strongly Gothic despite its furniture of another style.

To aid the reader in understanding the economics of interiors, we have added details about the prices of furnishings where we have been able to discern them from bills of sale, price lists, advertisements, or inventories.

Our survey ends at 1915, that classic terminal date that marks the great watershed at which World War I transformed western civilization. Paradoxically, however, by that date Elsie de Wolfe and those who shared her views had created a look that still survives.

A Documentary
History of
AMERICAN
INTERIORS

From the Colonial Era to 1915

1

The Early Seventeenth Century

1607–1675

THE common image of early Pilgrim settlements is still one of rude primitivism, yet it is clear from documents and inventories that Puritan New Englanders and Anglican Virginians introduced into their homes a refined stylishness as soon as practicable.

New England settlers received advice on what to carry out with them from England. Edward Winslow suggested bringing clothes, bedding, guns, paper, linseed oil for windows, and yarn for lamps. By the end of the 1620s, émigrés were advised to bring glass.[1]

By the 1640s, some New Englanders were living in moderate luxury; for example, Governor Theophilus Eaton of the New Haven colony owned an estate that amounted to a considerable £1,515.12.6.*[2] His hall, one of the few without a bed, was filled with tables, chairs, stools, and a court cupboard. The tables were covered with two Turkey carpets (£2), and there was his own "great chair with needlework" (13/4). A clock and candlestick were valued together at £3.12.6.

The parlor was a sleeping room with bed, trundle bed, livery cupboard, several stools, and a great chair. The governor had a study and a counting room, containing his books, a map, a globe, and £107 worth of silver. Downstairs, there was also a buttery and a kitchen that housed 253 pounds of pewter, three brass and five iron kettles and pots.

Following English style, the fabrics of some but not all bedrooms were of uniform color, and Governor Eaton had a green and a blue chamber. In Mrs. Eaton's chamber, however, the colors were mixed. His wife's room had "window"

The Theophilus Eaton House

---

* Throughout the Colonial period, transactions were figured in the English monetary system in which one pound (£1) equaled 20 shillings, and one shilling (1s.) equaled 12 pence (d.). Three shillings, six pence was abbreviated 3/6, the usage we have followed. Using the old gold standard in which an ounce of gold was worth $35, the mid-eighteenth-century pound was worth roughly $10.

curtains, but three other bedrooms had "hangings about the chamber," worth £2.15.0 in one of the rooms. These hangings were probably tapestries.

In the South, Nathaniel Butler, who produced his *Unmasked Face of our Colony in Virginia* in 1622, thought the poorest English cottages more sightly and comfortable than Virginia houses, which he called the "worst in the world."[3] The governor and Council responded that Virginia houses were for use rather than ornament and that those of the workingmen were better than the homes of workers in England. Persons of means, however, lived in much better houses, the Council claimed, and Butler's criticisms were unjustified. Already there was considerable disparity in construction and furnishing, for the records show that although one Virginia house was built at a cost of £20, another for Adam Dixon in 1622 had cost £100.[4] However, sturdy brick construction began soon after. John Hammond described a typical Virginia house in *Leah and Rachel* (1656): "Pleasant in their building, which although for the most part they are but one story beside the loft and built of wood, yet contrived so delightful that your ordinary houses in England are not so handsome, for usually the rooms are large, daubed and whitelimed, glazed and flowered, and if not glazed windows, shutters are made very pretty . . ."[5]

Virginia had become luxurious for some by the 1640s. To furnish but one chamber, a court allowed the widow of the wealthy Captain Adam Thoroughgood (1602–1640) a bed with appropriate linens and blankets, a table with a carpet, a cupboard and cupboard cloth, six chairs, six stools, six cushions, and a wicker child's chair. Implements included a pewter basin and ewer, a warming pan, a bedpan, andirons, shovel, and tongs. But there was real and unusual luxury in "six pictures hanging in the chamber" and in the silver that would adorn the cupboard: one saltcellar, one bowl, one tankard, one wine cup, and one dozen spoons. She also had iron knives and forks at a time when forks were rare even in England.[6]

By mid-century, E. Williams in *Virginia Truly Valued* was advising prospective settlers to bring canvas for sheets, bed rugs, blankets, a great iron pot, large and small kettles, skillets, frying pans, gridiron, spit, platters, dishes, spoons, and knives. In Virginia, as in New England, furniture could be provided by local craftsmen.[7]

New York settlements were influenced by the Dutch, and there, too, primitive earlier structures were followed by fashionable houses and furnishings for those who could afford them. The Dutch settlement, with access to the East India trade, had Oriental furniture, fabrics, and ceramics not commonly found in the English colonies.[8]

As in the later periods, those who had sufficient wealth looked to England for furniture and other decorative items, and the homes of governors, a few knights like Sir Christopher Gardiner, or the daughters or sisters of noblemen who ventured here,[9] as well as those of wealthy traders, were showplaces reflecting the latest European styles. In New England and Virginia, style was valued and emulated, and the rich were conscious of its fluctuations. About 1658, Colonel Richard Lee of Virginia took 200 ounces of silver to London to have it melted down and remade in order "to change the fashion."[10] Those with estates of £1,000 could furnish a house well, and those with more than £2,000 could furnish it luxuriously. The largest early estate we have found was that of Henry Shrimpton of Boston, who left £12,000 in 1666.

As in all periods that follow, the most stylish furnishings were confined to the homes of the wealthy. Houses of the poor remained simple and undecorated, and it might be years before new styles evident in more expensive items were transformed into subtle details of inexpensive pieces. In 1630, the skilled worker in Plymouth received 16d. a day or £20.13.4 for a 310-day work year. Such a man could ill afford looking glasses, silver, or tapestries, and inventories of the poor record little more than minimum basic furniture.

Table 1, below, presents the distribution of wealth in selected communities during the period. Only 3 to 11 percent of the householders could be counted among the wealthy. In 1643 in New Haven, 10 out of 122 householders had estates of £1,000 or more. Governor Eaton's was the largest at £3,000, and the other nine were listed at £1,000 even. Generally, the percentage of householders in the poorest group diminished as the century went on.

Seventeenth-century houses followed a somewhat similar evolution in the North and South, and, consequently, so did the function and decor of the rooms composing their interiors.

After a brief period in which the colonists built wigwams in Virginia and New England, "fair" houses began to appear,[12] following medieval designs the settlers had known in England. The earliest houses were one and one-half- or two-story structures with one room per story. The first-floor hall or common room was furnished for cooking, sleeping, and dining. A stairway led to a sleeping chamber above.

The second stage of construction introduced a two-room design, with chambers (bedrooms) over both the hall and the parlor. The hall continued to be the primary locus of family activity, with the parlor reserved for receiving important visitors. Both the parlor and the hall usually contained beds, with the better beds in the parlor. Late in the century, beds were sometimes lacking from either room, but not likely both.

A third stage of development brought new rooms to the house. Through the lean-to addition favored in New England or the lengthened construction more prominent in the South, the householder acquired a kitchen, which allowed cooking activities to move from the hall. This stage also often brought an additional first-floor bedroom and a buttery or storage room. Some houses went through all three stages as owners expanded them, but simple houses that were little more than a hall and chamber were still being built by the poor at the end of the century.

The Roger Mowry House in Rhode Island, a typical one-room design

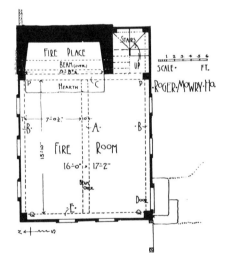

Floor plan of the Mowry House

Table 1. Size of Estates Figured in Pounds of Each Colony[11]
(figures are percentages of inventories falling into each category)

	£0–50	51–100	101–200	201–400	401–800	801+
HARTFORD COUNTY, CONN., 1650–80	18%	14	25	23	12	8
NEW HAVEN COLONY, 1643	33	12	12	17	18	8
MAINE, 1662–85	14	16	32	19	8	11
ESSEX COUNTY, MASS., 1635–55	28	24	24	17	4	3
NEW JERSEY, 1670–85	33	23	19	19	6	0
NEW HAMPSHIRE, 1639–75	17	19	30	24	7	3

FURNITURE

So far as one can tell from the few surviving specimens, the earliest American furniture followed English and European prototypes closely. Early craftsmen copied the basic lines of the Jacobean style, with its carved panel decorations, turnings applied to plane surfaces, and heavy turned legs. Often, these men reproduced stylistic variations from their home towns in England.

Simple chests and book boxes might be decorated and made more expensive through incised carving. Carver and Brewster chairs were turned, and, like the wainscot chair, were considered seats of honor and authority. Chairs with leather seats appeared in America by 1675, and the first rocking chairs date between 1650 and 1700. (Rockers were not considered elegant.)[13] Stools or benches without backs were more common than chairs in many houses.

Beds were either low post or the more expensive high post. Tables of oak frames with long, removable pine tops were common in cramped quarters, but more formal houses had oak stretcher tables with finely turned legs. The combination chair-table dates at least to the 1630s, and was readily adaptable to many purposes.

Early in the period, the simple six-board chest stored clothes, linens, and virtually anything else that needed a safe place, but later in the century more luxurious chests developed. The court cupboard was elaborate and expensive, offering a place to display and store utensils and ornaments, while the press cupboard provided equally ornate storage for clothing. Near Hampton, New Hampshire, court cupboards were made as late as 1720. Standing or hanging livery cupboards were found in few New England houses. Spice cabinets appeared late in the period.

Typically, the parlor in a house of moderate means included the best bed in the house, perhaps a trundle bed, one or two chests, a table, chairs or stools, and possibly a cradle. The hall usually contained a table with stools, benches, and chairs for dining. High-backed wooden settles, and occasionally a bed, were also found within the hall. A parlor without beds appeared in 1676 in Massachusetts in an estate of considerable wealth (£1,402), but the house also had a "little parlor" that contained two beds.

If a house had a kitchen, cooking equipment would naturally be found there. Without a kitchen, such utensils were in the hall.

Second-floor chambers were used for sleeping, domestic chores, dining, and storage. Rarely did a chamber lack a bed, but it was often only a low post or a trundle bed. Occasionally, flax or miscellaneous farm tools accompanied the usual chests and cupboards. By 1675, in stylish parlor chambers one might find a bed, two chests, a cupboard, and chairs or stools for as many as eleven. The well-furnished chamber might also include a close-stool and pan and a looking glass.

As American pictures of this era provide no clues to furniture placement, one must turn to European sources. Dutch pictures, the most useful, show the center of rooms as notably bare, with furniture placed against the walls, unless brought toward the center of the room for a specific purpose. Even then, it was moved only so far from the wall as was necessary to serve the purpose. Several pictures show tables and chairs or benches huddled along a fireplace wall or an outside wall.[14]

Massachusetts press cupboard

FLOOR COVERINGS

Early seventeenth-century floors were bare. Inventories mention carpets (sometimes quite valuable), but they were almost always table or cupboard coverings rather than floor coverings. However, portraits of the English royal family and nobility show Oriental rugs used as floor coverings early in the century.[15]

The inventory of John Whittingham of Ipswich, Massachusetts (1648), listed the furnishings of a chamber as silver worth £25 and a screen (10/-), wall hangings (£2), and "one Carpett £3.10.0." That carpet was not listed in association with the usual table or chest but with the pipe tongs, as though near the fireplace. In the kitchen chamber, along with parcels of cloth, was "6 yds. Carpeting £1.4.0." If a large, 6-yard piece was worth £1.4.0, one wonders whether the £3.10.0 carpet was of a different material or a much larger piece of the same. In any event, it is possible that this fashionable man who still owned land in England, and who had the second recorded set of window curtains in Essex County, may have had a floor carpet.[16]

PICTURES AND MIRRORS

Although European paintings reveal walls with pictures and maps hung on them, the inventories suggest that American walls were virtually bare. Pictures were almost unknown before 1700, except in the houses of the wealthy few who could afford to have their portraits painted.

Looking glasses appeared in moderate number by mid-century. In a few cases, mirrors were listed as "large" or "gret," but generally they seem to have been small and worth between 2 and 10 shillings. These early glasses probably had simple molded frames. Mirrors were usually found in the parlor or hall but sometimes in the chambers. Before 1675, it was rare for a house to contain more than one looking glass, and multiple mirrors were unusual even after that date.

TEXTILES

Fabrics played a far less important role in the seventeenth-century interior than they would in the following two centuries. Window curtains and richly upholstered furniture were notably lacking in the early period, but what few fabrics were evident added a bright note of color.

Turned chairs, joined stools, and settees offered no opportunity for upholstery beyond seat cushions. Continental prints and paintings show models of such simple cushions, often ornamented with tassels.[17] Virtually the only upholstered furniture was the leather seat chair, which appeared in inventories of those households of at least moderate means toward the end of the period.

Bed hangings undoubtedly received lavish treatment, for they were among the most valuable items in inventories. Unfortunately, no examples of seventeenth-century American work survive, and again one must be guided by Continental prints and paintings. A complete furnishing for a high post bedstead would include curtains and valances plus an assortment of bed rugs, blankets, and coverlets (£2 to £3).

Decorative fabrics were also evident on tables. Table carpets have already been mentioned (under Floor Coverings), but more common in inventories were tablecloths, items worth about 6 shillings. Often they were accompanied by napkins, worth 1 shilling each. Cupboards were likewise decorated with cupboard cloths and cushions in the well-appointed house.

In the uncommon instances where inventories mention fabrics, kersey and serge (varieties of wool), linen, and cotton are found most often. Sheets and pillowcases, tablecloths and napkins were usually of cotton or linen, while bed curtains and cushions were of wool.

Window curtains were very rare, but they did occur, generally in houses of the wealthy. Essex County probate records from 1635 to 1681 list only ten inventories with window curtains, the earliest in 1645. Early curtains were hung in pairs, sometimes on "rods" (note the plural), usually in the parlor, but sometimes in the hall or parlor chamber. Most of the estates with curtains were worth £175 or more.

Table linens likewise reflected degrees of wealth. Governor Winthrop had advised early settlers to bring linens, and some came lavishly supplied. He recorded one case in 1641: "A godly woman of the church of Boston, dwelling sometimes in London, brought with her a parcel of very fine linen of great value, which she set her heart too much upon, and had been at charge to have it all newly washed, and curiously folded and pressed, and so left it in press in her parlor over night. She had a Negro maid [who] went into the room very late, and let fall some snuff of the candle upon the linen, so as by morning all the linen was burned to tinder."[18]

The most elaborate display of linen was the "suit," a matching set of tablecloth, napkins, and side cloths. Tablecloths could be as long as 15 feet, depending upon the size of the table, and napkins, usually rectangular rather than square, might measure 42 by 29 inches. Napkins were vital to dining before the introduction of the table fork, new to England in 1611. Forks are known in America as early as 1640, but through 1681 Essex County inventories recorded none. In England and Europe, tablecloths and napkins were folded intricately in houses of taste, and the unfortunate lady of Boston was likewise having her linen "curiously folded." Fine linens were valuable and might account for as much as one-seventh of the value of household goods. Usually, linens were white or, occasionally, blue-striped.

WALL TREATMENT

In wooden houses, the most common wall treatment was wainscotting. Regional practices offered some variations, but in general exterior walls were wainscotted in horizontal boards, while interior walls were covered with vertical boards. Feather edging added refinement and expense.

Plaster or clay daubing can be dated to the 1640s in Connecticut and the 1650s in Virginia and Massachusetts, but the plastered or daubed wall remained relatively uncommon in New England. The lack of limestone deposits in tidewater Virginia, eastern Massachusetts, and Connecticut accounted for the use of clay daubing rather than lime plaster. (Lime produced in these areas was made from oyster shells.) Brick houses usually had daubed or plastered walls.

Throughout the colonies, wall surfaces included projecting corners of beams and posts. We know of no instances of wallpaper used in this period, but Governor Eaton of New Haven had tapestries on his walls.

ARCHITECTURAL DETAILS AND CEILINGS

In both North and South, seventeenth-century construction usually left the main ceiling beams exposed and decorated with chamfering, lamb's tongues, beading, or molding. In New England, the ceiling consisted of the entire exposed floor above, but in Virginia, the space between the main beams was sometimes plastered.

Doors throughout the colonies were made of vertical boards, sometimes decorated with molded or feathered edges. Staircases were narrow and steep. Martin S. Briggs has suggested a gradual evolution of stair design: first a stair encased with vertical boarding and no handrail; then a simple handrail with a square newel post; then a turned newel post, first with sawn, but by 1660 with turned balusters and molded handrail.[19]

Fireplaces in early houses were large, often 8 to 12 feet wide. In Virginia, hooded brick fireplaces were found in chambers and attics. Wenlocke Christison's house, built around 1670 in Talbot County, Maryland, contained a second-floor fireplace with a brick arch surmounted by a mantel shelf. Early large fireplaces were furnished with lugpoles rather than iron cranes.

LIGHTING

The fireplace provided an early basic source of light, and as late as the nineteenth century it was still the only source in some American houses.

Pine splints appeared by 1630. Rich in turpentine, these candlewood splints were placed on stones or pans near the chimney with no special brackets or holders. Use of such splints is documented in New England, Virginia, and the Dutch settlements.

Oil lamps, another source of light, did not appear often in inventories, but Francis Higginson (1630) wrote that the abundance of fish in New England provided "oil for lamps." Such lamps, called "Betty" lamps, would have been pans with supports for a cotton wick, usually made of iron and hung by a chair. G. Malcolm Watkins suggests that, like the English, the colonists were more inclined to use splints and candles than the oil lamps favored on the Continent.[20]

Candles were the preferred means of lighting, and in the early years they were also the most expensive. As late as 1634, lack of animals made it necessary to import tallow and candles. One candle sold for 4 pence—a considerable expense. By the middle of the century, domestic candle production was well under way.

The design of early candleholders is unclear, for examples traditionally thought to have been brought on the *Mayflower* are now dated at 1650. However, Jamestown archaeologists discovered a candlestick similar to that shown on the title page of *The Counter Scuffle* (Fig. 1, next page). A brass candlestick

A "Betty" lamp

dating before 1660 was unearthed on Cape Cod. It consists of the candle socket mounted on a saucer base with a long handle pierced by a hole for hanging. The 1652 inventory of a Boston merchant lists a dozen "wire" candlesticks, probably holders made from twisted iron. A variant of the candlestick was the lantern with its horn sheets for windows.

Candlesticks were generally collected together during the day to be carried into the chambers at night. Typical was the estate of the Reverend Peter Hobart of Hingham, Massachusetts (1678), with the seven candlesticks in a five-room house all collected in the buttery.[21]

COLOR

Green seems to have been the most popular choice of color in the seventeenth-century interior, at least if the Massachusetts records are indicative of colonial preferences in general. It was the color most frequently recorded for bed hangings and curtains, bed rugs, cushions for furniture, cupboard cloths, and painted

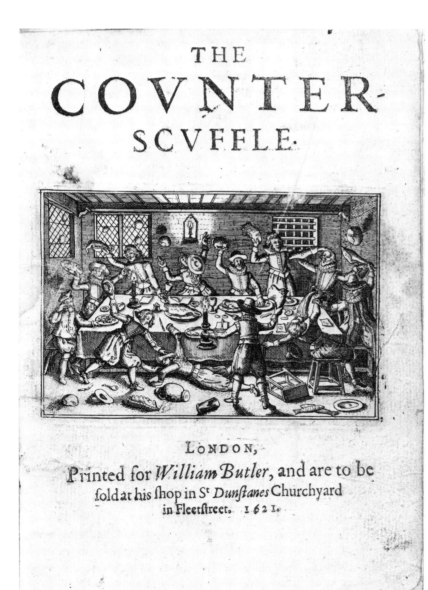

THE COVNTER-SCVFFLE.

LONDON,
Printed for *William Butler*, and are to be
fold at his fhop in St *Dunftanes* Churchyard
in Fleetftreet. 1621.

Figure 1. Artist unknown. Frontispiece engraving to *The Counter Scuffle* (London, 1621). Beinecke Rare Book and Manuscript Library, Yale University, New Haven, Conn.

This title page to a poem depicts an English table like those found in the colonies. Both the dress and pewter plates (rather than wooden trenchers) suggest a fairly high style mêlée. Each diner took what he wanted to eat or throw from a platter and cleaned his fingers with a napkin. The diners shared drinking vessels (goblets, jugs, and beakers), two knives and two spoons; there were no forks. All sat on benches or stools, except the man at the right who sat on a chair—not a popular furniture form at that time. Two candlesticks and a wall sconce provided light.

Figure 2. Title page engraving to Georg Philipp Harssdorfer, *Vollstandig Vermehrtes Trincir Buch* (Nuremberg, 1655). Beinecke Rare Book and Manuscript Library, Yale University, New Haven, Conn.

There is no evidence that Americans read Harssdorfer's book on carving and napkin folding, but American tables of the wealthy in 1655 probably looked similar. Unlike *The Counter Scuffle* (Fig. 1) of 1621, each guest had an individual plate. Knives appeared, spoons were absent, and forks were used only for carving. Four saltcellars surrounded the centerpiece, and guests shared glasses.[28] The tablecloth had been carefully folded (one of the arts taught in the book), and some Americans were quite particular about folding.

chairs. How bright these greens and other colonial colors were is unclear. American merchants wrote London suppliers that "sad" colors sold best, leaving little market for bright scarlet. Blue and yellow were the only other solid colors for bed hangings found in the 1650s and 1670s. Striped hangings were more popular early in the period than at the end. Somewhat distant seconds to green as the most popular color for bed rugs were red and blue, with white and yellow slightly less common. The only alternative to the green cupboard cloth was one of red and black in the 1670s. Red-painted chairs were almost as common as those in green, while blue made a strong appearance in the 1670s. Surviving examples show that chests and tables were likewise painted, and often carved or turned cabinetwork was decorated by red, white, and black paint.[22]

The wealthy followed English fashion in decorating each bedroom in a single color. Thus, Governor Theophilus Eaton had a chamber in which bed curtains and valances ("fringed and laced"), table carpets, cupboard cloths, and cushions were green. But not every fabric in the room matched. Some cushions were red, blankets were white, and there was a tapestry bed cover and carpet and Turkey work cushions. Another chamber was furnished in blue, but Mrs. Eaton's room presented a mixture of colors. Such color coordination was far from the minds of the poor, however.

ACCESSORIES

Accessories were limited to bare necessities in the houses of the poor. As one ascended the economic scale, accessories became more common and more valuable until one reached luxury in the homes of the very wealthy, who clearly used accessories as decoration.

Table service became more costly as the century moved on, and great changes are evident between *The Counter Scuffle* (1621) (Fig. 1) and the Harssdorfer title page (1652) (Fig. 2). These changes appear first in American houses of wealth, and only later in lesser estates.

Ceramics.   Ceramics were an important part of some early interiors, but not in every house, since for a time wood and pewter remained the most common table service. Both in the North and the South (from early in the century) domestic potters provided a limited production of inexpensive redware for daily household use: plates, bowls, mugs, jugs, dishes for cooking and baking, and milk pans. Inventories and archaeological evidence also reveal the presence of American Indian pottery in many seventeenth-century houses.

Imported wares supplemented domestic production. Most common was English and Dutch tin-glazed earthenware with blue decoration, generally known as Delft. In seventeenth-century America, Dutch ware predominated; posset pots, dated wine bottles, chargers, plates, and mugs were forms commonly imported. Sgrafitto ware with incised line decoration was another popular kind of earthenware. Archaeologists have discovered a rich diversity of imported ceramics. These discoveries together with notes on the forms and approximate dates of use are summarized in Table 2.

Current scholarship has revealed the presence of a few genuine Chinese porcelain drinking cups in mid-century Virginia, but generally very little found its way to the colonies. References to "Chany ware" in inventories refer to English majolica.

Most ceramics were confined to areas of food preparation. In early two-room houses they were found in the hall, while in the more elaborate buildings they were found in the kitchen or the buttery. Continental paintings and prints illustrate decorative placement of ceramics on court cupboards, and the parlor inventory of John Farrington of Dedham, Massachusetts (1676), lists four glass bottles, two stone jugs, and three gally pots in conjunction with a cupboard. "Gally ware" was an alternate term for plain tin-glazed majolica.

Clocks.   In an era when one might pay £20 for the construction of a house, a working clock was worth between £1 and £5, thus explaining why clocks, like silver, were confined to the houses of the wealthy. Essex County inventories covering 1635 to 1664 record only six clocks, and the people who owned them left estates of at least £227. From 1664 to 1681, only eight more clocks appear. These early clocks were wall or bracket clocks with pendulums (Fig. 5, page 22) or spring-driven table clocks. Where indication is given, the clocks were in the parlor.

A seventeenth-century Delft plate

Early Staffordshire plate by Thomas Toft

Table 2. Seventeenth-century Imported Ceramics

Medium	Origin	Form	Locus	Earliest Date
STONEWARE	Germany: Rhenish	bellarmine jugs: brown or gray	Maine, Mass., Va.	1640s
	Westerwald	jugs, ewers: blue and cream	Mass. Va.	1640s 1680s
DELFT	England: Bristol	vase	Va., S.C.	1680s
	Holland		Va.	
	Germany			
MAJOLICA	England: Southwark	pots, jugs, bottles, cups, saltcellar: purple sponge decoration	Va., Mass.	pre-1650
	Spain	bowls, platters, porringers	Va., Mass.	pre-1650
	Portugal: Lisbon	pans, bowls, dishes: pale blue and black; blue and white, Moorish designs	Va., Mass.	1644
EARTHENWARE	Italy	white slipware, sgraffito: designs of birds, flowers marbled slip with green or brown decoration	Va., Maine	pre-1650
	Spain or Portugal	two-handled bottles: cream with red decoration	Va.	pre-1650
	England: North Devon	chargers, jugs, plates, bowls, porringers, mugs: sgraffito, yellow glaze, white slip	Md., New England, Va.	1660s
	West Country	jugs: red with slip decoration	Va.	pre-1650
	Germany: Wanfried	redware with white designs of humans, animals, flowers	Va.	pre-1650
PORCELAIN	China	cup, blue decoration	Va.	c. 1650

Glass. Although American glassmaking began as early as 1608, the limited production in Virginia, Massachusetts, and New Amsterdam provided only a small part of the glass used in America—window glass, bottles, and possibly drinking glasses. Most glass was imported from England or the Continent, and Virginia archaeology has uncovered Venetian glass in the earliest settlements.

Bellarmine jug

In the early years, glass was relatively rare. Even the round, green wine bottle appeared in quantity only at mid-century, and bottles are notably absent in *The Counter Scuffle* (Fig. 1). Other than drinking glasses, from 1635 to 1664 the only table glass recorded in the Essex County, Massachusetts, inventories was one bowl. Later in the period, bottles appeared singly or in cases. These cases, worth from 5 to 13 shillings, are recorded variously as being in the hall, parlor, chambers, or even cellar.

Early Virginia sites have yielded lion mask stems, ladder stems, and, most common, inverted baluster stems. In sites dating to the third quarter of the century, Ivor Noel Hume excavated glasses with the same melon knop popular in London in the 1660s and 1670s. By the 1670s, Virginians were using the glass that George Ravenscroft had produced in England out of his newly developed flint glass.[23]

Glass seems to have been collected often in the kitchen, together with other items for preparing and serving food, but it was sometimes noted in the parlor or hall. In this early period, a single glass might be inventoried at 6 pence to 1 shilling. Fancy work cost more. Ravenscroft's[24] glass prices in London for his new flint glass in the 1670s were:

Beer glass, plain	1/6 @
Beer glass, diamond engraved	1/8 @
Claret glass, plain	1/- @
Claret glass, diamond engraved	1/3 @
Quart bottle, diamond engraved	4/- @

Soda glass ran about one-fifth the cost.

Pewter, Iron, Brass, and Tin.   Most metal accessories were kept in the kitchen or hall. If a house had a buttery, these items were sometimes divided between the buttery and cooking area. Iron was standard in every house, and most had some brass implements, but there were many houses with no pewter.

Pewter was important in houses of moderate means or better. In the early years, individual plates, trenchers, cups, or mugs were notably lacking in Pilgrim inventories, just as they were in *The Counter Scuffle* (Fig. 1). Only in the very best houses were there individual dishes. The most common items were "platters," which sometimes numbered as many as ten or eleven. Basins were common, often three to five to a household, and three or four porringers were standard. Less identifiable but common were pewter "dishes," which ranged in number from five to fifteen. Cups, plates, pint or quart mugs or cans, and candlesticks were much less common. A wide variety of items seldom appeared in pewter: chamber pots, saltcellars, flagons, fruit dishes, gill bottles, wine measures, sucking bottles, and tankards. The greater the wealth of the household, the more likely it was to have these less common and more luxurious items.

Most common in iron were pots, tongs, firepans, frying pans, skillets, spits, pothooks (or hakes), and trammels or adjustable pothooks. Only slightly less common were iron warming pans, gridirons, kettles, and dripping pans; not found in every house were chafing dishes, smoothing irons, skimmers, and shears.

In brass, it was usual for a house to have three brass kettles. Other common brass items were skillets, pans, and pots, but such pots were usually iron. Mortars and pestles occur often in brass; somewhat more unusual were skimmers, warming pans (iron was favored), spoons, and candlesticks.

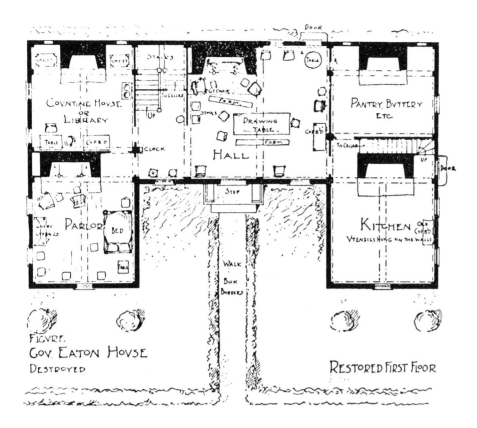

Figure 3. *Floor Plans, House of Governor Theophilus Eaton.* Isham and Brown, *Early Connecticut Houses*, pp. 101, 106; see Bibliography.

At his death in 1657, Theophilus Eaton of New Haven was the richest man in the colony. Using his inventory, Isham and Brown theorized the arrangement of rooms and produced not a seventeenth- but a nineteenth-century interior. Seventeenth-century prints show beds in corners, not standing at the middle of a wall, and unless in use, furniture was kept against the wall. Dutch prints commonly show draw tables placed beneath a window with a bench or form along the wall. Chairs and tables in use might be clustered around a fireplace, but otherwise the area in front of the fireplace was kept clear.

An early spoon

Tin occurred infrequently, although inventories record candlesticks, pans, saucers, and porringers. Similar to pewter were the uncommon Alcamy spoons. Alcamy was an alloy of copper and zinc, and late in the period, the English who produced these spoons in quantity plated some of them with tin.

Silver. Silver was comparatively rare. Only the wealthy had more than a piece or two. Richard Bailey could find no silver in any Pilgrim inventory,[25] and probate records of Essex County, Massachusetts, reveal that between 1635 and 1664 silver never amounted to more than 2.5 percent of the value of an estate. Thus, the largest collection of silver, worth £22, occurred in an estate worth £1,535. Most houses with any silver at all had but one or two spoons, and spoons were generally worth between 4 and 7 shillings each. The smallest estate in which silver appeared amounted to £69.

By far the most common silver items were spoons with the slip-end shape. Bowls were the next most common form, followed by caudle cups and dram cups, saltcellars, and porringers. Silver forks were known but very rare.[26]

By the middle of the century, America had acquired its first resident silversmiths, John Hull and Robert Sanderson of Boston; silversmiths were also working in New York by 1660. New England tended to follow the lighter lines of English prototypes, while New York adopted the massive, more boldly ornate Dutch tradition. Surviving examples show that these early silversmiths also produced salvers, baptismal basins, tankards, candlesticks, and chafing dishes. Even with an increasing number of craftsmen, silver remained the scarce possession of the rich. Essex County inventories for 1675 to 1681 reveal only three tankards, and no estate in Essex County inventoried before 1681 included silver candlesticks.

Usually, silver was collected in one room, but that room might be the hall, parlor, kitchen chamber, or hall chamber.

Treen. Treen or wooden ware provided an important part of a family's table service, especially early in the century. Large trenchers, either square or round, were shared among several diners. Very rare were small (6-in.) dessert or fruit trenchers, at least one set of which was used in Pilgrim Plymouth. Each of that set of twelve had a print for one of the months pasted on the top. A dessert course had first become important in English dining about 1600, and thus it is not surprising to find stylish service for such a course in at least a few American homes.[27]

2

The Late Seventeenth Century

1675–1715

INVENTORIES, orders, and letters reveal new decorative materials for almost every room in fashionable houses of the 1670s, as Americans copied the changing tastes of Charles II's England. The William and Mary style, named for the English monarchs who ruled from 1689 to 1702, likewise had its impact. However, documents suggest that the decorative changes of the 1670s had more impact than the evolutions of the 1690s and early 1700s; accordingly, we have grouped the styles of Charles II and William and Mary together.

As in all other colonial periods, wealthy Americans watched English styles closely, and either traveled to England, returning with household goods, or ordered them through London suppliers. From their houses and those of newly arrived royal officials, the latest styles, in turn, became models for local craftsmen.

William Fitzhugh (d. 1700) came from England to Virginia in 1670. The son of a barrister, he soon set himself up like a country nobleman, and in 1686 could write that he had 24,496 acres and a house "furnished with all accommodations for a comfortable and gentile living." The house had been built in 1674, and in the years that followed, orders to England brought pewter, a looking glass with an olive wood frame, brass andirons with fire shovel and tongs, iron chimney backs, a table, "leather carpets," tapestries, and silver. Four rooms were "hung" with tapestries. Ordering silver in 1688, Fitzhugh judged it "as well politic as reputable to furnish myself with a handsome cupboard of plate which gives myself the present use and credit."[1] Silver established status, and Fitzhugh was a satisfied customer, for he wrote that his silver arrived "just in time for a several days' visit from the Governor." The governor must have been impressed, for a decade later Fitzhugh's extraordinary collection included nineteen plates, three bread plates, eight dishes, a set of castors, a monteith (a large punchbowl with a scalloped edge), seven candlesticks, two pairs of candlesnuffers with trays, and a chocolate pot.[2] In Fitzhugh's house, seventeenth-century America was far from rustic.

In some cases, British fashions must have arrived only months after they appeared in London, but in the case of William Byrd I it took over a year. Byrd was building the first version of Westover in 1690 when he ordered a bed and curtains, chairs, table, looking glass, a dozen Russia leather chairs, and two oval tables.[3]

The effect of these efforts to furnish American rooms stylishly was impressive, even to Englishmen. John Dunton of London visited Salem, Massachusetts, in 1685 where he stayed with George Herrick (famous in the witch trials). Of his accommodations, Dunton wrote in *Athenianism* (1705): "My apartment was so noble and the Furniture so suitable to it, that I doubt not but even the king himself has been oftentimes contented with a worser lodging."[4] Furnishings exported from England to the colonies (cited in value of the exports in pounds) between 1697 and 1704 included[5]:

Upholstery ware	£47,441
Pewter	15,130
Tin and turnery ware	10,616
Chairs	4,735
Looking glasses	1,582
Chests of drawers	1,054
Plate	931
Cabinets	319
Escritoires	229
Joinery ware	202
Clock cases	63

Not all British goods that arrived in the colonies were special orders of the wealthy, for America was a regular market for British upholstered furniture and upholstery fabric, pewter, tin, and chairs. At the end of the century, most of these exports went to Virginia, Maryland, and New England; Carolina, Pennsylvania, and New York received somewhat lesser cargoes.[6]

In short order, craftsmen in the major cities were producing silver, pewter, and furniture in the late-seventeenth-century and William and Mary styles. But their limited output satisfied only a small part of the market and, as in other periods, imports supplied the bulk of fashionable items.

Although New York became an English possession in 1674, its residents and crafts reflected the Dutch background of the colony. Dutch influence in New York silver persisted until the 1720s,[7] and the *kas*, a form of cabinet not made in New England or the South, continued well into the Chippendale period. In comparing many inventories of New York with those of the South and New England, Esther Singleton concluded that the new, lighter styles in furniture had appeared in New York, while the older oak pieces were still found in many houses in the other colonies. Only the oak draw-leaf table survived in late seventeenth-century New York. A wealthy merchant might have thirty to fifty chairs in addition to stools and benches, while the poorer New York families had relatively few tables and chairs.

As in later periods, there was a rather even distribution of wealth throughout society (see Table 3 on page 20). Some were very rich, but the extremity of their wealth was far from what the nineteenth century would produce. In New York City, Esther Singleton found that during the 1670s almost one-quarter of

Figure 4. Frontispiece to John Shirley, *The Accomplished Ladies Rich Closet of Rarities, or the Ingenious Gentlewoman and Servant Maids Delightful Companion* (London, 1687). The British Library, London.

The frontispiece of Shirley's *Closet of Rarities* illustrates utilitarian aspects of the English seventeenth-century house. The distillery had large containers appropriately shelved, and such Southwark Delft drug jugs have been excavated in Virginia at a site dating between 1622 and 1652. Books arranged with spines toward the wall appear in several engravings. The two bedroom scenes, both without carpets, show a well-furnished bed and wicker cradle, and the kitchen and buttery had appropriate implements stored and in use. In the kitchen, note the spits, the large fireplace, and the tile floor.

the 368 householders had estates of 1,000 gilders or more. Ten had more than 10,000 gilders, with only three estates of 50,000 gilders or better. In the 1670s, £100 sterling was worth about 1,070 gilders.[8] Probate records from several areas show that an estate of £2,000 put one in the class capable of decorating a house with considerable fashion.

Sir William Phipps (1651–1695), Governor of Massachusetts, was born in Maine, one of twenty-six children of a gunsmith. His circumstances changed greatly in 1687 when, having gone to sea, he found a Caribbean wreck with treasure worth £300,000 sterling. He shared the treasure liberally with his men, keeping the still enormous sum of £16,000. Knighted by the king, he stayed in England three years and returned to Boston just before he was nominated governor.

His inventory showed a hall with no bed (a stylish extravagance if one could afford it), twelve cane chairs, a couch or day bed, two tables, a table carpet, two pairs of brass andirons, and a looking glass worth £8. The parlor

Table 3. Size of Estate Figured in Pounds of Each Colony[9]
(figures are percentages of inventories falling into each category)

	£0–50	51–100	101–200	201–400	401–800	801+
HARTFORD COUNTY, CONN., 1690–1700	16%	14	19	25	17	9
MAINE, 1690–1705	22	13	26	35	—	4
NEW JERSEY, 1690–1700	30	25	25	12	5	3

The Sueton Grant House, Newport, R.I., *c.* 1675

The Patterson House, Berlin, Conn., *c.* 1690

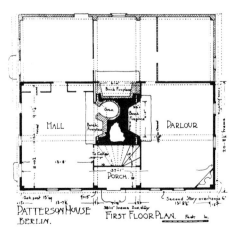

First-floor plan, Patterson House

had fourteen chairs, a couch, a clock (£20), a looking glass (£4), a candlestick, and a case of crystal bottles (£10). Lady Phipps's room had a bed and hangings of silk worth £70, a chest, dressing box, six chairs, tables, stands, and another clock (£10). The hall chamber bed with its silk curtains and eighteen cushions was worth £100; other furniture there included a "scriptore and stand," dressing box, twelve cane chairs, and a looking glass. "Chiny ware" decorated the mantel. A "White Chamber" was furnished more simply with a bed (£20), chest table, looking glass, and six Turkey chairs. Even the "Maid's Chamber" had a looking glass, but the "Chaplain's Chamber" did not. Other servants lived in the garret, but a black woman had a "little chamber." Kept modestly in the kitchen rather than displayed in a court cupboard (he did not have one) was £415 worth of silver. With these extraordinary possessions and his yacht, Sir William obviously did his best to imitate the fashionable life of a knight in England.

Seventeenth-century designs persisted well into the eighteenth century. Boston merchants last advertised new cane back chairs in 1715,[10] but in the country the style, or some forms of it, lasted much longer. In western and central Connecticut, bannister back chairs were made up to the end of the eighteenth century.[11]

Early buildings followed the medieval cruciform pattern, but a new symmetry that would characterize Georgian architecture was evident in Boston's Province House (1676–79) and Hutchinson House (c.1688). The same trend emerged in the Slate House in Philadelphia (1687) and the imposing structures at Williamsburg: the College of William and Mary (1695–1702), the Capitol (1702), and the Governor's Palace (1706–20). Stylish houses were organized on the central hall plan throughout the colonies. But in New England the center chimney plan was much favored, at times even by the wealthy, and continued throughout the eighteenth century. There, the lean-to became part of the original plan of some new houses, producing the salt box design commonly built by the end of the period. Some houses built toward the end of the seventeenth century later had a lean-to or other structure added, giving families new space for parlors, bedrooms, or storage.

The function of rooms continued much as in the previous era. The hall remained the center of family activity, a fact evident from its alternate names: dwelling room, fire-room, or even "house." The hall was in a state of transition, for some halls did have beds, especially in the South, while others did not, particularly in New England.[12] The trend everywhere was toward a hall free of beds. The parlor, on the other hand, had continued to be furnished with a bed as well as chairs and tables suitable for entertaining guests. The lean-to made possible the use of the kitchen as a room for food preparation distinct from the hall. The first rooms labeled dining rooms appeared, but such terms were rare. Most dining seems to have taken place in the hall.

FURNITURE

Inventories of the wealthy began to show a new luxury in the 1670s when Turkey work chairs appeared in increasing number, as more families were able to purchase such luxuries. Leather-covered chairs also became common. The posts and stretchers of these chairs had ball or spiral turnings, and American cabinetmakers did their best to emulate imported work. Less expensive were the large ladderback chairs with turned posts and rush seats.

New styles with regional variations were also evident in chests. In Massachusetts, the Jacobean press cupboard decorated with split, turned spindles evolved from an earlier form, while in Connecticut the sunflower chest added similar spindles to a paneled chest with drawers decorated with floral carving in low relief. Hadley chests lacked the spindles but had an all-over design in flat relief. Paneled surfaces with intricate moldings decorated other chests.

The arrival of William and Mary pieces is not so clearly evident in the probate record as is the change which had begun in the 1670s. But clearly the new William and Mary styles were imported and copied quickly, as Americans were eager to remain up to date.

The American William and Mary style depended upon the use of veneers, carving, ball feet, Spanish feet on tables and chairs, and characteristic turnings. Chairs and tables carried vase and ring, or block and vase turnings, while highboys and lowboys received trumpet turnings. The style also introduced a more extensive use of upholstery.

Beds remained much as they had, but half-headed bedsteads or half-canopied beds appeared in addition to high post, low post, and trundle beds.

Chairs assumed a new diversity by the turn of the century, with the expensive additions of the upholstered easy chair and the highly carved and elaborately turned cane back chair. Notable in the decoration of these chairs was the Flemish scroll. Less expensive but with many of the same motifs was the bannister back chair. Still less expensive was the simple slat back chair with simple turnings. Day beds appeared, adding a new note of comfort. Another new form was the corner chair.

Desks took several forms. The writing stand or desk on frame evolved from the earlier book box, but the fall front desk soon predominated.

FLOOR COVERINGS

Floors continued to remain uncovered, and not until the Queen Anne era is there definite evidence of floor carpets in use in America. "Carpets" in inventories again refer to table carpets of the sort seen in Figure 10, on page 37.

William and Mary cane back chair, c. 1690

Jacobean Turkey work chair

William and Mary lowboy

PICTURES AND MIRRORS

Pictures were still far from common in the average house. A few artists were painting portraits in New England, primarily in the English style, while the Dutch style was evident in the painting of Evert Duyckinck, who emigrated from Holland to New Amsterdam in 1638. Some Americans had their portraits painted in England, as Increase Mather did in London in 1688. Needless to say, such portraits were confined to the homes of the well-to-do.

Portraits were moderately common in houses of the wealthy in the South and New England. New Yorkers found special zest in collecting canvases, and not surprisingly, Dutch themes were common. Jacob de Lange (d. 1685), a wealthy surgeon and barber, had a rich collection of fifty-five pictures, including banqueting scenes, grapes, apricots, pomegranates, country scenes or landscapes, Abraham and Hagar, and scenes of break of day, winter, a cobbler, and country people frolicking. His coat of arms was worth £5, but all the other pictures together were valued at £24.11.6.[13] Other New Yorkers had pictures of Caesar, ships, and battles.

Mirrors or looking glasses, as they were always called, became progressively more common. They were relatively small compared to eighteenth-century mir-

Figure 5. Cornelis Troost. *Two Quakers Discussing a Marriage Contract.* C. 1730. Oil on canvas. Mauritshuis, The Hague, Neth.

Troost's Dutch scene was similar to Anglo-American usage. Note the tablecloth over the Oriental rug. The wall clock, similar to those that early settlers brought with them, was hung at the same high level as the birdcage. Delft plates were used decoratively, and simple curtains covered the lower section of the leaded windows. A mirror hung over a vase of flowers, but the only decoration given the plain walls was the floor molding of Delft tiles. The floorboards of the next story made up the ceiling.

rors, but still valuable. Ornate examples had scrolled walnut-veneered crests above rectangular glass. Simpler square mirrors with convex moldings were imported in considerable numbers from England and Holland.

Dutch pictures from this period show that while paintings and maps were hung high on a wall, mirrors were placed at eye level. Both mirrors and pictures were either blind hung or hung from an eye on the frame suspended from a nail and decorated with a bow.

TEXTILES

The householder of wealth had many imported fabrics from which to choose in furnishing a house fashionably. Not all imports were English products, for Chester County, Pennsylvania, inventories record East India pillowcases and Irish cloth. Those of wealth and fashion continued to coordinate colors within a chamber.

Leather finished with brass nails was the usual treatment of Jacobean or Cromwellian chairs. Beginning about 1650, Turkey work—a knotted fabric produced in England in imitation of Turkish carpets—became fashionable. In 1698, England produced 5,000 dozen Turkey work chairs per year.[14] In 1702, in Boston, six such chairs were valued at £3. Other pieces were upholstered with costly needlework; and camlet, serge, and damask appeared frequently in houses of fashion, with red, green, and blue favored colors for chairs. Other fabrics, according to Esther Singleton,[15] used in upholstery included: camak or camoca, darnix or dornix or darneck, perpetuana, kitterminster or kidderminster, drugget, dimity, calico, calimanco or callimanco, plush, mohair, paduasoy, horsehair, chaney or cheney or china, Turkey work, green cloth, crimson worsted, red cloth, red damask, leather, yellow damask, shalloon, say, watchet, linsey-woolsey, seersucker, blue-and-white cotton, fustian, silk muslin, chintz, Indian calico, tabby, taffety, sarcenet, and rateen.

Window curtains remained rare, confined only to chambers in fashionable houses. John Bowles, a Harvard graduate of 1671, who left an estate of £1,509 in 1691, had green window curtains in the chamber of his Roxbury, Massachusetts, house. They matched the green serge bed curtains with silk fringe.[16]

Probably bed curtains remained the most impressive display of fabric in the house, and a complete set included valance as well as side and end curtains. Several inventories stipulated that they hung from rods by hooks.

The estate of Colonel Francis Epes (1678) of Henrico County, Virginia, documents variation in fabric and value in a house of wealth. The most important bed, with camlet curtains and a double valance lined with yellow silk, was worth £24.5.0. A new, simple set of Kidderminster curtains was rated at 10/-, while "One old suite of Callicoe curtains and vallains" was only 5/-.[17]

WALL TREATMENT

Plaster walls were common in the South, but still relatively scarce in New England, except in houses of wealth. Some Rhode Island and Connecticut houses of about 1700 had plaster on exterior walls, while the interior walls were wainscotted in vertical boards. In houses of lesser means, wainscotting remained the norm throughout the period, and woodwork generally remained unpainted. Plaster walls were often treated with whitewash. If woodwork was painted, Indian red was a common color, but marbling was fairly common in Rhode Island.[18]

North or south, exposed posts and plates were part of the wall surface. These architectural members were often decorated with chamfering or carving, with variations depending on regional style and wealth of the householder.

A few lavish houses in Virginia had elegant tapestries. Colonel Francis Epes of Henrico County had a "suit of tapestry hangings" valued at £18.17.0, and in 1683, William Fitzhugh of Stafford County ordered tapestry from London for a room 20 feet long, 16 feet wide, and 9 feet high. By 1710, a room of the Governor's Palace in Williamsburg was done in gilt leather.[19]

Wallpaper was virtually unknown, but Michael Perry who died in Boston in 1700 had "painted papers." Americans who had been to England had certainly seen wallpaper and perhaps desired it as they did other things English and stylish. In 1675, William Salmon's *Polygraphice* included advice on appropriate wallpapers and pictures for particular rooms, and stylish Americans did their best to emulate these English norms. Proposed subjects appropriate to particular rooms included:

PORCH	rustic figures
HALL	shepherds, peasants, milkmaids, sheep, fish, fowl
STAIRCASE	monuments, buildings, ceilings to appear as though looking through clouds
GREAT CHAMBER	landscapes, hunting, fishing
DINING ROOM	The king, queen, coats of arms, chief nobility
BANQUETING ROOM	cheerful, merry pictures, Bacchus, Centaurs, etc.
GALLERIES	histories
CHIMNEY PIECES	landscapes
BED CHAMBERS	family portraits

Salmon suggested confining the picture of one's wife to the bedroom, especially if she were beautiful. To have it on general view might suggest untoward ideas.[20]

ARCHITECTURAL DETAILS AND CEILINGS

Beamed ceilings continued in the last period in which the exposed summer beam was virtually universal. In Virginia houses of great wealth like the Sherwood mansion in Jamestown (c. 1670–1680), ornamental plasterwork or pargeting might be found between the ceiling beams. Fragments document a stunning ceiling with an elaborate version of the insignia of the Order of the Garter. Houses of less, but still considerable wealth might merely have plain plaster between the beams.

Pargeting was unknown in New England, but plastered ceilings began to appear there late in this period. Many simple houses retained the practice of

Figure 6. Artist unknown. *The Hutchinson House.* Woodcut. *The American Magazine of Useful and Entertaining Knowledge* (February 1836), p. 237.

Colonel John Foster (d. 1711), who came to Boston in 1675, became a wealthy merchant and built this house sometime between 1681 and 1691. After his widow's death, it passed to the Hutchinson family and was thus the home of Governor Thomas Hutchinson (1711–1780), the only governor who did not live in Province House—because, he said, he had a better house of his own. Razed in 1834, it was so unlike other American dwellings of the 1680s that the date of the exterior has been much debated. However, a British officer who entered the house during riots in 1765 commented: "The structure and inside finishing seemed to be from a design of Inigo Jones [1573–1652] or his successor," thus documenting that to a learned eye the interiors must have been as elaborate and early as the exterior, which was original to the structure.[25]

using undecorated second-story flooring as a first-floor ceiling. Chamfering of plates and beams provided the decorative effect of ceiling moldings.

Mantels. Earlier fireplaces with huge wooden "mantel trees" continued to be built, but heavy bolection moldings began to appear in houses of wealth and taste, like William Penn's Philadelphia home (c. 1682–1683) and the Reynolds House in Bristol, Rhode Island (1698). The Bidwell-Mix House in West Hartford, Connecticut (1695–1700) is a very early example of a mantel constructed as an integral part of a paneled wall. The mantel has a shallow shelf. The "Ending of Controversie" (c. 1670) in Talbot County, Maryland, likewise has a mantel shelf surmounted by a framed panel with wainscotted wall on either side.[21] In finer Connecticut houses, the hearth was raised a few inches above the floor.

Doors. Batten doors from the previous period continued to be common, refined by edgings on vertical boards and even the battens themselves. During this period, the paneled door appeared. A two-paneled door with raised moldings is found in the Reynolds House (1698) in Bristol, Rhode Island, a three-paneled door is found in Wethersfield, Connecticut (1680), and a six-paneled exterior door appeared in the medieval-style house "Christs Cross" in New Kent County, Virginia (1690).

Stairs. Stairs in New England gained added refinement. The earlier simple enclosure in wainscotting (which continued in some construction) gave way to a newel post and stair rail supported by balusters. Generally, the balusters were turned, but in Rhode Island they were commonly sawn or carved in S shapes or in imitation of turnings. Whether stairs were built as a triple run or with winders, the balusters were placed on a molded box or closed string, with the area below finished off in wainscotting or more expensive paneling.

Floors in New England and the South were made basically of heavy plank.

Connecticut practice favored oak in a double layer on the first floor, with a single layer on the second. In Virginia, floors of Dutch or English brick were used occasionally.

LIGHTING

Candles were the most important form of lighting. Candlesticks were imported and made locally, with brass more common than pewter. Stylish baroque patterns appeared in imported brass and in the few silver candlesticks made in America. Wire candlesticks (twisted iron) are mentioned often in period inventories, and chandeliers or "hanging candles" also made their first appearance. An iron rush light holder was found in a late seventeenth-century chimney in Haverhill, Massachusetts, documenting the rush light as rare but present. Oil lamps were likewise used but not favored.

COLOR

In fashionable houses the English practice of coordinating fabrics in a single color continued. Red, green, and blue were favored colors. Turkey work added a new dash of color to American rooms, and perhaps not surprisingly some had coordinated Turkey work throughout a room. John Bowles, who died in Roxbury, Massachusetts, in 1691 with a substantial estate of £1,509, had six Turkey work chairs, six Turkey work cushions, and a Turkey work table carpet in the parlor. His parlor chamber was done in green fringed silk.

Paint added bright decoration to furniture at the end of the period. In New England, reds, blacks, and whites augmented carving and turning. At the end of the century, Hadley, Massachusetts, and Guilford, Connecticut, were producing chests painted with geometric or floral decoration. Painted graining in imitation of richer woods also appeared. Simple chairs were often painted in solid colors.

Painted furniture was prominent in the New York interior, where a large *kas* might be decorated with bunches of fruit, but the color was often a restrained monochrome rather than a bright, realistic depiction. Color Plate 1 is especially instructive, for it records the color choices of an artist adapting his picture from a black-and-white print.

ACCESSORIES

Using decorative accessories, Americans approximated British homes of wealth as best they could. Silver and china were more than utilitarian, adding greatly to the luxury of an interior.

Among the middle class and poor, however, attractive yet simple ceramic ware and pewter predominated, and wooden ware remained important in humble households.

Ceramics. Sgraffito ware gave way to the increasingly popular Delft imported from England and Holland. With the growing influence of Chinese shapes and decoration, Delft potters added reds, greens, purples, and yellows to

Delft plate with blue decoration

their plates, tea services, chocolate pots, coffee pots, sauceboats, tureens, and punchbowls. English stoneware, primarily from Staffordshire, also became increasingly important, with tulips and other flowers decorating posset pots, jugs, cups, mugs, and dishes. Combed ware was popular. A limited quantity of French soft-paste wares appeared. Chinese porcelains remained confined to homes of wealth.

Domestic production provided a limited supply of utilitarian redware, a small quantity of Delft (New Jersey, 1688–1692), and increasing quantities of stoneware (New York, Pennsylvania).

As in the previous era, except for decorative items, ceramics were found primarily in the kitchen or buttery.

Clocks. Although clocks were found in houses of at least moderate wealth, it did not follow that those of even great wealth had clocks. In Chester County, Pennsylvania, only 3 out of 123 inventories between 1682 and 1709 included a clock. Suffolk County, Massachusetts, inventories value clocks at between £1 and £2. These were probably wall or bracket clocks or spring clocks, for tall clocks were more expensive. Most clocks were still imported, even though makers appeared in Boston, Philadelphia, and New York. Two mechanisms were in use—the older foliot balance, and the pendulum mechanism, introduced in the 1660s, which rapidly replaced it. In 1707 and 1708, Boston clockmakers advertised that they could turn old clocks "into Pendulums."

The clock was generally kept in the parlor, but the Reverend Joseph Rowland of Wethersfield, Connecticut, died in 1678 with a clock in his kitchen.[22]

Glass. The well-to-do had increasing amounts of glass, often surprisingly stylish. Ivor Noel Hume excavated in Virginia one fragment of a cup or candlestick which he called "as handsome a piece of glass as ever graced the home of a seventeenth-century English nobleman."[23] Most glass was utilitarian, with a case of glasses in the parlor quite common. Over 70 percent of Noel Hume's finds were fragments of quatrefoil-stemmed glasses. Round bottles assumed a more squat shape.

But glass was still far from universal, for many households, even those of wealth, had no table glass at all. Ralph Fisbourn died in Chester, Pennsylvania, in 1708 with an estate of £1,762 and no glass other than some bottles.

Iron and Brass. With the exception of andirons, iron and brass were generally confined to the kitchen or hall. The principal implements were much the same as earlier in the century, but families had greater quantities of iron and even more of brass, especially in wealthy homes. A new addition to the household was the fire fender. Early examples stood between the hearthstones; the three-sided projecting version came later.[24]

Spinning Wheels. Spinning wheels were an important part of every household, and their locations were quite varied. They are recorded in the hall, perhaps most often in chambers, in the garret, and in the lean-to. Those listed in chambers or the hall were probably in use—those in the garret were stored.

Pewter. Pewter was common in the late seventeenth-century interior, with the quantity dependent upon the economic status and size of the family. The most common items were platters and plates. Porringers, basins, quart and pint pots (tankards or mugs), and chamber pots were perhaps the next most common, with flagons, saltcellars, and candlesticks less so. Virtually all pewter

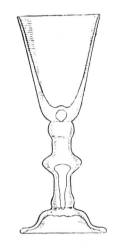

Typical late seventeenth-century glass

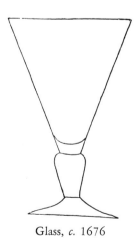

Glass, *c.* 1676

was imported from Britain or Holland, and importation meant that new English styles reached America rather quickly.

Appraisers in the 1690s valued pewter at 15 pence the pound, and some families had up to 150 pounds. Generally speaking, from 1690 to 1710, pewter accounted for 0.3 to 0.5 percent of an estate's value, although in some well-furnished smaller estates it could account for up to 1.6 percent.

Invariably, pewter was kept in the kitchen (if the house had one) or in the hall. It was not kept in the parlor.

Alcamy spoons continued to be made in quantity in England, where they were wholesaled at 6/- the gross.

Silver. Many families, like the Bowdoins, ordered the latest styles from London, but domestic silversmithing grew during this period. Silver remained an extremely valuable possession found in quantity only in the homes of the rich.

The increasingly varied diet of the well-to-do brought with it a new diversity of silver forms, as English and local silversmiths began to produce chocolate, tea, and coffee pots, mustard pots, sugar boxes, casters and dredgers for pepper, spices, or sugar. Other new forms were the spout cup and the rare and heavy monteith for punch.

Old forms were embellished with new motifs, using gadrooning, fluting, embossing, repoussé, engraving, and cast decorations. Regional styles of decoration developed, and certain old forms kept or lost regional popularity. Caudle cups survived in New England, as did two-handled punchbowls in New York, while porringers became popular in New York as well as New England.

Spoons, still the most common silver item, evolved during this period from the trifid pattern introduced about 1660 to the wavy-end spoon with rattail bowl prominent at the end of the period. New in this period were small "tea" spoons for use with coffee or tea.

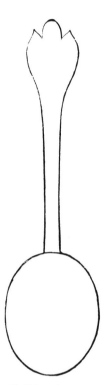

Trifid end spoon

Figure 7. Artist unknown. *Parlor Scene.* William Winstanley, *A New Help to Discourse* (Boston, 1722). New York Public Library, New York City.

Benjamin Franklin's brother James printed this William and Mary scene of gentlemen in their full-bottomed wigs sitting in tall, cane back chairs at a covered table. A lively discussion went on, with two of the men holding glasses by the stem as was the custom. A tankard, bowl, and pipe were on the table, and a period candlestick for lighting the pipe. The leaded casement windows are not curtained and there is no evidence of wall decoration.

3

The Queen Anne Style

1715–1750

Q UEEN ANNE" is the term used to designate early eighteenth-century furniture made in this country, and we have used the label to refer to the entire style that spread with the popularity of the furniture. Although chairs with the cabriole leg characteristic of Queen Anne began to appear in English furniture about 1695, the style did not become the general American fashion until the 1730s. Something new was clearly offered in a Boston advertisement of 1714 by a merchant who had "new Fashion" beds, chests of drawers, desks, tables, glasses, and bookcases. All had "come over in the last ship."[1]

The wealthy remained extremely fashion-conscious, often because they had studied or lived in England. It is now often assumed that it sometimes took a decade for British fashions to cross the Atlantic, but that was not the prevailing opinion at that time. Daniel Neal (1678–1743) of London published his *History of New England* in 1720. Of the Bostonians he wrote: "Their customs and manners are much the same with the English. . . . In the concerns of civil life, their dress, tables, and conversations, they affect to be as much English as possible; there is no fashion in London but in three or four months is to be seen in Boston. In short, the only difference between an Old and New Englishman is in religion."[2]

Neal was not alone, for about 1735 John Oldmixion (1673–1742) wrote: "A gentleman from London would almost think himself at home in Boston when he observes the numbers of people, their houses, their furniture, their tables, their dress and conversation, which, perhaps, is as splendid and showy as that of the most considerable tradesman in London."[3]

Typical of the quest for British fashion was Boston merchant Thomas Hancock, who died in 1764 leaving his nephew, John, the extraordinary fortune of £100,000. In 1737, he had built a house on Beacon Hill, ordering from London over the years carved Corinthian capitals, specially painted wallpaper, drinking glasses and decanters, and, in 1738, a "Handsome Chiming Clock" of the "newest Fashion."[4]

*Table 4. British Goods Shipped
to the Colonies*

(values in pounds)

| | Goods Shipped Between | |
	1720–28	1740–48
CHAIRS	£ 1,232	£ 377
LOOKING GLASSES	3,969	1,402
CLOCK CASES	234	26
ESCRITOIRES	5	7
UPHOLSTERY WARE	2,606	6,744
JOINERY WARE	282	557
TIN AND TURNERY WARE	2,193	3,798
PEWTER	25,484	65,493
PLATE	5,203	14,804

*Value of £100 Sterling in Currencies of Each
Colony Issuing Notes, 1740*[8]

NEW HAMPSHIRE		£553
MASSACHUSETTS	old tenor	525
	new tenor	175
RHODE ISLAND	old tenor	532
	new tenor	133
CONNECTICUT	old tenor	551
	new tenor	157
NEW YORK		166
NEW JERSEY		161
PENNSYLVANIA		165
DELAWARE		165
MARYLAND	hard currency	139
	paper	228
VIRGINIA		119
NORTH CAROLINA		966
SOUTH CAROLINA		795

Apart from such special orders, masses of British production came to the colonies in the regular course of trade, as Table 4 indicates.

The value of chairs and looking glasses sent to America decreased from decade to decade, but the value of upholstered furniture, silver, and pewter grew significantly. The bulk of these shipments was sent to New England, Virginia, and Maryland, with lesser quantities going to Carolina. New York and Philadelphia were important markets for looking glasses, but seemingly not for furniture.[5]

New designs spread in the colonies as local craftsmen copied imports and as British craftsmen emigrated here. The desire to own something like that possessed by a neighbor was the prime mover in the growing popularity of a new style, and marvelous documentation of the process survives in the specifications for the house that Charles Pinckney built in Charleston in 1746. The best parlor was to be wainscotted "as Capt. Shubrick's dining room is done." The back parlor was to have "chimney facings as in Capt. Shubricks back parlour," while the entry was to be fixed so that "the boards may be hereafter taken up as the same be paved as Mr. C. Justice Whitakers Entry is." For the dining room, Pinckney specified "this room is intended to be wainscotted and finished as Mr. Greemes is."[6]

American manufacture of decorative items was still in its infancy. Cabinetmakers, pewterers, and silversmiths were well distributed throughout the colonies, but wallpaper was not made in America until Plunkett Fleeson opened his shop in Philadelphia in 1739, the same year Caspar Wistar opened his South Jersey glassworks. Imports supplied what domestic output could not.

The disparity of wealth was great, but perhaps not so great as one might assume from reading reports of inventories. As in the Chippendale era, many colonies suffered from severe inflation as the paper currencies, which were the legal money in which accounts were kept, became less and less valuable in terms of silver coin. At the end of the era, several colonies attempted to correct for inflation by dubbing their earlier currencies "old tenor" (O.T.), which in Rhode Island (1740) was declared worth one-fourth the new tenor currency that replaced it. When converted into the English sterling rate, these bills were worth still a different figure. Thus in 1740, old tenor Rhode Island notes for £40 equaled £10 in new tenor notes, and about £7.13.10 in British sterling.

This numismatic detail is necessary for any comparative consideration of wealth in the colonies. Esther Singleton made much of the fact that South Carolina "personal estates of from £500 to £5,000 are found by the hundred, and in many cases the personal property runs into many thousands."[7] Arthur Middleton (1681–1737), president of the Council of South Carolina, left an estate of £25,000, a valuable property to be sure. But South Carolina had a bad inflation problem, and in 1737, £100 sterling was worth £753 in South Carolina currency. Thus, Middleton's estate was worth £3,320 sterling, the equivalent of a New York estate of £5,478 in New York currency. To the left are some guidelines in understanding figures that are as vexing today as they were for merchants then.

Table 5, on page 31, shows the distribution of estates during the period. A few were very poor, but most people lived a comfortable life with well-furnished interiors. Singleton noted that around 1731 a skilled carpenter in South Carolina

Table 5. Size of Estates in the Queen Anne Era, Figured in Pounds of Each Colony[9]
(figures are percentages of inventories falling into each category)

	£0–50	51–100	101–200	201–300	301–400	401–500	501–800	801–1,200	1,201+
MAINE, 1715–40	3%	8	14	11	14	3	20	12	15
HARTFORD PROBATE DISTRICT, CONN., 1715–29	14	9	15	16	10	5	13	10	8
NEW HAMPSHIRE, 1741–50	4	3	9	2	4	5	13	11ˣ	49

received 30/- a day, equivalent to 3/9 sterling, and a common workman 20/- per diem, or 2/6 sterling.[10]

The estate of Governor William Burnet, who died in 1729, shows what the style looked like by the 1720s. At his house in New York City he had twenty-four walnut chairs covered in red leather (@ 24/-), an easy chair covered with silk (£10), two tall clocks, a gilt cabinet on frame, a secretary with glass doors (£20), a plain tea table, a japanned tea table, a card table, and a backgammon table. In an era when forks of any kind were still somewhat rare, he had six dozen silver knives and forks (£72), plus twelve candlesticks and 1,172 ounces of other miscellaneous silver. The beds had red or chintz curtains, carpets covered the floors, and the walls were hung with tapestry (four pieces of it were worth £20). Another "fine piece of needlework representing a rustick" was worth £20. Pictures were everywhere. He had 151 Italian prints unframed (£15.2.0), 23 framed mezzotints, and 44 prints in black frames. He even had a harpsichord, clavichord, two trumpets, two violins, a tenor fiddle, a bass, and a set of nine "gouff" clubs (one of them iron). Here was all the elegance of London; and a visit to Burnet's house, or probably to any one of the royal governors' residences, certainly sparked orders to England from those who could afford such style.[11]

Craftsmen in smaller towns began working in the Queen Anne style somewhat later, but maintained it long after the Chippendale style had gained favor in the urban centers. Only in 1783 did John Wheeler Geer, a cabinetmaker in Preston, Connecticut, make the last of his fiddleback chairs, a country version of the style.[12]

Governors and those of wealth provided models for architecture and furnishings. A few practicing architects also offered plans for houses. Peter Chaffereau "newly come from London" advertised in Charleston in 1735, and George Harrison advertised in Philadelphia in 1746. The prominent architect of many Virginia houses in the Wren style, which remained popular in the Queen Anne era, was Richard Taliaferro (1705–1779) of Williamsburg. Although they were not advertised during the era, British books on architecture were in the hands of several builders, including Taliaferro.

The typical Queen Anne house was larger and more elaborately decorated with architectural elements than its predecessors. In New England, the center chimney design was common to the homes of virtually all economic classes, but the wealthy in urban centers in the North and in the countryside in the South were more likely to adopt the center hall design, with two major rooms on either side of the hall.

Room designations were generally what they had been in the previous

Central chimney design, the Benjamin House, Milford, Conn.

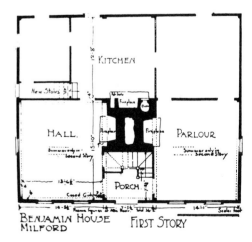

Floor plan of the Benjamin House

Figure 8. Charles Philips. *Tea Party at Lord Harrington's House.* 1739. Oil on canvas, 40¼ in. × 49¾ in. (1.02 cm × 1.27 cm). Yale Center for British Art, New Haven, Conn.

One might assume that no American interior was so glamorous as Lord Harrington's, yet evidence tells another story. Although the ceilings were not so high, the walls of Stratford (1725) and Sabine Hall (1729) in Virginia were if anything more elaborate, as were the mantels in the Cupola House, Edenton, North Carolina. Wealthy Americans had begun to use Turkey carpets on their floors, and virtually all the furniture had similar American counterparts. The Amberly-type flocked wallpaper, also used in America, was hung so that the repetitions of the pattern were not adjacent. This staggering of design came into fashion in England in the 1740s. There were differences, but the wealthy few who kept in touch with British fashion did rather well at emulating rooms such as this.[47]

period, with some new terms introduced but not generally used. The hall remained the principal gathering place for the family, and in houses of even moderate means, cooking was confined to the kitchen. The hall was used for family dining, but in the North the designation of that room or any room as a "dining room" was still rare. However, in the South references to dining rooms are relatively common.

The parlor, no longer a bedroom, continued as a room of such splendor as a family could afford. The terms "chamber" and "bed-room" were used somewhat interchangeably, but "chamber" usually referred to a bedroom on the second floor. Where a family possessed many books, a chamber might be designated a study and furnished accordingly with desk, chairs, and bookcases. During the period, it was common for at least one chamber to be furnished with a table and a considerable number of chairs. Garrets were sometimes used for sleeping, but usually they and cellars were areas for storage.

FURNITURE

Furniture designers placed a new emphasis on curves, particularly the **S** or cyma curve, Hogarth's line of beauty. This curve was evident in legs, feet, pediments, and skirts of case pieces. The pad foot was widespread, but in Pennsylvania and New York the trifid foot was popular, too, as was the slipper foot in Rhode Island. Early in the period, the Spanish foot was widely used on

Figure 9. Arthur Devis. *William and Lucy Atherton. C.* 1748–1770. Oil on canvas, 36 in. × 52 in. (91 cm × 132 cm). Walter Art Gallery, Liverpool, Eng.

The Athertons were English, but the scene could have been in America. If anything, American rooms of great wealth tended to be more ornate in both the Queen Anne and Chippendale periods. Americans were reluctant to take up their carpets in summer as the Athertons did, a fact that brought occasional criticism from foreign visitors. Devis's canvas is the only period illustration we have found, English or American, which shows a highboy, decorated here with a symmetrical arrangement of ceramics. Note the bare mantel shelf and the ornate oval mirror, a shape popular in the 1770s.[48]

Queen Anne drop-leaf table

An inexpensive Queen Anne chair

A more costly Queen Anne chair

fashionable urban pieces, and it continued much longer in country work. Shells were common enrichments, whether naturally carved on chairs or stylized into the fans that decorated highboys. Arched paneling of the same shape as in wall decoration found a place on the doors of secretaries and cupboards.

Regional characteristics were very evident in Queen Anne furniture, especially in the more expensive pieces. Most household furniture was produced locally, and cabinetmakers created variations of the Queen Anne style that gained local vogue. Favored woods were walnut, cherry, maple, birch, and pine (for painted furniture), but mahogany, introduced in England in 1724, became the prestige wood in America during the last years of the period.

Many of the wealthy continued to import much of their expensive furniture from England, but the English also exported a great deal of simple, plain furniture.

Two new forms indicated a growing refinement and secularization of American life. The card table—with its fold-over top—first appeared during this era (even though cardplaying was still illegal in some colonies), as did the tea table, which provided a setting for the new social ritual introduced in the 1720s. Advertised in Boston as early as 1725,[13] the first tea tables were rectangular; the tilt-top round table appeared in the 1740s. The Queen Anne idiom translated well into a variety of smaller tables, including the drop-leaf table, usually known as a breakfast table. A much larger version of the same table provided the favored Queen Anne dining table, which might seat up to eight comfortably.

Case pieces often received the most ornate decoration. Highboys or lowboys were most costly when made in walnut or mahogany; the painted maple highboy was less elegant and, therefore, less expensive. Desks persisted in a variety of forms. Desks on frame continued to be made, but they were less popular than the basic slant front desk. The secretary received great elaboration, with paneled doors, bonnet top, carved interior, inlays, and brass finials, often making it one of the most expensive and most spectacular items in an interior.

Chairs became the common form of seating, while stools grew comparatively rare. Such chairs ranged from the intricately carved Philadelphia examples in walnut or mahogany to the simple, turned, country versions with rush seats. Crown and York chairs with their bannister backs were regionally popular.[14] Complementing these side chairs and great chairs were the easy chair (much more common than in the William and Mary period), the settee, and the sofa. All three were upholstered. The settee and the sofa remained relatively uncommon, with the chief distinction between the two forms being that one could recline on a sofa.[15] The day bed continued to be made with standard Queen Anne decoration. Windsor chairs emerged in England in the 1720s, and occur in the inventories of Governor Patrick Gordon of Pennsylvania and John Lloyd of South Carolina in the 1730s.

Candlestands appear in expensive versions, but the simple turned baluster with cross base held a candle just as well in a house of lesser means. Cabinetmakers also provided combination candlestands and firescreens.

Corner cupboards or "boffets" were new, and they, too, might be simple or very elegant with carved, shell tops. In Connecticut, they were commonly placed in the hall in the right-hand corner as one stood with one's back to the fireplace.[16] A variety of pine cupboards, dressers, and china cupboards were found in virtually every house.

Generally, furniture was still placed at the periphery of the room, except when in use or when a piece had been designed as free standing and thus finished on all four sides. Symmetry was important in British rooms and seems to have governed American arrangements, too.[17]

FLOOR COVERINGS

The plain board floor continued. Mrs. Shiffer found no evidence of a floor carpet in Chester County, Pennsylvania, before 1775, and in 1766 John Wayles of Henrico County, Virginia, recalled: "In 1740 I don't remember to have seen such a thing as a turkey Carpet in the Country except a small thing in a bed chamber."

However, in houses of the urban wealthy, large Oriental or "Turkey" carpets began to appear.[18] Isaac Royall, Sr., died in Medford, Massachusetts (1739), owning a Turkey carpet in his best room valued at £40. Peter Faneuil's estate in Boston (1743) had one valued at £35. Less costly but still not inexpensive were English carpets that began to appear near the very end of the Queen Anne period. They are described in the Chippendale section. By the 1740s, Boston records indicate that carpets specifically designated for entryways and bedsides had appeared,[19] and Virginia documents record a "list" or striped rag carpet used on a Williamsburg floor in 1749.[20]

Also new was the painted floor cloth. The first floor cloth in York County, Virginia, inventories appears in 1739.[21] They were uncommon during the Queen Anne period, but the 1728 inventory of Governor William Burnet of New York listed "three, one valued at £8."

Bare wood floors continued to be sanded, and Boston papers for 1746 and 1747 carried advertisements for "scouring Sand for Floors." Floors themselves were sometimes decorated, but probably none at greater expense than that of William Clark in his Boston house of 1712. The floor of his south parlor was inlaid with diamond patterns and the Clark coat of arms in 300 different woods, including mahogany, ebony, and satinwood.[22] Some floors were painted with geometric or leaf decoration. Pumpkin yellow (yellow ochre) was common, and so were gray and brown. Indian red was used but required upkeep.

Smaller Oriental carpets continued to be used on tables, as is evident in John Smibert's portrait of Bishop Berkeley (1729), and Robert Feke's of Isaac Royall (Fig. 10). Even though small, these carpets were expensive and limited to families of considerable means.

PICTURES AND MIRRORS

Paintings, prints, and mirrors assumed new importance in the decorative changes of the early eighteenth century.

From their urban bases along the Atlantic seaboard, a small group of artists provided paintings for the homes of the wealthy. Many were recent immigrants.

Corner cupboard or boffet, Worcester, Mass., 1750

John Smibert from Scotland and Peter Pelham from England worked in New England, while Justus Englehardt Kuhn from Germany and Gustav Hesselius from Sweden worked in the Philadelphia area. Pieter Vanderlyn, a native of Holland, painted in New York City. In the South was Charles Bridges from England. Henrietta Johnson and Jeremiah Theus were centered in Charleston.

To these newcomers should be added the first important group of painters from older American families: Nathaniel Emmons (1704–1740), from Boston; Robert Feke (1705–1752?), primarily in Newport; Joseph Badger (1708–1765), also Boston; and several members of the Duyckinck family in New York.

The primary production of these painters was portraiture, but Theus did at least one landscape and Emmons's obituary mentioned his rivers, banks, and rural scenes.

Oil paintings were sometimes imported for sale, and Dutch pictures were advertised in Boston newspapers in 1738. Governor Gordon (1736) had two "Dutch" pictures and several others (probably Dutch by their subjects—one of them was an old woman frying pancakes).[23] A few wealthy Americans who traveled to London had their portraits done there.

A great diversity of subjects was available in prints. Maps and prints in gilt frames were advertised in Boston as early as 1713, where art was popular enough for William Price to open a "Picture Shop" in 1721. Portraits of British kings and queens were widespread, as were the works of Hogarth and others. Dealers also sold hunting, racing, fishing, fowling, and historical scenes. Many prints were hung in simple frames. Governor Burnet (1729) had twenty-three mezzotints framed, three of them glazed; presumably twenty had frames but no glass.[24]

Large paintings were generally confined to the more important public rooms in the homes of the wealthy. Yet prints and maps were spread all over the house. One man had eleven small pictures in his office, twelve small pictures in one bedroom, and five old maps and a mezzotint in another. In the hall along with the three large pictures he also had "4 Metzotinta Pictures of Indian Kings."[25] An advertisement from 1720 for prints offers suggestions for their placement in "an Gentleman's Dining-room or Stair-case."[26] Yet even in the homes of the wealthy, many rooms had no pictures, and many, perhaps most, houses had no pictures at all.

English pictures show that paintings and prints were hung quite high on the wall, and one 1745 Boston newspaper documented a similar American practice. Lightning struck the house of Jacob Wendell, Jr., of Boston and in so doing "scorch'd the Ceiling and some pictures that hung up near it."

During this period, looking glasses became more common, more ornate, and more expensive. Simple frames continued on some, but even these showed the graceful curves of the period in the shaping of the glass at the top. More elegant and more expensive were glasses with elaborate veneered crests, often with gesso and gilt decoration and sconces or candlearms. Popular but also relatively expensive were japanned mirrors. Courting glasses, with their simple wood frames and decoration resembling Delft tiles, were imported from Holland and Germany.

Mirrors, like pictures, were scattered about the house, but they were usually found in chambers. Although even small mirrors were expensive, many houses probably had at least one, but even in wealthy homes there might not be one in

Figure 10. Robert Feke. *Isaac Royall and Family.* 1741. Oil on canvas,
56³⁄₁₆ in. × 77¾ in. (1.42 m × 1.98 m). Harvard University Law School, Cambridge, Mass.

Isaac Royall (1719–1781), prosperous Medford, Massachusetts, merchant and arch Tory, maintained a residence of model elegance until he left for England in 1775. Jules David Prown estimated his income at over £1,000 per year. Two years before Feke painted this picture, Royall's father's inventory included two "Turkey Carpitts" valued at £40 and £30 each. The rug has been identified as a Transylvanian carpet. Few details of the room are evident, but there were no curtains at the windows.[49]

every chamber. Mirrors seem to have been hung at a lower level than pictures, for obvious reasons.

TEXTILES

Again, the wealthy paid attention to the finer points of textiles, and color coordination of chambers and public rooms remained a prime sign of the fashionable home. Advertisements chronicled the arrival of English, Scottish, German, and Indian fabrics of increasingly diverse color and variety.

Queen Anne furniture offered ample opportunity for display of expensive upholstery fabrics. Silk was the most valuable, followed by wool, then cotton. Both calico and chintz gained considerable popularity. Leather chair seats were common in fashionable houses.

Window curtains were no longer unusual, but they were still lacking in a great many houses. Quite often they were of the same material and color as the bed curtains, and the same hierarchy of fabrics applied to bed and window curtains. Green serge curtains frequently appear in inventories, as they did in the previous era, but the new style brought a strong appearance of red and crimson fabrics as well as patterned calicos and chintzes. In the South, a canopy of mosquito netting was called a pavilion.

Governor Gordon of Pennsylvania left five beds with curtains identified by fabric. The most valuable was one with mohair and silk curtains (£13.5.0), then a fustian wrought bed (£9.10.0), a bed with calico curtains (£6.5.0), one with seersucker curtains (£4), and finally a bed with "green" curtains (£2.16.0).[27]

WALL TREATMENT

During this period, wainscotting gave way to paneling, which in turn yielded to plaster and paper. The wainscotted dado likewise gave way to a simple chair rail.

Paneling appeared in Boston by at least 1695 and spread along the Atlantic coast during the next thirty years. At first, paneling was applied to the fireplace

Figure 11. Attributed to Joseph Steward. *George Wyllys*. C. 1770. Oil on canvas, 79¾ in. × 59¾ in. (2.03 m × 1.52 m). The Connecticut Historical Society, Hartford.

George Wyllys (1710–1796) was born to Connecticut's political establishment. The great-grandson of a governor, he succeeded his father as Secretary of State and was in turn followed by his son, with the three holding the post for ninety-eight years, Wyllys himself for sixty-one. Pictured here in his office, his hand rests on the Charter of Connecticut. The Queen Anne corner chair was similar to one made for Governor William Pitkin in Norwich,[50] and to the right was a slant-top accountant's desk with short Queen Anne legs. The round table is inexplicable in terms of American work, yet it bears strong resemblance to an English table of the early eighteenth century.[51]

wall and possibly to the other inside walls of a room, but later all walls might be paneled. Later still, more elegant paneling with fluted pilasters and Corinthian capitals became fashionable as Americans followed British architectural guides.

The rise of paneling generally marked the disappearance of wainscotting, but in Connecticut wainscotting was used in new construction as late as 1740 and it persisted for kitchens and back halls until the end of the century.

Plastering, likewise, gained a general popularity at all economic levels. The plastered wall might be decorated in several ways. The simplest and cheapest was to let it remain undecorated, but whitewash was the standard treatment of the plastered surface in many simple and not-so-simple houses. Painting a solid color gained acceptance in some areas.

A few people, such as Edward Bromfield of Boston (1722), Mann Page I of Virginia (1726), and Governor Burnet in New York (1729), had tapestries,[28] and those who followed English fashion may have covered walls with expensive fabrics,[29] but papering was common, especially by the 1730s. Wallpaper in America dates at least to 1700. Early paper was imported from England and sold in large sheets (22 × 32 in.) rather than the rolls that were developed by the 1730s when papering became common. New England urbanites were more likely to paper their walls than their New York counterparts, but in 1739 Plunkett Fleeson of Philadelphia made the first colonial wallpaper. Fiske Kimball noted that the rise of wallpaper and the plaster wall corresponded with the decline of paneling.

Many early papers had overall floral patterns, often in close imitation of textile designs.[30] Flocked designs were common and fashionable (Fig. 8). In 1738, Thomas Hancock of Boston ordered paper from London, asking for a chinoiserie landscape similar to a design he had found in Boston (he sent a sample) but with "more Birds flying here and there."[31]

The wealthy sometimes had wall paintings. Boston merchant William Clark built a large house in 1712, decorating the parlor walls with gilded pilasters with Corinthian capitals and landscapes and coats of arms; it was painted by a man brought from England especially to do the work.[32] The Vernon house in Newport, Rhode Island, received a splendid set of chinoiserie frescoes about 1740.

ARCHITECTURAL DETAILS AND CEILINGS

Batten doors gave way to the paneled door that became universal during the period. The casement window likewise yielded to the sash window, although casement windows were installed in new construction in Connecticut as late as the 1720s. Both doors and windows in the new style were surrounded with simple architraves.

Early stairways were sometimes simple, with crude steps and handrails, especially in the center chimney houses of New England. By 1720, however, especially in the center hall house, the stair assumed a new prominence, with considerable decoration. Early, simple flat banisters gave way to turned and, by the 1720s in Virginia, to twist-turned banisters. Newel posts, likewise, were elaborately developed in expensive construction. The Queen Anne stair was wider

Figure 12. Prudence Punderson. *Interior with Queen Anne Furniture.* C. 1770–1780. Needlework, 7 in. × 9 in. (18 cm × 23 cm). Private collection.

Prudence Punderson of Preston, Connecticut, who also produced the needlework picture seen in Plate 2, depicted a late, country Queen Anne interior. Three rush-seated chairs appear with Queen Anne backs, turned stretchers, and pad feet. Note that the chairs and table are all lined up against the wall. The tilt-top table is relatively plain, but the painted floor cloth shows a squared and diapered pattern of the sort that appears in other pictures late in the century. The simple frame shows how such needlework might be prepared for hanging.

and of more gradual ascent than earlier stairs,[33] and stairs were invariably of the open string variety.

After 1710, rectangular fireplace openings, with or without a mantel shelf, became an integrated part of the design of a paneled wall. Less common was a fireplace with an arched opening, a design popular in Virginia and Maryland in the 1720s and 1730s.

By 1720, Americans were beginning to install architectural mantels with fine carving and dentil moldings. At first, such work was confined to Pennsylvania, Maryland, South Carolina, and Virginia. Yet even as the style spread throughout the colonies later in the century, only families of wealth could afford such elaborate work.

The era presented a variety of ceiling treatments, of which the least expensive consisted of the exposed beams and floorboards of the next level. A more expensive variant encased the beams and plastered the ceiling between them. Generally, the flat ceiling plastered overall appeared after the beginning of the Queen Anne era, but it occurred as early as 1720 in Rhode Island. One notable and rare variant was the tray form dating to 1725 at Stratford, Virginia. Other expensive rarities in Queen Anne ceilings are cast plaster decorations documented at Westover in Virginia as early as 1730.

Ceiling moldings accompanying the flat plaster ceiling were generally variants of the simple bolection molding. Where wall painting included pilasters, the capitals formed parts of the moldings. Dentil moldings generally appear with the Chippendale styles, but examples of light dentil molding are found in Pennsylvania as early as 1721.

Cupboards over mantels appear by 1725; moderately rare in the Queen Anne period were overmantel panels bearing oil paintings. Corner cupboards were important. First appearing in the late seventeenth century, by the middle of the eighteenth century such cupboards were relatively common in moderately wealthy households and usually built in to the room where the family dined. Paneled doors were popular in the South, while New England and the Middle Colonies favored glazed doors.[34]

Figure 13. Artist unknown. *Tea Party in the Time of George I. C.* 1725. Oil on canvas. Colonial Williamsburg, Inc., Va.

The gentleman bought a tea service of great fashion and expense, with his China export tea bowls and saucers, and silver sugar bowl, tea caddy, sugar tongs, hot water jug, spoon tray, teaspoons, slop bowl, and teapot. The silver probably weighed at least 50 ounces, which at the official English rate of $5\frac{1}{2}$ per ounce would have been worth a minimum of £12. 18. 4 for the metal alone.[52] In 1729, Connecticut appraisers valued silver at 18 shillings an ounce, which would have given this set a value of £45.[53] The same artist produced another canvas with the same tea equipment.[54]

As window curtains were comparatively rare in the Queen Anne period, paneled, folding window shutters were a usual means to block out light. In simpler houses, sliding shutters (Indian shutters) were common.

Introduced during this era was the pattern of round-topped niches or doors flanking a fireplace, a pattern that appeared in 1720 in Rhode Island and in 1729 in Maryland (Fig. 24).

LIGHTING

Although rush and oil lamps persisted, candles provided the prime means of illumination. Candles could be made at home or bought commercially. Over the years, President Edward Holyoke of Harvard studied scientifically the three types of candles available, finding that spermaceti candles cost most yet burned longest. Bayberry candles cost more and burned longer than tallow. Bayberry candles disappear from his diary in 1743, while spermaceti was not mentioned until 1761. Rush candles were cheaper where they could be gotten. Long rushes soaked in grease or dipped in tallow gave a tolerable light, but they were seldom found in New England.[35]

Candlesticks reflected new styles. In both Massachusetts and Pennsylvania inventories, brass candlesticks were by far the most common, iron sticks the next most common, and pewter relatively rare. Although silver candlesticks survive as great monuments to the silversmith's art, neither Abbott Lowell Cummings in surveying Suffolk County, Massachusetts, nor Margaret Schiffer in studying Chester County, Pennsylvania, recorded a single silver candlestick in this period. Brass chandeliers were found in large rooms of wealthy homes; lanterns were used in halls, passageways, and on staircases.[36] Girls' handwork and useful lighting combined in the quill work sconce.

Iron candlestands fitted with brass candle sockets and drip pans appear as early as 1700. These candlestands were probably left in place, as were sconces, but each day the portable candlesticks were usually brought to the kitchen or hall to be made ready for night use.

COLOR

Rooms, particularly bedrooms, decorated in one basic color continued to be fashionable. Peter Faneuil, the Boston merchant, who in 1742 left an estate of £44,451, had one bedroom in green, another in yellow, and a third in blue.

Paint gradually became important, and paint dealers and painters appeared in major cities. A specialty of these painters was marbling and graining, which became a general fashion after 1725, even though marbling had appeared as early as 1705 when part of the Capitol at Williamsburg was ordered "painted like marble." Richard Marten advertised in South Carolina in 1736 that he did imitations of marble, walnut, oak, and cedar at 5 shillings the yard, the equivalent of 8½ pence sterling. Perhaps distinct styles in marbling developed by region, for a painter arriving in South Carolina from London advertised in 1743 that he did marbling "in a more complete manner than is generally done in this Province."[37]

Figure 14. Artist unknown. *John Potter and Family*. Before 1742. Oil on panel, 29½ in. × 63⅜ in. (76 cm × 160 cm). Newport Historical Society, Newport, R.I.

John Potter of Matunuck, Rhode Island, and his family gathered about a round tea table. The cups and saucers, creamer, slop bowl, and sugar bowl were all sprig-decorated pottery, while the teapot was of a different pattern. The service was fashionable enough, but not so elegant as silver.[55]

Paint dealers' advertisements list colors available. Warm tones predominated in the lists in Boston and New York newspapers, but in 1748 Peter Kalm wrote of New York: "The alcoves, and all the woodwork were painted with a bluish grey colour." Outside Philadelphia the mansion Graeme Park (1721–1722) had the woodwork likewise painted gray-blue. The dining room of the Governor's Palace in Williamsburg was painted pearl and the parlor cream.[38] Nina Fletcher Little has summarized the most common New England colors for woodwork as Indian red, green, yellow, ochre, and gray,[39] but many paneled walls in New England were left unpainted.

Mrs. Schiffer's study of Chester County, Pennsylvania, made note of all colors specified regardless of object. Black was the most prominent color between 1720 and 1749, while blue would lead the Chippendale list. Only one inventory specified the color of bed hangings—blue and white.

Colors advertised in Boston, in 1738,[40] include: white lead, Spanish white, spruce yellow, carmine, red lead, vermilion red, Indian red, ruddle-red ochre, Spanish brown, terra umber, leaf gold, and leaf brass. Additional colors, advertised in New York in 1748, included: Prussian blue, verdigris, English ochre, Venetian red, and umber. The number of references to particular colors in Chester County, Pennsylvania, inventories between 1720 and 1749 are interesting[41]: black, 48 references; white, 34; blue, 27; red, 21; brown, 15; green, 9; gray, 7; walnut, 3; snuff, 2; chocolate, yellow, winestone, olive, russet, and liver, all 1 reference.

ACCESSORIES

American homes of the wealthy became increasingly luxurious, with a growing number of accessories complementing other expensive furnishings. Colonists of middle economic status also began to include items that were more decorative than utilitarian; but the interiors of the poor remained sparse.

The appearance of Chinese porcelain added new elegance to tables that were increasingly set with forks as well as knives and spoons. A very few households even used silver plates. New styles of British glass quickly found their way to the American colonies.

Brass.   Brass was by no means prominent in every Queen Anne house. A valuable metal, it was appraised at 2 shillings per pound in Massachusetts in 1718 and 3 shillings in 1741. For many houses, a £6 kettle was a major investment.

Brass fireplace equipment was much more ornamental than iron work. Boston papers in 1737 advertised "brass doggs," presumably in a new style, for one appraised in Dorchester, Massachusetts, just five years earlier had described a pair of brass andirons as "old fashion." Nonetheless, they were worth £1. Such andirons were used in the best rooms in the house.

Brass implements were largely confined to the kitchen or hall. Many restorations today place warming pans near bedroom fireplaces, but inventories generally include one such pan per house, usually kept in the kitchen or hall.

Figure 15. Frontispiece to *The Pleasant and Profitable Companion* (Boston, 1733). American Antiquarian Society, Worcester, Mass.

The Boston artist showed a fine Queen Anne desk of uncertain structure. Because the support to the fall is not pulled out, one can only conclude that the man is writing on the slant top itself. Note that his inkpot is on top near the stand supporting the book. The gentleman sits on a turned ladderback chair in a style far different from the desk. The square floor could either be a painted floor or floor cloth.

Ceramics.   A few households still made do with wood and pewter, but the better-appointed residences had ceramics in increasing variety. Boston merchants advertised tea cups (without handles), coffee cups (with handles), saucers, bowls, teapots, salts, milk pots, sugar dishes, breakfast bowls, strainers, mugs, coffee bowls, handled cups, basins, patty pans, soup plates, and boats for spoons.

Earthenware and stoneware were produced locally in some areas, but most ceramics were imported from England or Holland. Chinese and Japanese ceramics came to America through England.[42]

From England, importation of stoneware and Delft continued as in the previous period—most of the Delft now coming from England rather than Holland. White salt glaze ware appeared in the 1720s. Blue and white ware was advertised prominently in the 1720s, but by the 1730s and 1740s there was more variety in the market: yellow ware from Bristol, yellow Liverpool ware, white earthenware and white flint ware from Liverpool, plus enameled ware and brown earthenware from unspecified sources. Rhenish ceramics, most notably mugs and chamber pots, were found in the lesser homes of Virginia. Chinese porcelain appeared increasingly, but so valued was it early in the period that one Boston citizen advertised the theft of a single tea cup in 1718.

Ceramics were often kept in the kitchen, along with pewter and brass, but increasingly gained a decorative as well as utilitarian place in the best rooms of the house. The more expensive the china, the more likely it was to be displayed. Typical are inventories in which fine glass and china are displayed in a boffet (or corner cupboard) in the parlor, while earthenware is kept in the kitchen.

The mantel frequently provided another display of ceramics. It is often said that Queen Anne mantels had no shelves or had shelves only in the kitchen. Inventories in Massachusetts and Pennsylvania prove otherwise as they list china, earthenware, and glass on mantel shelves. A Boston newspaper provided additional documentation in 1739 when it reported that a lightning bolt knocked "Earthen Vessels and Glasses" off a "Mantletree Shelf."

Another ceramic decoration that remained popular was the English or Dutch fireplace tile. A Boston advertisement reveals some of the varieties available in 1738: "Scripture (round and square), Landskips of divers sort, Sea Monsters, Horsemen, Soldiers, Diamonds, &c."

Clocks.   Careful readers of the Boston *News Letter* in December 1715 realized that a new style in clocks had literally arrived, for William Claggett advertised "a new Fashion'd Monethly Clock & Case lately arrived from London." In 1712, Joseph Essex advertised in Boston that he offered thirty-hour clocks, week clocks, month clocks, spring table clocks, chime clocks, quarter clocks, and quarter chime clocks. Generally, clocks were found only in houses of people of at least moderate means, and presumably most of those inventoried were tall case clocks, valued from £8 to £15. About 1720, both in Pennsylvania and New England, clocks were kept in the parlor, but by 1740 they were found perhaps as often in the hall or, as it was coming to be called, the dining room. In Chester County, Pennsylvania, only 2.4 percent of the estates between 1684 and 1699 included clocks. Between 1720 and 1749, that percentage had risen to only 4.3 percent.

Glass.   For those who could afford it, the markets offered an increasing array of glass imported from England. Few were able to benefit from the

left: Figure 16. Artist unknown. "He! He! He!" Frontispiece, with Tommy Trapwit, to Isaiah Thomas, *Be Merry and Wise, or the Cream of the Jests* (Worcester, Mass., 1786). American Antiquarian Society, Worcester.

Tommy smirks amid Queen Anne furnishings in one of Isaiah Thomas's many children's books of the 1780s. Like many period artists and printers, he showed a chair with a typical back but with straight legs seldom encountered in a museum or antique shop today.[56] The proximity of the table and chair to the fire in an iron grate—a feature found in many pictures—documents the role of heat as a major factor in furniture placement. Note that the firescreen, covered with a printed fabric, is more useful to Tommy for hanging his hat than it is for protecting his face from the heat.

below: Figure 17. C. L. Junker (?). *Interior of an Eighteenth-Century Tavern. C.* 1732. Wash drawing, 10½ in. × 14½ in. (28 cm × 38 cm). Courtesy of The New-York Historical Society, New York City.

Probably this tavern was English, for a print of the same subject by Charles Spooner (1720–1767) appeared in London with the title *The Sportsman Taking Refreshment* and the notation "Junker pinx^t." English or American, the drawing gives the flavor of the tavern rooms found in numerous American houses early in the eighteenth century. Decoration was minimal, and the room was filled with simple furniture, much of it surviving from the seventeenth century.

American glass manufactories, founded first in New York in 1732 and then in South Jersey by Caspar Wistar in 1739. The 1730s saw an increasing proliferation of forms. Boston merchants advertised wine glasses, jelly glasses, syllabubs, decanters, sugar pots, barrel cans, punchbowls, bird fountains, and candlesticks. Merchants also offered japanned glassware.

For those who did buy with taste in the newest styles, drinking glasses were the inverted baluster type (popular in England from 1720 to about 1735), or the later drawn stem glass (popular in England from 1730 to 1745). Both types have been found in Virginia. Colonel William Tailer, who died in Dorchester, Massachusetts, in 1732 leaving an estate of £9,366, had a lot of valuable glass. His five decanters were valued at 5 shillings each, his three dozen wine glasses were worth £2, and he had twenty-three glasses of other sorts worth £1.3.0. While his pewter was kept in the kitchen, the glass was in the hall, a room probably used as a dining room. Wealth and fashion did not dictate an elaborate collection of glass, for the Reverend Ebenezer Thayer who died in nearby Roxbury less than a year later had £137 worth of silver, but his only glass was some salts in the parlor. Purely decorative items appear in some accounts. In 1732, Colonel Thomas Jones of Williamsburg gave his wife flower bottles and six glasses with covers.[43]

Iron. Iron was an important, utilitarian part of every household. Numerous items are inventoried among cooking implements. Although firetools and andirons were used in many rooms, most other iron was kept in the kitchen or hall. Families of great wealth sometimes seem to have had larger collections of iron, but unlike the previous era, the quantity of iron in an inventory does not vary greatly with the wealth of the householder. Iron was used in almost every room with a fireplace. Andirons were necessities, often accompanied by cast iron firebacks, many of them produced in America after 1725. Early designs on these decorative additions to the fireplace included coats of arms, Cain and Abel, St. George, or floral motifs.[44]

Most iron was imported. English work tended to be more decorated than the simpler products of native blacksmiths.

Pewter. Pewter remained common, with the quantity again varying according to economic status and family need. Plates, platters, and basins continued the most common forms, followed by mugs, tankards, pots, and chamber pots. Candlesticks, saltcellars, spoons, and porringers are mentioned less often in Massachusetts inventories than they are in those of Chester County, Pennsylvania. Great quantities of pewter were imported from England in elaborate as well as simple forms. A Philadelphia merchant advertised imported pewter tea services in 1733, and Boston merchants offered dish covers and water dishes in the same year. Domestic pewter production became established in cities and towns, with New York craftsmen adhering to Dutch models rather than the English models followed in the other colonies. Generally, pewter designs followed new styles in silver.

Appraisers increased the value of pewter to 18 pence (1718) and then to 3 shillings (1733) the pound. China and glass were more common, yet still did not supplant pewter. In Massachusetts, pewter made up generally 0.15 to 0.3 percent of the average estate until the 1730s, when it rose again to roughly 0.4 percent, about the level it had been at the end of the 1600s. Fifty to 75 pounds of pewter was common as a household supply. The citizens of Chester County,

Pennsylvania, had comparatively more pewter in their estates, with the quantities ranging from 0.85 to 1.9 percent of the estate's value.

In New England and Pennsylvania, pewter continued to be an item for the kitchen or hall, but in Pennsylvania, it might be found in a "closet" in the chamber or in the parlor.

Silver. The Queen Anne style governed American silver about a decade before the style gained favor in furniture, moving away from the heavily ornamented William and Mary pieces to simple, curved lines, pear shapes, and cabriole legs. Chinese teapots and tea cups both had considerable influence on Queen Anne silver.

Importation from England continued among the very wealthy, and domestic silversmithing grew greatly, developing regional styles most evident in tankards. Spoons were still the most common silver items, with the rattail bowl supplanted by the double drop design. American silver forks remained rare, but James Logan of Philadelphia ordered six from John De Nys, a local silversmith, in 1718, and in New York, John Le Rous produced knives and forks shortly after 1723.[45] Trencher salts, porringers, casters, cans or mugs, chafing dishes, sauceboats, and tankards became more common for families who could afford them. Silver was inventoried at between 5/5 and 18/- the ounce, depending upon the currency. Colonel Henry Fitzhugh, who died in Stafford, Virginia, in 1743, had been educated at Oxford and married a member of the wealthy Carter family. His inventory included twelve silver plates (six of them valued at £33) and "one large two handled silver cup" worth £52.10.0.[46]

Silversmiths provided the most fashionable service for the new ritual of tea time. A full complement included a teapot, creamer, sugar bowl, tea caddy, spoons, and sugar tongs (Fig. 13). Tea services were displayed in the parlor with as much of the service as possible in silver, whether a few spoons or a full set.

Hanoverian rattail spoon
typical of the early
Queen Anne period

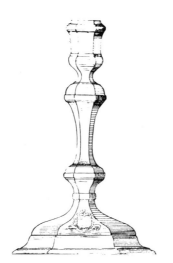

Queen Anne candlestick

4

The Chippendale Style

1750–1810

B Y 1750, the new English rococo was established in wealthy households of American cities. Papers in Boston, New York, Philadelphia, Baltimore, Annapolis, and Charleston advertised goods in the "newest" or "latest" fashions, and to the style-conscious reader it was clearly time to redecorate. As furniture of the new mode has generally been termed "Chippendale," we have called the whole period the Chippendale style. Claw-and-ball chairs can be documented in Boston as early as 1737, and in that same year Sir William Pepperell ordered chairs from London "of ye New fashion."[1] Joseph Richardson, the Philadelphia silversmith, began working in the rococo style in the late 1740s, about the time fashionable cabinetmakers there and in New York began producing chairs in the new designs.

Writing somewhat later, between 1769 and 1777, William Eddis, surveyor of customs in Annapolis, recorded the rapidity with which styles continued to cross the ocean: "The quick importation of fashions from the mother country is really astonishing. I am almost inclined to believe that a new fashion is adopted earlier by the polished and affluent American, than by many opulent persons in the great metropolis."[2]

Americans of wealth became very conscious of fashion. Some, like Peter Manigault (Fig. 20), were familiar with rococo from their own years in London. They often came back with silver, fabrics, or glass, and occasionally, like Robert Carter of Virginia, with portraits of themselves by Joshua Reynolds. Some visitors bought fashionable goods even though they disliked them. In 1758 Benjamin Franklin visiting England sent his wife in Philadelphia four silver salt ladles of the "newest, but ugliest, fashion."[3] He also bought carpet, tablecloths, upholstery and curtain fabrics, candle snuffers, coffee cups, table china, china, silver knives and forks, and silver candlesticks.

Others sought British fashion without leaving America, often without knowing what the fashion was. In 1758, George Washington depended upon a Bristol merchant for advice as well as supply: "In my last, I desir'd two pairs of work'd Ruffles at a guinea each pair; if work'd Ruffles shou'd be out of fashion send

Jeremiah Lee was one of the new wealthy merchant class.
Lee, who had just built a new mansion in Marblehead,
Massachusetts, had himself portrayed in a scene that never
existed—at least not in Massachusetts. The table here
and the one like it that appears in Copley's portrait of
Thomas Hancock (1764–1766) was derived from John
Vanderbank's portrait of Queen Caroline (1736) and
not from any object in North America. But such carpets
were in America, and after careful study it has been concluded that Lee probably stands on an Axminster woven
in an Oriental design.[79]

Copley documented several details characteristic of the
houses of his rich clients. The Chippendale chair is upholstered in a floral damask decorated with brass-headed
nails. Costly refinements on the chair were the molding
on the legs, the curls at the ends of the arms, and the Chinese fretwork at the top of the leg. The Oriental carpet
was deep red, white, and dark blue with touches of yellow
and black. The cushion on which the girl knelt was decorated with tassels.

such as are not." Fashion, whatever it was, was Washington's criterion in an order for china in the same year. "Pray let them be neat and fashionable or send none."[4] In 1773, Benjamin Fuller, a rich Philadelphia merchant, wrote an agent in Bristol, ordering "two genteel Cases for knives and forks, such as you would choose for yourself." The ivory-handled knives and forks for the cases were to be of the "best kind & newest fashion."[5]

Perhaps realizing the American quest for the fashionable, merchants exploited their London backgrounds. In 1775, Thomas Harper, a Philadelphia upholsterer and paperhanger, advertised that he "had the honour to serve a great number of the nobility in London with general satisfaction."[6]

Imported items in turn provided models for local craftsmen. The Hancock family of Boston received an English silver coffee pot in the new rococo style in 1746, and Benjamin Faneuil ordered one in 1751. It is likely that Boston silversmith John Coburn or the Symmes family had seen one of these pots, for Coburn made one almost identical for that family.[7]

English books added to the desirability of imported objects. Chippendale's *The Gentleman and Cabinet Maker's Director* (1754) was an obvious, though late, influence on some furniture design, while many books were in the hands of builders and interested students of architecture like Thomas Jefferson. Among the more common titles familiar to Americans were William Kent's *Designs of Inigo Jones* (1727), William Salmon's *Palladio Londonensis* (1734), Abraham Swan's *British Architect* (1745), Batty Langley's *City & County Builder's and Workman's Treasury of Designs* (1740), and Isaac Ware's *Complete Body of Architecture* (1756). Swan's *British Architect* was in such demand that a Philadelphia publisher issued it in 1775 together with selections from his *Designs in Architecture* (1757). In some cases, it is possible to see the direct influence of individual books. Thus, *British Architect* inspired mantels in the Lee House in Marblehead, Massachusetts, the Brice House in Annapolis, and Washington's Mount Vernon.[8]

Prints were probably another source of fashion design. Just as modern scholars have turned to them for decorative clues, so, too, the hundreds who bought them saw the latest fashions in British curtains, upholstery, wallpaper, carpets, and furniture.

American craftsmen in the major cities adopted the new styles first, as they found a ready market for copies of London models. In terms of population these "cities" would pass for small villages today, but at that time 10,000 people was a major concentration of economic productivity and an ample field for competition for status as most fashionable. Below is a list of the population of the largest cities in America in the 1770s:

1.	PHILADELPHIA, PA.	21,767
2.	NEW YORK, N.Y.	21,463
3.	BOSTON, MASS.	17,000
4.	CHARLESTON, S.C.	12,000
5.	NEWPORT, R.I.	11,000
6.	NEW HAVEN, CONN.	8,295
7.	NORWICH, CONN.	7,032
8.	NORFOLK, VA.	6,250
9.	BALTIMORE, MD.	5,934
10.	NEW LONDON, CONN.	5,366

Soon craftsmen in the smaller cities were copying the styles of the larger, and eventually by the late 1760s the styles moved to the countryside, where Chippendale furniture was being produced as late as 1805. Furniture provides probably the best examples of the process. In the 1760s, Philadelphia cabinetmakers produced costly highboys with latticework pediments. From 1767 to 1771, Eliphalet Chapin of Connecticut was in Philadelphia to work as a cabinetmaker and escape a paternity suit in Connecticut. He returned to his native state carrying Philadelphia styles with him. He produced highboys with latticework pediments, but the details were far simpler than the Philadelphia originals. Soon other cabinetmakers were copying Chapin's work, and with each imitation the style grew more and more distant from the original model.

American production of household furnishings expanded into almost every field. During the years preceding the Revolution, Americans were producing glass, printed textiles, wallpaper, Queensware, porcelain, and papier-mâché moldings. The impact of these new manufactures was usually limited and local, the bulk of the market being still supplied by imports.

Figure 20. George Roupell. *Peter Manigault and His Friends*. 1757–1760. Black ink and wash drawing, 10³⁄₁₆ in. × 12³⁄₁₆ in. (25 cm × 30 cm). Courtesy, Henry Francis du Pont Winterthur Museum, Winterthur, Del.

Peter Manigault (1731–1773), the rich and powerful Speaker of the South Carolina Assembly, gathered his friends at his house near Charleston, and one of the guests recorded the scene. Manigault says: "Your Tost Howarth." With dinner finished, punch appeared in a Chinese export bowl. Glass and silver were up to date, for glasses with drawn stems and bell bowls were popular in England in the 1750s, and the three silver candlesticks bear strong resemblance to those produced by John Cafe of London in 1753–1754, just the year Manigault returned to America from his legal studies in London.[80]

Some craftsmen and merchants began functioning as decorators or at least advisers on furnishing. Upholsterers, like Plunkett Fleeson of Philadelphia, were particularly likely to play that role in the cities. He advertised wallpaper, upholstery, furniture, papier-mâché moldings, and paper-hanging.[9] In the country, a cabinetmaker might fill much the same functions. Isaac Fitch of Lebanon, Connecticut, was a cabinetmaker who owned Gibbs's *Book of Architecture* (1728) and Morris's *Lectures on Architecture* (1734). He designed a house for Governor Jonathan Trumbull of Connecticut (1740–1809), spent weeks decorating one room in it, made furniture for the governor, and designed a "Carpitt."

Economic disparity was considerable, but far from the extremes to be found in the late nineteenth century. In reading estates and accounts during this period, one must keep in mind that accounts were usually kept in "lawful money" of the colony. Lawful money was basically paper money, which passed at a substantial discount from the sterling rate. Thus, British silver coins worth £1 sterling might be worth as much as £31 in lawful money in Rhode Island in 1762.

The currency problem is all too often neglected in interpreting estates and bills of sale, and because of inflation, readers are sometimes more impressed by the cost of items than they should be. For example, the £330 that John Townsend, Jr., charged for a large mahogany desk in 1767 sounds quite expensive, until one realizes that £330 in Rhode Island old tenor (currency before revaluation) was worth a more believable £10.12.0 sterling. New Hampshire, Massachusetts, Rhode Island, and Connecticut, troubled by the way in which inflation had departed from the sterling standard, revalued their currency several times. The former rates were called old tenor (O.T.). In 1774, a Massachusetts estate was worth the substantial-sounding figure of £9,031 in old tenor; in lawful money, the amount became £1,204.[10] The sterling value of that lawful money in turn was £1,003. If this sounds confusing now, it was then, and it grew worse during the Revolution with the appearance and rapid inflation of Continental Currency. In 1780, William Will, a Philadelphia pewterer, charged a customer £52.10.0 for three pewter plates. In 1755, a Plymouth, Massachusetts, cobbler had paid 10/8 for six pewter plates.[11] Will was a fine pewterer but his work was not that much more expensive; currency values explain the disparity.

In the chart at right, we have generally used actual lawful money figures where they seemed comparable, making comparisons to common sterling values where they might be helpful. The list gives some idea of the varying value of the money in circulation.

The property of the wealthy was in land or in wealth accumulated from shipping or trade. Ten thousand pounds was an impressive estate in any currency. Those who left estates of over £3,000 sterling were generally quite well-to-do, and from the inventories, those with estates of £500 lived in rather comfortable circumstances (Table 6, page 54). The figures in the table suggest a rather even distribution of wealth, with relatively few living in poverty, especially in the country.

The most elaborate houses and furnishings belonged to families of the greatest wealth, usually in the cities. The Hancocks, Apthorps, and Boylstons of Boston provided well for themselves through imports and the work of local

Value of £100 Sterling in Currencies of Each Colony Issuing Notes, 1760[12]

NEW HAMPSHIRE	old tenor	£2,666
	new tenor	427
	sterling notes	107
MASSACHUSETTS	old tenor	1,300
	middle tenor	325
	new tenor	130
RHODE ISLAND	old tenor	2,666
	middle tenor	666
	new tenor	333
CONNECTICUT	old tenor	2,666
	new tenor	761
	proclamation or lawful money	242
NEW YORK		167
NEW JERSEY		153
PENNSYLVANIA		159
MARYLAND	hard currency	154
	paper currency	146
DELAWARE		159
VIRGINIA		141
NORTH CAROLINA		190
SOUTH CAROLINA		700

Table 6. Size of Estates in the Chippendale Era, Figured in Pounds of Each Colony[13]

(figures are percentages of inventories falling into each category)

	£0–50	51–100	101–200	201–300	301–400	401–500	501+
LINCOLN COUNTY, MAINE, 1760–75	25%	16	25	15	4	4	11
LYME, CONN., 1760–75	32	18	13	9	10	4	14
STONINGTON AND GROTON, CONN., 1767–72	22	11	19	16	6	6	20
NEW JERSEY, 1761–70	16	16	22	14	8	6	18

craftsmen. In 1761, East Apthorp (1733–1816), a Bostonian who had taken Anglican orders, built himself a house in Cambridge, Massachusetts. His merchant father, who had died in 1758, left a comfortable estate of almost £20,000, and thus the Cambridge graduate of 1755 was able to indulge the tastes he had known in England. Peter Harrison (1716–1775), the Newport architect, helped design the house with details drawn from Swan and Langley. Wendell Garrett estimates that the land alone cost £2,000, and John Adams and others thought the residence more fitting for a bishop than a missionary.[14] In Albany, Philip Schuyler showered expense on furnishing a new house built in 1761–1762 at a cost, by his calculation, of £1,425.16.0.

Charles Carroll of Carrollton, at his death the last surviving signer of the Declaration of Independence, received the following advice from his father in 1772: "Lay out as little money as Possible in dress furniture & shew of any Sort, decency is the only point to be aimed at."[15] The Boylstons, however, thought otherwise, and a most awed John Adams recorded his impressions after returning from dinner at Nicholas Boylston's house on January 16, 1766: "Went over the House to view the Furniture, which alone cost a thousand Pounds sterling. A Seat for a noble Man, a Prince. The Turkey Carpets, the painted Hangings, the Marble Tables, the rich Beds with crimson Damask Curtains and Counterpins, the beautiful Chimny Clock, the Spacious Garden, are the most magnificent Thing I have ever seen."[16] Such was the impression many a householder was trying to create, but it took great wealth to succeed.

A number of the wealthy and leaders of fashion were Tories. Jules David Prown found that of 240 subjects for John Singleton Copley's expensive portraits, 55 percent were loyal to the Crown. Perhaps this is not surprising since many of those who followed the changing details of British decorative fashions might cling to the British model in their politics as well.[17]

At every economic class level, the best furnishings were reserved for the best room, with lesser quality distributed in rooms of lesser importance. Barbara Gorely Teller found a typical example in the 1780 inventory of William Checkley, a Providence customs official of moderate means. In his parlor he had a Scotch carpet, a claw-and-ball table, and a mahogany tea table with a porcelain tea set. His "keeping room," however, had a maple tea table, assorted china cups and a redware teapot, and leather-bottomed maple chairs. The kitchen had pewter plates and teapot.[18]

Residence of Colonel Jacob Ford,
Morristown, N.J., 1774

Vassal–Longfellow House, Cambridge, Mass.

Figure 21. George Harvey. *Schuyler Ogden and His Sister*. 1842. Oil on canvas, 17 in. × 14 in. (43 cm × 36 cm). Kennedy Galleries, Inc., New York City.

Schuyler Ogden and his sister stood in the front hall of the house their ancestor Philip Van Rensselaer built between 1765 and 1768, sparing no expense on an interior decorated with specially made rococo English wallpapers.[81] Between 1840 and 1843, the family had architect Richard Upjohn remodel the house, and the work in progress was thus responsible for the unusual juxtaposition of the encaustic tile floor and ornate Chippendale staircase. Note the Venetian carpet held down by brass rods.

Figure 22. Artist unknown. *English Conversation Piece. C.* 1750. Oil on canvas, 32½ in. × 28 in. (84 cm × 71 cm). Sold at Sotheby's, London, June 13, 1934; present location unknown.[82] By Kind Permission of Sotheby Parke Bernet & Co.

Every element of this English interior was to be found in America. Wallpaper of almost identical pattern has been found in Boston; Saybrook, Connecticut; and Dorchester, Vermont. Zechariah Mills of Hartford reproduced the same basic design in 1794. A grate filled the fireplace and a firescreen stood nearby. The canvas illustrates perhaps better than any the traditional arrangement of furniture against the wall. Only those Chippendale chairs actually in use were moved to the center of the room. The carpet, probably an Oriental, marked the house as one of considerable wealth.

The best room of the house was usually designated the parlor, if it wasn't styled more simply (in terms of location) "front" room or "north" room. "Hall" was falling out of the general vocabulary, and it became customary to name the room in terms of location, color, or size—east, green, or little room. By 1770, in New England, "keeping room" was another term for a parlor, sometimes a very well-furnished one. The term "sitting room" does not appear in Chester County, Pennsylvania, inventories until the 1780s, but a Massachusetts inventory refers to a "setting Parlour" in 1763. Dining rooms appeared in some number, usually among the fashionable well-to-do. Sometimes, dining rooms were on the second floor, without a dining table. In Maryland, "dining room" referred to an informal parlor used for entertaining and furnished with dishes and card tables. But many New England dining rooms *were* furnished with a large table and a number of chairs.

Other common first-floor rooms were studies (furnished with many books), kitchens, or butteries. Bedrooms, always called chambers, were named either for location or the first-floor room beneath, as in the kitchen chamber. The attic was called the garret.[19]

The fashionable Chippendale house followed the center hall plan, often arranged to allow an impressive staircase of twist balusters of the kind seen on page 55 in Figure 21. In some areas of New England, the center chimney plan continued to be built.

FURNITURE

Claw-and-ball chairs can be documented in Boston as early as 1737,[20] but the American version of the rococo, generally called Chippendale, began to emerge from the most fashionable shops of Philadelphia and New York in the 1740s. Boston and Newport cabinetmakers started work in the new style in the following decade, and by 1760 the mode was well established, although Queen Anne pieces continued to be made throughout the century. Country cabinetmakers produced Chippendale furniture well into the nineteenth century.

Generally, American craftsmen followed the simpler English styles of about 1720, rather than the more intricate designs of Thomas Chippendale in his *Gentleman and Cabinet Maker's Director* (1754).[21] Chippendale codified his era, bringing together many of the most elaborate designs of mid-century England. English design had continued in the direction begun earlier in the century, but with the addition of elements borrowed from the French rococo (shell motifs, cartouches, an emphasis on the curved line), the Gothic style (trefoils, lancet arches), and Chinese design (pierced fretwork). The ball-and-claw foot also has Chinese origins, but that motif had been used earlier in the century and was out of favor in England by the time Chippendale wrote.

Figure 23. Joseph Stewart. *John Phillips.* 1793. Oil on canvas, 78 in. × 68 in. (1.98 m × 1.73 m). Dartmouth College Collection, Hanover, N.H.

John Phillips (1719–1795), a Harvard graduate of 1735, made a large fortune in business and founded Phillips Exeter Academy in 1778. He was a very wealthy man, yet his New Hampshire house was far from the high style elegance seen in Virginia or in major urban centers. He sat on a Windsor chair next to a simple, baize-covered Pembroke with his floors covered with floor cloth. Note another floor cloth of contrasting pattern in the next room. The plaster walls were plain except for the painted base molding, and the wallpaper borders applied at ceiling, baseboard, and window. Window frame and base molding were painted the same color. The fringed curtains are a good example of a festoon design.

Expensive, high style ribbon
back chair with carved shells

Less expensive ribbon back chair

Inexpensive country version of
the ribbon back pattern

Regional characteristics flourished, most evident in expensive furniture, since the cheaper and simpler pieces offered little opportunity for characteristic decorations. Yet even simpler furniture often reveals its area of origin. With regional styles went regional preferences for certains forms. The late Charles Montgomery found that Salem produced many highboys, Boston produced fewer, and urban Charleston none. The chest-on-chest was likewise more popular in New York than Philadelphia;[22] the blockfront was common in New England, but rarely found in Philadelphia.

Mahogany had eclipsed walnut as the most prestigious wood for those who could afford it. Cherry was only a little less desirable in some regions, and maple and birch were less expensive everywhere. Moreau de Saint-Méry found mahogany common among Philadelphia wealthy, while lesser houses made do with painted green chairs.

Chairs for high style houses received careful carving; those in Figure 24 show the characteristic claw-and-ball feet and acanthus carving at the knees. The backs of these chairs were in the popular ribbon pattern. The straight leg was less expensive than the claw and ball. A still simpler version of the Chippendale chair is illustrated in Figure 27. Beyond the basic shape, its only ornament was the shallow carving on the ears. Rocking chairs appeared in number. Eliakin Smith of Hadley, Massachusetts, added rockers to many chairs during the 1760s.[23]

The sofa, comparatively rare in the Queen Anne period, became much more common. A Copley portrait dated 1771 shows a sofa decorated with brass-headed nails and furnished with extra cushions in the same fabric as the sofa.

The greatest efforts of the Chippendale cabinetmaker were reserved for case pieces, but curiously, few highboys, lowboys, or chests-on-chests appear in period paintings. It was apparently not fashionable to depict such pieces in portraits, but desks and secretaries do appear.

Case pieces varied widely in price with the degree of decoration. Most expensive was the claw-and-ball foot, less costly the ogee bracket foot, and least expensive the straight bracket foot. One must not assume that only claw-and-ball pieces were to be found in the wealthiest families. Washington, who spent considerable sums on his furniture, owned a kneehole dressing table with a straight bracket foot.

While no lowboys appear in the illustrations, period woodcuts depict an application Washington mentioned in a letter of 1758, when he ordered a card table from London to use as a dressing table. In Figure 26, Mrs. Cuyler sits by what may well be a demi-lune card table with a cloth and lace skirt added.

The illustrations document many uses of the large, round-tip table (see Plate 2). Illustrations show needlework, reading, dining, drinking tea, singing, and counting money being conducted at such tables. Rectangular tea tables appear, too, and they bear strong regional features.

Although the oval dining table continued to be popular, a new straight-legged drop-leaf form appeared (Plate 2). A smaller drop-leaf table, usually called a Pembroke, emerged during this period and found its way into many pictures. Marble-top or slab tables continued to be fashionable and expensive.

A study of Maryland inventories reveals that firescreens were most common in rooms with dining tables (Fig. 16 in Chapter 3). Candlestands were produced in great number but are rare in illustrations, while woodcuts (but not many paintings) show beds with full sets of curtains on straight tester frames.

Inexpensive Windsor chairs became increasingly popular during the Chippendale period. In 1784, Washington ordered eighteen for Mount Vernon, and William Paca of Annapolis had green Windsors in his entrance hall. Windsor candlestands were popular in Pennsylvania, but less so in Rhode Island and New Hampshire.

Placement. The illustrations indicate that furniture was placed close to the walls or in front of a fireplace. Several pictures document the importance of light in the placement of furniture. Without artificial illumination, a window was a necessary source for writing, reading, needlework, or dressing.

John F. Watson's *Annals of Philadelphia* (1830) included a description of a Philadelphia parlor. Watson assumed that if a chimney occupied one corner of a parlor, a "beaufet" or corner cupboard filled with china and silver occupied another. A tilt-top tea table occupied the third corner. When not in use, the tea table was tipped up and "stood upright, like an expanded fan or palm leaf in the

Figure 24. Samuel F. B. Morse. *The Family of Jedidiah Morse of Charlestown, Massachusetts.* 1811. Smithsonian Institution, Washington, D.C.

Morse, who painted this picture the year after he graduated from Yale, is shown with his parents and brothers. The Reverend Dr. Jedidiah Morse's *American Universal Geography* made the minister more famous than wealthy, but the family moved in fashionable circles. The Brussels wall-to-wall carpet shown here dates from about 1810, but the architecture and furniture are Chippendale. The same knee and foot appears on the chairs and the unusual library table. The globe was probably English, as James Wilson of Vermont made the first globes only about the time this picture was painted.

Figure 25. Benjamin H. Latrobe. *Game of Billiards.* 1797. Wash on paper,
7 in. × 10¼ in. (18 cm × 25 cm). The Papers of Benjamin Henry Latrobe,
Maryland Historical Society, Baltimore.

Billiard tables were confined to the houses of the wealthy and elegant. Governor
Christopher Gore had one about 1807 in Waltham, Massachusetts, as did the Lloyd
family of Wye House, Talbot County, Maryland, in the last decade of the eighteenth
century.[83] This room is plain except for the table. The windows, which are closed
even though one man finds it warm enough to go barefoot, have folding shutters
rather than curtains. The walls are bare and the board floor is uncovered, but a successful, level billiard table was an expensive *tour de force* of cabinetwork.[84]

corner." "A great high clockcase, reaching to the ceiling" filled the fourth
corner.[24] Further evidence that tall clocks often stood in corners, in Philadelphia at least, comes from a 1765 letter of Mrs. Benjamin Franklin to her
husband: "Your timepiece stands in *one corner*, which is, I am told, all wrong."
Thus, some apparently doubted the corner placement in the eighteenth century,
but these two sources document that a corner placement was common practice
in certain circles at mid-century.[25]

Watson continued describing the typical parlor. Along one wall was a writing desk and on another wall a tall chest or highboy: "Every householder in
that day deemed it essential to his convenience or comfort to have an ample
chest of drawers in his parlor or sitting room, in which the linen or clothes of
the family were always of ready access. It was no sin to rummage them before
company!"[26]

Pieces from earlier periods were at home in the Chippendale era. The
Reverend Michael Smith, who had lived in Williamsburg, wrote from London

in 1770 that "there are many of the eminent planters whose houses are pretty well furnished; but as much of that furniture is of an hundred years date, so it would serve an hundred years hence."[27]

FLOOR COVERINGS

The Chippendale era brought more coverings to floors as well as greater decoration to furniture. Available to the colonist, in addition to the floor cloths and Orientals, was an ever-increasing variety of English carpets. With a plentiful supply, floor coverings began to find their way into halls, back parlors, and dining rooms, as well as the best parlor; the appearance of the bedside rug is another sign of growing luxury.

Oriental carpets continued to be costly and rare in America. Maryland inventories, for example, record only two between 1760 and 1777. Nathaniel Cunningham, who died near Boston in 1748, owned a fine Turkey carpet valued at £60.[28] Franklin and Charles Carroll of Carrollton both found that in London a large Turkey carpet cost 10 guineas, no inconsiderable expense.

As alternatives to the more expensive handwoven Orientals, the English offered four kinds of carpeting. Most common in New England was the Scotch, Kidderminster, Kilmarnock, or, as it is usually called, ingrain carpet. The ingrain had no pile and both sides were serviceable. Wilton carpets, produced in Wiltshire, England, did have a pile made of loops that were cut. Selling for 8 to 9 shillings the square yard in London in 1777, Wiltons were used to cover stairs as well as floors. The Brussels carpet was similar to the Wilton except that the loops of its pile were uncut. Most valuable of the four British carpets was the handwoven Axminster (Plate 3). Abigail Adams priced Axminsters in England in 1787. With designs imitating Turkey carpets, they were 24 shillings per square yard, while other designs were 14 shillings.

As Axminsters imitated Turkey carpets, it is difficult to identify what kinds of carpets appear in paintings. After careful study of eighteenth-century carpets and Lee's inventory, Sarah B. Sherrill concluded that Jeremiah Lee (Fig. 18) may have stood on an Axminster copy of a Smyrna rug.[29]

Some of these carpets were sold in strips that the customer then assembled. The buyer of a Scotch carpet often bought a separate border to attach to the main body of carpet. Benjamin Franklin sent carpets from London in 1758 with this note: "There is enough for one large and two small ones, it is to be sewed together, the edges being first felled down, and care taken to make the figures meet exactly; there is bordering for the same."[30]

Painted canvas floor cloths continued to be popular even in the most fashionable homes. They were used either as regular carpeting for a room or as a summer substitute for a heavier carpet. Floor cloths were also used under dining tables, often on top of other carpets to protect them. Many floor cloths came from English firms. Charles Carroll, a barrister, wrote a London merchant in 1767 that he wanted two large painted floor cloths, "both made of the strongest and best Duck and Painted so as to bear mopping over with a wet mop."[31]

Many Americans, however, turned to local craftsmen who began producing these floor cloths in numbers. Advertisements in Annapolis (1760), Baltimore

(1764), Boston (1767), and Charleston (1768) show that this new American industry was widespread. A likely source of many floor cloth designs, particularly those imported from England, was John Carwitham's *Floor Decorations for Various Kinds* (1739). Carwitham's designs show marbling and geometric shapes (especially squares and diamonds) of the sort popular in America from the seventeenth through the eighteenth centuries. A 1761 Boston advertisement offered floor cloths imitating Wilton carpets, and in the 1770s, Boston craftsmen made at least one imitation of a Turkey carpet.[32]

Straw carpets remained popular for summer use all along the Atlantic coast. George Washington's orders in 1759, 1772, and 1789 document their acceptability in the most fashionable houses, as well as their inability to withstand many years of wear. Sometimes the straw replaced the heavier carpets, but a few householders simply laid the straw matting over the heavier carpet. Also evident during the Chippendale period were rag rugs—homemade floor coverings with a woof of long strips of rags and a warp of heavy thread.

Americans were proud of their expensive rugs and carpets, to some Europeans excessively so. Brissot de Warville and Moreau de Saint-Méry, French visitors to America, both criticized the Americans for leaving their floors carpeted in the summer.[33] Presumably, the civilized European took his rugs up: as Brissot said, "A carpet in summer is an absurdity."

Figure 26. Artist unknown. *Anna Wendell Cuyler.* C. 1765–1775. Oil on canvas, 26 in. × 20⅜ in. (66 cm × 51 cm). Albany Institute of History and Art, Albany, N.Y.

Anna Wendell (1736–1775) married Cornelius Cuyler (1735–1794) in 1763. Two years later, they moved to Schenectady, where presumably this scene was painted. The ribbons, watch, miniature, and chatelaine are signs of an affluence equally evident from the genealogy—Mrs. Cuyler's mother was a Van Rensselaer. She sits upon a Chippendale chair beside a fashionable curtained dressing table of the sort that appeared in several woodcuts depicting the sinful potential of worldly vanity. The window curtains, still relatively rare, were of a flowered fabric with a decorative fringe.

Painted floors continued popular, as in the previous period, and they were not confined to simple, country houses. Dorothy Quincy of Quincy, Massachusetts, had a floor in yellow ochre and black squares, and Harvard's Tutor Flynt also had a painted floor.[34]

PICTURES AND MIRRORS

Illustrations and inventories suggest a relative scarcity of pictures during this period. In several of the paintings illustrated in this book, the artist had space to decorate an otherwise bare wall but did not. Woodcuts usually show walls ornamented with moldings rather than pictures.

Few could afford the oils a new generation of artists were beginning to produce. Copley, Trumbull, Charles Willson Peale, Gilbert Stuart, and John Durand were painting large portraits, but they were expensive. Joseph Blackburn of Boston charged 10 guineas for a portrait in 1761, and a decade later Copley asked £19.12.0;[35] in 1768, George Mason of Boston advertised faces in crayons with glass and frame for two guineas (£2.2.0) each. Even the cheapest pictures by good artists were still costly. John Watson in his *Annals of Philadelphia* made special note that "picture frames of golden glare" were not to be found in Philadelphia before the Revolution.[36]

Most of the early American painters' work was devoted to portraits. Landscapes were rare but nonetheless fashionable. Washington in 1757 ordered "A Neat Landskip 3 feet by 21½ Inches" for his mantelpiece.[37] Henry Laurens of South Carolina likewise ordered an English landscape by size in 1756,[38] a common and logical way to fill a given space.

Watson describes the typical pictures of the Philadelphia area before the Revolution: "Small pictures, paintings on glass with black moulding for frames, with a scanty touch of gold leaf in the corners, was the adornment of a parlor." Mrs. Schiffer's investigations of Chester County, Pennsylvania, confirm Watson's recollections, but there were relatively few pictures in the average house. Many prints were imported from England during the period, and from the 1730s to the 1760s, Hogarth's prints were advertised from Georgia to Massachusetts. The inventory of Benjamin Prat in Boston (1763) included a colored Hogarth print in a gilt frame valued at £1.[39]

Mirrors received considerable ornamentation. Although Moreau de Saint-Méry thought mirrors uncommon in Philadelphia, John Elliott of that city, as well as craftsmen in Boston, produced looking glasses similar to the one pictured in Plate 2. Smaller and less expensive courting mirrors continued to be imported from Holland and Germany, and 75 percent of Providence inventories between 1760 and 1800 list such "Dutch looking glasses" in the bedrooms with values between £1 and £1.6.0.[40] Even small mirrors were costly.

Early in the Chippendale period mirrors were generally confined to bedrooms, but one must remember that occasionally beds were still to be found in the public rooms of the first floor. John Chamberlain of Chelsea, Massachusetts (1754), had a mirror worth £8 in a first-floor room, which also had a bed worth £18.[41] Typical of the later use of pictures and mirrors was the inventory of Captain Richard Bracket of Braintree (1760). In his "first & best Room" he had a mirror worth £3, a painted coat of arms, and six pictures, probably

Chippendale mirror

prints. The second room had a looking glass (worth 13/4) and five pictures. The third room and kitchen had neither pictures nor mirrors. No bedroom had any pictures, and only one (not the "best") had a mirror. Prints were sometimes collected in a stairway: Andrew Belcher of Milton, Massachusetts (1771), son of the governor, had forty-one pictures on his staircase.[42]

Small statuary gained new fashion. Dr. William Morgan of Philadelphia had been to the Continent and collected reproductions, which fascinated those, like Jefferson, who came to visit him. Jefferson, in turn, in 1771 projected a whole gallery of statues that he thought he ought to have.[43]

Washington sought to embellish Mount Vernon with plaster casts of Alexander the Great, Julius Caesar, Charles XII of Sweden, and Frederick the Great of Prussia, each to be about 15 inches high (with busts of the Duke of Marlborough and Prince Eugene somewhat smaller). In 1760, his agent wrote that there were no busts of any size to be had of Charles XII, and none in the sizes he wanted of the others. Copies could be made, but they would be "very expensive" —4 guineas each. He could, however, provide the following busts for 16 shillings each: Homer, Virgil, Horace, Cicero, Plato, Aristotle, Seneca, Galen, Vestal Virgin, Faustina, Chaucer, Spenser, Johnson, Shakespeare, Beaumont, Fletcher, Milton, Prior, Pope, Congreve, Swift, Addison, Dryden, Locke, and Newton. The British market featured classical and literary models at a time when Washington wanted military figures.[44]

TEXTILES

Where there were window curtains, good taste dictated that they be of the same or matching material as the chair seats, bed curtains, and slipcovers. In Philadelphia, Plunkett Fleeson charged £52 for bed and window curtains for one of John Cadwalader's bedrooms. In 1759, George Washington asked to have matching blue and white bed curtains, window curtains, and chair seats shipped from London; and Boston advertisements for the sale of Sir Francis Bernard's furniture in 1770 reveal that the governor had one coordinated bedroom done in crimson, another in yellow, and another in red and white. Benjamin Franklin documented the novelty of copperplate fabrics and the standards for their fashionable use when he explained what he sent his wife from London in 1758: "There are also fifty-six yards of cotton, printed curiously from copper plates, a new invention, to make bed and window curtains; and seven yards of chair bottoms printed in the same way, very neat. These were my fancy; but Mrs. Stevenson tells me I did wrong not to buy both of the same color."[45] Mrs. Stevenson was Franklin's landlady in London.

The most fashionable fabrics were imported, but many households continued to produce their own with spinning wheels and looms, which were usually kept in the garret or in one of the less important bedrooms. John Hewson of Philadelphia began commercial production of printed fabrics in the 1770s.[46] Boston, too, produced linen and calico printers, but it is unlikely that these domestic sources supplied much of the market.

Upholstery. Chippendale's book provided little guidance on upholstery fabrics, beyond noting that "French chairs" (Fig. 19) might be upholstered in Spanish leather, damask, tapestry, "or other sort of needlework."

Favored upholstery fabrics among Americans were silk damasks and wool or hair fabrics (china, mohair, moreen, or harateen). Leather and horsehair were also used to cover chair seats. Benjamin Lehman, a Philadelphia cabinetmaker, in 1786 specified prices of chairs varying with the upholstery. A mahogany side chair with the seat covered in leather was £1.14.0, while a damask seat cost 2 shillings more, and a horsehair seat brought the price to £1.16.6.[47] Moreau de Saint-Méry in the 1780s observed that horsehair was the most popular upholstery among the wealthy of Philadelphia, yet George Washington in 1765 was disappointed when some English chair seats arrived covered with hair. He commented that he "had a tryal of hair once before which were of no duration and from thence determined to have no more."[48]

Boston advertisements show that crimson was the favored color for chair seats. Lehman's price list notes that upholstering over the rails of a chair and adding brass nails increased the cost by 8 shillings. Slips seats were thus less expensive. By far the cheapest upholstery (if one may call it that) was the straw or rush seat, a form that was not confined to the houses of the poor. However, in wealthier households such chairs were likely to be found in the kitchen.

Slipcovers, popular in houses of fashion, were advertised in South Carolina, Philadelphia, and New York City.[49] Lord Botetourt, Governor of Virginia,

Figure 27. Attributed to John Brewster, Jr. *James Eldredge.* July 5, 1795. Oil on canvas, 54¼ in. × 41 in. (1.37 m × 1.04 m). The Connecticut Historical Society, Hartford.

Captain James Eldredge (1745–1811) appeared at home in Brooklyn, Connecticut. Nearby New London County cabinetmakers were already producing the Federal style, but it had made no impact on Eldredge's house. He sat on a simple, country Chippendale chair with straight legs and a baluster form splat.[85] The simple Pembroke table had straight, uncarved legs. The floor cloth was more up to date with its characteristic diapered pattern, but the greatest decorative effort went into the straight-hung curtains with their borders, fringe, and bow.

died in 1770 leaving a set of checked slipcovers for chairs covered in crimson damask.

Window Curtains. In the decades before the Revolution, window curtains had gradually come into favor in houses of fashion and wealth, but they appear in greater number in the illustrations than they do in inventories. Washington had window curtains (1759), as did Governor Bernard of Massachusetts (1770); yet curtained windows were still far from the norm in the average house. In researching records from Chester County, Pennsylvania, Mrs. Schiffer found that only 92 (or 3.5 percent) out of 2,594 probate inventories between 1750 and 1789 listed window curtains. Mid-century Massachusetts showed the same pattern. Only 20 percent of Boston families with estates of £5,000 or more had window curtains, and they were even rarer in Essex County.[50] Elizabeth Delhonde of Boston died in 1749 leaving an estate of £11,000, yet she had no curtains, even in a bedroom with furnishings valued at £192.

Mrs. Schiffer found that when inventories gave the location of window curtains, they were usually in second-floor bedrooms.[51] The room-by-room inventories of Suffolk County, Massachusetts, reported by Abbott Lowell Cummings show a similar pattern. In the thirty-seven inventories dating from 1750 to 1775, only four include window curtains. Where it is possible to locate these curtains, they occur in second-floor bed chambers—with the exception of one instance, in the parlor, and of a (surprising) two instances, in which they appear in the kitchen.

At mid-century, expensive imported wools, harateen or moreen, had replaced calico and linen as the most fashionable curtain fabrics, but in Massachusetts estates below £1,000, calico and linen remained prominent. Silk curtains, unknown earlier in the century in Boston and Salem, were advertised in Boston in the 1760s.[52] John Randolph of Virginia had silk curtains in 1775.

Perhaps the most fashionable form of window curtain was the festoon. Diagonal cords raised drapery so that it bunched at the upper corners of a window to form swags (Fig. 23). Tassels were an important part of the design, and in 1775, Ann King of Philadelphia advertised that she was the "first American tossel maker." Festoon curtains were advertised in Charleston (1751), Philadelphia (1754), and New York (1765). A Philadelphia advertisement of 1782 offered a set in a red and white copperplate print complete with "laths, lines, tassels, and brass pins."[53]

Equally advertised were Venetian curtains, a form that does not appear in our illustrations. Venetian curtains had one piece of fabric covering the entire window. Parallel cords lifting a wooden bar fixed to the lower edge of the curtain produced attractive bunching when the fabric gathered at the top of the window. Simpler, but still elegant, were what one advertisement called "plain" curtains, which were tacked to the top of the window frame and held back with tiebacks. A valance covered the tacking.[54]

Venetian blinds (to be distinguished from Venetian drapery) were a much-promoted alternate to curtains in Philadelphia (1767), Charleston (1772), and New York (1774). Governor Botetourt had them in Williamsburg in 1770, and they were in Independence Hall, but they seem not to have spread to New England.[55]

A look at fabric prices in England in these years, and some wall hangings' value at Sheffield Park, Sussex, is informative:

Fabric Prices in England (per yard)[56]

CUT VELVET	1741	25/-
GENOA SILK VELVET	c. 1725	32/-
CRIMSON GENOA SILK VELVET	c. 1725	36/-
CRIMSON VELVET	1752	27/-
SILK DAMASK	c. 1750	15/-21/-
CRIMSON GENOA DAMASK	1763	17/-
SILK AND WORSTED DAMASK	1759	6/6
MIXED DAMASK	1767	7/-
SILK TAFFETA		8/6–11/-
LUSTRING	1768	6/6
WOOLEN MOREEN	1760s	2/4–2/8
HARATEEN		1/9
SERGE		1/9

Comparative Value of Hangings at Sheffield Park, Sussex, England, 1776

(each chamber done primarily in one fabric)

RED DAMASK	£65
BLUE DAMASK	36
CRIMSON MOREEN	35
GREEN MOHAIR	25
BLUE CAMLET	22
CHINTZ	15 (housekeeper's room)
GREEN LINSEY	7 (cook's room)

Bed Curtains. The curtained bed was standard in houses of all classes, but the wealthy could afford more intricate hangings with festoons and scalloped valances decorated with gilt tape. Simpler beds had straight-hung curtains with little ornament. Silk was desirable if, like Peyton Randolph of Virginia, one could afford it. So, too, were the woolens harateen and moreen, but linen and cotton remained popular, even in the homes of the well-to-do. Randolph also had a set of chintz bed curtains worth £3 in a room with a marble table valued at only £2. Copperplate fabrics printed in red or blue were very popular and widely advertised.

WALL TREATMENT

Plastered walls were common throughout the period, with whitewash the standard treatment in simpler houses. Franklin lamented regular whitewashings, for they made a shambles out of a house. Two whitewashings, he held, were equal to one move, and three moves equaled a fire in devastating effect.[57] But the Chippendale era brought a new diversity to the walls of the wealthy and the moderately wealthy. Wall treatment varied by regions. For example, Moreau de Saint-Méry in the 1780s found Philadelphia walls still remained a plain gray even among the wealthy.

Painted Walls. The simplest decoration, and one that became more common during the Chippendale period, was the painted wall. A South Carolina advertisement of 1766 refers to painted rooms "in the new taste," yet, as noted in the previous chapter, painted rooms were well established in some areas in the Queen Anne period. However, during the Chippendale era there was a greater tendency to paint both the wall surface and woodwork. Less-expensive treatments might include woodwork painted a solid color, sometimes finished with a glossy surface (a highly desirable effect). More costly was graining imitating marble, mahogany, or cedar.

Wall Paintings. A few instances of wall murals survive from the Chippendale era but, in general, they are rare. Wall painting entered its great popularity in the Federal period.

Wallpaper. The most evident addition to Chippendale wall decoration was the widespread use of wallpaper. In 1748, Peter Kalm visited New York City and reported that wallpaper was virtually unknown there, yet in 1750 John Birket passed through Portsmouth, New Hampshire, and Newport, Rhode Island, and recorded that many houses there were well papered. In South Carolina, papering was perhaps seen as an alternative to decorating a wall with framed prints, for one merchant in 1765 advertised: "The expense of papering a room does not amount to more than a middling sett of Prints."[58]

Plain-colored wallpaper was used throughout the Chippendale period. Fowler and Cornforth note that plain blue paper was "particularly chic" about 1760 both in England and in France, where Madame de Genlis actually took down Gobelin tapestries to put up blue English paper.[59] In America, blue was likewise the most popular color for these plain papers, which were often hung with gilt borders. In 1765, Benjamin Franklin ordered blue paper decorated with gilt borders, a combination also used in the Governor's Palace at Williamsburg. In 1784, Washington ordered blue, yellow, and green papers to be used with gilt papier-mâché borders. Virtually all the illustrations in this chapter show walls without figured decoration, just the appearance plain paper or paint would have presented.

More elaborate papers found their way into houses of the well-to-do at considerable cost. In 1761, Philip Schuyler paid £14.1.0 for a set of painted papers and paper-mâché ceiling decorations from Squire of London. Chinese papers were fashionable with the very well-to-do, especially around Boston where they appeared as early as 1750. Later in the century, English imitations of Chinese papers were also popular in the Boston area.

In 1764, Thomas Lee of Marblehead, Massachusetts, ordered a set of wallpapers in the Gothic style then popular in England. Papers with architectural motifs were popular in New England in the 1750s and 1760s. Figure 22 shows a paper almost identical to one used in Paul Revere's house in Boston and in two houses in Connecticut, both built in the 1760s. That it was copied in Hartford in the 1790s documents the continuing popularity of the design.[60]

The 1770s produced a new diversity of papers in the American market. Flocked paper imported from England and France was widely advertised, and specimens survive in the Governor Wentworth Mansion of Portsmouth, New Hampshire, and in the Webb House in Wethersfield, Connecticut (1781). William Poyntell of Philadelphia was selling such paper in 1781 for 3/6 to 5/- a roll. In 1775, a room of the Dorothy Quincy House in Quincy, Massachusetts, was hung with French Reveillon paper with Pompeian motifs. Gilt leather hangings, fashionable in England, were advertised in America but apparently were little used.

ARCHITECTURAL DETAILS AND CEILINGS

Renovations and new construction in the years following 1750 were heavily influenced by the increasing number of British guidebooks for architects and builders.

Stairways continued to receive detailed treatment. In expensive construction, balusters were turned in elaborate spiral designs, or, in fewer instances—such as the William Paca House in Annapolis—Chinese Chippendale fretwork was substituted for balusters. Stair rails often ascended in a gradual curve to meet the newel post set apart from the line of balusters. Carved or scrolled step ends were fashionable, but in some areas paneled step ends, which had been popular in the Queen Anne era, continued in new construction to the end of the century.

As in the Queen Anne period, an arch was again a popular and expensive structural decoration in the entrance hall.

In the most important rooms, the greatest architectural details were usually lavished upon the mantel and fireplace. The fireplace might be faced with marble, the mantel shelf (usual in this period) supported with elaborate brackets, and the mantel surmounted with a carved, eared architrave with fine mold-

Figure 28. Richard Brunton. *Mrs. Reuben Humphreys. C.* 1800. Oil on canvas, 44½ in. × 40½ in. (1.14 m × 1.04 m). The Connecticut Historical Society, Hartford.

Richard Brunton was a prisoner in Connecticut's Newgate Prison when he did this portrait of the jailer's wife. Her furnishings show the fashionable best of a family of moderate means. The Federal style had made a mixed impact on Chippendale forms with a gilded urn added to the Chippendale fretwork mirror. The oval brass and enamel knobs were stylish at the end of the century. Sitting on her fan back Windsor, Mrs. Humphreys presides over her tea table, which is covered with a gray fabric that has a diaper pattern of sprigs and flowers, and is set with a creamware tea set with red floral decoration.

ings. The overmantel might also have a broken pediment, columns or pilasters, or scroll brackets at the sides. One must remember that such treatment was limited to the homes of the wealthy. The paneled walls and simple mantels from the Queen Anne period were still constructed during this time.

Ceilings likewise received attention in fine construction, with ornamental plaster figures of flowers, garlands, bows, and other sinuous rococo designs. A different ceiling ornament dominated by classical motifs would follow in the Federal era. A Charleston merchant advertised papers for ceilings in 1756.[61] Most ceilings, even in fine houses, were flat plaster surfaces without projecting beams. Highly unusual was the paneled bedroom ceiling found in a Springfield, Massachusetts, room (now in the Brooklyn Museum). The same treatment was found in a Hampton, New Hampshire, room (now in the Metropolitan Museum of Art, New York).

Complementing mantels and ceilings were appropriate moldings. Moldings with light dentil work continued to be found through the period, but more elaborate, heavy dentils gained high fashion status. These moldings were wood, cast plaster, or papier-mâché. Washington ordered papier-mâché moldings from London in 1757.[62] In less-than-important rooms and in simpler houses, plain ceiling moldings predominated.

Doors in houses plain or elaborate were paneled, but in expensive construction a door frame might rival the mantel in its fine detail, with a broken pediment or eared frame. Similarly, casement windows and corner cupboards received eared frames in expensive construction. Even though window curtains became popular during the Chippendale period, folding paneled shutters were still installed in fashionable houses.

One notable new architectural detail copied from the English drawing books was the Palladian window. First appearing in the South, it remained in high fashion in New England through the rest of the century, where it is perhaps more a Federal than a Chippendale feature.

Thomas Tileston Waterman suggests that about the year 1750, the chair rail assumed a new standard form as a pedestal shape with a flat top that became prominent in finer rooms; the earlier type ("like half of a stair rail"), which had been used throughout the Queen Anne period, continued to be used in less important rooms.[63]

Palladian window

LIGHTING

Candles were still the primary source of light. Spermaceti candles, made from the waxy substance in the head of the sperm whale, appeared on the American market late in the 1740s and were advertised as burning twice as long as the common (but less expensive) tallow candles. Bayberry candles were advertised in Boston in the 1750s and 1760s; one Boston chandler advertised wax candles "plain & fluted."[64]

Candles were comparatively expensive and used with economy, even in wealthy households. Philip Fithian, a Princeton graduate who had gone to Virginia as tutor to the children of Robert Carter, took careful note of the festive evening in December 1773 when Carter burned seven candles in a room at once: "The room looked luminous and splendid; four very large candles burning on the table where we supped; three others in different parts of the Room."[65]

Chippendale candlesticks were essentially Queen Anne shapes with rococo decorations added. The new designs appeared in silver and brass, although, as in the Queen Anne period, silver candlesticks were rare and found only in the homes of the wealthy. Of Paul Revere's 500 customers between 1761 and 1797, only 1 ordered silver candlesticks, a pair that cost £24.[66]

Candleholders appeared in increasing variety: wall sconces of brass or glass, mirrored sconces, glass chandeliers, and wooden candlestands with screw posts for adjusting the height of the candle. Looking glasses with candlearms could also be found in houses of the well-to-do.

Chandlers offered sperm oil for oil lamps, although what we now think of as the whale oil lamp was not developed until later in the century. These simple wick lamps in use in the period gained popularity in the 1750s; President Holyoke of Harvard noted in his diary for November 26, 1755: "First began to burn a lamp."[67]

The illustrations reveal that convenience was the primary standard for placing candlesticks within a room or on a table. Any attempt at a symmetrical arrangement was usually foregone when candles were in use. When candles were not in use, the portable sticks were still gathered in one central spot in the house, usually the kitchen.

COLOR

The tradition of rooms of distinctive colors continued. Sir William Pepperell (1696–1759), the only New Englander created a baronet, had four rooms in which the bed and window curtains were the same colors: red, blue, yellow, and green.[68] In 1759, Washington ordered a bed from England with blue or blue and white curtains, with the same fabric to be used for window curtains, chair seats, bed coverlet, and window valances. So furnished, the room would be "uniformly handsome and genteel."[69] Smaller estates give no clue of such variations in color from room to room.

The palette of colors available to the interior painter expanded. We get a hint of the distribution of color from an advertisement for the house of a Boston merchant who had failed. The building was sold to satisfy creditors in 1753. It had eight rooms, painted as follows: four in a lead color, one in green, one blue, one cedar, and one marble.[70] Cedar, marble, and other imitative painting were specialties widely advertised.

In her research of Chester County inventories for color, Mrs. Schiffer found very few references to rooms by color. In the 1770s, there was only reference to one "blue" parlor, one "green" parlor, and one "yellow" bedroom. This data suggests that color coordination of rooms was probably confined to the wealthy. Blue was the prominent color in general and especially in curtains, but green was more often found in curtains than in objects generally.[71]

The number of references to particular colors in Chester County, Pennsylvania, inventories (without respect to object) between 1750 and 1779 are: blue, 149 references; white, 144; black, 91; red, 69; brown, 56; green, 47; yellow, 12; scarlet, 7; gray, 6; purple, snuff, and pink, all 3; walnut 2; dove, crimson, orange, garnet, and ash, all 1 reference. Colors advertised in Boston and Philadelphia between 1763 and 1784 include:[72] flake white, cream, straw, ultramarine, blue, Prussian blue, blue smalt, verditure blue, verdigris, green, pea green, olive, spruce yellow, yellow ochre, yellow Spanish brown, Spanish brown, red, rose pink, drop lake, vermilion, carmine, red lead, Venetian red, mahogany, slate, stone, black, leaf gold, and leaf silver.

ACCESSORIES

Although the most fashionable and expensive items were found in households of the very wealthy, less expensive Delft and British Queensware began to add style to humbler houses. Even redware carried bright decoration, admittedly far from the rococo acanthus of the London silversmith, but also still far from the Spartan simplicity of earlier patterns.

Figure 29. Ella Emory. *Chamber in the Peter Cushing House.* 1878. Oil on canvas, 15½ in. × 26¾ in. (41 cm × 69 cm). Collection of Nina Fletcher Little.

Ella Emory painted several pictures of Peter Cushing's seventeenth-century house in Hingham, Massachusetts, as it stood in 1878.[86] The country bedroom was little altered since it was remodeled in the Chippendale period when the board ceilings were plastered over. The bed retained copperplate curtains in an English design from 1775 to 1785, showing sheep dipping and shearing. The desk decorated with painted graining was simple country work, but the easy chair with its serpentine wings was more sophisticated. The picture provides a fine representation of a wainscotted interior wall made up of feather-edged boards. Note that refurbishing had reduced the size of the hearth. Straw matting covers the floor.

American tables followed the British model closely, at least where a family knew of changed British styles and could afford to match them. Glass or silver candelabra, British drinking glasses, and extensive silver services all gave the late colonial table a real glamour. The elevated center decoration for a dining table had become a fashionable necessity in a few houses by the 1760s. In that decade, Washington and Charles Carroll, the barrister, both ordered a salver or "middle stand" as it was often called. Pyramids of salvers, syllabub glasses, and jelly glasses made a spectacular display. In the table setting, forks, usually iron, were no longer considered luxuries, but silver forks were still comparatively rare.

Brass, Iron, and Tin. Brass and iron provided an even wider range of implements than in the previous era. The value of brass fell from 3 shillings the pound in the 1740s to 1 shilling just before the Revolution. With the lower prices came proliferation of implements in even modest estates. Andirons and firetools brought the metals into virtually every room, but iron and brass were still primarily confined to the kitchen. The warming pan, too, still was usually found in the kitchen, though occasionally it turned up in a chamber or even in the front parlor.

Tin is mentioned fairly often in inventories, but like earthenware, specific pieces were rarely listed. Tin, again, was confined primarily to the kitchen.

Ceramics. The varieties of ceramics available in the Queen Anne era continued into the Chippendale, but with the addition of new wares as well. Some factories, like Bow and Chelsea, soon incorporated new rococo forms and decorations, thus keeping American rooms in touch with European styles. Advertisements and invoices chronicle the appearance of "new fashioned Turtle Shell Tureens" (tortoise-shell ware) (1754), Bow china (1754), Prussian plates (1758), Queensware (1769), Nottingham mugs (1770), and Staffordshire ware (1771). Wedgwood had introduced Queensware only in 1763, but by 1769, Washington had ordered not just Queensware but "ye most fashionable kind" from his London supplier.

The rise of creamware, of which Queensware was one variety, marked the end of Delft's popularity in America; English salt glaze ware likewise supplanted Rhenish stoneware, which had continued to be popular until about 1760. Very late in the period, the French alliance brought French tin glazes, notably Rouén faïence, to the American market. "Rhoan" ware was advertised in Baltimore in 1778 and Philadelphia in 1784.

In addition to these imports, domestic production continued; virtually every colony produced redware, and a Charleston pottery advertised locally made Queensware in 1771. Bonin and Morris of Philadelphia produced small quantities of porcelain from 1770 to 1772.

Forms popular in the previous era continued, with more variations in the sizes available—mugs could be quart, pint, or half pint. Chinese porcelains were still expensive, but increasing importation brought lower prices, and they were popular with all who could afford them.

As in the last period, the best china was usually kept in the parlor, the second best in the keeping room, and earthenware and other less valuable pieces in the kitchen, hall, or chambers.

Barbara Gorely Teller's study of Providence inventories from 1750 to 1800 is revealing and probably characteristic of all the colonies. Queensware was first

Queensware or creamware bowl, 1774

Bonin and Morris porcelain, Philadelphia, Pa., *c.* 1770

Chinese export plate

advertised in Providence in 1771, and thereafter 90 percent of all estates, even among the poor, contained at least one piece. Before the rise in popularity of Queensware, the less wealthy families (£200 or less) had favored either Delft or Chinese porcelain, while the middle- (£200 to £900) and upper-income (£1,000+) groups had shown a definite preference for porcelain. Perhaps not surprisingly, she discovered that families of wealth did not necessarily own many more ceramic pieces than poorer families.[73]

New in this period were ceramic figurines, advertised in Boston in 1762 as "curious fine China in statuary." In 1759, George Washington had written his London agent ordering "Sundry Small ornaments for chimy piece." The agent sent the following: a group with Aeneas carrying his father (£3.3.0), Bacchus (£2.2.0), Flora (£2.2.0), and "two ornamental vases with Faces and Festoons of Grapes and vine Leaves" (each £1.1.0). Each of the five items was "finished neat and bronzed with copper." The agent sent directions for their display:

The manner of placing them on ye chimney piece should be thus:

A group of Flora   Vase   Aeneas   Vase   Group of Bacchus

Symmetry was the guiding principle of an arrangement that cost Washington £9.9.0.

Glass.   By the end of the period, table glass had become common in houses of moderate as well as great wealth. Most glass was still imported from England, although American manufacturers began to produce greater quantities.

New, lighter designs had fiscal as well as aesthetic logic. The Glass Excise Bill of 1746, which taxed glass by weight, provided a strong motivation for the artist to achieve the same effect with less weight. Beginning in 1751, advertisements in Boston newspapers make reference to "new fashion" glass. Usually the phrase referred to the air twist stemmed glass or "wormed wine glasses" that had first been advertised in the Boston market in 1746. By 1761, glasses and decanters were also engraved or "flowered."

Glassmakers worked diligently to provide special glasses for specific purposes, and, inevitably, only the well-to-do could afford a full array of forms. The inventory of Governor Fauquier's glass is revealing. When the former Governor of Virginia died in 1768, he left: 5 beer glasses, 5 champagne glasses, 14 water glasses, 55 wine glassses, 59 syllabub glasses, 69 jelly glasses, 23 glass salvers, 15 decanters, and 8 cruets. He also had three sets of salvers that made up into large pyramids; the largest pyramid was valued at £15. Such pyramids were advertised in the Boston press in 1772.

Pewter.   Pewter remained an important part of the late colonial household. Plates, platters, and basins were the most common forms, and the porringer regained the vogue in New England it had never lost in Pennsylvania. Mugs, tankards, and spoons remained less common, with honey pots, colanders, salt boxes, hot water plates, and coffee pots found in relatively few inventories in New England. Chester County, Pennsylvania, inventories reveal a greater variety of forms.

Importation of pewter continued until the Revolution, after which it fell off sharply as domestic manufacture grew.[74] Queen Anne styles persisted until the end of the century. A few American pieces reflect English Georgian designs, but

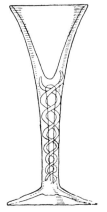

Air twist stem glass

as Eric de Jonge has remarked, "as far as the colonial pewterer was concerned, the rococo period never existed."[75] Regional variations continued, most evident in porringer handles, pots, and tankards.

The value of pewter fell in Massachusetts from 4 shillings a pound in 1754 to 1 shilling in the 1760s. In New England, pewter was found only in the kitchen or dairy, but in Chester County, Pennsylvania, it might also be in a front room or dining room.

Silver.   In American silver, the rococo style was evident in the work of Joseph Richardson of Philadelphia before 1750, a little over a decade after the style became popular in London. Silver in great variety was imported from England before the Revolution, and surviving examples and accounts suggest that such English silver served as model for the growing numbers of silversmiths in Boston and elsewhere.[76] Variations in decorative details offered ample opportunity for development of regional styles, especially in tankards and porringer handles.

The most common silver items were spoons in two sizes, large tablespoons and small teaspoons, the latter closer in size to today's demitasse than our teaspoon. Other tea implements were also popular, most notably sugar tongs, or

Rococo coffee pot, London, 1764

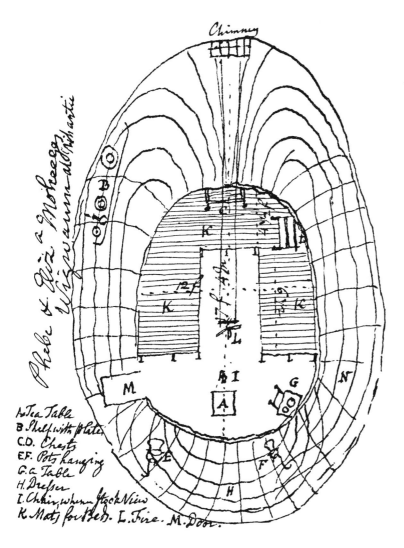

Figure 30. Ezra Stiles. *Phebe and Elizabeth Moheegan's Wigwam, Niantic, Connecticut, October 26, 1761.* Stiles, *Itineraries,* p. 153.

The future president of Yale recorded what can only be called a Chippendale wigwam. With its U-shaped platform or mats (L), the basic interior is much like those seen in John White's water colors of Virginia and North Carolina made between 1585 and 1587. In the intervening 170 years, the Indians had made increasing use of the white men's goods. This wigwam, home to twelve people, contained two chests (C, D), a dresser (H), a table with plates on it (G), a shelf with plates (B), and only one chair (I). The most unexpected item (and perhaps the most surprising to Stiles, too, since it was the first thing he noticed, labeling it A) was a tea table.

a cream pot (but not necessarily a teapot, an item of considerable cost). Porringers were common, but tankards or "canns" (mugs) were the most frequently found large pieces. Candlesticks, pepper boxes, chafing dishes, casters, salts, tobacco boxes, salvers, forks, and bowls all appear in American inventories, but they have no claim to being furnishings of the average household.

Silver was prominently displayed in the parlor or best room, often in a cabinet or corner cupboard.

PENNSYLVANIA GERMAN VARIANTS

The first German colonists settled in Pennsylvania in 1683, and thousands followed in the eighteenth century. The Dutch (1623), Swedes and Finns (1627–1755) also settled in the area. Naturally, each brought Continental decorative techniques with them, and by the Chippendale era, English, German, and other Continental styles blended together in the colorfully decorated creations of the Pennsylvania German craftsmen. For generations, German settlements in other colonies—notably the Moravians in North Carolina—also produced artifacts in Germanic styles.

Furniture often differed in form and decoration from that of New England and Virginia. Plank chairs and sawbuck tables were derived from medieval Continental design; the *schrank* was a large cupboard like a Dutch *kas*. Other forms were similar to those made in New England, and basic Chippendale chests were made as late as the 1840s.

Winterthur's research found that the average house late in the eighteenth century contained many benches and beds, but comparatively fewer chairs than houses of the English settlers. Typical German decoration for these pieces took the form of inlay, cutout and scalloped work, or painting. Hearts, tulips, leaves, grapes, unicorns, mounted horsemen, and swastikas were common and colorful in their painted furniture. Bride's chests were popular forms that received full, painted decoration, revealing distinct regional patterns.[77]

Winterthur uncovered the fact that Berks County houses of the Chippendale period had no floor carpets. Much of the furniture was unupholstered, but references in inventories to checked cushions were relatively frequent. Window curtains were almost unknown, but households contained great quantities of towels and tablecloths. The same folk designs naturally found a place in the decoration of fabrics.

Pennsylvania German sgraffito ware

Fraktur (illuminated writing) on birth and baptismal certificates (*taufschein*) offered opportunities for using the same motifs found on other decorative items. Framed, they added a bright note of color, usually red, to a white wall. Mirrors sometimes received unique frames. One such had a tall tracery of heart-shaped cutouts, while others were brightly painted and decorated.

Plain plaster walls were standard; however, as in New England, paneling and dentil molding found a place in some houses of moderate wealth. Fireplaces had no andirons or firebacks, and kitchen fireplaces were especially large. Five-plate stoves (attached to a parlor wall and fired from the kitchen) were popular, as were iron stoves decorated with typical Pennsylvania German motifs cast in the iron.

Most ceilings were plain, but in a few rooms, like the parlor of Conrad

Kershner's house (1755), now preserved at Winterthur, there was baroque molded plaster decoration. Kershner had a ceiling with grapevines painted a copper red and grapes painted purple.

Color was strong. Blue window frames and woodwork were often contrasted with plain white walls. Furniture brightly painted in reds and blue-greens also added color. In lighting, inventories show lanterns more common than candlesticks.

Winterthur's research in preparing the Kershner rooms found that Pennsylvania German houses of the late eighteenth century contained large amounts of pottery and pewter. Virtually every form of accessory received the same vibrant decoration. In earthenware, both sgrafitto and slip decoration produced the same designs and inscriptions found in fraktur. A mounted horseman was a favorite motif. Motto borders had disappeared from earthenware before 1812.[78] The Pennsylvania Germans' taste for color inspired English potters to create patterns termed "Gaudy Dutch" specifically for sale to them.

Fanciful shapes dominated Pennsylvania German iron work, whether door handles or toasters, and tin ware, produced in considerable quantities, was brightly decorated.

FRENCH VARIANTS

French variations of the baroque prevailed in the French settlements along the Mississippi. The household of Auguste Chouteau (1749–1829), founder of St. Louis, contained much imported from France; however, many of the larger pieces of furniture were made locally. Craftsmen worked in a variation of the Louis XV style, almost immune from the Chippendale style of the thirteen colonies. In a notable exception, Chouteau did own an armoire with claw-and-ball feet. Generally, furniture forms were those in the French tradition—buffets, bureaus, armoires, and commodes. Mirrors (all imported) seem to have been especially popular. Wallpaper was perhaps used in lower Louisiana houses, but in upper Louisiana walls were whitewashed and walnut woodwork was rubbed and waxed.

Pennsylvania German tin ware box

5

The Federal Period

1785–1815

AFTER the Revolution, Americans adopted new European styles, but often with a keen republican consciousness. George Washington, whom some had suggested as king for the new nation, wrote upon accepting a fashionable chimney piece presented by an English admirer that he feared for his "republican style of living."[1]

Americans heralded the Romans as models of civic virtue just as classicism began dominating European decoration. Significantly, American officers formed the Society of the Cincinnati, for they likened themselves to the poor Roman who had left his plow to defend the republic, only to return victorious (and still poor) to take up his plowing anew. During the Revolution, new building and decoration was minimal; but after Yorktown, Americans readily adopted the new classicism in decoration. Paul Revere made his first neoclassic teapot in 1782.[2] David Spear of Boston wrote his fiancée in January 1784 that a cabinetmaker was producing some "very good furniture." He commented that the chairs "are different from any you ever saw but they are very pretty, of the newest taste."[3]

The Scottish architect Robert Adam spearheaded the British development of what in America would be called the Federal style. Inspired by English and French studies of antiquity, Adam spent three years studying ruins, particularly Diocletian's palace at Spalato (Split), in Dalmatia. The student soon turned architect, and with his brother James published *The Works in Architecture of Robert and James Adam* (London, 1773), a book that stressed the unity of exterior and interior designs. Designs for walls and furniture were light, graceful, and delicate, with straight lines taking the place of earlier curves. Adam exteriors and interiors were soon the model for fashionable Britons, and in France comparable Louis XVI styles gained equal dominance.

Emigrants and travelers helped the new style cross the Atlantic. In 1785, John Penn, the governor's wealthy cousin, came to America and built a new, expensive house near Philadelphia in the Adam style. A few Americans, like

Thomas Jefferson, took their models directly from the ruins that had inspired Adam. Others, like Boston architect Charles Bulfinch, relied on the Adams' books and a close inspection of some of their buildings in England. Once back in America, Bulfinch—as well as English, Irish, and French architects who had emigrated—spread the new style with one spectacular building after another. Impressed with the new structures, other American architects adopted the form as their own; thus, Bulfinch's work around Boston inspired Samuel McIntire of Salem and Asher Benjamin of Greenfield. Like Robert Adam (and unlike most other American architects), McIntire concerned himself with interior design and furniture as well as architecture.

In 1790, *The Massachusetts Centinel* wrote that the practice of ordering art from Europe was "absurd and degrading."[4] Yet, even though nationalism encouraged patronage of local craftsmen, the fashionable wealthy continued to send to Europe for their furnishings, and European products were available in rural areas as well as urban centers. Charlton, Massachusetts, had a population of 1,965 in 1791 when Peter Whitney wrote of it: "There are a few dealers in European and India goods, as is usual in country towns."[5]

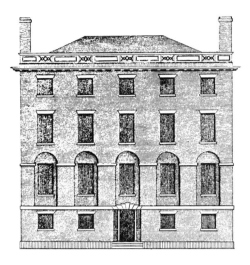

Asher Benjamin design for a large urban house, 1806

Figure 31. *Decorated Tray with Ebenezer Breed and Friends. C.* 1786–1792. Lynn, Mass., Historical Society.

A native of Lynn, Massachusetts, Ebenezer Breed (1766–1839) became wealthy as a Philadelphia wholesale shoe merchant. In 1792 he returned from a trip to England, found himself rebuffed by a fiancée, turned to drink, and lived in the Lynn poorhouse from 1800 until his death. The tray shows happier times in a fashionable parlor, probably in Philadelphia. Note the tall, steaming urn at the left in the typical Federal shape. English versions of such urns can be documented in America as early as 1786, and Paul Revere made his first in the style in 1791. The sofa was Chippendale, but the new Federal style was evident in the border of swags and urns, as well as in the decorated moldings on the door frame.

The new architecture brought elegance and luxury to Americans who could afford it. The earlier general purpose rooms became, in the Federal period, rooms with more specific functions. Suites of furniture were designed for specialized use. Thus appeared the American dining room complete with sideboard, knife boxes, side tables, and newly created dining tables. With notable exceptions (for example, Mount Vernon), the bedrooms became private rather than public rooms, located on the second floor, and visitors to the household were entertained by first-floor activities: conversing in the parlor, dining in the dining room, gaming in a game or billiard room, reading in the library, or performing in the music room. In Charleston, however, drawing rooms were often on the second floor.

Even the shapes of rooms were dictated by fashion. French practice made the oval or octagonal room a mark of distinction; thus emerged the Oval Room

Figure 32. Mary Buffum. *Miss Helen Townsend's Room. C.* 1887. Water color, 8½ in. × 11¼ in. (21.6 cm × 28.6 cm). Newport Historical Society, Newport, R.I.

Miss Helen Townsend lived in Newport in the late nineteenth century, and although the arrangement of furniture is characteristic of that era, the pieces are not. The tea table was a typical Newport style of 1740 to 1750, the sofa and side chair are both Chippendale, and the other items are Federal. The urn back chair was a design made throughout Rhode Island and eastern Connecticut, whereas the Pembroke table with its elaborate pierced stretcher is similar to one labeled by John Townsend. The breakfront bookcase and eagle mirror were typical New England Federal pieces. The base of the firescreen is typical of Newport Chippendale work, while the painted fancy chair, characteristic of the early nineteenth century, was the most recent addition to the ensemble. The corner post and window shutters show the room to be in an eighteenth-century house; but in the Federal era the chairs would have been arranged against the walls rather than set in a conversational grouping.

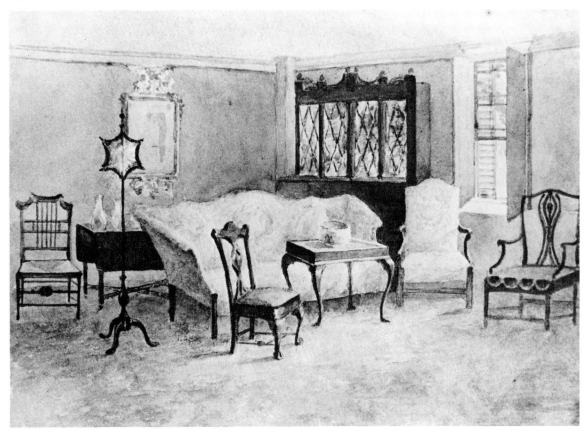

Table 7. Size of Estates in the Federal Era, Figured in Pounds of Each State[6]
(figures are percentages of inventories falling into each category)

	£0–50	51–100	101–200	201–300	301–500	501–1,000	1,001–2,000	2,001+
ULSTER COUNTY, NEW YORK, 1780–99	5%	7	40	14	14	12	4	4
LINCOLN COUNTY, MAINE, 1790–1800	18	14	23	15	10	14	3	3
LYME, CONN., 1790–1800	12	12	19	7	16	20	13	1
STONINGTON AND GROTON, CONN., 1795–1800	13	11	14	12	12	14	12	12
NEW JERSEY, 1786–90	15	16	22	15	13	12	5	2

of the White House and the oval dining room of the Gore Mansion in Waltham, Massachusetts.

The Federal period was the last before the rise of the new American industrial and trading millionaires. During this period, the dollar replaced the pound as the standard currency, and a fortune of several hundred thousand dollars numbered one among the very rich. When Washington died in 1799, his estate of $530,000 made him one of the richest Americans. Franklin had left $150,000 in 1788, and both fortunes were based largely on land holdings. When Alexander Hamilton died in 1803, his estate would have been worth $40,000 had it not been entirely consumed by debt. Financier Robert Morris was worth about $170,000 in 1787, and Charles Cotesworth Pinckney of South Carolina had an annual income of about $20,000 a year. These fortunes were extraordinary, as should be evident from Table 7. In Ulster County, New York, only 4 percent of the estates exceeded $5,000 (£2,000), while roughly 40 percent fell between $252.50 and $500. Data from Maine, Connecticut, and New Jersey show similar patterns, with wealth distributed rather evenly through the economic spectrum. In Lincoln County, Massachusetts, the three largest estates between 1780 and 1800 were each in excess of $17,000. The largest of the Connecticut estates was £33,992, an unusual fortune made in trade in a rural town where an estate of $5,000 meant relatively comfortable status.

During the Federal period, currencies remained unstable, accounts shifting from pounds to dollars, although some people never switched. In the conversion of pounds to dollars in the 1790s, states adopted different rates (Table 8). Thus, £1 was worth $4.29 in some states, but only $2.50 in others. McCusker's excellent manual for the Colonial period only goes to 1775, so that data for the Federal period are more difficult to find. Almanacks, newspapers, and arithmetics like *Dilworth's Assistant* (1805) are useful.

By the end of the period, new wealth was on the rise. Fortunes made in shipping grew; Thomas Handasyd Perkins of Boston accumulated $2 million in trade with India and China, and Stephen Girard of Philadelphia made over $1 million in trade and banking. By 1808, John Jacob Astor, whose financial success was just beginning, was able to invest $500,000 in his new fur-trading venture.

Those at the top of the economic scale were able to afford spectacular

Table 8.   Conversion of Pounds of the States into Federal Dollars[7]

States	Value of Dollar in State's Currency	Value of State's Pound in Dollars
NEW HAMPSHIRE, MASSACHUSETTS, RHODE ISLAND, CONNECTICUT, VIRGINIA, KENTUCKY, TENNESSEE	6/-	$3.33
NEW YORK, NORTH CAROLINA	8/-	$2.50
NEW JERSEY, PENNSYLVANIA, DELAWARE, MARYLAND	7/6	$2.67
SOUTH CAROLINA, GEORGIA	4/8	$4.29
BRITISH STERLING	4/6	$4.44

(Massachusetts accounts of the late 1790s used the sterling rate of $4.44 to the pound.)

Interesting is the value of 100 Spanish silver dollars in Continental currency, as accepted in the state of Connecticut.[8] In September 1777, 100 Spanish dollars were valued at 100 Continental dollars; in January 1778, 146; in July 1778, 303; in January 1779, 742; in July 1779, 1,482; in January 1780, 2,992; and in March 1780, 4,000.

Figure 33. Artist unknown. *Family Group. C.* 1815. Oil on canvas, 27½ in. × 38¼ in. (71 cm × 97 cm). Collection of Nina Fletcher Little.

Details of the room reveal this family to be one of moderate, yet substantial means and taste. The elaborate drapery with its valance and tiebacks is fashionable, but it is far from the intricate examples found in pattern books and houses of great wealth. Before the fireplace is an early appearance of what to the modern eye looks like a coffee table. The decoration of the overmantel is curious, surrounded as it is on only three edges with a paper border. The landscape, probably of London, and the framed needlework are hung by cords from a nail. The tole tray was both decorative and utilitarian.

Figure 34. Artist unknown. *Rhode Island Interior*. C. 1800–1810. Oil on canvas, 9½ in. × 11⅝ in. (25 cm × 30 cm). Collection of Mr. Fenton Brown.

Few pictures offer better documentation of the placement of fireplace implements. Probably most surprising is the brush hung around the corner. The mantel, like the whole room, is basically simple, and decorated only with a rather expensive clock and empty candlesticks. The near picture is allegorical, while the two smaller canvases appear to be portraits. A writing box is open on a Hepplewhite table against the wall, and a Hepplewhite dining table stands bare in the middle of the room. Curiously, no chairs appear. Two tones of buff in the walls contrast with white in the ceiling. The stylish curtains are red with gold tassels, and the ingrain carpet or floor cloth is red and green.

displays of the Federal style in the most elaborate houses. For example, the houses designed by Charles Bulfinch in Boston were regularly assessed at about $8,000 or more, and one was valued at $26,000 when it was finally furnished in 1806.[9]

Those people of lesser wealth had simpler and less fashionable furnishings. In the 1790s, in Connecticut, a common laborer received 5 shillings or 83¢ per day.

FURNITURE

Adam furniture appeared in Boston in 1784. In the following year, Samuel Walton of Philadelphia advertised "Household Furniture, of the newest and most elegant patterns, which have lately been imported from Europe."[10] By 1790, the style was generally available even in the smaller towns, but large Chippendale pieces were still being made as late as 1805.

above: Figure 35. Joseph Russell (1795–1860). *The Dining Room of Dr. Whitridge as It Was in the Winter, 1814–15, Breakfast Time.* 1849–1854. Water color, 7 1/16 in. × 9 1/2 in. (18 cm × 25 cm). The Whaling Museum, New Bedford, Mass.

below: Figure 36. Joseph Russell. *The Parlor of Dr. Whitridge, Tiverton, Rhode Island.* 1849–1854. Water color, 7 1/16 in. × 9 1/2 in. (18 cm × 25 cm). The Whaling Museum, New Bedford, Mass.

Even at the distance of thirty-five years, Russell recorded the persistence of earlier decor in one room of Whitridge's house and the impact of new Federal decoration in the other.

In the dining room, the only manifestation of the Federal style is the Hepplewhite table. The architecture, like the furniture, dates from mid-century. Even in winter the floor is bare in this country house, and, as in the parlor, a cushion with ruffles is found on a chair seat. The walls are plain white, while the plastered ceiling is tinted.

The parlor, a room reserved traditionally for special occasions, does show the impact of Federal styles. A freehand wall decoration is capped by a wallpaper border, but, as is usual in this period, the ceiling is plain white. Also typically Federal is the mourning picture with the weeping willow.

The wealthy continued to patronize Europe. In 1783, the year of the peace, John Hancock, the first signer of the Declaration of Independence, ordered from London a Wilton carpet, a silver tea urn, window curtains, twelve upholstered chairs, and a sofa. He wrote his supplier that he wanted a room "tolerably decent in its furniture but not extravagantly so."[11] William Bingham of Philadelphia bought furniture from the fashionable George Seddon of London, while Colonel James Swan used the expropriations of the French Revolution to fill his house in Dorchester, Massachusetts, with elegant French furniture in the latest styles. Washington, Adams, Jefferson, Madison, and Monroe obtained French furniture in a less dramatic manner.[12] The French look gained popularity, and many of the chairs in the White House were painted and gilded. Such chairs were not necessarily imports, as Philadelphia and New York craftsmen advertised comparable work as early as 1788.

American work followed English models closely. Adam's innovations in decoration were codified for the cabinetmaker in Britain and America in George Hepplewhite's *Cabinet-Maker and Upholsterer's Guide* (1788). Designs also drawing on French sources were to be found in Thomas Sheraton's *Cabinet-Maker and Upholsterer's Drawing Book* (1794), while the *Cabinet-Maker's London Book of Prices* (1788) contained designs for sideboards, one of several new forms to appear during the period.

As in the case of the sideboard, the Federal style brought the creation of new forms of furniture rather than redecoration of old ones. Wing chairs continued to be made, but the lolling or Martha Washington chair (Plate 6) assumed great popularity. The Pembroke table (Fig. 38) functioned as a tea table or occasional table. Other new forms were the breakfront (Fig. 32), the semicircular commode, and the basin stand. The work table was useful in the bedroom or parlor, while the parlor was the obvious place for the piano (Fig. 56 in Chapter 6), an instrument that had all but supplanted the harpsichord by the end of the Federal period. Characteristic of the South were the cellarette (a low case for storing or cooling wine) and huntboard (a small sideboard).

There is abundant evidence that Chippendale furniture continued to be popular in many areas, but for those who wanted the latest styles, the slant front desk was out,[13] its place taken by the breakfront, tambour desk, or cylinder fall desk. The lowboy was transformed into a dressing table with mirror, the chest-on-chest was occasionally adapted to the Federal style, but the highboy had reached a dead end. Sofas of the Chippendale period lost their many curves to the simpler lines of those seen in Plates 3 and 7.

The new style heavily depended on inlaid motifs of bellflowers, fans, icicles, shells, paterae, urns, and Federal eagles. Carving, too, embellished chairs and case pieces, and brass finials were added to case pieces as well as clocks (Fig. 32). Fine upholstery was garnished with lines or swags of brass nails (Plate 7). Painted furniture remained popular in country houses, and many a household bought sets of new painted fancy chairs.

Regional styles were evident, especially in at least moderately expensive pieces.[14] Wealthier families in the country were more likely to have work from urban centers than their less well-to-do neighbors, who might be quite content with the best a local cabinetmaker could offer. Several price books issued during the period offer some perspective on variation in price with the degree of decoration in a given piece.[15]

Hepplewhite side chair

Sheraton arm chair

Hepplewhite tambour desk

Painted fancy chair

Hepplewhite's arrangement of a wall, 1787

Placement within a room followed earlier patterns. Other than Figure 32, which shows a modern-looking grouping, most illustrations indicate furniture kept along the walls unless it was in use. Desk chairs were notable exceptions.

The best and newest furniture went into the parlor, with the second best in the dining room or sitting room, while chambers received the less desirable pieces. Some chambers, however, were furnished quite elegantly.

FLOOR COVERINGS

Floor coverings continued much as they had in the Chippendale period.

Oriental carpets remained expensive and desirable, but the lesser price made the British imports more common. In 1797, Washington ordered a Wilton carpet, provided it was not "much dearer" than a Scotch carpet.[16] Designs of these carpets varied greatly, so that it is often difficult to tell which variety appears in a picture. Washington wanted a floral Wilton, but they also came in geometric patterns. The Samels Family (Plate 3) probably had an Axminster. A Brussels carpet (Fig. 24), a newer fashion than Wilton or Axminster, was used in the dining room and other important rooms of the new White House whose construction began in 1792. Many varieties thus found their way to America, but a letter written from New York in 1790 said that only Scotch carpeting was generally available there.[17] Many of these varieties came in strips, which were sewn up with a border to fit a particular room.

Serious domestic production of fine carpets began in the 1790s. In 1794, Peter Sprague and his Philadelphia Carpet Manufactory produced carpeting for the Federal Senate chamber in Philadelphia. Similar to Axminster in weave, his carpets were woven in strips and sewn. Like their English counterparts, they were expensive. Washington paid $224.25 for a 15-by-17-foot rug for the Executive Mansion in Philadelphia.[18]

A floor covering that was increasingly being made in America but still also imported was the painted floor cloth. English floor cloth was quoted at $3 a square yard in 1802. Jefferson furnished at least one room of the White House with floor cloth, and pictures attest to its continuing use (Fig. 43). Jefferson planned to place a floor cloth under a dining table to protect either the floor or carpet beneath during dinner.[19]

Jefferson had also contemplated the use of straw matting to protect carpets under the dining table, but decided that the matting itself would become too greasy; yet matting, imported from India, Spain, and China, remained a standard summer substitute for carpeting. Mrs. Abigail Adams at least once used a floor cloth tacked to the floor as a summer replacement for a carpet.

As before, carpets were taken up in some houses during the summer. Moreau de Saint-Méry reported the Charleston custom of the 1790s: in summer, carpets were kept rolled during the mornings and then unrolled for the afternoon.[20]

Bare wood floors during the summer were sometimes sprinkled with sand swept into decorative patterns, and sand was often used year round on kitchen floors. Some floors clearly remained bare all year round (Fig. 35).

Homemade rugs began to appear. Rag rugs continued to be made, and in 1790 a Salem, Massachusetts, minister recorded a sewn rug made in the manner of a Scotch carpet. The braided rug was a few years in the future, although the yarn-sewn variation of the "hooked rug" was developed by the Federal period (Plate 6).[21] Small rugs found decorative and utilitarian uses. Figure 33 shows a small hearth rug ready to protect the large carpet. Decorative effects could also be achieved without carpets of any kind by stenciling a floor with geometric or floral designs, often in bright colors (Fig. 37).

Floor coverings were distributed in a house according to the use of the rooms. If a family had only one carpet or floor cloth, it probably went in the parlor along with the best furniture. Where there was more than one carpet, the best went into the most formal rooms. In addition to serving in place of carpeting, floor cloths were used in areas of heavy wear, notably halls and entrances.

PICTURES AND MIRRORS

Some Americans who had traveled abroad decorated their houses with Old World art. Thomas Jefferson had copies of Raphael's *Holy Family*, Leonardo's *Saint John*, Van Dyck's *Descent from the Cross* and *Crucifixion*, and Rubens's *Diogenes with His Lantern*. Such classic collections were extremely rare, but art was gaining in the average American interior.

The number of American artists—good and bad—grew appreciably. Portraits remained their most frequent and most lucrative productions. In 1796, Ralph Earl advertised full-length portraits at $60, and in 1801, Samuel King charged £11.14.0 for a portrait and £4.4.0 for a miniature. Silhouettes sold for 25¢, 75¢ if they were shaded and $2 if framed.[22] Pictures of George Washington assumed the symbolic role once accorded the reigning British monarch, landscapes began to make an appearance, and naval scenes were also in vogue at the end of the period. The artistically gifted produced mourning pictures to commemorate a departed parent, brother, or sister (Plate 15).

Frames, comparatively simple, were gilt or painted black. Oval frames, popular for portraits and mirrors, were mixed with rectangular frames in groupings (Plate 4).

Several techniques for hanging were acceptable. Smaller pictures could be suspended from brass rings hung on nails or suspended from colored cord threaded through a screw eye and hung on a nail. Generally, pictures were hung quite high. Only in Dr. Whitridge's house, where the ceilings were lower, did pictures hang at the level expected today (Fig. 36).

Pictures were hung singly or, if smaller, in groups. The Rumford parlor shows a large grouping arranged around the mantel, with oval and rectangular frames carefully balanced (Plate 4). Some paintings show pictures hung above doors, and an occasional illustration shows a room with bare walls; but in houses of the wealthy, the undecorated wall was unusual.

Chippendale mirrors with mahogany scroll work and gilt eagles continued to be popular into the 1790s. William Wilmerding of New York City sold such a mirror in 1794 for £8.[23] New designs in the Hepplewhite tradition featured gilt pediments and composition ornaments. New York versions often had an églomisé panel above the looking glass.[24] Convex mirrors, introduced late in the eighteenth century, frequently had candlearms and a carved eagle decoration. Such girandoles were made in England and America, but the Bilbao mirror with marble and gilt frame was a European import (the manufacture of this type of mirror has sometimes been attributed to Bilbao, Spain). Mirrored dressing boxes were popular.

In some areas, mirrors were more common than before, especially those with less expensive, simple frames. But Margaret Schiffer in Chester County, Pennsylvania, inventories noted: "Before 1800, looking glasses were usually placed on the first floor, in the parlor. The majority of houses that contained a looking glass had only one."[25]

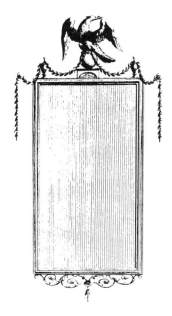

Mirror from Hepplewhite's *Guide*, 1787; see Bibliography.

Dressing glass, 1786

TEXTILES

High fashion demanded coordination of upholstery, window curtains, and bed hangings. In one room of John Penn's Philadelphia house, the window curtains and slipcovers on ten japanned chairs and two sofas were yellow printed chintz. Winterthur owns a cotton slipcover for a chair that matched a set of bed hangings,[26] and in 1797 for the White Room of his New York house, Aaron Burr used cotton dimity for chair upholstery, bed hangings, and window curtains.

Hepplewhite and Thomas Sheraton both stipulated fabrics as well as designs for fashionably appointed furniture. Sheraton depended heavily on silks and satins and an occasional chintz, but Hepplewhite had recommended that mahogany chairs should have "seats of horse hair, plain, striped, chequered, &c." Sheraton commended a set of dining chairs covered in red leather, and Hepplewhite praised leather as a covering for wing chairs.

In America, silk was the preferred upholstery in the most fashionable houses, but its use was limited to the best rooms. The President's House in Philadelphia had one room upholstered in yellow damask and another in a green-flowered damask. Horsehair was another popular covering for chair seats. The material was either made of pure horsehair or woven with a woof of horsehair (either black or dyed in brilliant colors) and a warp of cotton, linen, or wool. Leather seems to have covered few American wing chairs, but it was popular in chair seats.

Slipcovers, whether loose or tight-fitting, protected upholstery in summer and possibly in winter as well. Hepplewhite and Sheraton had both referred to slipcovers as more than seasonal upholstery, yet in pictures that show them, it is clearly summer (Plate 5, Fig. 31).

Window Curtains. Mrs. Schiffer's research indicates that window curtains became more common. Whereas only seven inventories of the 1780s included window curtains, fifty-three from the first decade of the 1800s included them. Between 1750 and 1800, curtains were listed most often on the second floor, yet the pictures show that by the end of the century curtains were firmly established in the public rooms of the ground floor.

Pictorial evidence documents the popularity of two types of curtains in the Federal period: straight-hanging curtains and the more fashionable festoon arrangement. Venetian curtains were notably absent, and it has been suggested that by the 1830s the Venetian curtain was considered "old fashioned."[27] Cornices were an important (and expensive) part of fashionable window treat-

Figure 37. Captain Simon Fitch (1758–1835). *Portrait of Ephraim Starr of Goshen, Connecticut.* 1802. Oil on canvas, 59 in. × 40 in. (1.50 m × 1.02 m). Courtesy, Wadsworth Atheneum, Hartford, Conn.

Nina Fletcher Little judges this floor to have been stenciled as there is no border, which would have been usual with a painted floor cloth. The illustration does not suggest great wealth, and one might suspect Starr to have been a moderate, middle-class subject, but the common Windsor chair supported a substantial merchant indeed. When Starr died, one of his sons inherited $60,000.

Figure 38. William Wilkie. *Nathan Hawley and Family.* 1801. Water color,
14 in. × 18⅝ in. (36 cm × 48 cm). Albany Institute of History and Art,
Albany, N.Y.

William Wilkie, one of jailor Hawley's prisoners in Albany, New York, produced
this record of the house near the jail. Although a middle-class family, the Hawleys
had a taste for art. In the far room, the plain plaster wall surmounts a low, paneled
dado, while in the near room, a high molding is surmounted only by a simple rail,
painted like the rest of the woodwork in contrast to the wall. The painted floor
cloth has wide, yellow-green stripes overlaid diagonally with narrow orange lines
enclosing blue-gray motifs. Inside shutters compensate for the lack of curtains.

ment. Joseph Moore of West Chester, Pennsylvania, died in 1799 owning eight
window papers or roller shades, which were raised and lowered with strings;
General Salem Towne of Charlton, Massachusetts, likewise had "paper curtains" in the kitchen. Such shades were raised and lowered with strings, an arrangement which Mrs. Trollope in 1828 found as inconvenient as it was ubiq-
uitous.

Damasks and satins in yellow, blue, or crimson were possibly the most
fashionable curtain fabrics; at least they were used in the President's House in
Philadelphia. Jefferson, who studied curtain styles carefully, also had curtains
of chintz and dimity, as did many of his contemporaries. A British fashion
magazine of 1807 called chintz draperies with silk fringes "truly elegant."[28]
Chester County inventories show calico and muslin as the most common curtain fabrics before 1800, while dimity and chintz begin to appear there in the
decade of 1810.

Bed Curtains.   Beds continued to carry full curtains, sometimes consuming as much as 56 yards of fabric on a single bed. High post beds with straight canopy rails were common throughout the period, as were the arched canopies of field beds. Sheraton wrote that the field bed was suitable for servants or children, but although American field beds often have plainer posts than those with straight valances, there is no evidence that Sheraton's advice governed American usage. Bed hangings in well-to-do houses might be made of silk or wool damask, while floral chintz or dimity bed curtains were common in houses of all classes, but not in all areas. Dimity and chintz bed curtains do not appear in Chester County inventories until the 1830s and 1840s. Some coverlets were imported, many were made at home, but a few were made commercially in new American manufactories.

WALL TREATMENT

Wall decoration emphasized wallpaper or paint. Paneling was less evident with the exception of the paneled dado, but a dado effect might also be created with a chair rail or wallpaper strip (Plate 3). Wallpaper edgings added decoration to otherwise plain plaster walls.

In the choice between paper and paint, many points had to be considered by fashionable householders. John Mifflin of Philadelphia had his entrances and staircase stained a dark straw color, but, as he wrote to Mrs. John Penn (then in London), the treatment was unsatisfactory. "The color did not take equally," and "whenever our servants strike a piece of plaster off, it cannot be repaired but will always remain a dent." He was most anxious to paper the stairway *if* such was the fashionable London usage of 1797. Alas, we do not know Mrs. Penn's report.[29] Earlier that year he had written to London asking for a figured stone-colored paper, an order he placed with reluctance, for paper was "not quite so fashionable as painting the wall would be." However, he noted, "the climate in America will not admit of the latter."

Wallpaper was increasingly popular, with the most expensive and fashionable papers coming from Europe. Upon his return from France in 1789, Jefferson papered his residence in Philadelphia with French papers: one room in a plain sky blue with a cornice paper of festoons, and another with plain pea green with a similar festoon cornice. More elaborate was a room papered with a lattice or trellis design.[30]

But domestic output was catching up, as American manufacturers in urban centers began producing papers based on French and English models. In the 1790s, Zechariah Mills of Hartford produced a wallpaper decorated with architectural details, a design copied from an English paper of the 1760s (Fig. 22). In 1800, Ebenezer Clough of Boston issued his famous "Sacred to Washington" paper, decorated with designs similar to those found on copperplate fabrics commemorating Washington. Mrs. Cooper's hall (Plate 5) is a fine example of a papered room, though we cannot identify the source of the paper.

Although wallpaper was not inexpensive, even families of moderate means could afford regular redecoration. When studied in 1923, the house of John Hicks, built in 1762, revealed up to fifteen layers of paper. Hicks was a carpenter of moderate means in Cambridge, Massachusetts. This decorative record, which documents changing fashion in wallpaper design, was discernible in three rooms. The hall was never papered until about 1830, but two upstairs rooms had been papered continuously since the original construction with periodic repaperings in 1790, 1800, and 1812. The second bedroom was papered twice again before 1830. The first paper dated to 1790 was a stenciled light floral pattern in white on a Pompeian red ground with a border in black, white, and green on a red ground; and the second paper, alternating large stripes of squares of varying sizes and broad floral sprays. The paper of 1800 in both bedrooms was likewise of vertical stripes of alternating vines and geometric patterns. In one room it was in a dark gray and white on a pale gray ground, and in the other maroon and white on buff. The 1812 paper showed large baskets of flowers, small rosettes, and a parrot and dove. The ground of the paper is gray but the accompanying border of tulips is in red, white, black, and two shades of green. Another paper from shortly before 1820 had a large brocade pattern in blue on a light blue ground. A similar paper in the same colors was applied over it about 1825.[31]

Stenciled walls gained vogue as an alternative to decoration with more expensive papers. Some itinerant stencilers early in the period limited their work to delicate borders at ceilings, above chair rails, and in corners, while later workers often covered the wall with bold patterns. Floral designs, vines, and urns were common, but some, like the stenciler of the Leman House in Washington, Connecticut, included a Federal eagle. One Massachusetts stenciler produced a pattern virtually identical to wallpaper, and in Maine, Massachusetts, and New Hampshire, one itinerant decorated walls with quarter fans and whorls reminiscent of the inlays of Federal furniture.[32]

More expensive than stenciling but less expensive than paper were hand-painted walls. Bartling and Hall advertised in New Haven in 1804 that they produced "that much admired imitation of stamped paper, done on the walls of rooms, far superior to the manner commonly practiced in this state."[33] Some artists produced freehand designs not unlike stencilers' patterns. Nina Fletcher Little, who has made a careful study of New England wall painters, has discerned the work of at least eight itinerants. One artist working about 1800 left a trail of his work in Vermont, Massachusetts, and Connecticut, while Jared Jessup, one of the few identified painters, worked his way along the Connecticut River Valley between 1805 and 1809. The Abiel Griswold House in Windsor, Connecticut, shows an elaborately painted trompe l'oeil decoration including convincing paneling and pictures.[34]

ARCHITECTURAL DETAILS AND CEILINGS

Elaborately furnished houses from New England to the South featured floral swags, carved urns or fruit baskets, and complex dentil moldings. The Banquet Room at Mount Vernon, an early Federal room almost giving the impression it was decorated by Wedgwood, is a fine example of Federal work. Another notable example of architectural detail was the Russell House in Charleston, costing $80,000 in 1809. In structures less costly the decoration was less intricate, but it was nonetheless inspired by the same principles.

Mantels often included a shelf for the display of figurines, clocks, or vases. One architectural feature evident for the first time in illustrations was a closet

(Fig. 33). Folding window shutters persisted in some houses, making curtains unnecessary.

Many fireplaces were rebuilt to accommodate coal grates, but iron stoves became more and more common (see "Heating Systems" in Appendix A). In the years after the Revolution, stoves were decorated with eagles, stars, Washington, and Franklin, but less political versions had the urns or garlands that characterized the period.

In summer, fireboards—either painted or decorated with wallpaper—remained in use to cover unsightly fireplaces. Iron stoves were filled with vases of flowers or branches (Fig. 36).

Illustrations reveal little about ceilings; most show basically light ceilings devoid of architectural detail. However, fashionable houses often had cast plaster or carved ornaments at the center of a ceiling, with matching fans or swag decorations at the border or in a cornice. In Salem, Massachusetts, Michel Félice Corné painted a seascape on a ceiling, but such was highly unusual. Less

Figure 39. Artist unknown. *Interior of a Moravian Boys' School. C.* 1800. Wash drawing, 9½ in. × 14 in. (25 cm × 36 cm). DeSchweinitz Papers, Moravian Archives, Winston-Salem, N.C.

Not a domestic interior, the drawing nonetheless shows two typical North Carolina secretaries. Light has governed the arrangement, causing the crowding of secretary, chair, and writing table at the far window. The map was hung at the same level as the tops of the secretaries and the hanging cabinet, and only the small calligraphic exercise between the window pushed higher, balanced by the larger frame below. A shaded candlestick was the only visible source of artificial light. The window casements were a basic German design brought to North Carolina by the Moravians.

Hall lamp

Hepplewhite girandole, 1787

elaborate and somewhat more typical were ceilings decorated with simple geometric painted or stenciled designs. Mrs. Little notes a house in West Sutton, Massachusetts, in which the ceiling had been stenciled with compass points, and some Masonic meeting rooms in houses were given deep blue ceilings with stars and an all-seeing eye.[35]

LIGHTING

Imported English or Irish glass or crystal chandeliers were expensive and elegant. Mrs. Cooper had such a chandelier, draped, as was common, for the summer. Equal in splendor to chandeliers were glass table candelabra with drops, of the sort owned by General Washington and Philip Schuyler of Albany.

Elegant but less expensive were Adamesque mirrors or urns with girandoles (Plate 3), and still less expensive were tin wall sconces.

Portable lighting devices were notably absent from most of the illustrations, perhaps not surprisingly since candles were still collected in one place each morning to be made ready for use during the evening. The very wealthy imported fashionable candlesticks and candelabra from England. American craftsmen followed the same designs in producing candlesticks, in order of diminishing cost and artistic detail, in silver, silverplate, brass, iron, tin, and wood. Iron or tin arms on a wooden shaft provided a serviceable chandelier, which incorporated lines of the Federal style, however minimally, and wooden candlestands with adjustable arms continued to be made in New England until the end of the eighteenth century. Rush lights and grease lamps remained in use in rural and frontier areas.[36]

Only at the end of the Federal period did whale oil emerge as an alternative to candles for fashionable lighting. In several rare instances gas lighting appeared. M. Ambroise had demonstrated gaslight for example, in Philadelphia in 1796, and similar demonstrations followed in Baltimore in 1802. The first regular domestic gaslight we have discovered was installed in Newport in 1806.[37]

New and still rare were Argand lamps. Jefferson gave a plated Argand to Charles Thompson, Secretary of Congress, for which he paid 31/6 in 1784.[38]

COLOR

The Federal period was the last in which a room was furnished throughout in fabrics of uniform color. Fashionable houses had more muted colors than did rural interiors, which favored stronger tones (Plates 5 and 11). The fashionable were often very meticulous about exact matching of color. Consider President Washington's directions for furnishing a house he leased in Philadelphia: "Whether the green, which you have, or a new yellow curtain, should be appropriated to the staircase above the hall, may depend on your getting an exact match, in colour, and so forth of the latter. For the sake of appearances one would not in instances of this kind, regard a small additional expense."[39]

In 1784, a Maryland painter listed the colors he used for interiors: verditure blue, Prussian blue, pea green, straw, stone, slate, cream, cloth, and pink.[40]

Many of the warmer colors advertised in the Chippendale period were absent. Frederick Kelly concluded that only in the post-revolutionary period was woodwork first painted white in Connecticut,[41] but white was not among the colors listed by the Maryland painter.

Margaret Schiffer's study of color in Chester County inventories regardless of object found blue the most common color again. Black stood a strong third on the Chippendale list, but between 1790 and 1809 it fell to the sixth most common color; green conversely rose from sixth to fourth. Most of her references are to fabrics and painted furniture.

The number of references to particular colors in the Chester County, Pennsylvania, inventories between 1790 and 1809 are:[42] blue, 220 references; white, 147; red, 81; green, 57; brown, 47; black, 45; yellow and gray, both 7; olive, scarlet, and rose, all 4; lead, 3; and purple, 2. Colors mentioned once include: chocolate, snuff, orange, lye, dark blue, Prussian blue, light blue, pale blue, pearl blue, olive green, and mahogany.

Late in the period, H. Reynolds in *Directions for House and Ship Painting*, published in New Haven in 1812, listed the following interior colors: pearl, ice, light stone, sea green, dark stone, red, purple, claret, and chocolate. He also provided formulas for mahogany, red cedar, cherry imitations, and a paint for marbling.[43]

ACCESSORIES

Generally, use of accessories continued much as in the previous era; but new designs of old forms often carried classical rather than rococo motifs. Late eighteenth-century table decoration included many delights for the eye rather than the palate. Galleried silver or silver gilt plateaus (elevated platforms to adorn a table) were decorated with porcelain or alabaster figurines. Edward Lloyd IV of Maryland had a 95-inch plateau with twenty-nine figures, while Thomas Jefferson ordered one in Paris for Abigail Adams with a paltry supply of only four figures: Minerva, Diana, Mars, and Apollo.[44]

Mantels continued to be decorated with imported fine ceramics, but flowers assumed a new decorative role there, too.[45]

Ceramics. The forms of ceramics remained much as they had in the previous era, but more countries provided imports.

After the opening of the China trade in 1784, a single ship might return with as much as 10 tons of porcelain. Although relatively inexpensive in China, where a tea and coffee set of sixty-one pieces cost $5, costs of shipping and sales increased the price; but it was less expensive than it had been in earlier decades and not beyond the reach of many families of moderate wealth. Simple floral designs or Canton ware were least expensive, Nanking ware brought a premium, and the more elaborate designs were the costliest. Washington's set of Cincinnati china contained 302 pieces and cost him £45.5.0 or about $150.[46]

Queensware, introduced in England in 1763, was imported in tremendous quantities. Liverpool ware with its transfer designs was also advertised widely, as was blue and white stoneware. Profits predominated over politics, as Liverpool potters produced jugs celebrating American victories over the British. At Mount Vernon, Washington had Canton or Nanking china for common use.

English porcelain imitating Chinese willow design

Albany stoneware jug, *c.* 1809

Some entrepreneurs began American factories to supply fine china. Peter Lacour advertised in Philadelphia in 1786 that he hoped to produce china and Delft, and in 1798, J. Mouchet announced that he produced "yellow or cream ware" at Red Hook Landing near New York. These domestic manufacturers advertised with the double appeal of nationalism and a close imitation of European or Chinese models, but they supplied little of the market.

Earthenware production increased throughout the states. The utilitarian ware found a place in most houses, but, increasingly, in wealthier homes it was confined to the kitchen. Typically, the best china was kept in a cupboard in the parlor or front room, while the more utilitarian pieces stayed in the kitchen.

Clocks. Clocks became more common in the average home as makers offered more affordable varieties, but clocks were still not inexpensive. The eight-day clock ($50–60) remained a prominent parlor fixture whose expense might vary with the richness of the case. Simon Willard's invention of the banjo clock in 1802 sparked many imitators. Although less expensive than the tall clock ($50–60), a standard banjo clock might cost $30, but the stylish presentation variation of the banjo never cost less than $80. Willard produced a much less expensive thirty-hour clock for $10 in 1802. The lighthouse clock, another Willard product, was both uncommon and expensive.

Very late in the period, Eli Terry of Connecticut and others introduced the shelf clock ($15).[47]

Glass. The most common pieces of glass were bottles, tumblers, and wine glasses. The case of bottles was again popular in this period, but it virtually disappeared from inventories by 1830. Decanters, cruets, salts, mustard pots, and candlesticks were also present, but in lesser numbers. Cut glass was advertised in Baltimore as early as 1786, yet it seems to gain a widespread popularity only toward the end of the period. American production of blown three-mold glass began during the War of 1812.

Although the American glass industry was making a strong beginning, considerable quantities were still imported. For example, between 1796 and 1798, 100,382 drinking glasses were shipped from Waterford, Ireland, to New York City. About a dozen American firms were producing simple glass items at the turn of the century. Glassmakers Henry William Stiegel and John Frederick Amelung had both tried to produce elaborate, fine table glass rivaling the

Opposite:
above: Figure 40. John Lewis Krimmel. *Quilting Party.* 1813. Oil on canvas, 16⅞ in. × 22⅜ in. (43 cm × 56 cm). Courtesy, Henry Francis du Pont Winterthur Museum, Winterthur, Del.

below: Figure 41. John Lewis Krimmel. *The Country Wedding.* C. 1819. Oil on canvas, 16 in. × 22 in. (41 cm × 56 cm). Pennsylvania Academy of Fine Arts, Philadelphia.

Krimmel probably used the same room and same props for both pictures. In both one finds the same tall clock (typical of Pennsylvania Chippendale work), fan back Windsor, silhouettes over the mantel, and mantel vase. Note particularly that the clock is placed at an angle in the corner. Of special interest is the early picture of Washington over the mantel, together with two naval scenes probably dating from the War of 1812.

Careful study of these pictures is well repaid in learning about the placement of many items. *The Country Wedding* shows the storage of jugs and crocks under a table and of boxes and food atop the linen press. *Quilting Party* documents the arrangement of glass and china in a cupboard and the use of a wooden knife tray at the table. The uncovered board floors are in keeping with the moderate circumstances of the household.

Figure 42. Artist unknown. *Connecticut Interior. C.* 1810. Water color with crystalline decoration, 14 in. × 12 in. (36 cm × 30 cm). New York State Historical Association, Cooperstown.

The artist, obviously defeated by perspective, nevertheless documented a slipcovered sofa, a stenciled wall, wallpaper borders, and a well-draped window. A painted floor cloth probably covered the floor. Although the art is primitive, the draperies are such that one would guess the subject was rather well-to-do.

European imports, and both failed because there was not yet a market for the work they produced.

Amelung's glass was engraved at the factory, but Mrs. B. Deschamps, a French émigrée to Philadelphia, advertised between 1795 and 1800 that she was ready to engrave the customer's glassware with "borders, flowers, garlands, cyphers, figures, escutcheons, &c."

Glass was generally kept in the dining room or parlor, usually on shelves or in a cupboard with china and silver. Figure 40 shows an undoubtedly typical arrangement. Generally, no glass was kept in the kitchen.

Iron and Brass. The basic forms of the previous era continued in both metals. Domestic production of brass andirons in the hands of such manufacturers as Paul Revere offered stylish work if not great volume. The most elaborate andirons were in the parlor, while simpler iron forms sufficed for the kitchen and chambers.

Pewter. Ledlie Laughlin, in his studies of pewter, found that the pewter trade, both imported and domestic, "declined precipitately" in Boston, Newport, and New York after the Revolution when china and other substitutes appeared in profusion. Yet in many parts of the countryside pewter flourished, with most of it made by domestic workers. Craftsmen in Philadelphia and Baltimore, together with those of Connecticut, North Carolina, and Georgia, created regionally important centers of production.

Regional styles were still evident in porringers. The pewter tankard, out of favor with the fashionable, was more or less obsolete, though the pot, can, or mug retained its place. Spoons were not only utilitarian but might be cast with patriotic decorations. Pewterers produced teapots in old Queen Anne designs and new Federal shapes.

Silver. Silver added a bright stylishness to the Federal interior, and as in previous eras, it was most evident in the homes of the wealthy.

With the exception of the tankard, which was seldom produced after 1800, forms continued as before, but with a close adherence to the neoclassical style that had gained vogue in England about 1770. Paul Revere produced two teapots in the new style in 1782, and by the end of the decade it was common. These teapots had straight sides, but the classic urn underlay many other Federal shapes. Coffee pots were based on the urn, but some smiths continued to produce the older pear shape as well.

Great quantities of silver were produced domestically, yet England remained the standard of fashion; advertisements assured potential customers that a smith's work was "in the most elegant and modern Fashion, agreeable to the European taste."

Regional variations were most evident in tea wares. New York teapots had more elaborate, bright, cut decoration than those from Boston, and Philadelphia work often had pierced fretwork decoration. Spoons continued to be the most common silver items in an inventory.

Silver was part of a family's wealth, and as such it was usually on display rather than concealed in the kitchen. Moreau de Saint-Méry, visiting in the 1790s, observed in Philadelphia that "before and all during dinner, as is the English custom, all the silver one owns is displayed on the sideboard in the dining room." However, a tea service or coffee urn might still be found on a parlor table or in the corner cupboard (Fig. 31).

Silver plate brought elegant designs at more moderate prices. For example, Revere charged £11.10.10 for a silver teapot in 1783. A plated one cost £6.11.3. A man who died in West Chester, Pennsylvania, in 1817 had two plated candlesticks worth $1.00 each and two others worth 75¢ the pair. Brass candlesticks were valued at 50¢ each.[48]

Cruet stands were popular silver additions to the fashionable table. The liquids kept in the small bottles were soy sauce, oil, vinegar, pepper sauce, bitters, and club sauce, which was more or less ketchup.[49]

Silver creamer in typical helmet shape, Philadelphia, Pa.

6

The Empire Style

1810–1830

THE Empire period was the last great style before mass production brought some uniformity to American interiors regardless of economic status. Elaborate forms of Empire looked expensive, and indeed they were. Like the styles that preceded it, Empire began among the fashionable wealthy of the major cities. As the style evolved, it spread from the cities to the smaller towns. Just as Boston and New York merchants advertised Paris and London styles, so, too, the small town craftsmen advertised the latest fashionable New York or Boston designs. America's nascent factory system did much to spread the elements of the Empire style, and thus the classic motifs of French designers were metamorphosed into the stencilings on Hitchcock chairs. The earliest American Empire furniture can be dated to about 1810, but by 1845, the style had run its course and had made almost no impact on rural interiors.

Mrs. Trollope's memoirs (1831) chronicled the progress the style had made in New York City: "The dwelling houses of the higher classes are extremely handsome, and very richly furnished. Silk or satin furniture is as often, or oftener, seen than chintz; the mirrors are as handsome as in London; the cheffoniers, slabs, and marble tables as elegant; and in addition, they have all the pretty tasteful decoration of French porcelaine, and or-molu in much greater abundance, because at a much cheaper rate. Every part of their houses is well carpeted, and the exterior finishing, such as steps, railings, and door frames, are very superior."[1]

The urban wealthy were able to follow the new Continental style rather closely. The basic motifs of Empire emanated from the new classicism at the turn of the century. Earlier classicism had emphasized Roman models, but designers now looked to Greece and Egypt. In France, the volumes of Percier and Fontaine and of Pierre La Mésangère codified the fashion, as did the works of Thomas Hope and George Smith in England. Unlike earlier pattern books, these volumes offered suggestions for drapery and wall treatment as well as furniture.

The same classical motifs that influenced the cabinetmakers also appeared in the work of other craftsmen. Wallpapers, for instance, depicted large architectural arches or heroes surrounded with classical decorations. Textile printers found Neptune and Minerva profitable designs for fabrics, and American silversmiths used snakes, sphinx heads, and acanthus leaves to decorate Greek and Roman shapes. The caryatids at the Erectheum in Athens inspired candlesticks, fireplaces, and carving on furniture.

The Greek influence was equally evident on the exterior of fashionable houses. Asher Benjamin, whose *Country Builder's Assistant* had first appeared in 1796, in later editions provided several designs that extended the gable end of a house so that it might be faced with a pillared portico. This emphasis on the showy portico caused many houses to be built with their gable ends toward the street. The main door was usually to the right or the left, but not in the middle of the portico. One entered into a narrow hall, and at the side of the hall was a double parlor, often divided with elaborate Ionic or Corinthian columns or by sliding doors that would separate the two rooms.

Further evidence of America's vision of the appropriateness of Greek and

Figure 43. Henry Sargent. *The Dinner Party. C.* 1820. Oil on canvas. Courtesy, Museum of Fine Arts, Boston, Mass.

Charles Bulfinch designed the Tontine Crescent in Boston in 1793, and when Sargent painted his canvases of No. 10, the dining room had not been redecorated as had the parlor (Plate 8). Especially noticeable are the floor cloth under the table, the large expensive mirror in a dining room, and the draperies, more decorative than functional. The placement of the cellar, wine box, and the setting of the table provide almost photographic documentation of a high style American dinner party during the dessert course. The pictures, hung rather high, were arranged symmetrically in relation to window, door, or object below.

Figure 44. Auguste Edouart. *The Family and Guests of Dr. Cheesman.* 1840.
Silhouette with wash on paper. Courtesy, The New-York Historical Society,
New York City.

Dr. John C. Cheesman held this reception at his house at 473 Broadway in New York
City. Moses Beach in his *Wealth and Biography of the Wealthy Citizens of New
York City* called Cheesman a "distinguished physician," with a fortune of $100,000.
Although slipcovers obscure the details, it is quite likely that Dr. Cheesman had ordered a parlor set similar to that which Samuel A. Foot bought from Duncan Phyfe in
1837. Foot had a day bed or meridienne, a curule stool, and a window bench, all of
which appear in similar Empire style.[10] Curious is the bareness of the walls, especially in view of the details of carpet, furniture, and draperies. Exceptionally large
patterns in carpets seem to have come into fashion about 1840, just at the time this
silhouette was taken.

Roman models is to be found in the names of cities settled during the period.
As the Erie Canal made access to New York State and the West easier, new
towns appeared, and the abundance of classical names is overwhelming: Troy,
Utica, Rome, Ithaca, Syracuse, Carthage, Corinth, and Hannibal.

For the first time, American householders had a few guidebooks to consult
on furniture, color, and decor in general. Hope and Smith, with their many
suggestions for furniture and curtains, were certainly known to major city
architects, cabinetmakers, and upholsterers. In 1825, Frances Byerly Parkes, or
Mrs. William Parkes as the title pages invariably called her, published her
*Domestic Duties or Instructions to Young Married Ladies on the Management
of their Household.* First published in London, the text was reprinted in an
American edition the following year. From 1828, *Domestic Duties* was available as one of the inexpensive titles in the Harper's Family Library series. By
1846, the book was in its tenth American edition; still in print in the 1880s, its
continuing popularity cannot be denied. Mrs. Parkes brought to the American
middle-class householder specific suggestions on decoration and, for the first
time, a philosophy or theory of a room. As will be seen more fully, she
counseled that each room had a spirit that should pervade its decoration.

Drawing rooms or parlors should be elegant and light, while dining rooms and libraries should be simple and plain.

If the Empire style was one of grandeur, it was also one of deception. In the pages that follow, we will meet one lady who painted a floor to look like a striped carpet and a family who had a wall painted to look like Dufour wallpaper.

FURNITURE

There are two distinct phases of Empire furniture, the first of which grew gradually into the second.

The first phase reflects the English Regency and French Empire styles. The details of the style appeared in such pattern books as Thomas Hope's *Household Furniture and Interior Decoration* (London, 1807), George Smith's *Collection of Designs for Household Furniture* (London, 1808), *Meubles et objets de goût* by Pierre La Mésangère (Paris, 1802–1830), and Percier and Fontaine's *Recueil de décorations intérieures* (1801). The Davis drawing (Plate 9) documents the persistence of the style until the 1830s, but it soon waned. In its purest American form it was limited to the stylish homes of the urban wealthy, especially in New York and Philadelphia, where French and British émigrés like Charles Honoré Lannuier, Anthony Quervelle, and Duncan Phyfe produced

Figure 45. Artist unknown. *Bedroom Interior. C.* 1830. Pencil, 4¼ in. × 6½ in. (10 cm × 18 cm). Cooper-Hewitt Museum, The Smithsonian Institution's National Museum of Design, New York City.

Inspired by the designs of Pierre La Mésangère, an architect produced a design for a well-furnished bedroom probably planned for the New York City area. The furniture is unusual in an American context, and the drawing is more useful in documenting the arrangement of a bedroom than in selecting particular designs for a restoration. The large carpet patterns suggest a date in the 1830s.

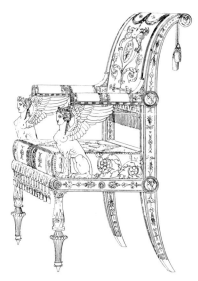

Chair design, Percier and Fontaine, 1812

notable examples. Presidents Madison and Monroe chose Empire pieces for the White House, some of them imported directly from France, others made in Baltimore.

New forms came into fashion with the Empire style: the Greek or klismos chair, the currule or Roman stool with a cross base, the Grecian couch, the pier table, and the sleigh bed. New carved motifs included sphinxes, lyres, eagles, winged supports, paw feet of lions and dogs, and dolphins. Palmettes, rinceaux, or cornucopias were often added, either in imported ormolu or gilt stenciling. The overall effect of this furniture was elegance and grandeur, yet lightness.

The second phase of the American Empire style was evident by the 1820s as cabinetmakers responded to changing European fashions. George Smith's later book *The Cabinetmaker and Upholsterer's Guide* (London, 1826) brought the English version of the new forms to American readers. Carving remained important for the elaborate paw feet of tables, sofas, desks, and sideboards, but gilded sphinxes, eagles, and dolphins disappeared. Late Empire furniture appeared heavier, more ponderous than grandiose, and cabinetmakers decorated with rich mahogany graining rather than ormolu.

Expensive versions of this second phase were produced by many of the same

Figure 46. Artist unknown. *Library of the Honorable Richard Rush. C.* 1836–1842. Water color. Philadelphia Museum of Art, Philadelphia, Pa. (Gift of Mrs. Frederick C. Fearing). Photography by A. J. Wyatt, Staff Photographer.

Richard Rush (1780–1859), son of the eminent Benjamin Rush, was Minister to Great Britain from 1817 to 1825 and then Secretary of the Treasury. The furnishings at Sydenham, his house near Philadelphia, ran from Federal to early Victorian, but the general appearance of the rooms was Empire, with the marble fireplace, the heavy moldings around the windows and doors, and the gilt mantel mirror. A variety of lighting devices were left in place during the day, and adjacent to the fireplace was a gas jet. Gaslight had become relatively common in London just before Rush's arrival there, and gas was introduced to Philadelphia in 1836.

Figure 47. Thomas Middleton. *Friends and Amateurs of Music.* 1827. Wash drawing, 13 in. × 19½ in. (33 cm × 51 cm). Carolina Art Association, Gibbes Art Gallery, Charleston, S.C. Photograph: Courtesy, Frick Art Reference Library, New York City.

This convivial ensemble could not have been much aided by the gentleman at the right playing his cello case, but the picture illustrates a good set of period dining furniture, including a heavy sideboard and a large center pedestal table. The eleven painted fancy chairs were decorative but not especially fashionable. The demi-lune sectional table at the left is a Federal piece. Such large collections of paintings were confined only to houses of wealth. Most of these were eighteenth-century canvases, and the placement of one over another was most unorthodox. The floor is bare except for the spittoon.

Late Empire sofa and mantel, *c.* 1833

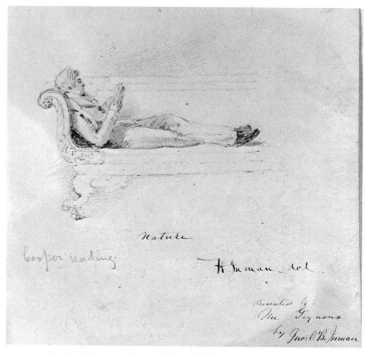

Henry Inman. *Cooper Reading.* Vassar College Art Gallery. Gift of Matthew Vassar.

Figure 48. F. Heinrich. *Mr. and Mrs. Ernest Fiedler, 38 Bond Street, New York City.* 1847. Oil on canvas, 44 in. × 60 in. (1.12 m × 1.52 m). Museum of the City of New York (Collection of Mrs. William L. Rich).

Heinrich depicted a high style double parlor toward the end of the period, when new styles had already made incursions. The caryatids were an extremely expensive adornment when first installed, and the piano was comparable in luxury. But the Fiedlers kept pace with changing styles and probably discarded many earlier pieces and decorations. Statuettes and statuary, rococo furniture decorated with carvings and fringe, and the splendid chandelier and mantel sconces show what a family of wealth and taste could add to such a room by the mid-1840s. The carpet, protected by a hearth rug, is a fine example of the fashionable floral patterns that gained popularity in the late 1840s.

craftsmen who had done the earlier pieces. In 1829, Anthony Quervelle, probably following Smith's *Guide*, made several tables for the White House. While the best carving might be found in the larger cities, craftsmen in smaller towns eagerly adopted the new forms and made the later style available to the middle classes of the smaller cities in a way the first phase had not been. Like many who followed American rather than European models, John Dewey of Litchfield, Connecticut, advertised in 1828 "a handsome assortment of cabinet work, made from the latest New York fashions." Possibly Dewey never heard of George Smith, but he copied those who had.

In the country, eighteenth-century styles persisted. The picture of Moses Morse, a cabinetmaker (Plate 11), reveals that by 1824 the Empire style had made no impact on his work or his house in Loudon, New Hampshire. But by the mid-1820s, Lambert Hitchcock and other enterprising capitalists began to mass produce furniture, which brought new styles to every part of the country.

above: Figure 49. *Drawing Room of the Mount. C.* 1860. From Calbraith B. Perry, *Charles D'Wolf of Guadeloupe, His Ancestors and Descendants* (1902).

right: Figure 50. Worthington Whittredge. *A Bit from the DeWolf House.* 1860. Oil on canvas, 12¼ in. × 12½ in. (30 cm × 33 cm). Collection of Mr. Stuart P. Feld.

In 1808, Russell Warren designed the James DeWolf house in Bristol, Rhode Island, for the uncle of General George DeWolf who appears in Plate 13. Architectural features, like the niche for the sofa, were Federal, but Sheraton and later Victorian chairs were mixed, some of them lined up against the wall, others formed into conversational groups. What might be taken for a Dufour or Zuber wallpaper was actually a mural attributed to Michel Félice Corné, illustrating the DeWolf coffee plantation in Cuba and scenes from Bernardin de Saint-Pierre's novel *Paul et Virginie*.[11] The fine chandelier was probably an early expense in keeping with the cost of the whole house, but the astral lamp on the center table represented mid-century lighting.

The Whittredge canvas shows how accurate a painting could be. The console table was a high style example of a fashionable but never very common Empire design. Seen clearly under the dome are wax flowers in a Vieux Paris gold porcelain basket supported by sphinxes. The large urn on the lower shelf was probably alabaster.

Hitchcock chairs added Empire motifs to the Sheraton fancy chair, achieving an inexpensive elegance through bronze stenciling. Hitchcock sold his chairs for $1.50 each.

ROOM FURNISHINGS

The Parlor or Drawing Room.   In her *Domestic Duties*, Mrs. Parkes offered helpful hints for selecting furniture. She held that mahogany was the most durable wood and the one capable of the best polish, but she approved of any wood with strong graining, especially rosewood or elm. She commented that "satin wood is going out of favor . . . as it is a poor, cold looking wood, without any variety of veining, and is incapable of receiving a polish, except by varnish."

The illustrations reveal that Americans at virtually every economic level furnished their parlors with many light, movable chairs, whether they were high style early Empire, later Hitchcocks, or Chippendale chairs retained from three generations earlier. Figure 53 demonstrates that as late as 1848, at least in New Bedford, Rhode Island, a parlor might be arranged in the eighteenth-century manner of placing the chairs against the wall.

With an increasing number of American piano makers and music publishers, music gained an importance in the life of the average middle-class

Figure 51. David Claypoole Johnston. *Family Group in Parlor. C.* 1835. Pencil sketch, 4 in. × 5 11/16 in. (10 cm × 15 cm). American Antiquarian Society, Worcester, Mass.

Johnston's drawings for book illustrations offer documentation of prevalent tastes late in the Empire period. Notable here is the tall case piano with its shirred fabric front. The clock on the mantel is out of scale with the room, as most such clocks were smaller. Note the meticulous symmetry of the mantel arrangement.

Figure 52. Artist unknown. *Vermont Room Interior. C.* 1830–1840. Oil on canvas. Private collection. Photograph: Courtesy, The Childs Gallery, Boston, Mass.

This interior is extremely busy, not only with its twelve inhabitants, but also with the strong design of the large patterned wallpaper and the elaborately festooned border. Note that no lighting devices are visible, and there are no curtains at the windows. The Hitchcock-style mirror, with its alternating bands of gilt and black, the blown glass in classical shapes, and the piano with the painting above it added refinement to a country interior. Only the grandmother had a rocking chair. We illustrate the typical frame along with the picture.

family. If the family had a piano or organ, it was likely to be in the parlor. Large, round tables occupied a central position in the parlor. Especially after the addition of better lighting in the Victorian Classical period, such tables remained logical gathering places for reading and discussion.

Pictures document a variety of Empire parlors. The DeWolf pictures (Figures 49 and 50, Plate 13) show what could be achieved in a late Empire style in Bristol, Rhode Island, while Figure 52 shows a middle-class, less prosperous family in their parlor in Vermont. Figures 57–60 illustrate country parlors furnished with painted furniture.

The Dining Room. The Sargent *Dinner Party* (Fig. 43) depicts an elegant dining room of 1821. Many of the furnishings are Sheraton, but the chairs seem to be early Empire. The painting proves that a basically Federal dining room might be found in the same house as a full Empire parlor.

The typical late Empire furnishings of the *Friends and Amateurs of Music* (Fig. 47) illustrate Mrs. Parkes's advice. She told her readers to furnish their dining rooms with "substantial" furniture, including a mahogany table, chairs, and sideboards. The musicians, however, have inexpensive Hitchcock chairs. For her, the ideal sideboard was "well proportioned to the room" and "massive without being clumsy."

The Library. During the early nineteenth century, the American publishing industry began to expand. Books were not inexpensive, but several publishers introduced less expensive editions, like the Harper's Family Library, the series that included Mrs. Parkes's book. The shelves of a secretary no longer sufficed to hold the family library, and specially built bookcases became more common in wealthier houses.

Bedrooms. An architect's design documents the furniture and its placement in a high style bedroom of about 1830 (Fig. 45). The bed with its complicated spread was based on a design in La Mésangère. Virtually the same items

Figure 53. Joseph Russell. *South Parlor of Abraham Russell, New Bedford.* 1848. Water color, 7⅛ in. × 9⅝ in. (18 cm × 25 cm). The Whaling Museum, New Bedford, Mass.

Abraham Russell's house in New Bedford, Massachusetts, was raised on July 6, 1803, and in 1848 the family still placed many of their chairs around the edge of the parlor, an arrangement common in the eighteenth century. Except for the Empire table, the furniture was a simple variant of the Federal style. In many houses the center table became a focus for family gatherings, but note that the table was "centered" toward the light. A fireplace with flanking columns and rather heavy entablature was standard in the Empire period, and the one seen here was likely a modification of the original Federal construction.

found in this sketch were included in the contents of a bedroom in the Broadway house auction of 1834. That bedroom contained a high post bedstead, a wash stand with marble slab, two mahogany footbenches, a mahogany candlestand, and andirons, shovel, and tongs. *The Itinerant Artist* (Fig. 61) offers a glimpse into a country bedroom. The low post bed (complete with trundle) survives from the eighteenth century, but the simple chair may be of more recent manufacture.

FLOOR COVERINGS

Floor coverings had become usual, even in the country. In well-to-do and middle-class houses, wall-to-wall carpets predominated. The Sargent *Tea Party* (Plate 8) shows the essence of high style with its French Aubusson, a carpet consistent with the fine furniture. Both the wealthy and middle classes of city, town, and

Figure 54. Alexander F. Fraser. *Asking a Blessing*. C. 1830–1842. Oil on canvas, 14⅛ in. × 20¼ in. (36 cm × 51 cm). Milwaukee Public Museum, Milwaukee, Wis.

This painting may be copied from—or it may be the original of—a Kellogg print of the identical scene published in Hartford between 1830 and 1842. Somewhat strange is the niche with the classical bust on a shelf. The walls are unusually plain and dark for the period, but the picture provides good documentation for a period table setting or the selection of toys. Such cruet sets were popular, as were dish covers. The family will have water from blown tumblers rather than stemmed goblets. A floor cloth protects the large patterned carpet underneath.

country used Scotch or ingrain carpet (Plate 10) or the somewhat more expensive Wilton (cut pile) and Brussels (uncut pile) carpets. Such carpets were generally imported from Britain, but in 1833 the Hartford Manufacturing Company of Thompsonville, Connecticut, began domestic production of ingrains. The figures in the carpet designs, whether floral or geometric, were larger than those of the Federal period.

The painted floor cloth remained as a means of protecting valuable dining room carpets, both in fine houses and simpler settings (Figs. 43, 54). Floor cloths appeared in Chester County, Pennsylvania, inventories as late as 1847. Designs might be geometric, in imitation of more expensive floor coverings. In 1827, a Boston man offered to paint such imitations for $1.37½ to $2.25 per square yard.[2]

Hearth rugs protected carpets in front of fireplaces (Figs. 44, 46, 48). John Thomas Avery (Fig. 59) had his floor decorated with shirred or yarn-sewn rugs, types becoming more popular throughout the countryside. Shirred rugs were made by sewing strips of fabric onto a fabric backing, while hooked rugs were made by pulling loops of fabric through a coarse backing. The Talcott Family portrait (Fig. 60) shows a Roman or striped carpet, a brightly colored form common in the country.

Painted floors became rarer, but still survived in the country (Plate 11). In New Hampshire in 1830, Mrs. Ruth Henshaw Bascom painted her parlor floor red, green, blue, yellow, and purple in imitation of a striped carpet. Only the primitive scene in Figure 61 shows a bare board floor.

A short-lived innovation was the paper carpet, patented in 1819 by Francis Guy of Baltimore, who treated wallpapers to make them as durable as canvas floor cloth yet 50 percent cheaper. Intended principally for summer use, they were never well received.

PICTURES AND MIRRORS

Even in the country, a room appeared empty without pictures and mirrors. Symmetry was the rule for Empire hangings alike in city, town, and country. Paintings and prints tended to be hung in matching pairs, often at eye level and somewhat lower than in the Federal period. However, Sargent's *Tea Party* and Rush's study (Plate 8 and Fig. 46) show that pictures could still be hung at great height in a fashionable setting. The Rush study further illustrates that a mantel mirror might be surmounted by a large picture above it. (See also Fig. 64 in Chapter 7.)

A considerable number of small pictures or prints could be placed in balanced groupings, or a fair number of larger pictures could be placed singly around the wall. Toward the end of the period, single paintings with elaborate frames dominated whole walls. Almost all the illustrations show blind-hung pictures and mirrors.

Period paintings commonly included portraits and landscapes, and as the century continued, landscapes became larger and more remote geographically in their subject matter. Genre scenes were less common (Figs. 46, 53), and religious themes are notably lacking until the 1840s.

The subject matter of art did not vary with the householder's economic

Figure 55. J. Johnston. *The Chess Game. C.* 1830. Oil on canvas, 27 in. × 35 in. (69 cm × 89 cm). Lyman Allyn Museum, New London, Conn.

Johnston depicted a prosperous, upper middle-class family at leisure in their parlor, possibly somewhere near Boston. The klismos chairs and the table are less expensive versions of the early Empire style, and a late, painted fancy chair appears against the wall at the left. The tall organ with its shirred fabric front was an expensive addition to the family's recreation. The landscapes with their ornate frames are symmetrically arranged, but the portrait is probably an eighteenth-century ancestor. The carpet is more typical of Ralph Earl's portraits of the 1790s than of other examples from the 1830s.

status, but the quality did. The best artists were patronized by the urban wealthy, but the walls of houses in the smaller towns and in the country were decorated by traveling artists whose "primitives" were certainly high fashion for many of the towns they visited. Mrs. Parkes warned that "where pictures are exhibited, a person of good taste will rather prefer to possess a few of high merit, than to have the walls covered with inferior performances."

Frames. Frames fell into two categories: wide gilt bolection moldings and, later, ornate plaster frames with extensive gilding. Frames of either category were not inexpensive. For prints, small black Hogarth frames continued to be popular.

Sculpture appears in two middle-class interiors (Figs. 51, 54); both show fairly large busts displayed upon small shelves. Within a few decades, sculpture would become much more common.

Mirrors or looking glasses grew in size and number in the American interior, a proliferation made possible by growth of the American glass industry. Some large mirrors appeared to be almost an integral part of a building, but in most instances the mirror was obviously removable. Symmetry reigned in the hanging of a looking glass—usually hung between two windows or centered over a mantel or piano. Only in Figure 51 does a mirror hang otherwise, but there it is flanked by portraits.

TEXTILES

During the Empire period, the Federal practice of coordinating the fabrics throughout a room seems to have been given up. No one advocated a wild display of clashing colors, but none of the illustrations shows the same fabric used for upholstery, bed curtains, and window curtains.

Table 9.   Suggestions for Empire Upholstery,
Based Primarily on Smith, A Collection of Designs for Household Furniture

Piece	Material	Color and style if given
PARLOR CHAIR	leather	"color of no great consequence," loose or stuffed cushions
PARLOR CHAIR	leather	red morocco with printed Grecian ornaments in black; French-stuffed, with tacks or brass molding
LIBRARY CHAIR	velvet or leather	black
TÊTE-À-TÊTE SEAT	fine cloth velvet calico	
DRAWING ROOM CHAIRS	silk painted satin painted velvet superfine cloth chintz	red or blue
SOFA	leather or cloth	blue or green with printed ornamental borders
OTTOMAN	superfine cloth calico of chintz pattern	red or green with gold gimp (twisted edging) or fringe of fine worsted
DRAWING ROOM SOFA	satin silk velvet	ornamented borders painted in water colors
CHAISE LONGUE	silk cloth calico	red and green or blue with gilt; in a moderately furnished apartment, one might use calico with a small pattern "of the chintz kind"
WORK TABLE BAG	lustring silk	blue or red with silk gold fringe
FIRESCREEN	silk or velvet	blue with gold fringe, painted designs
FOOTSTOOL	leather velvet printed cloth	red, blue, or green

Table 10. Suggestions for Empire Curtains, Based Primarily on Smith and Mrs. Parkes
(numbers indicate order of preference for fabrics)

Room	Spirit of decor	Style of curtains	Fabric	Color
DRAWING ROOM	elegant, light	continued	1. plain-colored, silk or figured damask 2. lustring or tabarays 3. calico with a mellow glaze 4. Salisbury flannel, commonly used but not good for large curtains	warm colors, large patterns
		glass	muslin	white
DINING ROOM AND LIBRARY	simple, plain	Roman	1. superfine cloth or cassimere 2. undressed moreen 3. maroon calico	scarlet or crimson
BEDROOM		straight-hung, draw		

Upholstery.   Smith and Hope offer suggestions for high style upholstery, which are summarized in Table 9, but most paintings reveal few large upholstered pieces. Slipcovers appear in two fashionable rooms (Figs. 44, 46).

Window Curtains.   The pictures present a great variety in window curtains from plain to elaborate, yet some well-to-do households still lacked curtains. When Isaac Pennock died in 1824 leaving $110,000, only one of his six West Marlboro, Pennsylvania, bedrooms had curtains, and his parlor and dining room were filled with expensive furniture, yet neither room had curtains. George Smith's *Cabinetmaker and Upholsterer's Guide* was the direct (or more likely, indirect) inspiration for many American drapery arrangements (see Table 10). Fabrics were to carry out the spirit of each room. For a drawing room, which should be elegant and light, what he called "continued" draperies were proper. Plain-colored satin or figured damask were preferable materials, with lustring and tabarays, calico glazed, or a small chintz pattern less than desirable fabrics.

Dining rooms and libraries were to have simple and "plain" decorations, and "Roman" curtains were most appropriate, although Smith's Roman curtain hardly seems simple or plain. For these curtains, cassimere or superfine cloth was specified, with moreen in second place, and calico in third. In both rooms, scarlet and crimson were the right colors.

Roller shades and venetian blinds were popular in many houses (Fig. 58).

Bed Curtains.   Bed curtains became increasingly rare as heating improved, and theories of the effects of night air changed. Nonetheless, Mrs. Parkes offered some suggestions for bed hangings—she favored moreen or chintz lined with colored calico. She detailed the usual furnishings of a bed: a bolster, two pillows, a feather throw with a strong linen bed tick, and for cold weather Whitney blankets. To dress up a bed, a counterpane of Marsellois or Marcella cloth—a white woven honeycomb material—gave a handsome appearance. Popular late in the period were reversible or Jacquard coverlets, many of them produced by itinerant weavers who charged from $2 to $5.50 for weaving the customer's yarns.[3]

WALL TREATMENT

Illustrations from the period indicate plain walls of a pale hue in the houses of the rich and the middle class, and Mrs. Parkes advised that walls "of light colors were the most general."

Wallpapers gained favor, expecially as the American manufacture of them

Figure 56. Ambrose Andrews. *The Family of Philip Schuyler*. 1824. Water color, 9½ in. × 12⅛ in. (25 cm × 30 cm). Courtesy, The New-York Historical Society, New York City.

Although certainly an Empire interior from the painted chairs and the gilt pier mirror, this water color nonetheless provides the best early illustration of an inlaid Hepplewhite piano. The walls are plain except for a thin wallpaper border applied about 3 inches below the ceiling. Atop the Pembroke table in the far room is a footed jewel or sewing box in a typical Empire shape. The Schuylers were another Empire family without curtains, but they have the same wall-to-wall floor covering with its small diaper pattern in both rooms.

Figure 57. Joseph H. Davis. *The Tilton Family.* June 13, 1837. Water color on paper, 10 in. × 15½ in. (25 cm × 38 cm). Abby Aldrich Rockefeller Folk Art Collection, Williamsburg, Va.

John Tilton of Deerfield, New Hampshire, married Hannah Barstow of East Kingston, New Hampshire, on December 19, 1830, seven years before Davis painted them. Working in New Hampshire and Maine, Davis executed over 100 similar family groups, many showing painted furniture and carpets with gaudy designs as in this picture. His brush perhaps caught the spirit rather than the exact design of numerous carpets, and his works invariably convey the sense of bright color common to a number of country interiors.

advanced. Mrs. Parkes thought that paper was particularly appropriate for the drawing room: "The rich, gold-flowered, and deep crimson embossed papers are much in vogue for large rooms, in which warm colors, and large patterns may be assembled together without inconsistency." The Vermont residents in Figure 52 certainly assembled a variety of "large patterns" in their parlor. In small rooms, Mrs. Parkes held that simplicity, lightness, and cheerfulness should prevail. She also advised that in adjoining rooms, sharp contrasts of color should be avoided.

The illustrations present a variety of wallpapers. Popular in late Empire decoration were papers with small flowered sprig designs (Fig. 60), or large floral patterns with applied borders.

Strong vertical stripes are more characteristic of earlier Empire (Plate 13). Also fashionable with early Empire were French scenic papers. From the first decade of the century on, the firms of Zuber and Dufour produced a variety of papers based on such themes as Scott's "Lady of the Lake," the voyages of Captain Cook, or the travels of Telemachus. Advertised in Boston as early as 1817, these papers were never common because of their high cost. American and British papers were advertised at 25¢ to $2.50 a roll, and the French papers were presumably still more expensive. They were, however, a consistent presidential favorite. John Quincy Adams ordered a set of Dufour's "Vues d'Italie" in 1818,

Figure 58. J. Collins. *Nathaniel Coleman and Wife.* 1854. Water color, 6 in. ×
8½ in. (15 cm × 23 cm). Burlington County Historical Society, Burlington, N.J.

The Colemans' parlor, though sparse, is informative. They inherited their Queen Anne
mirror, but they have added a set of venetian blinds with a scalloped valance, a built-in
cupboard, and a door with glass panels. The stand beneath the mirror was Federal, the
larger table Empire, as were the four painted fancy chairs and rocker. It was summer,
and the fireplace was filled with a plain fireboard, while the simple mantel was garnished with flowers and two oil lamps. Note the tole tray and footstool stored under
the table; the other footstool is safely out of the way against the wall.

Andrew Jackson chose Dufour's "Telemachus in the Island of Calypso" for the
hall of the Hermitage, and Martin Van Buren bought Zuber's "Landscape of the
Hunt" for the hall of his house at Kinderhook, New York. One would think
that James DeWolf had such papers (Fig. 49), were it not that the DeWolf
genealogy records the walls were covered with paintings of the family's Cuban
plantations supplemented with scenes from *Paul et Virginie*, undoubtedly copied
from the Dufour paper.

Stenciling survived in the country. The work in Plate 11 has been identified
as the product of an itinerant who was active in southern New Hampshire and
northern Massachusetts in the first quarter of the nineteenth century.[4]

Wall painting flourished as itinerants traveled in New England, Virginia,
Ohio, and southern New York. Many painters imitated the expensive French
papers, but in New England the stylized work of Rufus Porter between 1825
and 1840 was easily distinguishable.

ARCHITECTURAL DETAILS AND CEILINGS

Designers incorporated architectural details from Greek, Roman, and, sometimes, Egyptian originals. Typical is the Davis design for a double parlor (Plate 9), with its well-carved Ionic columns, a doorway modeled on the north porch of the Erectheum, and its combination of egg and dart moldings along with a honeysuckle pattern. The Fiedlers (Fig. 48) had a similar molding, plus additional scrolled brackets supporting the entablature between the two rooms. Both parlors show similar door frames.

Several of the fireplaces in the illustrations are survivors from eighteenth-century styles, but characteristic high style Empire fireplaces are to be found in Plate 9 and Figures 48 and 62. Both the latter show the caryatids so much advocated in the pattern books of the period.

Some high style rooms had cast plaster decorations in the center of the ceilings (Plates 9 and 13, Fig. 43), but the majority of ceilings in houses of all classes were plain.

LIGHTING

Oil lamps were well developed, and their manufacture was spreading. The Argand lamp, which used sperm oil or lard oil, went through several transformations to emerge by the early 1840s as the "sinumbra" lamp, which would project no shadows. "Agitable" or "common" whale oil lamps began to appear about 1800 (Fig. 58). In 1830, Isaiah Jennings invented a new "burning fluid," a mixture of alcohol and turpentine, a formula modified in 1839 and labeled camphene. This new fluid was meant for an Argand-type lamp, but since it was subject to violent explosions, it failed to supplant earlier fuels even though it produced a fine light.

Candles still provided the major source of lighting for most Americans. Simple candelabra and candlesticks were found in a variety of forms and materials, but classic early Empire candlesticks appeared in the high style parlors like the caryatid sticks in Plate 8 or the wall brackets or tall lamp stands in Plate 9.

Mantel garnitures of marble, brass, and crystal prisms and matching chandeliers appeared toward the end of the period (Fig. 48).

Hall lamp

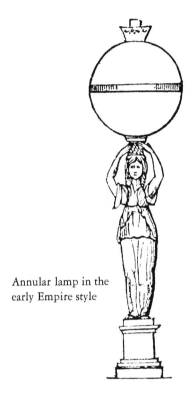

Annular lamp in the early Empire style

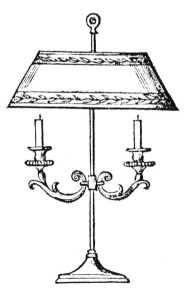

"Cheap candlestick for reading and writing," 1845

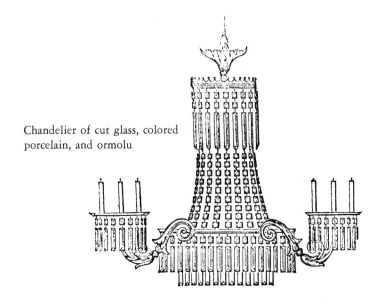

Chandelier of cut glass, colored porcelain, and ormolu

Gas made a minimal first commercial appearance when a Baltimore gas company was organized in 1816. It had seventy-three customers in addition to the city by 1821, and they paid an average bill of $68.49 per year, an amount affordable only by the well-to-do.

COLOR

Strong, dominant colors are evident during the period in both high style and country settings. Smith and Mrs. Parkes emphasized reds—crimson, maroon, and scarlet fabrics, as well as red morocco leather—as particularly apt for dining rooms, libraries, and parlors. In these rooms, one was advised to achieve a simple, plain, yet sober effect. By contrast, lightness was appropriate to the drawing room, where the reds seemingly did not dominate, and where Mrs. Parkes thought warm colors and papers with large patterns should reign. She was particularly fond of "a rich, gold flowered, and deep crimson embossed paper." For painted walls, light colors were to be preferred.

Figure 59. Artist unknown. *John Thomas Avery, Aged Eleven.* 1839. Water color. Collection of Mr. and Mrs. Samuel Schwartz.

John Thomas Avery's picture is in the Empire group because of the painted and grained Empire stand by the window. Otherwise, the room is typical of the Federal style, even though the picture is dated 1839. Stenciling provided a decorative border atop the walls and around the window, with a special tulip design reserved for over the window. The clock is covered with the same enthusiastic painted graining and may be a very late example of Chippendale work. Scatter rugs, probably shirred in this instance, appear in few pictures of this period. These are of matching design in yellow and orange on a black background.

Figure 60. Deborah Goldsmith. *The Talcott Family.* 1832. Water color on paper, 14 in. × 18 in. (36 cm × 46 cm). Abby Aldrich Rockefeller Folk Art Collection, Williamsburg, Va.

Again bright colors appear in a country interior, this one in New York State. The subjects were Mary Talcott, age seventy; Samuel Talcott, thirty-eight; Betsey Talcott, thirty; and Emily Talcott, three months. The linen press is late Federal, but the painted side chairs and rocker were new. The Talcotts avoided the problem of choosing a contrasting color for woodwork by applying the floral wallpaper over the window frame, but then they painted the lower edge of the window itself, the windowsill, and the baseboard a solid powder blue. The striped rag carpet provided a stunning array of color from bright yellow to red, orange, green, brown, black, and blue.

In Plate 9, strong blue and yellow appear in the sofa and fire screen, while the walls are plain and muted. The carpet is a sea green. Strong blue, crimson, and green were consistently popular colors in rugs, curtains, and upholstery.

More subtle schemes were organized around beige and chocolate. In Plate 8, muted walls contrast with the bitter green of the curtains and the Aubusson rug, while in Plate 13, the entire room is done in shades of beige and brown.

Mrs. Parkes wrote that less gaudy colors should be used in the bedrooms, where "quiet cheerfulness" should prevail. There she suggested lustring for bed and window curtains in the more subdued colors of plum, pink, cinnamon,

Figure 61. Charles Bird King. *The Itinerant Artist. C.* 1825–1840. Oil on canvas, 44¾ in. × 57 in. (1.14 m × 1.45 m). New York State Historical Association, Cooperstown.

Around the central scene of an artist painting a portrait are details that document a country interior of the Empire period. The fireplace area shows kitchen activities, and through the open door one glimpses a bedroom with furniture from an earlier period except for the fiddleback fancy chair. Note the drying towels on the cord stretched before the hearth. Interesting in the main room is the board suspended just below the beams on which provisions are stored, out of reach of children and animals. This painting provides a wealth of documentation for the clutter of a rural family "at home." Such collections of household implements were characteristic from New England through the newer settlements of the Midwest.

lilac, green, garnet, light blue, and brown. In the country, strong colors were no less evident (Plate 11) than in prior periods.

ACCESSORIES

Mantels began to collect a great number of decorative objects: candlesticks or other lighting devices (from simple oil lamps to elaborate girandoles); glass domes over French clocks, stuffed birds, or flower arrangements; and urns.

Flowers appear in many illustrations, and in Figure 55 a caged bird was part of the decor.

Dining room scenes document the contents and arrangement of appropriate accessories at differing economic levels. The Sargent *Dinner Party* (Fig. 43) includes a display of silver, wine coolers, and decanters notably lacking in *Asking a Blessing* (Fig. 54).

Good documentation of the fashionable table is readily forthcoming from Robert Roberts's *The House Servant's Directory*. Governor Gore's English butler undoubtedly set standards followed in few houses, but he is explicit on the meticulous arrangement of the dining table. Plates were to be exactly the same distance from each other and glasses exactly the same distance from the table edge. Settings were calculated for service and effect: "If you have a salad to go in the center of the table, lay a silver waiter under it, so as to raise your salad bowl more majestically."

Likewise in arranging the sideboard, the governing principle was "that ladies and gentlemen that have splendid and costly articles, wish to have them seen and set out to the best advantage." The glasses for dinner were to be arranged in a crescent, "as this looks most sublime." In arranging dishes on the side table, art was everything. If there were any empty spaces after the necessaries were out, "ornament them with some spoons and your sauce ladles; having the bowls uppermost, as they show to most advantage."[5]

Figure 61 documents accessories more common in the country household.

Ceramics. Most fine ceramic ware was imported, but utilitarian ware was made locally. Relatively little of the pottery carried Empire design.

Porcelain, usually dinner sets or tea services, arrived in quantity from China: the Fitzhugh pattern ornamented by an American eagle; blue and white ware in the more expensive Nanking varieties and the cheaper Canton; and between 1815 and 1830, the rose medallion and mandarin patterns. Chinese copies of French porcelain also found their way to America.[6]

French and English porcelains in turn found their way to the American market. In 1817, President Madison received a French porcelain service for the White House. His personal set of white and gold French porcelain, 286 pieces, was appraised at $600 that same year.[7] English pottery found large market and little domestic competition. The most notable addition to the market was Staffordshire printed transfer ware. Originally printed in a deep blue, these widely advertised plates carried historical and scenic views of American life. One maker, William Adams of Staffordshire, had even toured America in 1821–1823 to see these places first hand. Liverpool jugs, plates, and bowls with transfer print scenes of military victory or patriotic devotion also found a strong market. Advertisements show that pictorial china had a national market—plates showing the State House in Boston sold in Cincinnati as well as in Massachusetts.[8] British potters aimed their wares consciously at the American market.

Domestic manufacture of porcelain began anew in 1816, when Dr. Henry Mead of New York City produced a vase in the high Empire style with caryatid handles. His output was minimal, but by 1826, William Ellis Tucker of Philadelphia was producing considerable quantities.

Stoneware and redware production was widespread and flourishing. The stoneware industry grew when the Embargo of 1807 prevented the importation of British ware. Decoration of both stoneware and redware was often minimal,

Philadelphia porcelain
in a typical shape

Dr. Mead's New York porcelain

Liverpool transfer ware pitcher

but Pennsylvania German potters continued to produce sgraffito designs on redware.

Better-quality ceramics were kept in the dining area, while more utilitarian items were confined to the kitchen.

Table 11 shows some ceramics prices in the years of the Empire style.

Table 11. Ceramics Prices: An Empire Sampling[9]

1815		
JOHN NORTON & SONS,		
BENNINGTON REDWARE PRICES		
1 dozen large platters	(wholesale price)	1.00
1 dozen small platters	(wholesale price)	.67
1821		
40 dozen creamware plates		
(auction estimate) (50¢ per dozen)		$20.00
1822		
1 dozen Chinese tea cups and saucers, gilt		
edges, sepia or brown painted design, French		
pattern (wholesale price)		$4.00
1826		
209-piece set of blue and white, Chinese		
dinner ware (Nanking) (wholesale price)		
(average price 34¢ a piece)		$72.00
1826		
157-piece set of blue and white, Chinese		
dinner ware (Canton) (wholesale price)		
(average price 9.7¢ a piece)		$15.25

7

Victorian Classical

1830–1850

THE Victorian Classical style was the first that saw virtually every decorative item for the house mass produced. Across America, but especially in New England, manufacturing plants began to appear wherever water would power lathe or loom, and wherever canals and railroads had been built to carry the products of these new factories to urban centers and the countryside.

We have organized this last major style (before the first stages of eclecticism) around the appearance of the popular pillar and scroll furniture, which offered the American public its third and final variant of the Empire. This furniture was well established in urban centers by the early 1830s, but would be judged passé by 1853.

In this later transformation of Empire, ornament, like furniture, became heavier. Basically the same standards governed the furnishing of rooms as in the late Empire period, and Mrs. Parkes's ever popular *Domestic Duties* reached its tenth edition by 1846.

Americans found another guidebook to domestic taste in J. C. Loudon's *Encyclopaedia of Cottage, Farm and Villa Architecture and Furniture,* published in London in 1839. Never reprinted in America, it was nonetheless consulted here and was a great influence on A. J. Downing. Later in the period, Thomas Webster and Mrs. Parkes published their *Encyclopaedia of Domestic Economy.* The original English edition of 1844 was reprinted by Harper's in 1845, and in 1849 by Henry Bill of Norwich, Connecticut, whose salesman received a large number of orders in the Midwest.[1] The book discussed Gothic, Elizabethan, and rococo, as well as the high style early Empire, but more or less regarded late Empire as the norm.

Mass production, good transportation, and wide circulation of guidebooks meant the demise of regional styles and to some degree a similar appearance in goods both inexpensive and expensive, but the economic disparity between the poor and the very rich was growing ever greater. The word "millionaire" appar-

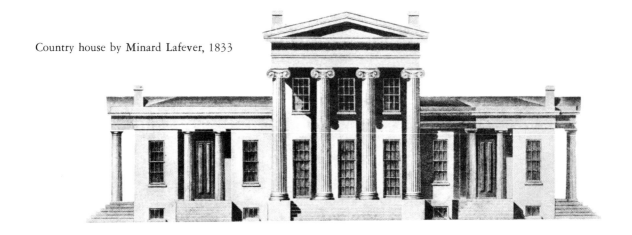

Country house by Minard Lafever, 1833

Ionic House by Shaw

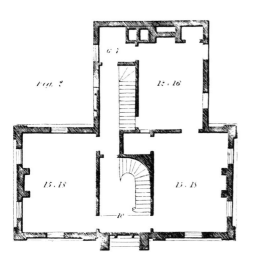

First-floor plan

ently was coined in 1843 to describe Pierre Lorillard, banker and snuffmaker, who died in New York leaving $1 million. John Jacob Astor was worth about $20 million in 1847. Estimates at the time held that there were perhaps twenty-five millionaires in New York City and nine in Philadelphia. Several cities had a few citizens worth over a half million, and there were several hundred in New York who were worth between $100,000 and $500,000, many of them the new manufacturers. These people could afford the most expensive variations of the late Empire style.[2] A. J. Davis had gained prominence during the era as one of the foremost architects in America. One of his designs was built in Kentucky for $30,000, an extraordinary expense. More common was the $1,400 Ionic house Edward Shaw presented in his *Rural Architecture*, and in the *Architecture of Country Houses* (1850), A. J. Downing included several designs that could be built for under $1,000. These were the houses in which the great majority of Americans lived.[3]

James Gallier's *American Builder's General Price Book and Estimator* (1833) has enabled us to estimate the costs of furnishing a Victorian Classical house and the wages paid to builders. The plasterer received $1.75 a day for his efforts, the mason $1.62½, and the common laborer $1.00. Ornament may take on new significance when we realize that the columns separating double parlors (Fig. 48) often cost the equivalent of 200 days work by one laborer.

The Victorian Classical style faced competition from the Gothic, Elizabethan, and rococo styles by the mid-1840s, and by the time of the New York Crystal Palace Exposition of 1853, it was all but dead. Reviewing the few pieces

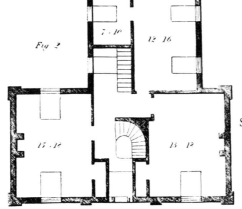

Second-floor plan

of furniture that were exhibited at the exposition, Professor Benjamin Silliman, Jr., condemned them as "ponderous and frigid monstrosities."[4]

Pauline W. Inman recorded the typical manner in which the Victorian Classical style came to the house of a newly married couple in 1840. Polly Eldridge Miner and Nathan Smith Bennett came from Bridport, Vermont, families of prominence but not great wealth. Shortly after their marriage they went to New York City, where they bought a Victorian Classical mahogany bureau with mirror, six curly maple chairs, and a pillar and scroll mahogany sewing table. For $34.18 they purchased 46 yards of two grades of fine ingrain carpeting.

In 1846, they went to New York again, spending $148 to redecorate with a sofa, bed, side table, eight mahogany chairs, mahogany stand, work table, pier glass, and center table. Additional trips to Boston and Troy filled their house with other late Empire items. About 1847, Mrs. Bennett subscribed to *Godey's Lady's Book*, which brought news of decoration and fashion. She had her collected issues bound in 1854.

Perhaps most significant for our study, in 1849 she took a room-by-room inventory, and by matching accounts with the inventory one can develop a good picture of the expenses and sources for furnishing a middle-class house in the 1840s.

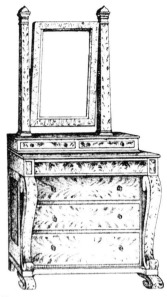

Bureau with mirror from Hall's *Assistant*; Mrs. Bennett bought one much like it for $35

Figure 62. Auguste Edouart. *New York Interior*. 1842. Silhouette with water color, 19 in. × 28⅛ in. (48 cm × 71 cm). Courtesy, Henry Francis du Pont Winterthur Museum, Winterthur, Del.

An interesting contrast to Edouart's portrait of the Cheesman family (Fig. 44) with their Empire furnishings, this Victorian Classical parlor has furniture with a heavier, though no less formal look. The draperies with a pier mirror in the center are virtually identical in both pictures. The center table is similar to examples by Duncan Phyfe produced between 1834 and 1840. An astral lamp was fashionable lighting, just as the door frame was high fashion with its egg and dart molding and anthemion decoration. Note that a rocking chair is at home in this formal room.

A Typical Middle-class Interior of 1849: Polly Bennett's Household Inventory[5]
(with added notes on sources and prices from her records)

KITCHEN

1 cooking elevated Rotary
1 Clock with L. Glass
1 Cherry light stand, bought locally[?], 1840 $3.00
1 calico stuffed Settee and pillows
1 Rocking chair stuffed
6 splint bottom chairs, bought locally, 1840 $6.00
1 pine table, bought locally[?] $3.50
Map U.S.A.

do—Illinois
" Nepolian [Napoleon]
Wood box and c. baskets
Brass mounted shovel and tongs
Comb basket, combs and brushes
2 white w[indow] curtains
1 stool, and rag carpet

[The following are kitchen and table ware not mentioned in the inventory but known from her accounts:]

Iron
    Frying pan, bought locally, 1840   32¢
    Coffee mill, bought locally, 1840   92¢
    Set Knives & forks, bought locally, 1840 $1.00

Silver, plate, etc.
    6 silver tablespoons ⎫
    12 silver teaspoons ⎬ New York, 1840 $33.00
    1 pair silver sugartongs ⎭
    Britannia teapot, bought locally, 1840 $1.00
    Britannia castor, bought locally, 1840 $1.25

Tin and wood
    Bread tray, bought locally, 1840 $1.00
    Tea board, bought locally, 1840   75¢

China
    1 set Gold band china, bought Troy,
        1846 $13.00
    Gold band tray, bought Troy, 1846 $1.00
    1 set crockery, bought locally, 1840 $21.57
    6 plates edged, bought locally, 1840   50¢
    1 dish, bought locally   12¢

Glass
    1 dozen pressed, fluted tumblers,
        bought Troy, 1846 $1.25

BED ROOM

1 Bed french stead, bought locally[?], 1840 $7.00
1 Mahogany dressing table
1 High chair
1 set book shelves

1 painted curtain and one calico
Rag carpet, vessel and lid
July 1849, two new maps Vermont and N.H.

SITTING ROOM

1 Ing[rain] carpet, bought N.Y.C., 1840   75¢ per yard
1 Stove and pipe
1 Mahogany Dressing Beauro with L. Glass attached,
    bought N.Y.C., 1840 $35
1 Large L. Glass Mahogany and Gilt, bought N.Y.C.,
    1840 $10
1 4-feet Dining Table, bought locally, 1840 $6
1 Mahogany light stand, work table[?], bought N.Y.C.,
    1840 $9
1 Stuffed green Settee and pillow

1 Hearth brush and Duster
1 Hearth Mat
2 Oil Cloth at doors
2 cotton colored Spreads
6 Curley Maple Chairs, bought N.Y.C.,
    1840   each $2 or $3
1 Large Rocking Chair Maple,
    bought N.Y.C.[?], 1846 $9
1 small R. chair and beauro and glass
    (Lucy's)
White curtins with fringe
4 glass window pins

PARLOR

1 Brusles [Brussels] carpet 18¾ by 16¾,
    bought N.Y.C., 1846 $1.50 per yd.
1 Hearth Rug—Wilton
1 Haircloth Sofa stuffed, bought N.Y.C., 1846 $32
8 Haircloth Chairs   "   (mahogany), bought N.Y.C.,
    1846 $24
1 Center Table Marble Top, bought N.Y.C., 1846 $18

1 pier Table Marble Top, bought N.Y.C., 1846 $16
1 Globe Lamp [solar lamp], bought Troy, 1846 $4.00
2 China Vases [gilt mantel vases], bought Troy, 1846   75¢
1 Large Mahogany frame L. Glass, bought N.Y.C., 1846
    $12
4 Glass window pins
Some nice Books on Table

UPPER AND LOWER HALL
1 Willow Cradle
Ingrain Carpet in U. Hall, bought N.Y.C., 1840   66¢ per yd
1 Muslin curtin Ruffled
Stair Carpet Vernician [Venetian]
13 Brass Stair Rods
Vernician carpet in L. Hall
1 4-feet dining Table and C. Spread table,
    bought locally, 1840 $6
Dotted Muslin Curtin, Door Window
1 Peacock Feather Brush
5 Band boxes in U. Hall
2 curley Maple Chairs in L. Hall,
    bought N.Y.C., 1840 $2 or $3 each

BED ROOM
1 Sofa Bed stead and Bed, bought N.Y.C., 1846 $22
1 Mahogany light stand, bought N.Y.C., 1846 $5
3 Curley Maple Chairs, bought N.Y.C., 1840
1 Ingrain carpet, bought N.Y.C., 1846   75¢ per yd.
1 Looking glass
3 Muslin Wd. curtains
1 Blue and White vessel and lid,
    bought locally[?], 1840   40¢
1 "   "   " wash bowl and pitcher,
    bought locally[?], 1840   50¢
1 "   "   " soap and brush dish
Books and Pin Cushions
1 Wash stand cherry

LARGE CHAMBER
2 Beds—1 high Post and 1 French, Fr. bed,
    bought locally[?], 1840 $4
1 Ing carpet—Yellow Brown and White,
    bought New York, 1840   78¢ per yd.
1 Wash Stand-bowl and Pitcher
2 Bits Oil Cloth
1 Brusles [Brussels] Hearth Mat
6 Wood Bottom Chairs
1 R. [Rocking] Chair cushioned (green)
1 L. Glass M. [Mahogany] and Gilt,
    bought N.Y.C., 1840 $2.25
1 Show case and Toilet
4 Painted W. [window] Curtains
1 set white bed curtains
1 foot stool—2 white vessels
A quantity of Books and boxes

BED ROOM
1 Bed and French bed stead
1 Toilet copperplate cover
1 curly maple chair, bought N.Y.C., 1840 $2 or $3
1 stool copperplate cover
1 Rag carpet striped
1 Looking Glass
1 copperplate w curtain
white vessel
8 Pictures of Presidents, U.S.A.

May 1849
At this time I have five good feather beds and bedsteads
one Sofa one high post and three french
two striped under beds and three brown linen

FURNITURE

John Hall's pattern book *The Cabinet Maker's Assistant*, published in Baltimore in 1840, documented the ascendancy of the new pillar and scroll style. The flattened **S** curve replaced the columns still evident in the furniture of the early 1830s, and the earlier winged foot was transformed to an **S** or **C** scroll on its side.

Victorian Classical case pieces were large and massive, with broad, plain surfaces, perfectly suited for new mass production techniques. Compared to earlier work there was a notable absence of gilding, but veneer figures were arranged for spectacular flame effects. Instead of the scroll foot, some pieces in the new style had a bulbous turnip-shaped foot, low and squat on sofas or tall and fluted on pianos.

The urban and rural wealthy and fashion-conscious chose mahogany, but in the country it was a rich era for painted furniture, often in the same pillar and scroll designs.[6] Hitchcock and his competitors produced painted fancy chairs by the thousand, and they were popular at all economic levels. Inventors earned patents for space-saving, convertible furniture, like the sofa, patented in 1831, that folded into a bed.[7]

Victorian Classical footstool

Victorian Classical sofa

Figure 63. S. W. *A Hartford Family. C.* 1840–1850. Oil on canvas, 30⅛ in. ×
33⁵⁄₁₆ in. (76 cm × 84 cm). White House Collection, Washington, D.C.

Lavish expense produced such a room for this unfortunately anonymous family. The
raised moldings of the paneled dado are gilded, as are the moldings on the door
frame and door; heavy picture frames and the gilt lamp on the piano add to the luxurious effect. The wallpaper, probably an expensive import, had a pink-and-green
design on a gray-green background. Two forms of a sewing stand appear at the left,
the taller behind the mother and the small red one on the stool. The rug is a typical
high fashion design of this period, with red and blue stars on dark blue background.
The father's chair is upholstered in a cream, red, and green fabric.

In 1850, Downing published his *Architecture of Country Houses,* an American guidebook to be discussed in the Gothic chapter. He thought the Gothic
suitable for libraries or dining rooms and the Louis XIV style as best for
modern drawing rooms, but he commented that "the furniture most generally in
use in private houses is some modification of the classical style. . . . Modern
Grecian furniture has the merit of being simple, easily made, and very moderate
in cost. Its universality is partly owing to the latter circumstance, and partly to
the fact that by far the largest number of dwellings are built in the same style,
and therefore are most appropriately furnished with it."[8]

In spite of its universality, Downing offered no illustrations of the style,
promoting instead the Gothic, Elizabethan, and rococo, which eclipsed the
Victorian Classical within a very few years.

FLOOR COVERINGS

Carpeting was standard in all but the poorest houses, but there were exceptions: Aurora, Illinois, interiors of 1845 showed well-dressed families in reasonably fashionable settings with plain board floors.[9] In the 1830s, stylish designs, whether octagonal, star-shaped, or circular, were large, roughly 3 feet in diameter, but in the early 1840s, even larger, 4-foot designs gained vogue. Wall-to-wall carpeting was the norm, with or without separate boarders. Figure 65 shows the manner in which two strong but different patterns met beneath a door.

Varieties of carpeting continued much as in the Empire period, but ingrains were especially popular. Mrs. Bennett bought a Brussels carpet for her Vermont parlor and protected it with a Wilton hearth rug, but the rest of her floors were covered with ingrain carpet or rag carpets. Every room had carpeting of some sort.

In carpeting, too, American manufacturers began supplying the market. By 1834, the government counted eighteen to twenty factories producing 21,600 yards of the more expensive Brussels carpet, 31,500 yards of three-ply ingrain, 954,000 yards of cheaper ingrain, 132,000 yards of Venetian carpet, and 8,400 yards of damask Venetian.[10] With increased production, the balance began to turn in favor of American goods over imports.

Oriental carpets continued to be expensive and seldom appeared, even in the rooms of those who could obviously afford them. However, Oriental motifs provided designs for a number of factory-produced carpets.

Many floor coverings were made at home. The striped woven carpet was in its last stages (Fig. 72), but braided and shirred rugs would continue for decades.

PICTURES AND MIRRORS

Pictures and prints were household accessories for families of all classes, but many fashionable rooms show surprisingly bare walls, as though starkness gained a temporary vogue in the early 1840s (Fig. 44, Plate 12).

American artists were increasing in number. Thomas Sully, probably the most prominent portraitist, received an average of $100 for a portrait, while itinerant Matthew Prior advertised portraits for $10 to $25. Landscapes predominate in the illustrations in this book, vying with religious allegories for popularity. In 1833, Thomas Cole received $250 for a landscape.[11] Prints offering similar themes were less expensive and provided similar decorative effects.

After an initial start in the Empire era, lithography became another American industry, producing great quantities of historical scenes, city views, fires and disasters, sporting scenes, sentimental allegories, and just about anything else that would sell. Mrs. Bennett had a set of the eight Presidents in 1849. The following year, a Maine innkeeper bought an updated version with ten Presidents for which he paid 62½¢.[12]

Silhouettes continued to be a popular and inexpensive artistic addition to the household. Auguste Edouart (Fig. 62) led the field in quality and probably quantity of silhouettes, producing some 10,000 during his decade in America. These silhouettes are more valuable than many paintings in documenting the American interior. Yet most silhouettists limited themselves to heads; many maintained permanent studios, while others were itinerants.

Frames varied from the expensive gilt, rococo plaster frame, which would remain popular for the rest of the century (Fig. 63), to plain gilt frames, to the simplest black moldings. Small pictures and silhouettes were often put in simple black or curly maple frames with small rings for hanging attached to the top. In the country or back room, maps, drawings, or prints might be nailed or glued directly to the wall.

Maps were popular as decoration (Fig. 73). Several firms produced colored maps backed on cloth with black turned rollers and small rings for hanging. Mrs. Bennett hung maps in her Vermont home. In the kitchen were maps of the United States, Illinois, and the exploits of Napoleon. A bedroom had maps of Vermont and New Hampshire.

Pictures were basically hung high, with exposed cords usually running from a nail about 6 inches from the ceiling. Some illustrations show ribbons decorated with bows instead of cords. Many pictures are hung flush with the wall,

Figure 64. *Parlor, Residence of William Rodes, Richmond, Kentucky. C.* 1860. Courtesy, The Filson Club, Louisville, Ky.

William Rodes built Woodlawn in Madison County, Kentucky, in 1822, and this photograph reveals that paintings were at times hung over scenic wallpapers in elegant settings. (The arrangement of a painting over a mantel mirror also appears in Fig. 46.) Note the use of a small hearth insert in a large fireplace that has late Federal details, and the arrangement of fireplace accessories.

Figure 65. Oliver T. Eddy. *The Children of Israel and Sarah Ann Griffith.* 1844. Oil on canvas. Maryland Historical Society, Baltimore. Photograph: Courtesy, Frick Art Reference Library, New York City.

The Griffith children appear in their fashionable double parlor in Baltimore. Between the parlors, the wide-fluted pilaster strip seems a vestigial remnant of the columns that appear in other pictures; note the sliding doors (barely evident) that can close one parlor off from the other. A mirror hangs between the two windows. The carpet in the parlors has a large circular, stylized floral pattern, but the hall carpet has a pattern of smaller geometric shapes.

but the shadows in the Hartford interior (Fig. 63) show the angle at which some pictures and mirrors tilted out from the wall.

Mirrors or looking glasses were now part of virtually every interior and in almost every room. Spectacular pier mirrors were still large, heavy, and expensive, and overmantel or wall mirrors might be given a frame as intricate as any picture (Fig. 63), but smaller mirrors in simple frames or built into dressers abounded. Mrs. Bennett bought a dresser with a mirror attached, and she had mirrors in the sitting room, the parlor, and in all but one bedroom. One of these looking glasses she bought for 44¢ in 1840.

TEXTILES

In textiles, Empire taste continued into the Victorian Classical period. More and more of the textiles used in American homes were produced domestically, and the American manufacturer did his best to imitate English designs. New presses made multicolor printed fabrics possible. Typical was the Hudson Calico Works. In 1836, it had forty-two hand block printers, but it also had five printing machines imported from England; two of these machines could print four colors simultaneously while the other three printed three colors. The factory produced a total of 5.4 million yards of printed cotton a year, a significant percentage of the 120 million yards produced nationally that year.[13]

Upholstery.   Mrs. Parkes had said almost nothing about upholstery in her original book, but Loudon and the Webster and Parkes *Encyclopaedia* offer several suggestions. For a sofa, both Loudon and the *Encylopaedia* list horsehair first, with Loudon offering moreen and damask as sober alternates while the *Encyclopaedia* suggests chintz or silk. For drawing room chairs, silk is the first choice. Loudon mentions only chintz as an alternate, but Webster and Parkes list flowered satins, painted velvet, superfine cloth, worked worsted, or chintz. The *Encyclopaedia* specifies morocco leather or horsehair for library, parlor, or easy chairs.

Figure 66. Samuel F. B. Morse. *The Goldfish.* 1835. Oil on wood, 29⅝ in. × 24⅞ in. (76 cm × 64 cm). National Collection of Fine Arts, Washington, D.C.

The subjects, Mrs. Richard Cary Morse, the painter's sister-in-law, and her children Charlotte G. Morse (Mrs. Aspinwall Hodge) and Elizabeth Ann Morse (Mrs. Samuel Colgate), appear in a very ornate hall. The classical inspiration has been carried into the ceiling as well as the columns. The chair and table are good examples of more expensive Victorian Classical furniture, while a wicker cradle might be found at many economic levels. The squared floor is either marble or, less likely, floor cloth in imitation of marble. Note the small stool under Mrs. Morse's foot.

It is difficult to say how closely these standards were followed. Most up-holstery appears plain and dark, looking more like velvet or plush than silk or horsehair. Plate 12 shows a sofa covered with moreen, Figure 70 an easy chair upholstered in leather, and in Figure 63 the formal piece is upholstered in anything but a solid color. The chair in which the father sits is probably covered in a floral chintz.

Loudon suggested slipcovers or loose printed cotton upholstery as an alternative to regular upholstery in heavier fabrics (Fig. 44). Plate 12 shows a dust ruffle along the front of a sofa. The ruffle was topped with a decorative tape. Wherever cushions appear on sofas or chairs, they match the upholstery.

Window Curtains.   Webster and Parkes informed their readers what they already knew: that curtains were decorative *and* "necessary to exclude cold air."

The writers of the period agreed that the best curtain design was a simple hanging on a gilt rod from large brass rings with no drapery swags or cornice. Loudon offered a figure illustrating such Grecian curtains, together with a description of the pulley mechanism for drawing them back and forth. The *Encyclopaedia,* however, included a few more elaborate curtain designs with swags and cornices. Mrs. Parkes held that drawing room curtains should be plain damask or chintz. The English edition said drawing room curtains should "never" be moreen, a phrase the American editor of the book modified to "seldom." White muslin under curtains or blinds was appropriate. For the dining room, moreen and crimson or scarlet cloth were correct, but chintz was never proper. No suggestions were given for other rooms.

From the evidence available in the pictures, American curtains had grown somewhat simpler, and very few swags appear. Generally, heavy drapes were fixed in position and drawn back, held by a tieback; but in some houses, intricate Empire curtains complete with swags and tassels lived on into the 1840s (Fig. 62).

Simple curtains appeared in the country (Fig. 72). Roller shades came plain or in the fancy, factory-produced designs of the 1830s and 1840s. More details are given in the Gothic section.[14]

Venetian blinds were popular during this period.

Bed Curtains.   Most of the new beds were of the French type, which could be draped but usually were not. Loudon illustrated the field or tent bed, which he said was "in universal use," but he refused to illustrate a fully curtained bed, claiming that they took more fabric than a cottager could afford. Mrs. Parkes advised those who did want curtain beds to use moreen or chintz lined with colored calico for the curtains. Woven reversible coverlets were popular, sometimes borrowing motifs from rugs.

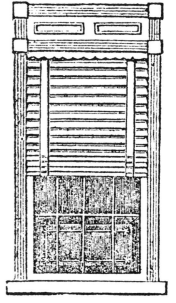

Venetian blinds in a typical window frame

WALL TREATMENT

Throughout the period, readers of Mrs. Parkes's continuously popular *Domestic Duties* were reminded that "Painted walls, chiefly of pale colours, are at this time most general; but, in a drawingroom, I prefer paper. The rich, gold-flowered, and deep crimson, embossed papers, are much in vogue for large rooms, in which rich, warm colours, and large patterns, may be assembled together without inconsistency, and without offending the eye to that degree which a similar selection of colours would occasion in small apartments, where simplicity, lightness, and cheerfulness should prevail."[15] In 1842, Loudon advised that paint was best for a plaster wall in *any* room.

Gallier's price list includes some notes on English and French wallpapers. (Nothing is said of American varieties.) French paper came in sheets 18½ inches wide and 9 yards long, at a cost of 25¢ to $1.00 per sheet. English paper was 20 inches wide and 12 yards long, with prices "as variable as its quality." Sizing and hanging papers cost 25¢ to 32¢ per piece.

The American wallpaper industry, expanding with machine printing, made inroads on English and French imports, but by 1850 there were only six American factories producing wallpaper. Papers both imported and domestic were widely advertised and available, yet many Americans seem to have preferred plain walls, as the illustrations indicate.

In instances where paper does appear, vertical stripes with floral embellishment dominate the design (Figs. 63). Another period paper (possibly American) incorporates large medallions on a marbled background. Popular, too, were "rainbow papers," which had alternating light and dark bands of the same color with a design overprinted.[16] The Atwoods had a paper covered with arabesques, which they also used to cover the fireboard (Plate 15). Borders of swags and palmettes carried basic Victorian Classical motifs. Such borders could be purchased by the yard and installed by a professional paperhanger or by the householder and his family. Borders were often used with a painted rather than papered wall.

Willy helps his parents hang a wallpaper border. Courtesy of Old Sturbridge Village, Sturbridge, Mass.

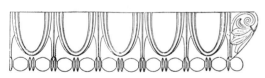

Asher Benjamin designs for moldings

ARCHITECTURAL DETAILS AND CEILINGS

The Greek revival brought a full complement of appropriate architectural details. Moldings ranged from intricate anthemion designs to a simpler egg and dart. Such details may seem surprisingly inexpensive in Gallier's list, for cast plaster cornices 8″ tall were 30¢ the foot, while 1½″ cornices were only 7¢ the foot; but a plasterer's laborer was paid but a dollar a day.

Similar motifs might be included in the corner blocks of door and window frames. Columns between double parlors were still a mark of elegance.

Mantels were relatively simple in most rooms, typified by the design seen in Figure 68. The cost depended upon the ornamentation, and could run quite high. Gallier quoted a chimney piece with Grecian Ionic fluted columns with an ornamented panel and molded shelf at $21.25. With plain Doric columns and Doric capitals it was $14.25, while a very plain one with pilasters and no ornamented panel was $11.50. Marble mantels began at $25, but a fancy "dining room" chimney piece in Irish black and Egyptian marble ran $150 to $250. Caryatid columns with Corinthian capitals for fireplaces ran $200 the pair (Fig. 48). Fireplaces were often filled with iron inserts carrying simple Greek revival designs, and the Victorian Classical look found its way onto cast iron stoves. (Fig. 71 shows a simple box stove dating from the 1830s.) Fireboards continued to be used in summer. One from Sutton, Massachusetts, was a potted fruit tree surrounded by polychrome tiles.

Ceilings in the most fashionable houses either were decorated with rosettes or remained plain.

LIGHTING

The market offered a wide variety of lighting devices, but gas was preferred where it was available. Introduced in the Federal years, its use spread during the Empire period, and it began to have a major impact in the Victorian Classical era. The Philadelphia Gas Company, chartered in 1835, started operation in 1836, and a year later had 670 customers using 6,814 burners. Richard Rush's library shows what is probably a gas jet (Fig. 46) and a similar jet from the 1850s appears in Figure 73.

The Argand lamp and the astral lamp dominated the Victorian Classical era. The Argand lamp remained popular for use on mantels and in chandeliers, but cast a bothersome shadow for reading, making the annular, astral, or sinumbra (the terms were basically synonymous) the preferred table lamp. Available in very elegant forms, these lamps burned whale oil. Similar in appearance to the astral lamp but designed to burn cheaper oils and even lard was the solar lamp. Solar lamps are distinguished visually by the location of the reservoir; in the

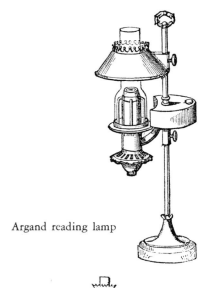

Argand reading lamp

Annular lamp

Figure 67. Benson J. Lossing. *Washington Irving's Study at Sunnyside. C. 1850.* Pencil drawing. Henry E. Huntington Library and Art Gallery, San Marino, Calif.

Benson J. Lossing was an active historian and artist who traveled widely to document his books. His sketch of Irving's library at Sunnyside along the Hudson River in New York provided a record for his own work, and it is equally valuable today. Although lace curtains were at the window, the plain Turkey red curtains and valance on the far wall dominated the room. Two pictures over the black marble fireplace are set on the mantel rather than hung.

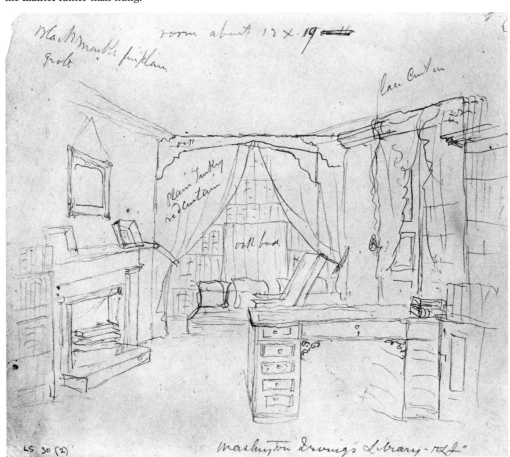

Figure 68. Amasa Hewins. *Interior with Lady at Piano.* 1836. Oil on panel,
17½ in. × 14 in. (46 cm × 36 cm). Courtesy, Wadsworth Atheneum, Hartford,
Conn. (J. J. Goodwin Fund).

The intent of the man lurking in the doorway is not clear, but Hewins is extremely
precise with detail in the period piano with its stool, the Argand chandelier, the
French clock, and fireplace equipment including a hearth brush hung from a hook on
the wall. The exact date of the picture helps to document the popularity of carpets
with large designs. The picture with its ornate frame is hung high, as was the custom
in previous eras.

astral lamp, the reservoir is round and located within the shade, but in the solar
lamp it is located beneath the burner. Plate 15 shows what is possibly a solar
lamp with a richly decorated shade and prisms.

Although of French invention, most lamps were produced domestically. By
1845, Christian Cornelius of Philadelphia had become the largest manufacturer
of lamps, but in New York City Baldwin Gardiner gained prominence for his
products.

During this era, camphene lamps continued to be made despite the increasing outcry about their safety. Simple wick oil lamps persisted in the country, as

did candles, but in many houses candlesticks were more for decoration than lighting. Pottery grease lamps remained in production and use until mid-century in areas settled by the Germans (Pennsylvania, Ohio, Tennessee, and North Carolina).

In contrast to earlier periods, illustrations in this chapter show parlor lamps left in place during the day, but sometimes small lamps were collected in one spot to be made ready for the evening, just as candles had been before. Miss Leslie's *House Book*, published in Philadelphia in 1840, recommended a portable kind of lamp not seen in our pictures: "Small japanned lamps are the most convenient for carrying up and down stairs, and for lighting to bed. Every

Figure 69. James Harvey Young. *Charles L. Eaton and His Sister.* 1848. Oil on canvas, 53½ in. × 41 in. (1.37 m × 1.04 m). Fruitlands Museum, Harvard, Mass.

Charles L. Eaton and his sister lived in Medford, Massachusetts. They stood near a massive baluster table, probably marbelized wood, which supported an elegant astral lamp. Single-arm Argand lamps with tulip globes flanked the black marble fireplace, but the carpet is the most interesting feature of the room, with its design based on a combination of Oriental and floral motifs. It has a wall-to-wall repeating pattern without a border.

evening before dusk, as many of these bed lamps as may be wanted by the members of the family, should be arranged on a japanned waiter with a brass lamp of larger size burning in the middle, and a few paper matches on one side." The ideal spot for this lamp depot was a small table or shelves at the first landing of the stairs or in the entry or hall below.[17]

COLOR

In her *Domestic Duties*, Mrs. Parkes, in probably the first discussion of color theory many householders ever encountered, advised that colors should be selected using the same rules that regulated "drawings": "Yellow, red, and blue, are contrasts in all their shades, and the harmonizing tints are discovered by the union of two of them. These colours have different qualities; blue is of a cold and unassuming nature, yellow illuminates, and red warms. . . . And, though yellow, blue, and red . . . are contrasting colours, yet, still greater contrasts to each may be procured by the union of two of them; for instance, blue and red form violet, and violet is the greatest contrast to yellow. The other intermediate colours, also of green and orange, form the greatest contrasts to red and blue." The dominant color of the drawing room thus would "please the eye best by having its contrast blended with it, by the proper intermediate colours." The same rule presumably applied to other rooms.[18]

In dining rooms, the carpet and curtains should be harmonious with the wood of the table and chairs, but somehow, she assumed, the curtains would always be crimson or scarlet. In any room with many pictures, the wall, carpet, and curtain colors should absorb rather than reflect light. Deep olive green or dull crimson, were considered ideal.

Loudon adopted the same rules of harmony and contrast and advised the householder to plan a room's color scheme around the carpet. Carpet and walls of the same color gave a "deficiency of force and of effect, from want of contrast," but they should not be of "different colours, equally attracting the eye," for that effect did not create a unified whole. Harmony of color was best,

Opposite:

above: Figure 70. Richard Woodville. *Soldier's Experience.* 1844. Water color, 11 in. × 10 in. (28 cm × 25 cm). Walters Art Gallery, Baltimore, Md.

below: Figure 71. Richard Woodville. *Old '76 and Young '48.* 1849. Oil on canvas, 21 in. × 26⅞ in. (53 cm × 69 cm). Walters Art Gallery, Baltimore, Md.

Woodville produced two versions of the same scene five years apart, providing a revealing contrast of styles in the 1840s. In the earlier version, the visiting captain finds the conservative (note the knee breeches) and probably impoverished revolutionary veteran surrounded by eighteenth-century furniture and mementos. He had only a few newer items, like the iron stove and painted chairs. An interesting detail was the cushion on the back of the veteran's chair and the skirt around the legs.

In the later version, Woodville made his veteran a fashionable man of wealth, complete with three servants. The vertical striped paper was obviously new, as was the marble mantel with its columns. The veteran's leather-covered chair was likewise recent. The Revolution is not forgotten with the Trumbull portrait of Washington (1792) and his engraving of the Declaration of Independence. A bust surmounted the earlier secretary, but the clock, lighting, and vases on the mantel are of recent fashion. The table shows that a small white cloth might be spread over a larger cover left intact during dinner.

and strong carpets should be matched with subdued curtains and walls. He suggests the following combinations:

Carpet	Walls and Curtains	Ornamental Borders on Wall
brilliant crimson	white, yellow, or drab	crimson
bright blue	white, yellow, or drab	blue
green	red, black, or white	green
yellow	dark gray wall, black curtains	yellow

Note the absence of greens and blues from both walls and curtains.

Gallier's prices list painter's colors by the pound, and again blue is missing and green (sometimes dangerously made from arsenic compounds) was very expensive. Common yellow was the most economical at 12¢ a pound, while Venetian red was 14¢. Red lead, stone, "lead color," and white lead all sold for

Figure 72. Marcia Ann Jennings Kilbourn. *Interior of Joel Jennings Home.* C. 1840. Oil on canvas, 9½ in. × 16 in. (25 cm × 41 cm). Old Sturbridge Village, Sturbridge, Mass.

In a painting by her granddaughter, Zillah Walker Jennings (1766–1852) is shown in the Brookfield, Massachusetts, room in which most of the furniture dates from the Federal period or earlier. More or less matching the design of the coverlet was the floral wallpaper that went over the ceiling moldings. The floor practically tells the history of New England floor coverings. By the door is a floor cloth in a design typical of the 1790s. The striped carpet was popular in the Federal era, too, and braided rugs can be documented as early as the 1820s. The plain ceiling provides a good illustration of a summer beam, which means that Mrs. Jennings's room was the front parlor; the picture thus documents a bed in a country parlor shortly before the middle of the nineteenth century.

Figure 73. Artist unknown. *T. C. H. Martin as an Infant.* 1857. Water color. Courtesy, Museum of Fine Arts, Boston, Mass. (M. and M. Karolik Collection).

Bedroom illustrations are uncommon, and although this is late in the period, it nonetheless shows a sleigh bed, veneered dresser, and covered table, all in the Classical Victorian style. Boxes and trunks stacked in the corner plus the London newspaper on the bed suggest that the Martins have just arrived from England. Despite the flowers, the mantel is arranged for use rather than decoration. The small hanging shelf holds equally small books, and a wicker wastebasket is near the window. A censer and flowers kept the room fragrant.

16¢ per pound, while chocolate color was 18¢. Black and "straw color, mixed with chrome" were more expensive at 25¢ per pound, while a "good" green cost 50¢. No other powders were listed, but Gallier mentioned other colors in his painting quotations, and there greens do appear. Four coats of oil paint in basic lead, stone, chocolate, or white were 20¢ per yard, French gray, fawn, or olive green 23¢. "Warm tints," lilacs, light greens, and peach cost 24¢, and for 28¢ per yard one could have French green, deep green, yellow, blue verditer, scarlet, or lake.

As an aside, Gallier recommended painted classical decorations: "A considerable degree of ornamental effect might be economically produced by painting on plain cornices and walls, as was practiced by those great masters of taste, the ancient Greeks, in some of their temples." Just how "economical" these decorations were is unclear, for Athenian scroll and lotus corners each cost 60¢. Painted graining ran 6 to 18¢ per foot depending upon the wood being imitated (Amboyna was the most expensive), while marbling ranged from 6 to 14¢ per foot.

One price suggests a possible New York style in 1833. Running water had appeared, and pipes had intruded into the American interior. Gallier quotes prices for painting pipes, with a surcharge "if finished green."[19]

The illustrations generally follow the guidebooks. Reds, crimsons, and scarlets with contrasting greens were common. Many walls of fashionable houses were finished in light colors, but some had adopted the darker drab. Some of the country scenes indicate brighter color schemes, but the Atwoods (Plate 15) have adopted the muted drab characteristic of the era.

ACCESSORIES

Imports still remained in high fashion for those who could afford them, but new domestic production brought basic decorative accessories into houses of moderate wealth.

Ceramics.   On the more expensive porcelains, gilt eagles, griffins, caryatids, and urn shapes exhibited classical themes, but the less expensive pottery reflected the classical style only minimally.

Porcelain imports in varying quantities continued from Britain, France, and China. From China came Canton and Nanking ware (both very popular early in the period), from France the expensive Sèvres, and from England Coalport, Copeland, Derby, Minton, Rockingham, and Worcester wares. American porcelain reappeared when William Ellis Tucker opened his Philadelphia factory in 1826. Although painted with American landscapes, the gilt decoration followed French models, and both Tucker and the public judged the product in terms of its success at imitation. Some of his pitchers, however, were original shapes. Before closing in 1838, the factory also produced cups with presidential portraits.

A simple and common porcelain was the gold band pattern, a plain white plate ornamented only with a gold rim and a gold circle at the center. Mrs. Bennett chose this for her household in 1846, paying $13.00 for a dinner set.

Domestic pottery also imitated imported Liverpool and transfer print Staffordshire creamware, whose traditional deep blue designs now gave way to prints in pink, sepia, black, or green. The inventory of William Whitby of East Vincent, Pennsylvania (1840), shows the quantity in which printed wares entered some homes:

2 Set of printed Tee ware
7 printed pitchers
printed bowls
2 9/12 doz pink printed plates
1 do printed Soups
9 printed pink Oval Mete dishes
12 green printed plates[20]

Banded creamware or mocha continued to be imported in the first years of
the period, and English lustre ware remained popular in the 1830s and 1840s.
Pitchers and jugs were the most common, but some householders had whole tea
sets.

Henderson's American Pottery Manufacturing Company in Jersey City produced stoneware (some with acanthus decoration) and an imitation of light
brown English Rockingham ware. Rockingham or Bennington ware gained a
national market during the rest of the century. Another British pottery to gain
a large American market was spatterware, a brightly decorated form of pearl-
ware popular in simpler houses in New England, New York, Pennsylvania, and
the Midwest. These pieces, too, were imitated by American potters.[21]

Earthenware factories all over the nation provided reasonably priced utilitarian stoneware. Redware continued to be produced throughout the period,

Figure 74. Eastman Johnson. *Girl and Pets.* 1856. Oil on canvas. In the collection
of The Corcoran Gallery of Art, Washington, D.C.

Although later in date than some of the pictures used to illustrate this period, this
study shows a timeless fascination with pets and a footed goldfish globe very much
like the one Morse painted twenty years earlier (Fig. 66). The little girl is apparently
in a back room, which is not an illogical spot in which to keep guinea pigs. The
room has fallen from earlier grandeur. The molding on the wall behind the girl and
the window shutters suggest refinements beyond keeping animals and plants. The
little girl sits on a simple chair with turned posts and a rush or woven seat. Unwit-
tingly, Johnson documented a cactus as an indoor plant as early as 1856.

although inexpensive Staffordshire imports displaced much of the earlier redware market. For example, by 1845 the Brooks Pottery of Goshen, Connecticut, gave up making domestic ware and shifted to stove pipes and flower pots.[22] Redware slip decorations and inscriptions did not reflect the late Empire style but occasionally spoke for the era. In the year of the panic, 1837, George Wolfkiel produced redware plates reading "Hard times in New Jersey."

Better ceramics were kept in the dining room, while utilitarian items were stored in the kitchen. (See below, for typical prices.)

Silver and Britannia Metal. Victorian classical hollow ware was heavier than Empire work, with new squat, bulbous shapes trimmed with melon reeding and classical or floral decoration. By the 1840s, repoussé ware had become very popular, and though often rococo in design, it found its way into many Victorian Classical interiors.

Silver tea sets were basic for those who could afford them, and wealthy households might also have silver covered dishes, sauceboats, pitchers, or fruit baskets. Silver was now generally kept in the dining room, and inventories record few instances of silver kept on a tea table in the parlor.

Spoons remained the most common flatware. In 1840, Mrs. Bennett bought six tablespoons and a dozen teaspoons in the common, and by then traditional, fiddleback handles. Silver knives and forks were sometimes made, but silver spoons were commonly used with Sheffield steel knives and forks with wood, bone, or ivory handles. Mrs. Bennett spent $33 on her silver, but her knives and forks cost only $1.00.

Imported and domestic silver plate was similar in appearance to silver, yet

Typical Prices of Victorian Classical Ceramics[23]

PORCELAINS   American China Manufacturing Company,
    prices for undecorated items, 1832–38

Pitchers $1.00
Teapots $1.00–$1.25
Coffee pots $2.00
Plates $4.00 a dozen
Cups $1.50 a dozen
Saucers $1.50 a dozen
French vases (amphora-shaped) $1.50
Fruit baskets $2.00
Tumblers $3.00 a dozen
Cup plates $1.50 a dozen

ROCKINGHAM WARE   O. L. & A. K. Ballard, Burlington, Vt.

1 gallon pitcher 75¢
1 quart pitcher 35¢
Ewer and basin $1.25
Teapots 40¢ to 70¢

VERMONT STONE WARE,   August 1840

1 gallon pots $3.00 a dozen
1 quart jugs $1.00 a dozen
3 gallon sweetmeat jars $7.00 a dozen

Plate 1. Attributed to the Van Cortlandt Limner. *Lady Undressing for a Bath. C.* 1710. National Gallery of Art, Washington, D.C. (Collection of Edgar William and Bernice Chrysler Garbisch).

The significance of this plate lies in the color, for the American artist copied a French print by N. Bazin entitled *Femme de qualité déshabillée pour le bain* (1686). The colors represent what the painter believed to be typical of a fashionable room. Note that the pilasters and the moldings of the panels have been highlighted. The coloring suggests that the floor was painted, but the original print had a clear, plain board floor. The print also showed ornamented moldings and cornices, and porcelains arranged on a shelf over the door.

Plate 2. Prudence Punderson. *The First, Second, and Last Scene of Mortality. C.* 1774–1784. Needlework, silks on linen, 12⅝ in. × 16¹¹⁄₁₆ in. (33 cm × 43 cm). Connecticut Historical Society, Hartford.

Prudence Punderson (1758–1784), who lived in Preston, Connecticut, was the daughter of Ebenezer Punderson, a Tory graduate of Yale (1755). The survival of the eagle-topped mirror (now at the Connecticut Historical Society) proves that her needlework picture was in part based upon real objects and demonstrates the elegance found in many Tory country houses. The tilt-top table with claw-and-ball feet shows unusual refinements. The chair has an intricate back and fretwork at the knees. In the last scene of mortality, a decorated coffin lies atop a Chippendale drop-leaf dining table with fluted legs.

Plate 3. Johann Eckstein. *The Samels Family.* 1788. Oil on canvas. Courtesy, Museum of Fine Arts, Boston, Mass. (Ellen Kelleran Gardner Fund).

Interior decorated in English styles. Even after the Revolution, well-to-do families continued to follow English fashions.

Plate 4. Countess Rumford (?). *Piano Recital at Concord, New Hampshire.* 1799–1811. Water color. National Gallery of Art, Washington, D.C. (Collection of Edgar William and Bernice Chrysler Garbisch). See notes, p. 388.

This painting of a stylish parlor is very informative about the placement of pictures and the dominance of red and green colors. The chairs were probably English.

Plate 5. "Mr. Freeman" (?). *Elizabeth Fenimore Cooper in Otsego Hall.* 1816. Water color, 21½ in. × 25½ in. (56 cm × 66 cm). New York State Historical Association, Cooperstown. See notes, p. 388.

Otsego Hall was built in Cooperstown, New York, in 1798. The heavy white trim and dentil moldings stand out against the strong yellow wallpaper.

Plate 6. Artist unknown. *The Sargent Family of Charlestown (?), Massachusetts.*
1800. Oil on canvas, 38 in. × 50¼ in. (97 cm × 127 cm). National Gallery of Art,
Washington, D.C. (Collection of Edgar William and Bernice Chrysler Garbisch).

The Sargents were obviously a family of some wealth, and the anonymous painter
took great pains to record the details of their room. The chairs are typical Salem designs; the Martha Washington or lolling chair is covered with a particularly elegant
brown-and-cream India cotton. One is not sure whether the paired birdcages represent
late Georgian symmetry or separate pets for each of the two older girls.

Plate 7. Ralph Earl (1751–1801). *The Angus
Nickerson Family of New Milford, Connecticut.* 1791.
Oil on canvas, 43½ in. × 58½ in. (1.11 m × 1.50 m).
The Springfield Museum of Fine Arts, Springfield, Mass.

Earl depicted a well-to-do Connecticut family whose
decor reflected the latest fashions. Especially notable are
the cascaded curtains at the windows, the pair of oval
mirrors, and the cabriole sofa with the squab cushion,
which was to become a popular Regency feature. Note
the wall-to-wall carpet with its design; very similar designs appear in many canvases the artist painted in Connecticut in the early 1790s. The fringed cover of the
writing surface of the desk also appears in several Earl
pictures.

Plate 8. Henry Sargent. *The Tea Party.* C. 1821–1825. Oil on canvas. Courtesy, Museum of Fine Arts, Boston, Mass.

Sargent illustrated the double parlor of Number 10 in the Tontine Crescent, Boston, redecorated in the latest Empire taste to a degree and quality only those of wealth could afford. One of the rare features of this canvas is the illustration of two rooms completely under artificial illumination.

Plate 9. Andrew Jackson Davis. *John C. Stevens House.* C: 1830. Water color on paper. Courtesy of The New-York Historical Society, New York City. See notes, p. 388.

John C. Stevens lived at College Place and Murray Street in New York City. Davis is often considered the principal early advocate of the Gothic taste, yet he used the high Empire style in 1830, a late date for Empire. The only trace of the Gothic here is the diamond panes of the French doors in the back room. The bright colors show the dazzling effect the Empire style could create.

Plate 10. Erastus Salisbury Field. *The Family of Joseph Moore.* 1839. Oil on canvas, 82¾ in. × 93¼ in. (2.11 m × 2.36 m). Courtesy, Museum of Fine Arts, Boston, Mass.

This large canvas documents the use of bright color at 18 Pleasant St., Ware, Massachusetts. The ingrain carpet is a brilliant yellow, green, and red. The walls are gray, in contrast with the draped red curtains, the green shutters, and the white woodwork. The thread stand on the small table looks somewhat lost beneath the heavy pier mirror with its veneered border. Although the seats of the chair are somewhat different, the decoration indicates they were both made by Lambert Hitchcock.

Plate 11. Joseph Warren Leavitt. *Moses Morse.* C. 1824. Water color, 7 in. × 9 in. (18 cm × 23 cm). Collection of Nina Fletcher Little.

Moses Morse was a cabinetmaker in Loudon, New Hampshire. The interior gives a strikingly Federal appearance, documenting the persistence of the earlier style in New Hampshire when other areas had changed to the Empire taste. Vivid colors and the crisp designs of the stenciling are the only enlivening features of an otherwise sparse interior.

right: Plate 12. Frederick Spencer (1806–1875). *Family Group.* 1840. Oil on canvas, 29⅛ in. × 36⅛ in. (74 cm × 91 cm). Brooklyn Museum, New York City.

Spencer shows a respectable middle-class family at their country home. As in other pictures dating from the early 1840s, the carpet has a large patterned design and a border. The sofa and marble-top table were moderately expensive but not extravagant pieces, and the table documents the decorative effect of books.

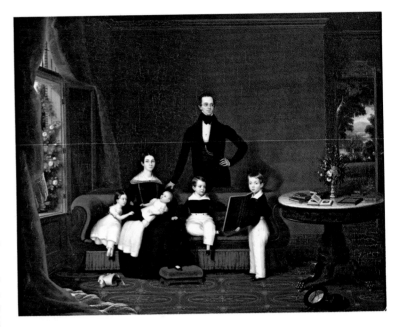

below: Plate 13. Artist unknown. *General George DeWolf and Family.* C. 1835–1840. Water color with crystalline decoration. Collection of Mr. and Mrs. Gerald E. Myers.

General George DeWolf built his house, which he called The Lindens, in Bristol, Rhode Island, in 1810 at a cost of $65,000. The interior is quite fashionable with its striped wallpaper, bright carpet, swagged drapes, and ornamented ceiling. The mahogany table with carved legs and the large-patterned rug were typical furnishings of the 1830s.

left: Plate 14. Oliver T. Eddy. *Jane Rebecca Griffith.*
C. 1840. Oil on canvas. Maryland Historical Society,
Baltimore.

It is not surprising to find a Baltimore girl in her
hall surrounded by furniture similar to the designs of
John Hall's *Cabinetmaker's Assistant,* published in
Baltimore in 1840. The columns flanking the doorway
are typical of high style architectural detail, but the
walls are notably plain. The carpet, which is not the
same design as the hall carpet seen in the picture of
the other Griffith children (Fig. 65), has large geometric patterns. The walls and columns are tan, the
ceiling somewhat darker; the upholstery is red and
the carpet is green, red, black, and brown.

below: Plate 15. Henry F. Darby (1829–1897). *The
Reverend John Atwood Family of Concord, New
Hampshire.* 1845. Oil on canvas. Courtesy, Museum
of Fine Arts, Boston, Mass. (M. and M. Karolik
Collection).

Here is the quintessence of Classical Victorian life,
evolving around the new center table, which with its
solar lamp became the focus of family life in the
evenings. The mantel and the exposed girt in the
corner are likely clues as to the eighteenth-century
origin of the house, but recent redecoration has brought
the room up to date. Inexplicable is the straight-hung
drapery in and under the piano.

Plate 16. Worthington Whittredge. *A Window on the Hudson.* 1863. Oil on canvas, 27 in. × 19 in. (69 cm × 48 cm). Courtesy of The New-York Historical Society, New York City.

Whittredge portrayed the interior of an unknown Gothic house along the Hudson during the Civil War. The ceiling is in the Gothic style, but the pedestals are Louis XVI, while the small table at the right and the larger secretary at the left are Victorian Classical. The arm chair is Elizabethan and the étagère Renaissance.

Plate 17. Nicholas Biddle Kittell. *Mr. and Mrs. Charles Augustus Carter.* 1848. Oil on canvas, 24 in. × 22¼ in. (61 cm × 56 cm). Museum of the City of New York.

At home on Bleecker Street, the assistant superintendent of the New York Hospital created an interior made Gothic by the simple points of the furniture.

Plate 18. George H. Story. *The Family* (or *The Departure*). 1872. Oil on canvas, 38 in. × 48 in. (97 cm × 122 cm). Addison Gallery of American Art, Andover, Mass.

Pictured here is the family of Reuben Dennon, a Boston banker. The upholstery on the Elizabethan-style dining chairs is elaborate, and the table has a typical rectangular shape. The details are not clear, but it is possible that the cupboard on the far wall is also in the Elizabethan style. The carpet under the dining table is protected by an Oriental rug.

Plate 19. J. A. S. Oertel. *Visiting Grandma.* 1865. Oil on canvas, 24 in. × 20 in. (61 cm × 51 cm). Courtesy of The New-York Historical Society, New York City.

Oertel's painting shows a fashionable New York City interior of 1865 with almost all the furnishings in the rococo style. Only the large leather-covered upholstered chair in which Grandma sits is in another style. Notable is the use of a rug under the center table, on top of a wall-to-wall floral-patterned carpet.

right: Plate 20. Hans Heinrich Bebie (*c.* 1824–1888). *Conversation Piece: Young Ladies in an Interior.* 1873–1875. Oil on canvas, 29 in. × 36 in. (74 cm × 91 cm). Baltimore Museum of Art, Baltimore, Md.

The furniture in this painting is in the proper taste of the period. In the parlor is a set of rococo furniture consisting of three chairs and a matching console table with a marble top. The covered round table is probably in the same style. The same demure figures on the candlesticks reappear at the top of the mirror. The door frame and wall decoration are ornate and typical of the patterns of the early 1870s, and the canvas documents an early use of portières.

Plate 21. Cornelia A. Fassett. *Mrs. Martha J. Lamb Seated in Her Library.* 1878. Oil. Courtesy of The New-York Historical Society, New York City.

Martha J. Lamb (1829–1893) sat in a Renaissance library, but she must be considered one of the creators of the enthusiasm for the Colonial Revival. Not only was she editor of *The Magazine of American History* from 1883 until her death; she also published *The Homes of America,* a survey of American domestic architecture since the seventeenth century. Only the furniture gave Mrs. Lamb's room a Renaissance look. Neither wall, carpet, nor window carried motifs of the style.

Plate 22. Artist unknown. *Anonymous Family Group. C.* 1880. Water color. Henry Ford Museum, Dearborn, Mich.

Simple versions of the Renaissance style found their way into thousands of American houses. The factory-produced secretary shown here echoes the designs, but lacks the decorative carving, of the more expensive Renaissance pieces. Another minimal sense of Renaissance decor is the painted outline on the roller shade adjacent to the desk. The wallpaper with its small border is typical of 1880.

Plate 23. Edward L. Henry. *The Parlor on Brooklyn Heights of Mr. and Mrs. John Bullard.*
1872. Oil on panel, 14⅝ in. × 16⅞ in. (38 cm × 43 cm). Private collection.

Bullard, who lived at 220 Columbia Heights, became a millionaire in the tanning and leather business. His parlor was furnished in a splendid version of the Renaissance style. The color shows well the contrasting dark banding in the woodwork and the collective splendor of the gilt frames. This plate shows why the early 1870s are remembered as an era of reds and tans; even the fringe on the chandelier is in a basic red.

Plate 24. Edward L. Henry. *A Lover of Old China*. 1889. Oil on board, 13½ in. × 11¾ in. (36 cm × 30 cm). The Shelburne Museum, Shelburne, Vt.

Henry depicted authentic colonial interiors and his pictures thus stand in contrast to the contemporary Colonial Revival. Mrs. Livingston Murray, the artist's aunt, shows some of her treasures to Richard Ely of Philadelphia. The dentil moldings reveal that a period house is the setting for the Philadelphia corner cupboard—the lower shelf of which holds a collection of Chinese export porcelain. The chair in the window is Queen Anne, while the Empire style is evident in the side table, sofa, draped curtain, and large-patterned carpet.

Plate 25. Louis C. Tiffany. *Morning Room.*
C. 1881. Harrison, *Woman's Handiwork,*
frontispiece; see Bibliography.

Mrs. Harrison provided a rare color view of a
room by Tiffany and Associated Artists. The
colors are more subdued than in many of their
rooms, but their typical style is evident. The
design of the upper wall is carried into the
ceiling, which is a shade lighter in color, and
the color of the lower wall is used on the woodwork and furniture. The mantel seems to have
been decorated with tiles, some of them possibly the iridescent glass for which Tiffany was
already known. Tiffany glass fills the transom of
the window.

Plate 26. Artist unknown. *Entry Hall in the
Eastlake Style.* 1884. Lyman Allyn Museum,
New London, Conn.

Several features make this plate from *Godey's
Lady's Book* useful. One sees how a harmonious
color scheme might unify eclectic elements in
a hall. Note that an Aesthetic paper was combined with a Renaissance frieze of the same
colors, while the color of the woodwork and the
paneling of the ceiling and paper create a
similar unity. Parquet floors gained great popularity during the 1880s, and so did the
stained glass seen in the doors down the hall.

Plate 27. William H. Lippincott. *Punch and Judy Show.* 1896. Oil on canvas, 21¾ in. × 31¾ in. (56 cm × 81 cm). Vassar College Art Gallery, Poughkeepsie, N.Y.

By comparison with other interiors of the period, this drawing room is strangely uncluttered. The English Restoration revival chair that forms a base for the stage has no affinity with the mass-produced Grand Rapids furniture on the audience's side of the room. The pictures were hung spaciously against a paper with relatively indistinct design. The mantel shelf was covered with a simple lambrequin and the piano had a shawl on its top as well as two violins. The small frames were almost dwarfed by the unusual owl clock, while two statues flank small pictures and a vase on the bookcase. Polar bear rugs were popular throughout the nation during this decade.

Plate 28. Artist unknown. *Boston Interior.* C. 1890. Water color, 5¾ in. × 6 in. (15 cm × 15 cm). Collection of Edgar deN. Mayhew.

As in Mrs. Lamb's room, a profusion of frames in various shapes are clustered on the walls. Note that the picture above the Venus was hung catercornered, as was the draped mirror in the opposite corner. The Moorish furniture, Renaissance table, and rococo chandelier (complete with Cupid) give an eclectic appearance to the room. The draperies might be called Louis XV.

Plate 29. Artist unknown. *Living Room Design. The Craftsman* (October 1905), p. 71; see Bibliography.

Gustave Stickley himself described this room as: "Chimney piece in a Craftsman living room." Note how the seats and casements on either side bring the whole end of the room into direct relation with the chimney-piece in the middle, and also how the line is carried around by the bookcase and casement at the right side and the piano at the left. Note also the division of the wall spaces by the wainscot, the space plain plastered above, and the frieze that carries a decoration in stencil. One might add that the frieze design is repeated in the rug. Yellow and green comprise the basic color scheme, with reds and blues used sparingly as contrasts.

Plate 30. Will H. Bradley. *Living Room Design. C.* 1901. Letter press for *Ladies' Home Journal* (there in black-and-white), 6⅛ in. × 7⅞ in. (15.55 cm × 19.95 cm). Metropolitan Museum of Art, New York City (Gift of Fern Bradley Dufner).

Bradley produced this design as part of the series he did for the *Ladies' Home Journal.* All six of the rooms were colorful, and in most of them basic red tones dominated. The furniture is all in the rectilinear version of the Art Nouveau.

right: Plate 31. *Writing Corner in a Chintz Bed-room.* 1913. De Wolfe, *The House in Good Taste,* p. 83; see Bibliography.

Here Miss de Wolfe used her favorite chintzes in one of her best-loved color schemes. Almost unusual in her later work were pieces in dark or natural wood tones like the desk and stool.

Plate 32. *Dining Room. C.* 1915. Wallick, *The Small House for a Moderate Income,* p. 24; see Bibliography.

Wallick offered a design with many themes common to Elsie de Wolfe's work. Woodwork and furniture were painted ivory, and chintz was used for portières and lampshade.

Figure 75. Hanson. *Evening Prayers. C.* 1840. Oil on canvas, 13¾ in. × 21¾ in. (36 cm × 56 cm). National Gallery of Art, Washington, D.C. (Collection of Edgar William and Bernice Chrysler Garbisch).

Hanson provided a great many details about a country dining room. The tattered wallpaper, dating from an earlier period, is finished with a thin border. The six painted chairs with simple gilt decoration are later versions of the Windsor, and the typical clock is on a small shelf finished with a scalloping similar to the one on the corner shelf. One painting is obviously religious, and the other two may be religious allegories, which were very popular topics.

much less expensive. Electroplating brought a great expansion of the industry in the late 1840s.

Less expensive was German silver (copper, zinc, nickel) or Britannia metal (tin, copper, antimony). Britannia metal soon became another major industry, and Ashbil Griswold of Meriden, Connecticut, was an important manufacturer. His factory produced coffee pots and mills, spoons, waffle irons, and signal lanterns, employed 250 people, and earned an annual income of $200,000.[24] Some of the items produced by the Britannia factories carried neoclassical designs, but many followed basic eighteenth-century shapes that pewterers had produced for generations. Mrs. Bennett bought a Britannia castor with cruets for $1.25 (Figure. 54).

In *Domestic Duties*, Mrs. Parkes advised that silver be polished twice a week. She recommended a mixture of "levigated hartshorn" (powdered deer or calf bone) and turpentine. In houses of wealth with a great deal of silver and many servants, the silver should be kept in a "proper plate-chest" or "strong closet" under the supervision of the butler, who should count it every night.

Typical pewter shapes for coffee and teapots, *c.* 1830

8

The Spanish Southwest

1560–1850

S PANISH settlements, like the English, followed the decorative styles of the mother country as much as possible, yet the isolation of the Spanish colonists plus their lack of materials and tools kept their furnishings almost primitive until the very end of the colonial period.

Spanish styles were naturally prominent in five principal areas of colonization. Florida was colonized in the 1560s and remained in Spanish hands until ceded to the British, at which point most of the Spanish left. It passed again to Spain in 1783, but there was little interest in recolonization, and it was finally taken over by the United States in 1821, with almost none of the old Spanish decoration still intact. New Mexican settlements date from 1598. After the Pueblo Revolt of 1680, there were no Spaniards in New Mexico until recolonization in 1692. The area remained Spanish until 1821 when it became part of Mexico; the treaties of 1848 and 1853 brought it to the United States. Arizona followed a similar pattern.

The colonization of Texas began only in the 1680s, and Texas likewise became Mexican territory in 1821. After the Louisiana Purchase of 1803, Americans began settling in large numbers, and in 1836, they declared and defended an independent republic. The United States annexed Texas in 1845. California had been explored and claimed by several nations since the sixteenth century, but permanent Spanish settlements did not begin until 1769. California, too, became Mexican territory in the 1820s, and then part of the United States in 1848.

During the era of colonization, Spanish decoration evolved from Renaissance to baroque to rococo to the Spanish version of the Empire, the *Fernandino*. Major capitals of the Spanish empire in South America and Mexico followed these trends closely. Mission buildings in Texas and Arizona reflect the baroque to some degree, but New Mexico and California heard only the faintest echoes of these changing styles. In large measure, the stylistic developments of the mother country went unnoticed.

Indian basket

Recovering the details of these earlier interiors is difficult, as few houses and few of the decorative arts survive to provide a comprehensive picture of the early centuries.

HOUSES

Early buildings from Florida to New Mexico were constructed from readily available materials—cochina limestone in Florida and sun-hardened adobe in the Southwest. The earliest surviving example is the Governor's Palace in New Mexico, built in 1610 with techniques borrowed from the Pueblo Indians. Projecting through the thick adobe walls were the characteristic wooden beams or *vigas*, which supported the flat, gently sloping roof of mud placed over branches. Originally part of a building 400 feet long and intended as a fortification, the Governor's Palace was extraordinarily large, but its construction was typical of the most humble houses. A coat of mud finished the walls. The width of the house was dictated by the length of the *vigas*, rare and valuable in a region where wood was not plentiful. Need and economic conditions dictated the length of the house as connecting rectangular rooms were strung out together. The most common houses had one or two rooms.

The Spanish tradition of sparse furnishing was exaggerated still further by necessity, since so few furnishings were available even to the wealthy. By the late eighteenth century, the residences of governors and the interiors of some churches had gained considerably in decor, but even by the mid-nineteenth century, the average visitor to the Spanish settlements of California described them as crude and "without the smallest pretention to architectural taste or beauty."[1]

Isolation was a prime cause of decorative simplicity. The set of tools given each priest in the establishment of a new mission grew dull or broke and could not be replaced. Goods not made locally had to be brought overland from the coast or Mexico (a distance of 1,800 miles from New Mexico), a necessity that increased cost and limited size. The opening of the Sante Fe Trail in 1821 was a great boon for the Southwestern interior.

In the late eighteenth and early nineteenth centuries, a few houses in the style that would become somewhat common in the Mexican period appeared. Adobe construction continued, but these larger houses were built along three sides of an open garden patio surrounded by a covered walkway into which each room opened. By the early nineteenth century, these larger houses included a diversity of specialized rooms: sleeping rooms for family, servants, and guests, implement rooms, cheese and milk rooms, hide and tallow rooms, and small family chapels. In California, these large expensive houses had pitched, red tile roofs not generally found in New Mexico, where the flat roof persisted. But even in California, the average house remained the small adobe with a flat, tar-covered roof.

In the 1830s, the two-story house with surrounding second-floor balcony gained popularity in the Monterey, California, area. American Consul Thomas Larkin completed such a house in 1837.[2] A few similar houses were built elsewhere in California, but the many poor continued to live in small adobes. In *Two Years Before the Mast*, Richard Henry Dana included a brief description of the Monterey houses he saw in 1835:

The houses here, as everywhere else in California, are of one story, built of clay made into large bricks, about a foot and a half square and three or four inches thick, and hardened in the sun. These are cemented together by mortar of the same material, and the whole are of a common dirt-color. The floors are generally of earth, the windows grated and without glass; and the doors, which are seldom shut, open directly into the common room; there being no entries. Some of the more wealthy inhabitants have glass to their windows and board floors; and in Monterey nearly all the houses are plastered on the outside. The better houses, too, have red tiles upon the roofs. The common ones have two or three rooms which open into each other, and are furnished with a bed or two, a few chairs and tables, a looking-glass, a crucifix of some material or other, and small daubs of painting enclosed in glass, and representing some miracle or martyrdom. They have no chimneys or fire-places in the house, the climate being such as to make a fire unnecessary; and all their cooking is done in a small cook-house, separated from the house.[3]

In 1859, Dana revisited California—ten years after the Gold Rush had brought a vast influx of Eastern settlers, their tastes, and so far as possible their styles. To his eyes, San Francisco was transformed into "one of the capitals of the American Republic," a "solid city of brick and stone." San Diego, on the other hand, "had undergone no change whatever." He found an old friend there in "a familiar one-story adobe house with its piazza and earthen floor."[4] Clearly, time was on the side of the Eastern styles, but in some areas the Spanish traditions held on to the end of the century.

A tarimita

FURNITURE

In the late seventeenth and early eighteenth centuries (the earliest period for which any evidence can be found), interiors of the Spanish settlements were sparsely furnished. Even in a well-to-do house, furniture consisted only of a rawhide chest imported from Mexico,[5] and locally made hanging shelves (*repisas*), chests, small stools (*tarimitas*), and *alacenas* (cupboards built into the wall).

By the late eighteenth and early nineteenth century, furniture was more diverse in form and more colorful in its decoration, but still far from the elegance of Spain or Mexico City. Typical forms in a house of some wealth were tables, tall *trasteras* with grilled doors for the storage of valuables, low chests without legs, *tarimitas* or stools, and chairs. As in early New England, arm chairs were traditionally reserved for the clergy. Alan C. Vedder has argued that regional styles of decoration developed, making, for example, New Mexican furniture readily distinguishable from furniture made elsewhere in the Southwest.[6] New Mexican cabinetmakers normally decorated with chip carving and incised lines, reserving relief carving of traditional Spanish motifs (rosettes, pomegranates, and lions) for special chests. Paint highlighted carving and added supplementary decoration. Early furniture was primarily made from pine.

In the nineteenth century, both forms and decorations proliferated. The *trastera* continued to be probably the most impressive piece in the household, but the early grilled doors with turned stiles sometimes gave way to plainer, paneled doors. Later in the century, *trasteras* sometimes held meat rather than

A trastera

Figure 76. *Interior of an Adobe House, San Juan Capistrano, California. C.* 1870. History Division, Los Angeles County Museum of Natural History, Los Angeles, Calif.

This rare photograph shows a simple and primitive adobe interior. The seating was provided by simple benches and broken chairs. Note that trunks were stored on benches along the left wall. The far end of the room had two makeshift bedrooms with blankets used to create dividing walls. The exterior walls of adobe had no frames around the doors. The floor was of dirt. The spool bed along the far wall matches the post of another seen in the foreground. Corner shelves were popular in the Southwest.

valuables or china, the typical assignment of the earlier forms. Chests with legs supplanted earlier floor chests in the most fashionable houses, but plain six-board chests continued to be made for the storage of grain as well as household items. The hutch-top chest appeared by mid-century. Tables continued in a diversity of shapes. Elegant California families had large refectory tables, but perhaps the most interesting were the New Mexican serving tables 14 inches high, which were used for dining while the family sat on the floor around them. Built-in adobe *bancos* (low ledges along a wall) and *tarimitas* provided common seating, supplemented by pillows or *piquitas* (little pillows). Cross sections of logs supported on simple legs also provided simple seats.[7] Eighteenth-century-style chairs continued to be made, but in the second quarter of the nineteenth century new European and American styles, based on Empire and Sheraton designs, appeared in New Mexican chairs. In the remote areas, whittled hard-

A chip-carved chest

A chair with chip-carved decoration

wood chairs with rawhide provided the Western approximation of the ladder-back chair. *Repisas* continued to hold holy figures, books, and other small objects, and the *alacena* remained popular.

Chip carving was the standard decorative technique for this primarily pine furniture, and such carving flourished after the Santa Fe Trail made new tools available. Painted designs of flowers, urns, and animals made chests and *trasteras* colorful additions to a room.

In California, near the coast, the wealthy of the early nineteenth century were able to make some claim to fashion with furniture imported from Peru and China. Furniture was a sign of status to Californians, even in the 1820s. In 1874, the widow of Governor Luis Antonio Arguello remembered that the poor during her husband's administration (1822–1825) had had little furniture, but since they did not know how to use it, they felt no sense of deprivation.[8] In the Spanish tradition, Californians in the early nineteenth century sometimes had grandiose beds. Sir George Simpson described those in Monterey in 1842: "Among California housewives the bed is quite a show, enjoying, as it does, the full benefit of contrast. While other furniture consists of a deal [pine] table and some badly made chairs, with probably a Dutch clock and an old looking glass, the bed ostentatiously challenges admiration with its snowy sheets fringed with lace, its piles of soft pillows covered with finest linens or the richest satin, and its well arranged drapery of costly and tasteful curtains."[9]

Generally, however, beds had been unknown in the New Mexican settlements, and most people slept on the same mattress on the floor, which rolled up during the day served as a seat. By 1835, Richard Henry Dana found that even the "common" houses of California had two or three beds, but in New Mexico beds were not prevalent until the 1840s.

The opening of the Santa Fe Trail in 1821 and the arrival of American settlers in Texas, Florida, and California heralded the advent of mahogany furniture and East Coast styles. In 1843, the first piano arrived in California, and the following year American Consul Thomas Larkin ordered for his house in Monterey:

4 dozen chairs, with arm and rocking chairs
1 pair of sofas, 6½ or 7 feet long
1 pair of sofas that can be used as beds
2 ladies work tables
2 wash hand stands
1 pair large dining tables for a hall
1 pair heavy round tables
2 pairs mirrors, each different pattern
4 large National pictures, handsome frames
4 pair large candlesticks of different patterns, with large glass shades[10]

Many new settlers brought their furniture with them, like the lady who brought mahogany chairs with horsehair seats from Buffalo to Monterey.[11]

Even the Larkins had limited furniture. In the 1840s they planned a ball, and after borrowing chairs from the neighbors they still did not have enough. Large pumpkins provided the extra seating. In 1851, a ball in the house of James W. Magoffin of El Paso, Texas, raised exactly the same problem, and there the guests sat on trunks and the floor.[12]

Chinese furniture was imported to California in the 1820s and gained special vogue in the 1840s, in some houses by choice, in others by necessity. A man visiting a lady in Monterey wrote: "In her salon I noticed many bureau lamps, tables, pictures, and vases of Chinese make. I made bold to inquire the reason why she preferred Chinese furniture to French or American. She replied that in the olden times she was not allowed to choose, that French or American furniture was not to be had in the country, and therefore she had no choice but to furnish her apartments with articles of Chinese make."[13] Particularly popular were nests of brightly painted, leather-covered chests, but also available were marble-top tables, rattan chairs, rosewood desks, and lacquered shaving boxes.

By the 1850s, the Eastern styles were common among the well-to-do of Florida, California, and Texas; New Mexico and Arizona remained stylistically more insulated until the completion of the national rail system sent boxcars of Eastern furniture to the Old Spanish dominions. Even then, some New Mexican styles persisted until the end of the century.

FLOOR COVERINGS

The standard floor of the adobes was compacted earth, which over time gained great hardness. By mid-century in Texas, such floors were sometimes covered with canvas.[14] Early in the century, however, wealthy households in California might have wooden or tile floors, and by 1850 board floors were common there, but kitchens had dirt floors as late as the 1870s.

Loosely woven woolen rugs, called *jergas*, were used in houses that could afford them in the eighteenth and nineteenth centuries. Checked patterns predominate in surviving examples. Later, braided and hooked rugs were added. By 1849, San Francisco shoppers could buy ingrain carpet at $1 a yard or Brussels carpet at $2.50.[15] Chinese straw matting, often used in bedrooms, was also available.

PICTURES AND MIRRORS

In the nineteenth century, prominent California families imported religious paintings from Spain. Spanish and Mexican framed prints of varying quality and cost were popular with those who could afford them, and as American commerce with the Southwest grew in the later nineteenth century, Currier and Ives produced a series of colored lithographs of saints especially for that market. Their *Sacred Heart of Mary* was dated 1846. In 1853, one Monterey resident owned "3 Chinese pictures & frames."[16] Several art forms came together in the *nicho*—an embossed tin frame of a drawing of a saint. The *nicho* was commonly hung in a corner.

Santos (religious decoration) in two varieties were important parts of the Catholic household of the eighteenth and nineteenth centuries. *Retablos* or paintings of saints were done in tempera on gesso-covered boards and varied greatly in size. *Bultos*, or religious figurines, were another frequent devotional and artistic addition often kept on a *repisa*. Archbishop Lamay did his best to suppress *santos* after 1851, and thus most date from before that time.

Figure 77. Alexander F. Harmer. *Donna Mariana Coronel Grinding Corn.*
C. 1885. Oil on canvas. History Division, Los Angeles County Museum of
Natural History, Los Angeles, Calif.

Harmer documented the simple kitchen equipment used in an adobe house. Donna
Mariana grinds her corn with a *mano* on a *metate*; the ground corn was caught in
what appears to be a wooden bowl. This laborious grinding needed to be done daily.
The accessories all seem to be of native stoneware, with the exception of a brass bucket
and the circular Indian basket partially filled with corn. The storage cupboard is very
primitive, as is the small table against the wall.

Prominent California families had large mirrors early in the century. After
the opening of the Santa Fe Trail made tin common in New Mexico, mirrors
were sometimes included in tin wall sconces. They might also be encased in
special tin frames without candlearms.[17] Early Yankee traders found a ready
market in New Mexico for small mirrors.

TEXTILES

The decorative use of textiles in the traditional houses was limited to the
blankets that hung on the walls, bed furnishings, and *piquitas*. Blankets, a major

New Mexico industry in the eighteenth and nineteenth centuries, were decorated with a variety of Spanish and Indian motifs. The Chimayo blanket introduced from Mexico carried traditional patterns of the seventeenth century. The Rio Grande blanket was woven commonly with diamond patterns, and other blankets were made by sewing strips together. Indigo, brown, and cream were prominent colors for these sewn blankets, with yellows, reds, and greens also appearing.[18] Women put great decorative effort into *piquitas* adorned with Spanish and Moorish motifs.

As American influence grew, lace window curtains appeared in California as early as the 1830s,[19] and the arrival of mahogany furniture in the next decade required upholstery previously unknown in the Spanish settlements.

Embroidered *sabanillas* provided a *tour de force* of home decorative work, as the *colcha* stitch was used to cover these large cloths with colorful designs. The finished work might be used as a hanging or bedspread.[20]

WALL TREATMENT

Walls were generally whitewashed adobe. Whitewash on interior and exterior walls might be tinted, and nineteenth-century New Mexican householders sometimes added stenciled decorations.[21]

Early Texas settlers from the East, however, soon built in wood rather than adobe, and several houses of the 1850s have walls of horizontal boards painted and decorated with elaborate designs reminiscent of Robert Adam. Ceilings of joined boards were decorated similarly.[22]

By the 1850s, wallpaper was available in California and used on adobe as well as plaster walls.[23]

ARCHITECTURAL DETAILS AND CEILINGS

Architectural decoration was limited to *alacenas* or cupboards, built into the walls, and simple shutters at the windows, for doors and windows had only the most minimal frames and decorative moldings were virtually unknown. (For an exception in California, see *Antiques*, April 1978, p. 822.) The Governor's Palace in San Antonio, Texas (1749) has hooded fireplaces, and New Mexican houses of the early nineteenth century had simple corner fireplaces; but in California, Richard Dana noted of common houses, "they have no chimneys or fireplaces." Cooking was done in a separate kitchen.

Doors were often hung on rawhide or pivoted on dowels rather than hung from iron hinges. Doors varied from the simplest construction to the later four-paneled doors pictured in Figures 76 and 77, to those with panels decorated with pierced work.[24]

New Mexican adobe construction included *bancos*—low ledges along a wall, for seating. Window shutters or bars were a necessity as glass was very expensive and almost unknown in some communities. In Monterey, in 1824, it has been noted that the rich had iron bars at their windows, the poor, wood.[25] Eastern settlers brought Eastern styles, and in 1847, Thomas Larkin ordered windows with the weights and pulleys common in the East.

New Mexican fireplace

Zuni interior
showing a *banco*

In most settlements, ceilings were the exposed beams or *vigas* and the roofing materials they supported. However, in nineteenth-century California, unbleached cotton or lightweight canvas was tacked to the beams and held in place by molding strips around the walls, thus making a fabric ceiling. The painted corbels that decorated the *vigas* in New Mexican churches seem not to have been used in domestic construction.[26]

LIGHTING

Until the advent of oil lamps in the 1820s, candles provided the principal illumination. In early nineteenth-century California, candles were even used during the day in some houses, as the few small windows in the thick adobe walls admitted little light.[27] Elaborate tin wall sconces, candelabra, and chandeliers added a decorative touch after the 1820s when tin became available to New Mexican craftsmen.

Whale oil lamps and lard oil lamps provided alternate lighting in later years. Kerosene did not appear until the 1860s. Pine flares were not used inside, but were important outdoor lighting.[28]

COLOR

Blankets hung from poles on walls, *santos*, painted chests, and possibly a *jerga* or rug added what color there was to an eighteenth-century room. The interior of a well-to-do house of the early nineteenth century was very colorful, with bright painted furniture, *jergas*, blankets, and occasional wall hangings.

Eighteenth-century furniture often had its relief carving heightened with color, in one case brown-black, in another red and green. Some pieces were painted in solid colors. In the nineteenth century, florid, multicolor decoration gained fashion in New Mexico. Gesso and water-color paints were applied to carved work; or, much like Eastern tin ware, pieces were given a dark ground color (black or indigo) and decorated with flowers and animals in bright pink, yellow, green, red, and blue. In many cases, furniture was decorated by the same *santeros* who produced religious pictures and statues.

Some small items were not painted but instead blackened with a mixture of soot and pitch and then decorated with straw inlay.

ACCESSORIES

The quantity and quality of accessories varied greatly with economic status and access to trade routes, but even later houses appeared sparse, far from the profusion beginning to clutter the East Coast dwelling.

An unusual feature of some houses, especially those belonging to members of the Penitents sect, was the private chapel. Typical furnishings of such a chapel included several *bultos*, larger carved figures, a chest for storing religious articles, a missal stand or lectern, several crucifixes, a large triangular candle-holder, whips for self-flagellation, and a human skull as a reminder of mortality.[29]

Ceramics. Standard ceramic ware was earthenware, much of it produced by Indians following European models. Imports were costly, but the wealthy sometimes had Chinese porcelain, and finds near San Diego have uncovered rather early pieces. In the 1840s, ironstone and English china entered the California and New Mexican markets. In some California houses of the early nineteenth century, large earthenware jugs brought from Guadalajara held cool drinking water, which was mixed with wine and sugar for refreshment.[30] By 1849, one Monterey bride had china that was little different from what she might have known back in Buffalo. She wrote her sister "our china is white—very nice not French china except the coffee cups and fluted bowls."[31]

Copper and Iron. As copper and iron implements were imported and expensive, they were found in few households. Copper came from Mexico, Peru, or Russia, while brass was brought overland to New Mexico from Missouri. Pots, kettles, and pans were normal forms. About the 1840s, the English found a ready market for large iron plates or *comales*, which were put on top of low ovens made of stone and adobe, becoming a stove top.[32]

Clocks. In nineteenth-century California, clocks came primarily from England and New England, although a few were from Germany. Sir George Simpson visiting Monterey in 1842 took special note of Governor Alvarado's German tall clock with a miniature calliope or organ that played old folksongs, a surprising item in a Spanish settlement.[33] Needless to say, clocks were rare.

Silver. Silver was a sign and form of wealth. As in the East, silver passed from generation to generation. In the 1850s, the family of Don José Antonio de la Guerra in Santa Barbara had a collection dating to the 1770s, when a platter and plates were made. A *brasero* to hold coals for lighting fires dated to the late eighteenth century, and a mug or beaker was dated 1804, about the time other mugs and a wine cup were made. They also had a silver

Typical Southwest tile of the late eighteenth century

writing stand with two candlearms.[34] These pieces were made in Spain and Mexico; some Russian silver also survives in the San Francisco area.

Stone. Indian stoneware was an important part of domestic life. Mortars and pestles were important for grinding, but corn was commonly ground with a *mano* on a *metate*. Some families used these tools on a low table, but in Figure 77 the slanting *metate* is put on the floor, while the *mano* was used like a rolling pin to grind the corn. An Indian bowl or basket held the finished corn.

Tin. Tin was important in the interiors of nineteenth-century New Mexico. It first appeared with the opening of the Santa Fe Trail, and tinsmiths quickly adapted it to decorative frames, candlesticks, and religious items as well as utilitarian household utensils and containers.

Wood. Wooden plates and implements were common before imports supplanted them.

Nineteenth-century New Mexican interiors also often used geranium plants for decoration.

9

Gothic and Elizabethan Styles

1836–1870

The Gothic Style

WITH the rebuilding of the English Houses of Parliament in 1836, interest in a Gothic revival, which had appeared sporadically for almost a century, gained new momentum on both sides of the Atlantic. By the end of the decade, Gothic villas, cottages, and schools were beginning to appear in America. If Augustus Welby Pugin was responsible for the English revival, two Americans took equal credit for promoting the style in their country: Alexander Jackson Davis and Andrew Jackson Downing.

Davis published his *Rural Residences* in 1837, and Downing followed with *Cottage Residences* (1842) and *The Architecture of Country Houses* (1850). Both of these men held the Gothic style to be correct, proper, and picturesque for a growing America, and Gothic buildings sprang up over the countryside. New York State, especially the Hudson River Valley, took the lead in Gothic construction, but Connecticut and the rest of New England soon caught up. Downing's *Country Houses* was the source of many Gothic dwellings as far afield as Colorado and Oregon. Sharp gables, gingerbread vergeboards, and pointed windows were very much in style.

Some Americans were inspired to remodel earlier houses, just as James Fenimore Cooper transformed Otsego Hall in 1834, but many of Downing's readers built new homes, and those who could afford it began moving into what were now called villas.

Downing defined a villa as "the country house of a person of competence or wealth sufficient to build and maintain it with some taste and elegance." In his estimation, the scale of a villa required "the care of at least three or more servants." Estimates for the designs of his villas ranged from $2,300 to $14,000 in 1850. Downing described the villa as "the most refined home of America—the home of its most leisurely and educated class of citizens."[1]

Figure 78. *The Drawing Room at Kenwood. C.* 1850. Downing, *The Architecture of Country Houses*, p. 384; see Bibliography.

In 1842, A. J. Davis designed Kenwood, a house built near Albany, New York, for Joel Rathbone. Downing used one of its rooms to illustrate the ecclesiastical or high-pointed arch (overmantel mirror) or the low, flat, Tudor Gothic arch (oriel window). With the exception of the Elizabethan arm chair, the furniture was Gothic, as was the fireplace inset; however, the carpet was more typical of the 1840s than the Gothic style. The walls were plain, and the statuettes of the knight and lady who watch over this early Gothic room will reappear in many later rooms (e.g., Fig. 81).

Less elaborate and less expensive was the cottage, which Downing termed "a dwelling of small size, intended for the occupation of a family, either wholly managing the household cares itself, or, at the most, with the assistance of one or two servants."[2] The estimated cost of cottage designs ran from $330 to $3,000.

Alexander Jackson Davis became the most prominent creator of Gothic villas. Perhaps the best known is Lyndhurst, the house he built for New York merchant William Paulding in 1838. Davis designed the furniture as well as the structure.

In this era, Gothic motifs pervaded almost every decorative form, including silver, fabrics, wallpaper, lighting fixtures, pottery, china, and glass. Despite advice from the writers, relatively few houses seem to have been completely furnished in the Gothic style. Many households had a Gothic room, and still more, a few pieces of Gothic furniture.

The standard roster of rooms in houses of at least moderate stature included a dining room, library, hall, and two of the following three: parlor, living room, or drawing room. An uncommon refinement in some villas was a boudoir or ladies morning room. The kitchen usually had a number of small adjuncts like a pantry, scullery, or porch. Of great interest are closets or large dressing rooms as part of the original design, and, in a few rare plans, a water closet room or "bath room" or both. Basements of a villa might include a laundry, serving room, larder, and servants' hall as well as a kitchen. Servants' rooms were generally in the attic.

Downing's simple "small cottage for a working man" had only a living room and bedroom on the first floor and two bedrooms and two closets on the second.

Downing's plan for a Gothic villa, estimated cost $7,500; 1850

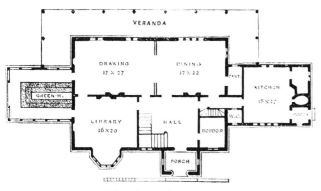

First-floor plan of villa

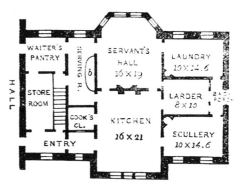

The working basement of a large house

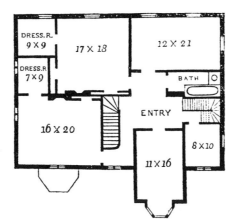

Second-floor plan of villa

FURNITURE

An important guide to Gothic furniture was J. C. Loudon's *Encyclopaedia of Cottage, Farm, and Villa Architecture and Furniture* (London, 1839), a work owned by America's influential designer A. J. Davis. Loudon presented several styles of furniture (Grecian, Victorian Classical, and Gothic), but he urged consistency in one's choice of decor. Gothic furniture was right, and seemingly only right, in a house with a Gothic exterior. He added that "the expense of the

Figure 79. *Front Parlor, Residence of Samuel Welles, 57–59 Summer Street, Boston.* C. 1870. Boston Atheneum, Boston, Mass.

Usually, furniture determines the prevailing style of a room, but the Welles parlor is a notable exception. In about 1845, the family redecorated the parlor in the Gothic style, but kept the high style early Empire furniture and mantel. Clearly, the Gothic architecture overshadows the earlier furniture. There was nothing Gothic about the floral wallpaper or carpet, but they were surely added during the renovation. Drapery rods appear empty above the windows, but the windows themselves were covered by painted roller shades of the sort widely advertised. The chandelier is an excellent example of the Victorian Classical style.

Gothic style is the only serious objection which can be made against it."[3]

Another influential book of the mid-nineteenth century was Thomas Webster and Frances Parkes's *Encyclopaedia of Domestic Economy*, already mentioned. Webster and Parkes copied many of their plates and ideas from Loudon, but when they came to the Gothic style they wrote with restraint: "We omit chairs in the Gothic style, as they are never used, except the house itself be in the same style; and we may observe that this style is, in general, very ill adapted for domestic furniture, and except it be designed by artists of great taste, and who are very well acquainted with Gothic architecture, and what little remains of ancient furniture, attempts at imitation are generally very miserable, besides being extremely expensive."[4]

One of the first Americans to design Gothic furniture was Alexander Jackson Davis. Finding no suitable Gothic cabinetwork, Davis turned to designing furniture himself.[5] But the great American publicist of Gothic furniture designs was Downing, who included a section at the end of his influential *Country Houses* in which he illustrated a variety of styles and differentiated between cottage furniture and villa or city furniture. The cottage furniture was simpler in design and less expensive, in contrast to the villa furniture, which was more detailed and more costly.

Both Loudon and Downing suggested contents for each room of the house. Loudon's English standards were more expensive, whereas Downing continually offered a less expensive "cottage" variant in addition to the more expensive villa style.

For the drawing room, Loudon held the furniture should be of oak, painted and gilded. In his illustration of a drawing room, the drawing room table is of oak, circled with ebony and striped with gold; there is also a piano, music stool, and music stand, a canterbury (low rack for music, magazines, or large books), and a firescreen.

For a bedroom, Loudon recommended a bed, bed steps, wardrobe, dressing table, cheval glass, and wash stand. He offered no pictures of Gothic bedroom furniture, for any cabinetmaker familiar with Gothic ornament, he thought, could easily "gothicize" a standard bedroom piece.

Downing emphasized the difference between cottage and villa furniture: that for the cottage or country should be "chaste, simple, and expressive." It should also be durable and comfortable. Unlike Loudon, Downing was willing to mix furniture styles in the cottage or country house.

In the country drawing room, according to Downing, one wanted a round center table, comfortable upholstered chairs, a sofa or ottoman, and a piano—"Even in simple cottages the piano will be found." He especially stressed useful small pieces for the cottage, most of which would probably be used in the drawing room. Thus, he suggested small tea tables, a ladies work table with a silk bag, a small portable basket stand, a whatnot or étagère, hanging shelves, and a writing desk. Downing saw these pieces as necessary whether they were in the Gothic style or not. For example, the hanging shelf could be Gothic, but for the basket stand he suggested "rustic work varnished in the Swiss manner."[6]

Country bedrooms were seldom Gothicized: "Elaborate bed-room furniture in the Gothic style is seldom seen in country houses in the United States." He suggested the Elizabethan style for the bedroom or the Victorian Classical style; either style could be provided in painted bedroom sets.

Gothic chair

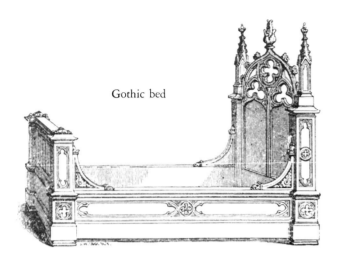

Gothic bed

Iron bed

Iron umbrella and hat stand

For the villa, Downing offered elaborate Gothic beds, tables, and drawing room or library chairs. Such expensive furniture was to be covered with "rich stuffs" and highly carved. This high style furniture was available from Roux in New York City.

Gervase Wheeler of Norwich, Connecticut, wrote *Rural Homes or Sketches of Houses Suited to American Country Life* in 1852. Even more than Downing, Wheeler was concerned with the details of interior furnishing, and he devoted particular attention to summer furniture.

For summer use, he recommended rattan furniture on both aesthetic and humanitarian grounds. Such furniture was available from Messrs. Berrian in New York City, who supported the needy through their sales. This rattan furniture was made either at the House of Refuge in New York, where "between three and four hundred boys [were] at work upon case seats," or in the suburbs of New York, where there were "a number of Germans who have in their employment at least two thousand girls occupied in this manufacture." The furniture was light, strong, and inexpensive.

Wheeler thought iron furniture could be useful in the hall, where a family would need an umbrella or hat stand. Iron beds were also good, but Wheeler was adamant that iron furniture should only be painted black. "Graining it oak is an absurdity," and it must not be painted white because "white on iron always seems a mask." And chocolate brown looked like rust.[7]

FLOOR COVERINGS

Floor coverings in the Gothic style followed the general canons of the mid-nineteenth century. One might imagine that the most appropriate carpet for a Gothic interior would be one with a Gothic design. Loudon suggested a library carpet that "consists of an imitation of wainscot, has a quiet subdued tone of color, and accords well with furniture made, or painted in imitation, of oak."[8] Although at least one Gothic carpet of probable American origin survives, the pictorial evidence suggests that few American interiors were as pure as Loudon might have wished. Some Americans of the mid-1840s had adopted the new floral designs that replaced earlier geometric motifs (Plate 17).

Loudon had recommended Scotch or Kidderminster carpets with small patterns. Less expensive substitutes were green baize, drugget, or homemade paper carpets, which he said were surprisingly durable. Loudon still offered the suggestion of painted floors for lobbies or passageways. He advised that whatever the design, wall-to-wall carpet should be tacked in place temporarily. Better than wall-to-wall was a rectangular carpet with margins of wooden floor ex-

Figure 80. Chester Harding. *Mrs. Abbott Lawrence*. 1845–1850. Oil on canvas, 27½ in. × 22¼ in. (71 cm × 56 cm). Courtesy, Museum of Fine Arts, Boston, Mass. (Gift of The Misses Rosamond and Aimee Lamb).

The Lawrences were a prominent and wealthy mercantile family of Boston, and Abbott Lawrence in 1847 gave $50,000 to start the Lawrence Scientific School at Harvard. Katherine Bigelow Lawrence (1793–1860), the subject of the canvas, married Lawrence in 1819. The Gothic arm chair had a gilt quatrefoil in the back and a light quatrefoil design on the seat rail. An accomplished needlewoman, Mrs. Lawrence possibly made the writing portfolio on the top of the table and the wicker sewing basket on the floor.

Figure 81. *Dining Room, Jenks Residence, Mt. Vernon Place, Baltimore.* 1885. Maryland Historical Society, Baltimore.

The Jenks family remodeled a Baltimore house built in 1843 by J. H. Thomas. Earlier classical detail was seen through the open door, but the dining room was redecorated in the Gothic style, and thus this picture documents the persistence of the style to the end of the nineteenth century. The chairs and sideboard with its massed display of silver incorporated Gothic tracery, as did the door. The wall had been specially designed to match the decor, with pointed arches like those in the triptych mirror, but the carpet had nothing to do with the Gothic style.

posed at the edges, for the careful housekeeper could rotate such a carpet regularly to ensure even wear.

Gervase Wheeler also recommended small patterns, for a large pattern, he held, destroyed the apparent size of the room. To his eye, the new designs of shaded flowers and other plant decorations were out of place on the floor: crushing living flowers under foot, even to inhale their odor, was a barbarity, but to tread on odorless worsted ones seemed senseless. For the hall he advocated Indian matting.

Loudon advised that stairs be carpeted. "Stair carpets give an air of great comfort and finish to a house; and a cottage should never be without one."[9]

PICTURES AND MIRRORS

One might expect Gothic interiors to be adorned with endless scenes of medieval ruins and romantic settings. Several artists produced such works, for example, Thomas Cole's *Voyage of Life* series, but these prints and paintings do not appear in any of our illustrations. Much more evident are family portraits and genre scenes.

Pictures were still hung rather high, undoubtedly because of the high ceilings.

Figure 82. Lilly Martin Spencer. *The Ward Children.* 1858. Oil on canvas, 92 in. × 68½ in. (2.34 m × 1.73 m). Collection of The Newark Museum, Newark, N.J.

Marcus Lawrence Ward, Sr., of Newark was Governor of New Jersey from 1866 to 1869. His four children appear with a superb Gothic chair, surely made for the family. (The chair reappears in Fig. 176.) The carpet is typical of the dark floral and fern designs shown at the English Crystal Palace Exhibition in 1851.

Figure 83. *Interior in a Simple Gothic Style. C.* 1850. Downing, *The Architecture of Country Houses*, p. 383; see Bibliography.

Although architecturally very comparable to Figure 78, the effect of this "simple" parlor is much less luxurious. Both figures illustrate oriel windows surmounted by Tudor arches, but the overmantel in the simple interior has a decorated Tudor arch rather than the Rathbones' full-pointed arch. Kenwood's furniture is decidedly Gothic, while that pictured here is debatably so. Though Downing has used oval picture frames in a Gothic interior, Kenwood's rectangular frame with spandrels at the top is more in keeping with the style.

The illustrations document a variety of hanging techniques: blind hanging, hanging with tassels and cords from a nail, or hanging with long cords from a picture molding or rod.

Loudon realized that the right place might not be found for each picture in a "moderately sized house," and therefore, "the best mode is to place them in a gallery built on purpose, if they are numerous and where justice may be done to them."[10]

Painted roller shades with appropriate designs gained vogue during the Gothic period. In 1844, the New York Transparent Window Shade Manufactory advertised "vignettes, arabesque scrolls and roseate centres, sculptural views, fancy sketches, Gothic landscape centres, Tintern Abbeys, moonlight views, the Euro and Episco Gothic and Corinthian designs—besides an almost innumerable number of cheaper patterns from one dollar and upwards." Such shades with varying designs remained popular until the 1880s. They were raised with strings until after the 1850s and 1860s, when spring mechanisms were invented.

TEXTILES

Loudon, Webster and Parkes, and Downing provide few references on the use of textiles.

Loudon does offer an illustration of what he calls a "Gothic Curtain and Cornice," but it is not evident to us what makes it particularly Gothic. The valance is of cloth and fringed in a vaguely Gothic arch, but there are no crockets or cusps such as one might have expected. Gothic curtains were likewise possible in even "the humblest description of Cottages": "A simple cottage curtain, opening in the center, may be formed by nailing two pieces of dimity, coloured calico, or printed cotton, to a square cornice, either painted, or covered with a piece of paper bordering; these curtains may be looped back by a piece of sash line or coloured cord, twisted around hooks fixed to the architrave, and will thus form a kind of Gothic drapery across the window."[11]

For villa or townhouse curtains, Downing suggests brocades, satin, or velvet in colors that harmonize with the upholstery. He recommends chintz for country curtains. Undercurtains were of lace or thin organdy.

There is very little reference to upholstery fabrics. Loudon praised a parlor

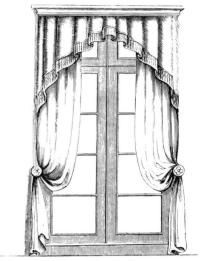

Gothic curtains and cornice from Loudon

Figure 84. Louis-Henry Mignot. *Lady in a Rocking Chair.* November 1846. Pencil on paper, 5¾ in. × 11³⁄₁₆ in. (15 cm × 28 cm). William Rockhill Nelson Gallery of Art, Kansas City, Mo.

Two separate scenes fill a sketch labeled "New York." On the right is a simple Gothic fireplace insert with the shelf above arranged symmetrically with a clock, candlesticks, and paper fans. Such unframed drawings pinned or glued to the wall appear occasionally in bedroom pictures. The other part of the sketch shows a larger fireplace with formal Federal details. The girl sits in an excellent example of a Boston rocker, the chest is typical of the Victorian Classical style, and the carpet has a large pattern appropriate to the 1840s.

Gothic parlor stove

set done in damask, while Downing was quick to recommend leather (usually tufted) for library and dining room chairs. For sofas he preferred figured damask, worsted, or silk. Horsehair is notably absent.

Cotton fabrics with Gothic designs appeared about 1830.

WALL TREATMENT, ARCHITECTURAL DETAILS, AND CEILINGS

Predictably, Downing's architectural details emphasized perpendicular lines, pointed arches, and deep moldings. He preferred pitched ceilings with the beams exposed. He praised the shadows cast by bold moldings: "Those who love shadow, and the sentiment of antiquity and repose, will find most pleasure in the quiet tone which prevails in the Gothic style."[12]

Fireplaces and the iron fittings manufactured to insert into earlier fireplaces carried Gothic motifs of varying degree. Among the most spectacular Gothic pieces of any genre were the cathedral-like iron stoves.

Downing offered the homeowner several options for wall treatment. Wallpaper had the virtue of being economical and easy to apply. Curiously, he was

Figure 85. A. Mayer. *City Bedroom. C.* 1860. Water color. Courtesy, Museum of Fine Arts, Boston, Mass. (M. and M. Karolik Collection).

Mayer resided in America between 1850 and 1867, and since he spent most of his time in Brooklyn, it is likely that this bedroom was there. The bed is a simple, veneered, Victorian Classical–style sleigh bed, but the wash stand and dresser with mirror are typical of the mass-produced bedroom sets that Downing promoted in 1850. Like the cuts he illustrated, these pieces were painted and "ornamented" with floral decorations. Unusual items in the room are the folding chair and the metal stand beneath the window.

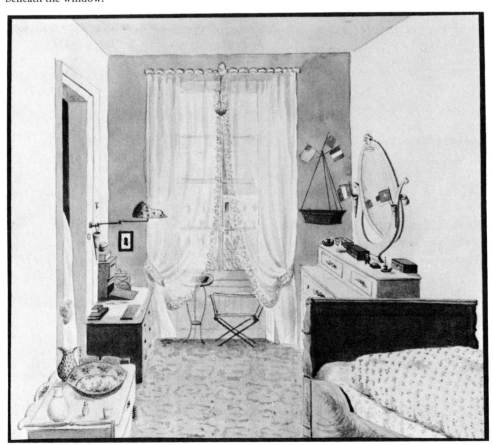

Figure 86. Erastus Salisbury Field. *The Smith Family. C.* 1865. Oil on canvas, 36 in. × 47 in. (91 cm × 119 cm). Abby Aldrich Rockefeller Folk Art Collection, Williamsburg, Va.

Gathered in their parlor, the Smith family was typical of the mid-century middle class at home. Such valances in the Renaissance style with their cords and tassels were often found in homes of great wealth, but there they would have surmounted heavier drapes not edged with lace. The sofa on which Mrs. Smith is seated is a basic rococo shape, with an unusual decoration of C scrolls. Such large floral patterns flowed in great quantity from American carpet factories. The walls.are unusually bare, even for the 1860s.

critical of wallpaper imitative of church windows or carved work, preferring a simple flocked paper made to imitate woven silk or worsted. Another acceptable alternative was a fresco paper that would "give the same effect as if the wall were formed into compartments of panels, with suitable cornices and moldings."[13]

For painting walls, two options were available: distemper and oil paints. Distemper was a water-base preparation that had the virtues of quick application, no smell, economy (it cost about one-third the price of oil paints), and a softness and delicacy of color rarely seen with oils. Its disadvantages were that the distempered wall could not be washed and it stained easily. Downing described oil paints as "entirely satisfactory," even though the application was tedious and the odor considerable.

Suggestion for a Gothic wall panel, 1892

Downing's more elaborate designs show coffered ceilings, often with a wooden or cast plaster boss at the center. Somewhat simpler (and less Gothic) interiors indicate the use of plain plaster ceilings.

LIGHTING

Gothic hall lamp

Neither Loudon, Downing, nor Webster and Parkes say anything about appropriate Gothic lighting, but the *Encyclopaedia* illustrates a hall lamp with Gothic details. From the book's discussion of lighting, it is clear that the householder had a wide choice of lighting techniques. Astral lamps continued to be popular. Lamps for camphene or burning fluid were still made, candles remained important, but they were not the usual means of lighting among the fashionable. Gas was available in the urban areas, although kerosene lamps were not developed until the 1850s. In the country, rushes and grease lamps continued to be used.

Although not prominent in the style books or our illustrations, Gothic lighting fixtures were produced in some number. They were decorated with Gothic arches, trefoils, cusps, and crockets for use with candles, oil, and later, kerosene. Producers included Cornelius and Company of Philadelphia, William Shaw of Boston, and Clark Coit and Cargill of New York City.

COLOR

Downing warned that inattention to color could ruin an otherwise successful decor. The first rule of color is that for each room a dominant color must be chosen to act as a unifying element. Next, each room has two principal areas of color, the carpet and the walls, and the colors of both "should harmonize—that is to say, if they do not agree in color, they should be selected so as to contrast harmoniously." A successful color scheme could be ensured by avoiding common problems. First, avoid a predominant bright and intense color on walls or floor, for it may overpower all the rest. Second, pale and deep colors should be mixed with careful regard to their degrees and strength; and third, there must be "media" that "united and harmonize an assemblage of bright colors." The latter rule he explained by saying that "a confusion of parts of equal strength [of color] should always be avoided."[14]

Downing's preferences for the colors to be placed in particular rooms are summarized in the listings at the top of page 173.[15]

Downing was careful to stipulate that woodwork, if painted, should always harmonize with the prevailing tone of a room. It should never be the same color as the predominant tone, and only in a city or villa drawing room should it ever be white.

Gervase Wheeler specified for the wall of a library a ground of rich, deep blue, with a painted diaper pattern in brilliant red or orange. For dining rooms, he recommended sage green or a color that went by the name of "fallen leaf," a shade of brown. Wheeler preferred woodwork lighter than the color of the wall.[16]

Both Downing and Wheeler favored white ceilings for a papered room, but an alternative was to paint them in delicate, neutral colors.

Room	General spirit of room	Colors recommended
HALL	cool, sober, simple	gray, stone color, drab
DRAWING ROOM	beautiful, elegant, light, cheerful	generally light colors Town: white relieved with gilt Country: ashes of pearl, pearl gray, pale apple green; gilt should be used sparingly in the country
DINING ROOM	rich, warm	stronger colors with more contrast than in drawing room, yet overall the effect to be simpler; in general, substantial without being clumsy
LIBRARY	quiet, grave	fawn or another neutral tint for walls; woodwork dark oak or other wood painted and grained to resemble oak
BOUDOIR	delicate, feminine	no colors specified
BEDROOM	variable from light and cheerful to simple and chaste	variable

ACCESSORIES

The appearance of the étagère or whatnot made almost mandatory the accumulation of items to put on it, and Loudon urged even the humble cottager to collect: "There will be room for other ornaments of a smaller description than busts and sculpture, such as curious stones, spars, ores, or other minerals, or coins, and objects of art and antiquity. The public taste for articles of this description has improved in an astonishing degree within the last twenty years."[17]

Loudon also advocated books as decoration, and added that "every cottager ought to possess a general encyclopaedia and to take in a newspaper."[18] During this period, Harper & Brothers brought out a new series of inexpensive, popular, and instructive titles, binding them in black with a gold-tooled Gothic arch and crocket on the spine.

Wheeler provided a complete account of necessary accessories, for these were no trifling matter. In the hall we find brackets for flower vases, a thermometer, and a weather glass (barometer), and "a cabinet of dried grasses or other little museum curiosities." For the drawing room one needed hanging baskets of flowers and a statue of the little "Fisher Boy," "so truthfully suggestive of quiet home life." Wheeler also suggested Wedgwood vases in floral shapes, available at Collamore's on Broadway in New York City. The library received special attention, for it was "the magnetic gathering place of a thousand tasteful trifles—relics, specimens, objects of art, curiosities, suggestive nothings —which serve to make talk independent of politics, dress, fashions, and scandal."[19]

The illustrations show the use of a considerable number of decorative items by no means confined to an étagère. Small vases of flowers, items kept under bell jars, dishes of fruit, and small pieces of china added notes of interest but did not yet appear in profusion.

Gothic pitcher

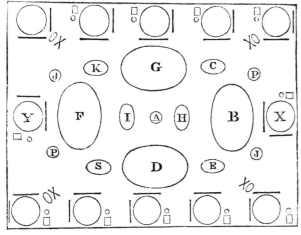

A, Castors.	F, Scolloped Oysters.	K. Parsnips.
B, Boiled Turkey.	G, Boiled Ham.	PP, Pickles.
C, Oyster Sauce.	H, Potatoes.	JJ, Jelly.
D, Roasted Ducks.	I, Turnips.	X, Host.
E, Gravy for Ducks.	S, Celery.	Y, Hostess.

Mrs. Beecher's dinner table

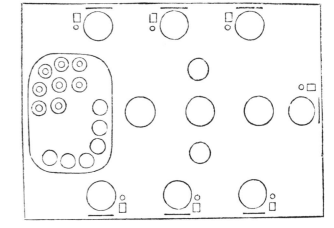

Mrs. Beecher's tea table

Table Arrangement. In her *Domestic Receipt Book,* Catherine Beecher provided diagrams for setting a dinner table and a tea table. These arrangements seem typical of all styles (Gothic, Elizabethan, rococo, and Renaissance) from the 1840s to the 1870s. The printed caption of the dinner table diagram shows the placement of serving dishes, while her text specifies that each place should be furnished with a knife (parallel to the edge of the table), a fork (at right angles to the edge), a napkin (the square), and a cup plate (the small circle). Cup plates held one's cup while one drank out of the saucer. Drinking from a saucer, quite acceptable in the 1840s and early 1850s, was out of style in the most fashionable homes by the beginning of the Civil War.

At each place on the tea table was a knife (parallel to the edge of the table), a napkin (square), and a cup plate (circle). On the waiter or tray were tea cups and saucers, sugar bowl, slop bowl, creamer, and two or three containers for tea, coffee, or water.

The Elizabethan Style

Although contemporary with the Gothic, the Elizabethan style was more limited in its impact. Downing offers it as a general style, and it fostered considerable furniture, yet there were comparatively few consistent interiors. Downing thought this seventeenth-century style would have a special appeal for immigrants (it would remind them of familiar interiors in Europe) and for collectors. One might not furnish a whole house in the style, but collectors could "fit up a library, or some one or two rooms in their house, in this style, and will find more pleasure in hunting for old Elizabethan chairs than in the possession of the finest and most faultless reproductions of any modern school of art."[20]

Downing offered a design for a collector's library, a design he adapted directly from H. W. and A. Arrowsmith's *The House Decorator and Painter's Guide* (London, 1840). Downing furnished the Arrowsmiths' library and changed only two details: his central doorway was flanked by spiral columns, and double spiral columns also stood at either side of the fireplace. The Arrowsmiths had introduced stop fluted pilasters by the door and a cabochon at the fireplace. Downing's changes created more unity between the architecture and the design of the furniture, and undoubtedly revealed what he thought the essence of the Elizabethan style to be.

Figure 87. E. L. Henry. *Family in Victorian Interior*. 1872. Oil on wood panel, 11¼ in. × 8½ in. (28 cm × 23 cm). Courtesy of Mr. Ira Spanierman.

The dining room chairs and small stool in the foreground are good examples of Elizabethan revival with their rich upholstery and deep fringe. The wall covering and mantel are in the Renaissance style, while the folding screen is Chinese; the mistress of this fashionable house is seated on a Turkish frame chair of the kind popular in the late 1860s. Henry has documented typical glasses of the period and a splendid epergne. With an unabashed Victorian love of duplication, the family has placed an Oriental rug on a wall-to-wall carpet.

Elizabethan cottage bedroom set by
Hennessey, $36

Hennessey's more expensive Elizabethan
bedroom set, $70–100

In general, there is little evidence that many Americans followed such Elizabethan designs in furnishing a house or even a room, yet sporadic examples do appear throughout the nineteenth century.

FURNITURE

What passed for the Elizabethan style in American furniture of the nineteenth century was in fact derived from baroque furniture of the English Restoration of 1660 to 1688. It was far from true Elizabethan furniture. The salient characteristic of this "Elizabethan" revival was spiral or spool turning. Such turnings formed the posts and legs of chairs, the legs of smaller tables, towel racks, and spool beds, the last being one of the most characteristic pieces of the period. Turnings were the only distinctive feature of the Elizabethan bedroom

Opposite:
above: Figure 88. H. W. and A. Arrowsmith. *Design for a Library. The House Decorator and Painter's Guide* (London, 1840).

below: Figure 89. A. J. Downing. *Library in the Elizabethan Style. The Architecture of Country Houses* (New York, 1850), Fig. 185.

Downing furnished the Arrowsmiths' design for an Elizabethan library. The three chairs have spiral turnings with upholstered seats and backs, and the center rectangular table has a heavy fringed cover. The carpet is too indistinct to suggest a characteristic Elizabethan pattern, while the ceiling follows the Arrowsmiths' design exactly—even to the inclusion of coats of arms. Downing has also included the same row of portraits atop the bookcases, but he has substituted turnings in the architectural work.

Figure 90. Samuel Bell Waugh (1814–1885). *Mrs. Stiles and Grandchild.* 1843. Oil on canvas, 35 in. × 27 in. (89 cm × 69 cm). The Helen Foresman Spencer Museum of Art, University of Kansas, Lawrence.

Mrs. Stiles, who was probably a resident of Philadelphia, sat in a chair with pronounced spiral turnings similar to those found in a design published by Downing seven years after this picture was painted. The canvas provides a good lesson in color preferences, revealing a great partiality for reds. Her square table, rather than a round one more common in the Victorian Classical style, was covered with a gold cloth that fell to the floor. Her foot rested on a thick red cushion with gold tassels at each corner, and the carpet with its large hexagon pattern was red and gold with touches of green. The walls were a reddish brown and the drapery almost crimson.

set that Downing suggested for a simple cottage. Such a set cost only $36 and was available in black walnut, maple, or birch from Hennessey of Boston. Another bedroom set for the more luxurious cottage featured applied spool turnings at the corners of pieces finished in natural dark wood or painted with vignettes on a drab ground. Hennessey's more expensive set also had marble tops and ran from $70 to $100.

Downing said that Elizabethan furniture was generally found in libraries, drawing rooms, and bedrooms, and that it was particularly appropriate in a Gothic interior. "Though not strictly in keeping with that style, yet its intricate picturesqueness and constant use in this way have given it a kind of right there which it has not intrinsically by its origin. It is so much richer and more domestic than strictly Gothic furniture."[21] Downing showed three Elizabethan chairs in his Gothic interior from Kenwood. Elizabethan chairs were far from exact copies of the Charles II originals. The backs were higher, and Downing suggested an upholstery of velvet and "rich stuffs" for the central back panel, with fringe bordering the seat. Comfort was more important than authenticity.

ARCHITECTURAL DETAILS AND CEILINGS

Gervase Wheeler was probably the first writer to devote special attention to the aesthetics of hardware furnishings. Porcelain was especially recommended because it was easily cleaned. Bell pulls, tiebacks, door knobs, ends for speaking tubes, escutcheon plates, and coat hooks were all usefully made of porcelain and available from Baldwin and Many of New York City. Porcelain had the additional advantage of being easily decorated to follow particular styles; thus,

Figure 91. Artist unknown. *Library, Residence of George B. Chase, Boston, Massachusetts.* 1876. Charles Wyllys Elliott, *Book of American Interiors,* p. 91; see Bibliography.

This library, decorated by Ware and Van Brunt, documents the persistence of the Elizabethan style into the 1870s. Elliott described the black walnut center table as a *tour de force* of the Elizabethan style, as were the bookcases, mantel, and ceiling. The walls were dark, covered with a diaper-pattern leather paper in brown, black, and gold. The carpet was two shades of crimson, as was the upholstery, while the curtains were a harmonious olive brown. Seven paintings are modern landscapes, but over the mantel is a large portrait of Sir William Pepperell, probably the one done by John Smibert in 1747.

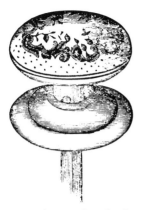

Elizabethan door knob

one could hardly do better than a door knob "called by the trade 'the Elizabethan pattern,' I presume, from a resemblance in its decoration, to the detail of that period." The center of the knob was white, with the outer edge buff and the figure in maroon. The maroon was in turn powdered with gold, making the knob well suited to a "dark or black walnut door."[22]

Figure 92. *Hall, Residence of Mr. and Mrs. James Lancaster Morgan, 7 Pierpont Street, Brooklyn, New York.* 1880–1882. Museum of the City of New York.

James Lancaster Morgan had become a millionaire in chemical manufacturing. The Elizabethan chairs with their rich upholstery and fringe match the spiral turned pedestals flanking the door. The Elizabethan theme is almost swamped by the Turkish portières and the Renaissance hat stand. Portières were often advocated as an alternative to sliding doors, but here the Morgans have used them in addition to the sliding doors. The weighted apparatus for raising and lowering the gas chandelier appears clearly, and the chandelier, like the ceiling and wall, carries classical decorations.

10

The Rococo Style

1850–1870

ALONG with Gothic architecture and its characteristic interior appeared the Italian villa and its frequent counterpart—the rococo interior. Downing realized that not everyone wanted a Gothic house, and he therefore gave several plans and elevations for Italian villas, a style he thought blended well into the American landscape.

Italy had gained a new romantic image in the American mind. Through novels such as Helen Hunt Jackson's *Ramona* and Nathaniel Hawthorne's *The Marble Faun*, the Italian landscape became almost as familiar to readers of American novels as it was to American artists and sculptors, who began to see a year's study in Italy as a minimal prerequisite to creativity. The Italian villa acquired any needed propriety when Queen Victoria and Prince Albert constructed Osborn House on the Isle of Wight in that style.

The villa is characterized by relatively flat roofs supported on deeply projecting brackets, arcaded windows and verandas, and most important, a campanile rising taller than the surrounding roofs, thus, as Downing put it, "bringing all into unity and giving picturesqueness."[1]

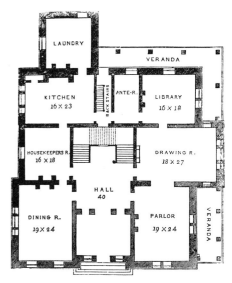

Floor plan of the King villa

Tuscan or Italian villa by Richard Upjohn, built for Edward King, Newport, R.I., 1845

Figure 93. George Platt. *Parlor Design.* 1840–1850. Ink and wash on paper,
7 in. × 12½ in. (18 cm × 33 cm). Collection of Mr. Russell Lynes.

Platt's drawing, possibly for his own rooms at 49 Seventh Avenue in New York City,
shows a rococo interior by one of America's first professional decorators. The furniture was consistently expensive rococo, with many of the pieces probably designed by
Platt himself. Note particularly the firescreen (standing nowhere near a fireplace)
and the two round tables at either end of the sofa. The walls have received an elegant
treatment with papers or painting creating a sense of framed panels. There is a dado
and frieze design, but the ceilings are plain except for the plaster rosettes. At each
window is a simple fringed valance with glass curtains beneath. Larger pictures were
consistently hung over smaller ones.

The Tuscan villa was a much more expensive dwelling than the Gothic
cottage (Downing estimated the cheapest at $3,800), and such lavish designs
appealed to the new captains of industry, many of whose factories were mass
producing the decorative items to furnish such houses. O. S. Fowler, the noted
phrenologist, commented that just as "beautiful birds build tasty nests," so too
"a superior man (builds) a superb villa."[2]

Although Italian traditions supplied the exteriors, French models inspired
the interiors. Unlike the somewhat limited impact of the Elizabethan style, the
rococo decor was widely popular, with manifestations in virtually every form of
interior decorative art.

The key characteristic of rococo interior decoration is the S curve or serpentine line, which permeates all decorative elements in the room from the cabriole
legs and curving backs of the furniture to the gold picture frames, the valances
over the curtains, and curving lines of a fireplace and mantel. It is carried to the
ceiling in the loose curves of the plaster work and, to a degree, also reflected in
the loose floral designs of the carpets.

The first interior decorators had begun to appear in urban centers. George

Platt (1812–1873) of New York City was one of the pioneers. In the early 1840s, he began listing his occupation in the city directory as "decorations," and by 1850, Downing described him as "the most popular interior decorator in the country." Downing recommended the advice of such a decorator for furnishing "villas of considerable importance."[3]

FURNITURE

American cabinetmakers were already producing rococo furniture when Downing published his *Architecture of Country Houses* in 1850, and the popularity of the style increased greatly after its prominent exhibition at the Crystal Palace Exposition in London in 1851 and, subsequently, the smaller Crystal Palace Exposition in New York in 1853. James Watson Williams, a Utica lawyer, built a Tuscan villa in 1850 and furnished it with rococo furniture. He owned several books by Downing and the catalogues of both Crystal Palace exhibitions.[4]

Downing promoted the rococo revival in his book, but he was not always clear what he was reviving. He spoke of several styles of "modern" French furniture and offered drawings of pieces he liked. Curiously, those he termed "Louis XIV" are most clearly derived from real Louis XV examples, and the problems of Downing's labels aside, it was the Louis XV fashion that provided the basic rococo style.

Although it may appear delicate and fragile, furniture in this style is often extremely strong because of its construction. John Henry Belter of New York City, who gained several patents for his techniques, layered an average of six to eight veneers together, with each layer set at right angles to the grain of the surrounding layers. Belter was the leader in creating expensive versions of the style, but other names were also prominent: in New York City, Joseph Meeks, Charles A. Baudoine, Gustav Herter, and Alexander Roux (Downing advised buying from Roux); in Philadelphia, George Henkels, Daniel Pabst, and Gottlieb Vollmer; in Boston, Augustus Eliaers; and in New Orleans, François Seignouret and Prudent Mallard.

Rococo parlor set

In an elaborate profusion of intricate decoration, the rococo offered expensive-looking (and expensive) furniture, which appealed to the socially and financially established and hopeful alike. In 1852, Baudoine sold James Watson Williams a rococo rosewood parlor set including two tête-à-têtes, four arm chairs, and four side chairs. The price was $340. Williams also paid Baudoine $160 for a pair of rococo card tables. Mr. Williams and his wife looked two years to find the right étagère, a relatively new furniture form that was finding a place in every proper parlor. In 1853, he could report prices ranging from $65 to $500, and two years later he bought one in rosewood from Julius Dessoir of New York City for $150.

Mahogany remained in vogue, but it had become expensive and difficult to acquire, as heavy harvesting of the forests of Santo Domingo had depleted the

Figure 94. A. J. Volck. *Entertaining in the Parlor.* 1862–1863, Pen and pencil drawing, 5½ in. × 8⅜ in. (15 cm × 20 cm). Maryland Historical Society, Baltimore.

One of the few pictures to illustrate a room furnished completely in the rococo style, this drawing shows an elegant Baltimore parlor during the Civil War. The furniture, decorations, and even the sewing machine emphasize the rococo S and C scrolls. Rococo motifs are especially strong in the low table at the right, which supports a bust of Jefferson Davis, photograph albums, a Bible, alabaster doves perched on an urn (modeled after a Pompeian mosaic), and a shell vase complete with writhing serpent. Through the arch is a picture gallery with a high cove ceiling.

Figure 95. *Parlor, Residence of Henry Wadsworth Longfellow. 105 Brattle Street, Cambridge, Massachusetts. C.* 1868–1870. Society for the Preservation of New England Antiquities, Boston, Mass.

Originally designed by Peter Harrison in 1759 for John Vassall, and later owned by the Craigie family, this house eventually passed to Henry Wadsworth Longfellow, who created the mixture of eighteenth- and nineteenth-century styles. In the corner is a Chippendale corner chair and two French Louis XVI arm chairs that he bought from Mrs. Craigie in 1841. The rococo furniture he added included the large arm chair and the center table with the marble top. The Satsuma vase imparts a modest Oriental note to the room. The lattice grill in the fireplace is not a fireboard but a grill for circulating hot air. Gas was introduced into the house in 1856, at which time Longfellow bought the fine rococo chandelier.

supply. A fashionable substitute, which some thought even better, was rosewood. White or colored marbles were frequently used as table tops.

Even more than Gothic, the rococo style gave a look of lightness and grace in sharp contrast to the often ponderous Victorian Classical style that had preceded it. Downing referred to a "rage for very light and fancifully carved chairs for drawing rooms," and the balloon back chair was clearly an example of such furniture, although it was equally at home in the bedroom. Other light furniture included papier-mâché chairs imported from England.

The popularity of elaborate rococo furniture waned at the end of the Civil

War, as is evident by the bankruptcy of the previously flourishing Belter firm in 1867. Not only did the depression following the Civil War restrict the funds available to buy such expensive furniture, but new styles were appearing to catch the eye of those who might have afforded such expensive work. But not all rococo furniture was the expensive production of prominent cabinetmakers. For several decades, other manufacturers mass produced the rococo in large quantities, usually in walnut upholstered in black horsehair.

FLOOR COVERINGS

Period guides say nothing about appropriate rococo patterns, but paintings and photographs do offer documentation of designs and the general use of wall-to-wall carpeting. Floral or geometric-floral designs remained popular in the

Figure 96. Matthew Wilson. *Portrait of Horace Fairbanks.* 1873. Oil on canvas, 96 in. × 71 in. (2.44 m × 1.80 m). The St. Johnsbury Atheneum, St. Johnsbury, Vt.

Horace Fairbanks was Governor of Vermont (1876–1878) and president of the Fairbanks Scale Company. His great wealth was reflected in the decor of a room in which there is furniture from several periods in addition to the notable rococo chair on which he sat. The wall bookcase is Gothic, the console table and the desk combine elements of Elizabethan and Francis I, and the footed dish is Pompeian. The floor is an excellent example of parquet work, and like many, the tall curtains flow out onto the floor.

Figure 97. A. D. Shattuck. *The Shattuck Family.* 1865. Oil on board, 20 in. ×
16 in. (51 cm × 41 cm). Collection of Mr. and Mrs. Eugene Emigh.

At the summer house of the Shattuck family in Great Barrington, Massachusetts, Mrs.
Jesse Shattuck, mother of the artist, holds her grandson, William Shattuck, on her
lap. The kneeling figure is Marian Colman Shattuck, who holds a goldfish bowl to
delight her son. The light coloring of the walls and the lacy curtains give an open,
summery effect to the room. Mrs. Shattuck is seated on a balloon back chair of the
sort produced in great number. The **S** curves of the chair are repeated in the table
at the right with its cross legs. The diamond pattern of the carpet is red, blue, and
grayish-green. On the wall is Sir John Everett Millais's popular print of *The Hugue-
not* (1851) and an unidentified *Madonna and Child* still in the possession of the
family.

1850s. Three pictures from the mid-1860s reveal a preference for carpets with
medium or small diamond or square patterns. By the 1870s, floral designs had
regained popularity. In Governor Fairbanks's study (Fig. 96), no carpet con-
ceals the elaborate parquet floor. Such floors gained a widespread popularity
beginning in the 1870s.

Kidderminster carpet design shown at
the Crystal Palace Exhibition, 1851

PICTURES AND MIRRORS

In 1850, Downing gave the following advice on art in the home: "There are few persons living in cottages who can afford to indulge a taste for pictures. But there are, nevertheless, many in this country, who can afford engravings or plaster casts, to decorate at least one room in the house. Nothing gives an air of greater refinement to a cottage than good prints or engravings hung upon its parlor walls. In selecting these, avoid the trashy, colored show-prints of the ordinary kind, and choose engravings or lithographs, after pictures of celebrity by ancient or modern masters. . . . Next to prints of this kind, medallion casts, in plaster, of celebrated antique subjects—one or two feet in diameter—are fine objects to hang upon the walls, and may now be had in the cities for a small sum."[5]

Downing mentioned Goupel, Vibert & Company in New York City as a good source for acceptable domestic art.

The illustrations document the typical use of pictures. Both oils and prints appear, with landscapes and religious scenes dominant. Portraits are virtually

Figure 98. Artist unknown. *The Thames Children of Selma, Alabama. C.* 1850. Oil on canvas. Abby Aldrich Rockefeller Folk Art Collection, Williamsburg, Va.

The anonymous artist produced a posthumous portrait of three children now thought to have died in an epidemic about 1845, and incidentally documented the appearance of the rococo style in Alabama by mid-century. Much of the rococo furniture in the South was imported from France for the great plantation houses. The chair follows Louis XV models rather closely, but the thin-legged table is an adaptation. The Brussels carpet with its floral and fern motif is in sharp contrast to the plain walls, but the draperies have vine decoration as well as an unusual fringe.

Figure 99. Artist unknown. *The Carryl Children of Salisbury Centre, New York.*
C. 1850. Oil on canvas, 47¼ in. × 38 in. (119 cm × 97 cm). Fruitlands
Museum, Harvard, Mass.

The most notable piece of rococo furniture is the marble-topped pier table at the
left surmounted by a plain, tall mirror. The sofa and the arm chair are in the same
style, but do not appear to be so elaborate. The two square stools with needlepoint
covers, like the marble fireplace, date from the 1820s or 1830s. The sculptures on
pedestals are religious, probably both depictions of Christ. Such figures, like those
Downing recommended, might be either plaster or marble. Supporting the figures
are brackets based on medieval prototypes. The manner in which the picture behind
the vase is hung is most unusual in any era, and the sofa is likewise placed diagonally
in the corner. The children are playing on an oilcloth set atop a carpet with a strong,
radiating geometrical pattern.

absent. In general, walls display fewer pictures than will be found in the following decades. Frames for both pictures and mirrors come in considerable variety,
from those that reflect the sinuous curves of rococo design to those with

Figure 100. Erastus Salisbury Field. *The Family of Deacon Wilson Brainerd.* 1858. Oil on paper on linen, 35¾ in. × 43¼ in. (91 cm × 109 cm). Old Sturbridge Village, Sturbridge, Mass.

Deacon Brainerd and his family lived in rural Palmer, Massachusetts. Field was not quite photographic in portraying the furniture, but he does document the presence of a carved yet simple rococo parlor set. No other hints of the rococo style appear in the room. The carpet is a characteristic factory product, and the dark wall is plain, relieved only by a single picture hung from tasseled cords. The thin curtains are embroidered with a running floral design.

straight, simple sides. Frames with rounded arch tops appear on both prints and mirrors in the 1860s. Mirrors were common, but not always inexpensive. Large mirrors with highly ornamented frames could cost as much as $270. Pictures and mirrors were usually blind hung at eye level.

TEXTILES

Samuel Sloan, in his *Homestead Architecture* (1861), offers suggestions for the upholstery of rococo furniture and for appropriate draperies. Wool rep was recommended for library and dining room upholstery and draperies, while silk rep, either plain, ribbed, or striped, was recommended for parlors. Haircloth was a standard familiar covering, but an interesting variation could be found in colored haircloth worked into stripes or diamond figures.

There is a general uniformity in the draperies of the more fashionable houses, where they are heavy and elegant. In Figures 96 and 99, the draperies are cut so full and long that they spread over the floor. Several pictures show valances with rococo motifs, and many have tassels hanging from the center of the valance and on the cords holding the draperies to the tiebacks. Glass curtains were sometimes hung under heavier draperies.

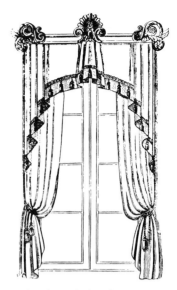

Loudon's design for rococo curtains with gilt cornice

WALL TREATMENT

In general, walls were relatively plain. The Maryland interior of 1862 (Fig. 94) reveals a subtle vertical stripe, and the wall is divided into elongated vertical panels, but whether by moldings or painted or papered designs is not clear. Generally, the walls were covered with a solid color, and with the exception of the Shattuck house (Fig. 97), they had a flat surface.

ARCHITECTURAL DETAILS AND CEILINGS

Few houses had the elaborate and expensive ceiling treatment seen in the gallery room of the Maryland house (Fig. 94). Most had flat ceilings with relatively simple ceiling moldings. The Oertel picture (Plate 19) shows an elaborate rosette in the center of the ceiling. Door frames sometimes received rather ornate treatment (as in the Baltimore house), but it was in mantels and fireplaces that rococo details were most obvious.

Rococo reflecting grate

LIGHTING

Rococo designs are evident in the gas chandeliers shown in several illustrations in this chapter. While gas was available to the urban dweller, those in the country relied on earlier forms of lighting, many of which continued to be popular in the cities too. The Argand whale oil lamp was widely used in its astral lamp form, and a stream of patents tried to assure the public that lamps for burning fluid or camphene were safe. Kerosene was discovered in 1854, and the opening of the Pennsylvania oil fields later in the decade brought a new standard lighting fluid to the entire nation. In time new kerosene lamps would carry rococo decorations, too. In the humbler homes candles, rush candles, and lard oil lamps were still used.

COLOR

Samuel Sloan, in his *Homestead Architecture*, suggested draperies of a color different from the walls, carpets, or upholstery, "as a good contrast is more pleas-

Candelabra   Parker's sinumbra lamp

ing than sameness, even though the material be rich."[6] In general, the walls are rather dark, and the Carryl children (Fig. 99) had a ceiling as dark as the wall. Several pictures in this chapter illustrate door or ceiling moldings painted a lighter color than the surrounding wall area.

ACCESSORIES

The rococo style saw a relatively restrained use of decorative accessories, with the high Victorian profusion still to come.

In general, the same objects and arrangements described under the Gothic period apply to the rococo style. Accessories that carried strong rococo themes are the following:

Ceramics. China companies produced numerous patterns with rococo motifs, swirling floral designs, or intertwined grapes and vine leaves. Likewise, the shape of some china produced during this period had the sinuous edge of the **C** or **S** curve.

Glass. American glass houses produced a number of pressed designs that carried rococo themes on virtually every article of table glass.

Silver. As always, silver was a medium quick to reflect new designs. Expensive and elaborate pieces carried heavy repoussé work in grape and vine patterns. Manufacturers of silver plate offered simplified versions of these designs at much-reduced prices.

Terra cotta flowers

11

The Eclectic Decades

1865–1895

B Y the Civil War, the concept of one *right* look was dead. The introduction of the Gothic, Elizabethan, and rococo periods had followed each other in rapid sequence, and the three more or less coexisted during the 1850s, with writers generally proclaiming the merits of each rather than opting for one at the expense of the other two. The 1860s and 1870s saw the addition of many new styles and the disappearance of none. The last decades of the century brought still more new styles and more refined variations of those begun earlier.

The Renaissance style, which had begun before the Civil War, remained popular to the end of the century, although it was considered an elaborate style especially appropriate to the homes of the very rich. Later, decorators would make fine distinctions between German and Italian Renaissance. A wealth of French revivals began to fill the pages of magazines on decoration, and the bewildered reader could have spent hours trying to distinguish the Francis I, Henri II, Henri IV, Louis XIII, Louis XIV, Louis XV, and Louis XVI styles, all of which were highly recommended. In the 1890s, there was even a revival of the Empire style. English styles, too, gained a new vogue in revival forms as writers commended the design merits of Elizabethan, Jacobean, Queen Anne, Chippendale, Sheraton, Adam, and Hepplewhite. In many ways, the Colonial or "Centennial" Revival is difficult to distinguish from a revival of late English styles.

In the 1870s, American and English decorators looked increasingly to exotic sources for inspiration, and Japanese, Chinese, Turkish, Moorish, and Persian influences appeared. The Aesthetic Movement in England, with its designs by William Morris and Lewis F. Day, had a distinct following in America, and Charles Eastlake himself inspired a separate look. Several exotic forms were eagerly proposed by their creators but never caught on. Egyptian and Pompeian revivals did find some following, but the advocate of the Aztec revival found few copying his designs. An American chauvinism appeared countering the importation of foreign styles. "Why not," one writer in *The Decorator and*

Furnisher asked, "formulate a style based on the American Indian?" He sketched appropriate furniture and at least one interior, but the Wigwam style, as he called it, had no followers we could find.

The most obvious impact of these diverse styles was in the furniture, but each movement usually had appropriate wallpapers, ceiling designs, color schemes, and accessories that could provide an integrated interior if that was what the householder chose. Often, he or she did not.

Many details of these eclectic designs were drawn from books like Owen Jones's *Grammar of Ornament*. First published in London in 1856, it remained in print until 1910. In 112 color plates, Jones described stylistic characteristics of 19 cultures, many of which, perhaps not coincidentally, emerged as prominent or abortive interior designs late in the century. The Elizabethan, Renaissance, Greek, Chinese, Persian, Moorish, Turkish, and Arabian styles appeared early in the eclectic period, and all are represented in Jones's book. Medieval and Celtic ornament found a place in late Gothic, while Egyptian, Indian, Pompeian, and Hindu had more limited impact. Late in the century, designers saw unrealized potential in Roman and Byzantine styles, and Jones's "savage" ornaments were perhaps the origin of the proposed American Wigwam style.

Advice on decoration was readily available for those who sought it out. Samuel Sloan's *Homestead Architecture* (1861) had offered general suggestions for furniture and interior decoration, but like many writers, Sloan's concern was primarily architectural. Catherine E. Beecher and her novelist sister Harriet Beecher Stowe published their *American Woman's Home* in which they provided suggestions for decoration, in 1869. Charles Eastlake's *Hints on Household Taste*, published in England in 1868, was reprinted in New York in 1872. His book first presented American readers with what must be called a philosophy of the interior. Furniture, papers, floors, and all decorative elements were to be selected according to the principles of honesty and strong construction.

The years 1877 and 1878 saw the publication of several major books on decoration. *The House Beautiful: Essays on Beds and Tables, Stools and Candlesticks* was a reworking of articles Clarence Cook had published in *Scribner's Monthly*. Influenced by Eastlake and the Aesthetic Movement, Cook offered moral advice on honesty of furniture and simplicity of life, as well as illustrating furnishings in all styles.

Such diversity was not evident in a little book reprinted by a Philadelphia publisher in 1877, *Suggestions for House Decoration in Painting, Woodwork, and Furniture* by Rhoda and Agnes Garrett. Published in London the previous year, the authors criticized current decoration and praised antique furniture, a subject of obvious appeal to those who had visited the Philadelphia Centennial Exposition. The Garretts' praise of the Queen Anne style surely gave the Colonial Revival a strong initial push.

Modern Dwellings in Town and Country by H. Hudson Holly was ready for Christmas giving in 1878. Holly fashioned his book out of articles he had written for *Harper's Magazine*, and his text concerned both the architecture of a house and its interior decoration. Some of Holly's suggestions were labeled "Anglo-Japanese" or "Neo-Jacobean," but most of his illustrations were drawn from Eastlake or the Aesthetic Movement.

Harper & Brothers published another entry in the market in 1878: Harriet Prescott Spofford's *Art Decoration Applied to Furniture*. Like Holly, she extracted her text from her *Harper's Bazar* articles. Unlike the other authors with whom she competed, she offered distinct chapters on a number of styles: Gothic, Renaissance, Elizabethan, Jacobean, Louis XIV, Louis XV, Louis XVI, Pompeian, Empire, Moorish, Queen Anne, Oriental, and Eastlake. She also included chapters on each room in the house. Her illustrations document her debt to Eastlake and the Aesthetic Movement.

America received another offering on taste in 1881 when Scribner and Welford published *The Decoration & Furniture of Town Houses* by Robert W. Edis. Issued earlier that year in London, the book together with Eastlake and the Garretts supplies ample evidence that after 100 years of independence, Americans were still turning to England for decorative trends.

The sale of such books indicated a ready market for advice on decoration, and the 1880s saw the emergence of two American periodicals on interior decoration. *The Decorator and Furnisher* appeared in October 1882 with A. Curtis Bond as editor and Clarence Cook, Robert Edis, and Lewis F. Day as frequent contributors. At first the journal was just as useful to the professional decorator as it was to the householder, for it chronicled changing styles in carpets and wallpapers, printed reports of new products, and provided hints for successful decoration. The magazine advocated no particular style as most correct or proper, and, significantly, in 1890 it ran a competition for rooms designed in each of the following: Colonial, Italian Renaissance, Louis XV, Louis XVI, Romanesque, and "Adams." Under the editorship of W. R. Bradshaw, the magazine remained eclectic and useful, and it began to draw articles from German and French as well as English sources. By the mid-1890s, change was evident in its pages. Advertisements for stained glass and the latest wallpapers gave way to those for bicycles, corsets, and face creams. Articles on picturesque rural America failed to maintain the subscription lists in spite of the management's lowering the price from $4.00 to only $1.00 per year. Under editor Edward Dewson, the magazine expired with the October 1898 issue. Its pages remain a rich source for documentation of late nineteenth-century interiors.

Home Decoration, edited by Mrs. Josephine Redding, appeared in January 1886, and gave extensive coverage to ladies' decorative needlework. Apparently never serious competition for *The Decorator and Furnisher*, it perished with the June 1889 issue. Its columns, too, are useful documentation of this period.

Like *Home Decoration*, many books of the time were devoted to needlework as a way of beautifying one's house. *Beautiful Homes* by Henry T. Williams and Mrs. C. S. Jones (New York, 1878) offered suggestions on decoration in general, but most of its pages sketched needlework embellishments for tablecovers, curtains, doilies, draperies, lambrequins, and upholstery. *Woman's Handiwork in Modern Homes* by Constance Cary Harrison (1881) emphasized the Aesthetic Movement and publicized the work of Louis Tiffany and Candace Wheeler. Other guidebooks like *Treasures of Use and Beauty* by a "Corps of Special Authors" (published in Springfield, Massachusetts, in 1883) offered chapters on preserving or "embalming" natural flowers, needlework decoration, and china painting—a subject much emphasized in *The Decorator and Furnisher*.

With obvious public interest in decoration, publishers offered readers glimpses into the fashionable homes of the wealthy, in such works as *Artistic Houses* published in 1883. The book offered photographs plus details on who did the decoration of the rooms using what materials. Several photographs from *Artistic Houses* are reproduced in this book. It must have been such interiors that *The Decorator and Furnisher* had in mind when in 1892 it described the apartment New York City banker Lewis G. Tewksbury had just furnished for $75,000 as a "Typical American Interior." The rooms illustrated in a book like *Inside of a Hundred Homes* by William Martin Johnson probably struck most readers as more typical. The author offered room-by-room scenes from houses of smaller scale than those in *Artistic Houses*, providing details on the furnishings and color of each room. The splendor of the rich was again evident in *Stately Homes in America* by Harry W. Desmond and Herbert Croly (1903), a book which the subjects of *Artistic Houses* would have admired.

By 1903, however, a new quest for authenticity and simplicity was under way, and the eclecticism of earlier decades was passé; this quest is the subject of later chapters. The rest of this chapter is devoted to patterns of decoration common to *all* styles prominent or proposed from 1865 to 1895. The variations of each style will then be described in individual sections.

But before passing on to the general principles of the eclectic period, we must note the nature of the rooms to be decorated, for each required a separate spirit.

Many writers dropped the earlier distinction between the formal parlor and the family living room, and most of them used the term "drawing room" to describe this general public room.

Only Williams and Jones (1878) speak of two such rooms. For them the parlor was a room offering a liberal display of elegance and decoration, where the most handsome and rarest items were on display for the entertainment of guests. The Garretts and Mrs. Spofford described the drawing room along the same lines: a room of light, airy elegance, with gay and beautiful decorations. Mrs. Spofford referred to the room as having a definite "feminine character." Cook dogmatically refused to speak of a parlor and counseled the homeowner to have a "living room" with no formal, unnecessary furniture or expenditures; yet to Cook the living room should be the largest and most pleasant room in the house. Williams and Jones saw their separate living room, as opposed to the parlor, as a place of attractive comfort, the room in which the real life of the family took place.

All the writers surveyed saw the library as by no means an extravagance in even the most modest house, for it was held that a family needed a retreat. Williams and Jones saw it as simple yet substantial, while Mrs. Spofford defined its spirit as one of culture and somber refinement.

Writers agreed that the hall was particularly important as it gave the visitor his or her first impression of a house and its occupants. Spofford and Cook both stressed that the hall should offer an immediate sense of cordiality, hospitality, shelter, shadow, and rest.

The dining room evoked two images. Mrs. Spofford and the Garretts opted for the traditional role as a place of solid wealth, comfort, and substantial permanence. Mrs. Spofford held that if one could afford but one sumptuous room, it should be the dining room. Williams and Jones and Cook, however, stressed brightness, a cheerful look, and even festive colors.

On the character of the bedroom there was consensus. Spofford and Cook emphasized the importance of light and air in the decoration, while the Garretts urged comfort, convenience, and avoidance of an effect of gloominess. Williams and Jones emphasized quiet, subdued colors, urging that the room should be a place of "warm, cozy comfort" in winter and of "cool, refreshing daintiness" in summer.

The decades of eclecticism were well supported by the industry that burgeoned after the Civil War. Furniture was no longer only the product of the craftsman or of the small factory, for large-scale production grew as towns like Grand Rapids, Michigan, began manufacturing vast quantities of comparatively inexpensive furniture. American mills made wallpapers, textiles, and carpets in increasing quantity and quality. Large amounts of goods were still imported from Europe and the Orient.

To help the householder, bewildered by the vast selection of goods available and styles suggested in the guidebooks, there was an ever-increasing number of professional decorators, especially in urban centers. For many, interior decoration was an adjunct to another profession: Louis C. Tiffany was primarily an artist in glass, Hudson Holly was an architect, and Leon Marcotte was a furniture manufacturer. By the end of the century, women like Candace Wheeler were establishing significant reputations in the emergent profession. Miss Wheeler's article on decorating as a career for women, originally published in *Outlook*, was soon reprinted in *The Decorator and Furnisher*.

Housing in this period ranged from the simple, cramped type of apartment seen in Figure 188 to palatial villas and townhouses. More so than in any earlier era, interiors reflect extreme economic disparities. Cornelius Vanderbilt died in 1877 leaving a fortune of $105 million; in June 1892, *The Tribune Monthly* in New York City compiled a roster of millionaires, name by name. Over 4,000 Americans fell into this category, and many of their homes are illustrated in the chapters that follow.

But most were not in the millionaire class. In the 1870s, the average unskilled worker made about $350 per year, while the most skilled of the 10 million Americans who were wage laborers earned about $1,040. The middle class, including business and professional people, had incomes ranging from $1,000 to $10,000 per year. In 1867, Ticknor and Fields of Boston published an anonymous little book entitled *Six Hundred Dollars a Year: A Wife's Effort at Low Living*. It offered household economies in everything from furnishing to cooking in order to produce the most attractive house on a minimum income of $600. Even on $600 they had a servant named Biddy; "low living" was not necessarily unattractive, but those on minimum incomes lived in a decorative world far different from that of the Vanderbilts.

Calvert Vaux's design for a simple surburban cottage built on a 25-foot lot for a plumber in Newburgh, New York, cost about $1,500. Thousands of such houses were built. A more fashionable house in the Queen Anne style, Hudson Holly estimated, would cost $6,500 in 1878. Holly described other houses with estimates running up to $17,000, but these were modest compared to the creations of the new battalion of industrial millionaires and their decorators.

LeGrand Lockwood of Norwalk, Connecticut—a railroad financier of the Civil War—led the way with his Elm Park House, begun in 1864 at a total cost of $1.5 million. Jay Cooke followed with the $2 million he spent on a seventy-two-room house, Ogontz.

In addition to the villa, the cottage, and the townhouse, the apartment was

PERSPECTIVE VIEW.

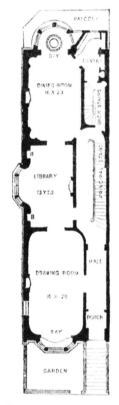

PLAN OF PRINCIPAL FLOOR

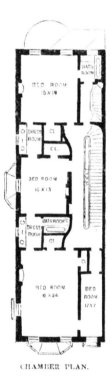

CHAMBER PLAN.

Vaux's design for a townhouse,
estimated cost $20,000, 1857

Holly's design for a house to cost $6,500

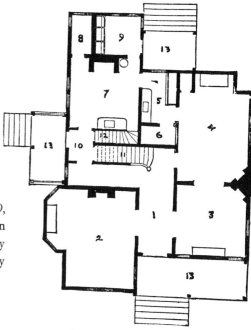

Floor plan of Holly's design

gaining new importance as the urban home of millions of Americans. In 1869, Catherine Beecher and Harriet Beecher Stowe had considered apartments in their *American Woman's Home.* Their floor plan of the typical four-story building with a 22-foot front and no side windows, "as is the case with most city houses," had four identical apartments.

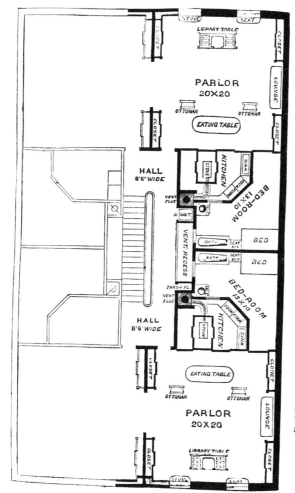

Beecher and Stowe's floor plan for apartments, each housing four

Wall arrangements for the Beecher and
Stowe apartments

We illustrate their suggested treatment of the walls of one of these apartments, with emphasis on efficient storage as much as decor. Sliding doors conceal the kitchen; each apartment contained a bath tub and water closet, a bedroom, and a parlor. With proper arrangement and "close packing of conveniences," the apartment could house four people comfortably, and two such apartments connected together could house ten.[1]

Apartments were clearly becoming the urban way of life, for by 1900, 94 percent of Manhattan families lived in rented apartments. Comparable statistics were Boston (81 percent), Cincinnati (79 percent), Philadelphia (78 percent), and Chicago (75 percent).[2]

FURNITURE

Of the guidebooks, Mrs. Spofford's offered the fullest account of what was needed to furnish the artistic house. The following list is based upon her chapters.

Furniture for the Well-Furnished House, Based on Spofford, Art Decoration Applied to Furniture
(items marked with an asterisk were optional, recommended only if there was room)

DINING ROOM
An extension table, strong, heavy, shape optional
Dining chairs, morocco seats, host and hostess chairs taller
than the side chairs
Sideboard
Buffet with glass doors
Carving table or dinner wagon
Butler's tray with trestle

HALL
A chest, an ancestral chest is most desirable
Curio cabinet
Umbrella and cane stand
Sofa or lounge
Two or three chairs, high-backed, old-fashioned
Antlers for hanging hats
*Cabinet for canes, umbrellas, fishing rods, guns
[Cook would add a mirror]

LIBRARY
Bookcases
Desk
Steps
Small movable bookcase
Lectern
Heavy library table
Portfolio stand
Globes
Collector's cabinet
Comfortable chair
Footrest

BOUDOIR OR LADY'S SITTING ROOM
Lounge
Two comfortable chairs
Prie-dieu (if one is devout)
Desk or escritoire
Sewing table and workbasket
Easel
Piano

DRAWING ROOM
Chairs, deep and luxurious
Varying chairs "of the light fanciful kind"—black lacquer
with wicker seats
Sofas
Lounges
Ottomans
Hassocks in profusion
Footstools in profusion
*Circular divan
Piano, if there is not a separate music room
*Center table, shape optional, but round is "more friendly"
Folding screen
Easel
Davenport
Etagère
Corner shelves
Side tables
Tall cabinet for curios, relics, minerals, etc.—the "main
piece of furniture in the room"
Hanging cabinet
[Cook adds a desk or writing table and a portfolio stand]

BEDROOM
Bed with high headboard, low footboard,
brass bed acceptable
Cheval glass, between windows
Lounge
Easy chair
Footstools
Toilet table
Wash stand
Lofty chest of drawers
Screen—if no separate dressing room
Wardrobe—if no closet
Writing desk

Clarence Cook suggested items of furniture in his text, but offered no systematic room-by-room survey. All the authors agreed that it was far better to let a room stand empty even for two years than to fill it with inferior cheap furniture. Manufacturers supplied most of the items listed in the table in each of the major styles.

The author of *Six Hundred Dollars a Year* listed necessary furniture for the more frugal household, and these items, together with their average prices, follow:

Furnishings for the Frugal House, Based on
Six Hundred Dollars a Year

PARLOR		
40 yards tapestry carpet at $1.00 a yard	$ 40.00	
Walnut haircloth sofa	30.00	
Four walnut chairs, at $3.00 each	12.00	
Walnut center table	5.00	
Cloth cover	2.00	
Small pier table with marble top	8.00	
Piano and stool	200.00	
Two window shades of white linen	2.00	
Total		$299.00
FURNISHINGS FOR THREE CHAMBERS		
75 yards of ingrain carpet at 75¢	$ 52.50	
Three cottage sets at $40.00 each	120.00	
Beds and bedding	50.00	
Crockery ware	6.00	
Muslin curtains	3.00	
Total		$231.50
DINING ROOM		
20 yards carpet at 75¢	$ 15.00	
A good second-hand table	5.00	
Six cane seat chairs at 1.50 each	9.00	
Cutlery	10.00	
Stone china dinner set	10.00	
Tea set, white French china	5.00	
Window shades	1.00	
Total		$ 55.00
Kitchen furniture and cooking utensils	30.00	
Hall furniture and stair carpet	30.00	
Total cost of house furniture		$645.50

Perhaps the most astounding single item among the parlor furnishings was the $200 piano, an object accounting for two-thirds of the cost of the parlor. Such culture was considered necessary during this period, even in houses of self-proclaimed "low living."

A somewhat paradoxical addition to the interior decorated with refined taste was rustic work, a type of furniture that fitted into no particular style but introduced a "pretty effect" into the home. Companies sometimes produced rustic furniture, but plant stands, fire fenders, and picture frames were usually homemade out of varnished sticks and roots.

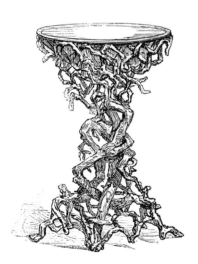

Rustic table

A fully ornamented fireplace
in summer

FLOOR COVERINGS

By the late 1870s, decorators were faced with the choice of covering their floors
with either the traditional carpet, usually wall-to-wall, or smaller rugs. Rugs
gained a number of advocates, such as Clarence Cook, who held that the rug
could be moved and turned over daily for cleaning and thus held less dust. The
combination of wood floors and rugs was therefore cleaner and healthier.

Carpets continued to have their defenders. Mrs. Spofford presumed that
carpeting would cover almost every floor, and even Cook was forced to concede
that carpeting was appropriate for covering unattractive floors or stopping
drafts through poorly constructed ones. Most writers anticipate that the carpet
will be laid with a border, generally in a darker shade than the field.

Articles in *The Decorator and Furnisher* allow some generalizations on
changing styles in carpets. The carpets of the 1870s were comparatively drab
and dark, but by the early 1880s, there was a taste for bright, even "flaming"
colors. In 1885, new styles were described as "stylish, and yet subdued," and in
1889, the latest fashions in carpets were reported as employing few colors in
restrained tints.

Not every style had an appropriate carpet; in many interiors, the pattern of
the carpet had little to do with the style of the rest of the room. But color
coordination of the carpet with other decor was imperative to the tasteful eye,
and the standards of combination are discussed under color.

When writers spoke of rugs, they inevitably meant Orientals, which were costly. Yet most writers thought the expense was worth it, for the Oriental provided both optimum wear and design.

Gaining increasing popularity in the 1870s and 1880s was an alternate floor covering, the parquet floor or "wooden carpet," as it was often called. The householder with an unattractive or drafty floor might cover it with parquet. Among other manufacturers, George Halbert of Brooklyn produced a popular flooring ¼-inch thick. The pieces of parquet were shipped prepared in place and glued to cloth, and the local carpenter simply shaped the floor to the room. Usually, an installation included a border 3½ to 5 inches wide. The cost for such flooring varied from $1.50 to $18 a square yard. Decorative practice required a border of roughly 2 feet of parquet between the wall and an area rug. *The Decorator and Furnisher* for October 1890 states: "The combination of an oriental rug and a floor of wood is very artistic."

Carpet designs were often borrowed from Oriental rugs and occasionally taken from wallpapers, but it was not unknown for a wallpaper design to be copied from a carpet.

Pattern for a stained floor
in imitation of tile

PICTURES AND MIRRORS

Art was an important part of the tastefully decorated house, for pictures and statues provided an educational stimulus to the minds of the young, and they revealed a great deal about the cultural attainments of the adults of the house.

Pictures were the prime means of adding such artistic culture to one's interiors. Oils were fine for those who could afford them, while etchings and engravings provided less expensive but less colorful decoration. In 1885, *The Decorator and Furnisher* reported that the strong market for etchings of the previous few years was diminishing. Colorful and not so expensive were colored lithographs and chromolithographs. Currier and Ives produced thousands of hand-colored prints before the Civil War, but in the 1860s, Louis Prang began his series of chromolithographs, that is, lithographs printed in color. Prang— and others—issued historical and scenic views of American life, and a series of accurate reproductions of paintings from the Renaissance to the present. Thus, the rural parlor could be furnished with Bierstadt's *Sunset in the Yosemite Valley*, a print costing $12.00, or with Raphael's *Sistine Madonna*.

Frames. Oil paintings appear in increasingly heavy plaster and gilt frames with intricate cast details. To go with prints the Beecher sisters selected for the ideal parlor, they suggested rustic frames made at home from branches still covered with bark. But by the 1870s most of the illustrations show prints displayed in simple black frames with wide mats.

Cook provided a full discussion of hanging pictures. Nails in plaster caused cracks and the inconvenience of summoning a carpenter. The brass or iron picture rail, which appears in several of our illustrations, supported pictures well but was unattractive. The best technique involved hanging pictures from a picture molding placed along the bottom of the frieze. Sensitivities were high in the 1870s and 1880s; in January 1885, *The Decorator and Furnisher* held that picture cords suspended from one point on a picture rail would create triangles that would detract from the lines of the picture. The distracting shape was all the more obvious because the cords were often "bright red." The author echoed what Cook had written—the cords should descend straight from the molding.

The modern restorationist should bear in mind the advice offered during the period: In seeking colored cords to support pictures, one must be sure the cord will continue to bear the weight. Thus, *The Decorator and Furnisher* recommended copper wire rather than cord.

Cook advised that pictures be hung at eye level; often, he noted, they were hung too high. *The Decorator and Furnisher* for January 1885 offered another fine point of hanging: Oils should not hang flat against a wall but should tilt slightly forward, in order that the brush marks could be seen better. Other writers were equally adamant that pictures should not tilt at all.

Statues, originals or casts, were another important part of the cultural aspect of a house. Writers often paid little attention to the style of the room into which the statue was introduced. Cook depicts a statue of Minerva in a room filled with Aesthetic, Eastlake, and Oriental items; to his eye, the only incongruous effect was Minerva's nudity—"A nude Minerva would have shocked a Greek."

Those acquainted with Victorian morality may wonder why so many nudes appear. Issue after issue of *The Decorator and Furnisher* carried designs for walls, screens, or panels showing nudes seated, leaping, or flying. The magazine discussed the issue directly in 1893 in "The Nude in Art." The article was primarily an interview with artist Napoleon Sarony, who claimed that his favorite art form became immodest only when there was a "knowing look" in the eyes.[3] Without the knowing look, a nude was thus a fit subject for the chaste Victorian interior.

Between 1860 and 1890, John Rogers sold over 100,000 of the cast plaster groupings that were to make his name a household word, yet none of the guidebooks recommended them, and Cook saw the Rogers groups as far inferior to the fine reproductions of classical statues available.

TEXTILES

Eclectic rooms used many fabrics in different styles and colors, but in the carefully planned room the colors at least were chosen to harmonize.

Upholstery. Each season brought a new array of upholstery fabrics in a wide range of color and designs. Mrs. Spofford counseled her readers to choose fabrics and designs appropriate for the individual style of the pieces covered, but even within these limits the growing textile market offered many choices. Most expensive were imported tapestries, for which one could pay $25 to $40 to cover the back of a single chair.

Tufted upholstery is commonly associated with the Moorish style, but during the eclectic period tufting was also used in many other styles, too. Upholstery materials appropriate to particular styles are discussed in the sections that follow.

Slipcovers. Slipcovers seldom appear in the illustrations, but they were used, even in very fashionable houses, especially for summer.

Window Curtains. Window curtains were an important and characteristic part of every decorative style, and where possible we have illustrated drapery designs for each style. Eastlake advocated very simple straight curtains hung from rings, but others urged the homeowner to adopt elaborate hangings with highly ornamented flat lambrequins.

Several elements were involved in an elaborate set of draperies, and it may be well to set forth the basic terms. The line cut at left shows a window with double curtains taken from Williams and Jones's *Beautiful Homes*. From the wooden cornice, which has been ebonized and gilded, hangs an embroidered lambrequin edged with fringe and tassels. Beneath the lambrequin is a set of figured damask curtains and a set of point lace curtains or undercurtains. Behind both sets of curtains is an embroidered fine muslin roller shade. Williams and Jones comment that the drapery they illustrate is very expensive, but that the enterprising homemaker could prepare a cheaper substitute of the same design using velveteen and Swiss muslin. Expensive or reasonably priced, the full design would include cornice, lambrequin, two sets of curtains (or at least the effect of two sets), and an undershade.

Price was not the only element to be considered in selecting a drapery fabric. The Garretts held that the beauty of drapery was in the folds, not the pattern of the fabrics, and thus they disapproved of rep, then the standard fabric for dining room draperies, for it produced awkward folds. Serge, waste silk, or velvet, they held, were much better. *The Decorator and Furnisher* for October 1888 offered several rules dealing with the relation of fold, fabric design, and surrounding walls. The size of the pattern in the curtain materials should be proportional to the size of the foldings in the curtain design: large patterns were fine for large folds and small patterns for small folds. Against a figured wall, plain or bordered rather than figured curtains were best. Period suggestions for colors of curtains are to be found in Table 12 in the section on color.

Other window coverings were popular during the eclectic decades. Venetian blinds were controversial. Some decorators liked them, but the Garretts found them unacceptable. Roller shades were highly popular and often used behind window drapes. Frequently they were plain, but several companies still specialized in producing shades ornamented with simple designs or even completely covered with landscape scenes.

Bed Curtains. Bed curtains had a new renascence during the eclectic period, and their designs were usually in keeping with the canons of individual styles.

Portières. Prominent in these decades were portières or curtains in the doorways between rooms. Portières possibly had their origin in the Moorish style, as some accounts refer to the expensive Baghdad portières used when the style was "first" introduced. By the 1870s and 1880s, however, the form was well established and adapted to a variety of styles. As with window curtains, the portières could be very elaborate, with cornices and lambrequins, or simple straight drapes hung from rings on a pole.

The eclectic decades were an era of ladies' needlework, and there was virtually no limit to the ways in which a seamstress might decorate her house. Williams and Jones's book is a compendium of needlework. They offer designs for decorating upholstery, for making hanging corner shelves, lamp mats, lamp shades, card and letter racks, wall pockets, table scarves, and lambrequins for

Fully draped window, 1878

mantels. Such needlework appears in houses of moderate means, but it is lacking in photographs of interiors furnished at great cost.

WALL TREATMENT

Motifs of wall decoration varied with the individual styles, but virtually all styles divided the wall in the same way. In the 1870s and 1880s, a commonly advocated system of wall decoration involved a three-part division. Mentioned in many guidebooks but appearing in few pictures, the three parts divided the wall surface into dado, wall or filling, and frieze. This division was popularized in part by the Aesthetic Movement, which produced many wallpapers for each division, sometimes with extra decorative borders between the dado and filling or the filling and frieze. A dado might be paneled rather than papered.

Designers offered decorators coordinated sets of dadoes, fillings, and friezes, but householders were at liberty to match or mismatch designs as they chose.

The frieze received a great deal of attention, for in it the most representational details were to be found. Frieze designs might include scenes of medieval life, Japanese processions, characters from the Bayeux tapestry, birds in flight, as well as conventionalized urns or swags. At times, these scenes were painted by an artist directly on the wall, but more often printed papers were used. Stenciling was another means of frieze decoration. As the 1880s progressed, the fashionable frieze became narrower, for in 1884 *The Decorator and Furnisher* commented that broad friezes were not *yet* out of fashion.

In the 1880s and 1890s, relief decoration added a three-dimensional aspect to walls. Embossed wallpapers or applied panels were the more commonly accepted techniques or relief decoration. Lingomur (a wood fiber product), Lincrusta Walton (canvas treated with layers of thickened linseed oil), Japanese papers (embossed designs filled with fibers), Anaglypta (an English pulp paper), and stamped leather all offered a variety of designs appropriate to particular styles. Papier-mâché might also be used. The Stereo Relief Decorative Company of Boston offered a large line of metal or composition relief panels for friezes, borders, and fillings. The company described its work as much more "life like" than decoration possible with Lincrusta Walton or papier-mâché.

Many writers saw walls as the beginning of a decorative scheme, for the colors of upholstery and carpets were dependent upon those of the walls. Before choosing a color for the wall, one was advised to decide whether oil paintings were to be hung. If so, fairly plain walls in crimson or olive green were in order as a background for the gold frames. Without pictures, one was free to explore the limits of creativity being poured into new papers each season. The illustrations show that few people with oils limited themselves to plain crimson or olive walls.

Designs of paper varied greatly; by the end of the period, manufacturers offered papers specifically designed to complement individual styles.

In 1881, Clarence Cook developed generalizations about regional styles in the decoration of walls. In the 1860s, there had been widespread sentiment favoring plain white plaster walls. That began to change about 1870, at least in New York, where white or delicate tints relieved with gold came into fashion when the city followed the lead of the French. Philadelphians clung to their

Wall pocket

white walls out of a "Quaker love of neatness," and Bostonians did the same, preferring to invest their money in the "solid comforts of life" or in education.[4]

The discussion of individual styles that follows includes illustrations of appropriate papers where possible.

ARCHITECTURAL DETAILS AND CEILINGS

In general, especially in houses of fashion and wealth, architectural details and ceiling designs were dictated by the specific style followed, and such details are discussed under the individual styles.

In lesser houses, however, discernible styles in architecture and ceilings are lacking. In such houses, ceilings were usually plain, perhaps with a central cast plaster rosette, and walls were plain plaster surfaces, perhaps with a picture rail at varying heights from the floor. Houses of some grandeur often had a simple ceiling molding lacking in plainer homes. There was usually a baseboard about 6 to 8 inches high. Several stylish Texas houses of this period have horizontal board walls. Log or board walls were a necessity rather than a stylistic motif in simple frontier houses.

Mantels reveal individual styles more than any other architectural detail, but simple marble or wood mantels almost defy classification. With the advent of central heating, architects sometimes omitted mantels and fireplaces as needless. Occasionally in the renovation of a house, owners added them for charm rather than out of necessity. In 1880, J. Pickering Putnam produced *The Open Fireplace in All Ages*. A sentence from the first page summarized his thesis: "We should be prompted to respect the open fireplace, as funishing the best substitute for the life and health giving rays of the sun, and to discard all such systems of heating as are opposed in principle to that employed by nature."[5]

In 1881, Clarence Cook, noting regional variations in ceilings, observed that while the younger decorators of Boston had achieved excellent results by papering ceilings, New Yorkers had been reluctant to accept anything but white ceilings, unless an artist of the quality of Tiffany or Samuel Colman were available to do the painting. In his estimation, the future and good taste both lay with the Bostonians.[6]

COLOR

Color was an important consideration in any interior design, and in the century of Darwin, writers devoted considerable attention to the scientific theory of color.

With the exception of Frederick A. Parsons, who in 1892 argued in *The Decorator and Furnisher* that the primary colors were red, green, and blue-violet, writers followed the Brewster-Chevreul theory that there were three primary colors—red, yellow, and blue.

The standard color chart, which came to be known as the Brewsterian color circle, was useful in showing decorators complementary colors. Most theories stressed that a color harmonized best with the color directly across the circle from it. Thus, blue and orange, red and green, and yellow and purple were

Table 12. Table of Color Harmony, with the Carpet as the Basis of Each Color Scheme, from The Decorator and Furnisher[7]

CARPET.	WOODWORK.	WALLS.	FRIEZE.	CORNICE.	CEILING.	UPHOLSTERY.	DRAPERY
Black bear rug.	White mahogany and bronze.	Yellow striped paper or silk.	Painted.	Different tones of yellow.	Light yellow.	Yellow self-tones, rose.	Red and ivory
Chocolate.	Ivory enamel	Ecru, warm.	Old rose.	Chocolate, ecru, old rose.	Light warm ecru.	Old ivory, ecru and chocolate.	Capote blue.
Citron.	Bronze.	Old gold.	Citron.	Light gold, citron, old gold.	Light gold.	Old gold, red and citron.	Empire blue.
Claret.	Antique oak.	Olive green.	Gold.	Antique oak.	Vellum.	Red.	Bronze.
Deep sienna.	Antique oak.	Bottle green.	Indian red.	Deep sienna.	Deep ecru	Brown and Indian red.	Indian red.
Ecru or fawn.	Old ivory.	Light old ivory.	Ecru.	Deeper ecru and Indian yellow.	Very light ivory.	Ivory, with Indian yellow.	Blue and ivory.
Gobelin blue.	Fawn color or antique oak.	Dull drab (dark).	Gobelin blue or red.	Dull drab, Gobelin blue, or red.	Light drab	Drab, Gobelin blue, & little Gobelin red.	Rose and Nile.
Golden brown.	Black walnut.	Sage green.	Golden brown.	Ochre.	Light ochre.	Sage green & brown	Red and bronze.
Indian red.	Yellow brown.	Deep dull olive.	Indian yellow.	Olive.	Yellow olive.	Indian yellow & red.	Indian yellow.
Indigo.	Mahogany.	Deep Pompeian red.	Bright deep olive.	Olive, red, blue.	Light olive.	Deep Pompeian red.	Yellow.
Indian yellow.	Oak or cherry.	Indian yellow.	Deep Indian yellow.	Indian yellow.	Light Indian yellow.	Ind. yellow, cardinal red, olive or blue	Heliotrope.
Leather.	Antique oak or cocobola.	Bottle green.	Maroon.	Leather.	Deep ecru.	Deep bottle green and maroon.	Orange.
Old green.	Antique oak.	Dull sage.	Pompeian red (dull).	Dull sage, ochre.	Light greenish ochre.	Brown, with Pompeian red.	Capucine red
Old rose.	Rosewood.	Sea green.	Old rose.	Old rose and sea green.	Light sea green.	Sea green, grey, old rose.	Old rose, with sea green.
Olive.	Black walnut, cherry or mahogany.	Indian red or Indian yellow.	Dark blue, dk. Indian red, dark Indian yellow.	Olives	Light olive or ochre.	Deep Pompeian red or Indian yellow.	Copper bronze or Empire red.
Oriental rug.	Mahogany.	Pompeian red.	Same as wall.	Mahogany.	Buff.	Deep yellow.	Oriental stuffs.
Pompian red.	Olive.	Dull blue.	Dark Pompeian red.	Olive.	Cream.	Olive and red.	Tones of Pompeian red.
Red orange.	Ash.	Ochre.	Bright olive.	Ochre and light dull orange.	Pale ochre.	live, yellow and orange.	Two tones of olive.
Sage green.	Cherry.	Ochre.	Pompeian red.	Sage green, ochre.	Light sage green.	Pompeian red, dull blue, olive, sage.	Pompeian red, Nile or sage.
Violet.	Butternut.	Violet and yellow.	Violet and gold.	Violet and gold.	Yellow.	Warm green.	Old gold.

natural harmonies. Using the color circle, the decorator knew how to harmonize the subtle tertiary colors as well. Several articles in *The Decorator and Furnisher* explained color theory in considerable scientific detail, considering problems of juxtaposition of colors and the influence of distance upon perception of color.

Most writers urged the householder to begin the color scheme of a room with the carpet, but some suggested taking the wallpaper or woodwork as the basic given. Whatever the beginning, the decorator should devise a color scheme and stick to it until the decoration of a room was complete. Table 12, above, was one of several such charts in which *The Decorator and Furnisher* offered coordinated color schemes. In this chart the carpet—in the left-hand column—was the "given" of the plan; but one would not have said that *only* a Pompeian red wall was right with an Oriental rug.

In general, the approved pattern of color arrangement put darker colors and sober, somber shades on the floor and lower walls, while the higher parts of the walls and the ceiling were lighter and sometimes even bright or brilliant. Note that white never appears as a ceiling color in Table 12.

Colors seem to have been generally dark and heavy in the years after the

Civil War. In the early 1880s, there was a demand for bright colors in wall-papers, carpets, and fabrics; but by the middle of the decade, reports of new designs emphasized the subtle and muted tones of the colors. Such moderation continued into the 1890s, when one writer commented that "all fine color is restrained."

Often the names given to colors were revealing, for secondary and tertiary tints were much preferred. Thus, one spoke not of red or blue, but of peach bloom or tender blue, soft olive, or ethereal green. Cook likened the shades he mentioned to the canvases of Burne-Jones and Alma Tadema, and to the work of William Morris, and thus chose such names as mistletoe green, pomegranate flower, and duck's egg.

By the end of the century, the interior decorator faced a problem unknown earlier. One now needed to ask whether the color scheme of a room was to be seen primarily under natural or artificial light. In the 1890s, *The Decorator and Furnisher* carried several articles on this problem and offered the following generalizations: Gas produced a creamy, orange light, while oil offered a "dull tint with a dull drab cast," and incandescent electric light was a pale orange tending toward red. These observations, together with the maxim that "color destroys its own kind but intensifies the opposite when mixed together," meant that under gaslight, blue tended to look green and green tended to look blue. Two remedies were available. Colors could be mixed initially in the original painting to counteract the distorting effects of artificial light; or one could put correcting colored globes on the lights themselves.

ACCESSORIES

Accessories assumed new importance, for they told a great deal about a family. The absence of accessories or a multitude of small items of no special value was revealing, and to Mrs. Spofford, "the mere shape of a lamp shows whether people buy what their neighbors buy, or have any individual taste of their own to exercise."[8]

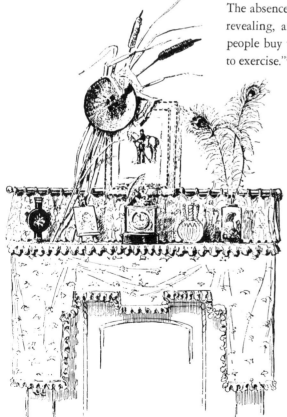

Cretonne lambrequin for a mantel

Many accessories carried the motifs of individual styles, yet it was a characteristic of these decades to bring together a diversity of styles for the enrichment of life. Thus, in the same room, one intentionally gathered Japanese ivory carving, French bronzes, Venetian glass, pre-Columbian gold, Navajo baskets, Sèvres china, Chinese jade, and Moorish weapons, even though the basic decorative style might be Louis XVI. This penchant for varied collecting led to what the modern eye calls "Victorian clutter."

The drawing room was the most obvious place for a rich display of accessories, and within that room the mantel was the natural focal point. The arrangement of mantel accessories in Cook's illustrations was notably asymmetrical, but the plates in Spofford, Eastlake, and Edis show the symmetrical arrangements advocated by *The Decorator and Furnisher* in October 1884. After cautioning that too few were better than too many accessories, the magazine advised that irregularity of height contributed to the variety of small objects, and that in the properly arranged mantel the taller objects were on the ends and in the middle. The February 1892 issue presented the aesthetic principle of such a setting. When lines connecting the tops of objects formed angles pointing up, the mantel seemed to be "frowning"; but pointing down, the same objects were smiling with "the impression of motion and life."

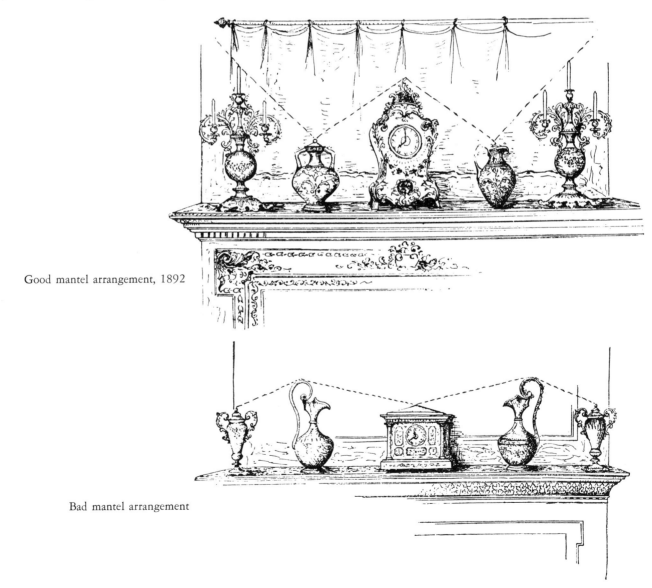

Good mantel arrangement, 1892

Bad mantel arrangement

A well-decorated dinner table, 1890

Plants as decoration

The dining room was the natural setting for decorative accessories of a different sort. Almost with one voice the writers endorsed the presence of a massive sideboard laden with rare china and glass. Obviously, such items were not for daily use. In 1878, Cook criticized most householders for choosing plain white china for their tables. Such china, imported from France, was of high quality, but he thought it produced a rather colorless, stark table. White detracted from food and, as he put it sensitively, "Fruit does not know how to behave itself when it is put into white china dishes."[9] To remedy this dire problem, Cook suggested buying diverse lots of old china, English earthenware, French faïence, or Canton ware. Eclecticism could apply to china as well as a room, but like the room, dishes needed to harmonize even though they might not match.

During the 1880s and 1890s, home china painting became very popular, and the magazines regularly featured china designs. Such decorated china was for use as well as display.

In December 1890, *The Decorator and Furnisher* illustrated a grandly set table; this linecut (above) can provide details for preparing period settings. The magazine commented, Cook notwithstanding, that white china was probably the best, as it did not clash with flowers and other elements of color in decoration. Deep blue or richly painted china prevented the use of flowers. Red and white dominated the suggested color scheme of a table: a crimson plush table scarf and white linen and china might be complemented by red and white roses.

In the early 1890s, color luncheons were popular, and the magazines and cookbooks were ready with plans for a successful event. At a "carnation" dinner or luncheon, there was a carnation beside each plate, pink shades over the lights, pink jellies and sherbets, and, or course, the hostess wore a dress decorated with pink ribbons. Other themes documented were a red dinner, a yellow and mauve dinner, a green luncheon, or a daffodil lunch. At the last the table was decorated with daffodils and yellow ribbons, and the menu included consommé with yellow custard, sole with a saffron-colored sauce, eggs in yellow aspic, and orange cake with yellow icing.

A living accessory was the plant. Miss Beecher and Mrs. Stowe promoted houseplants (ferns and mosses) as educational, beautiful, and inexpensive. Publications from the 1860s and 1870s indicate that an aquarium was another popular living accessory.

Among decorative acccessories, silver was most responsive to changing modes, and many companies produced flatware patterns to accompany particular styles. Glass, however, did not generally reflect the individual styles. Manufacturers produced some 300 different patterns, some of which, like Lincoln Drape or Cable, commemorated historic events such as the Atlantic cable's completion in 1866. Few of these many patterns were designed to match furniture styles and wall decoration. Ceramics were likewise less responsive to evolving style, but householders placed little emphasis on matching their china with the prevailing decor of a room.

China and glass protected with worked doilies

Renaissance Revival

In 1878, Harriet Spofford wrote that there was "nothing more luxurious" than the Renaissance style, and countless householders agreed. From the early 1860s to the mid-1880s, it won support from the fashionable urban dweller; it continued to be popular in rural areas and less fashionable homes until the end of the century.

Mrs. Spofford in her *Art Decoration Applied to Furniture* saw the basic Renaissance style as beginning in the Italian Cinquecento. She distinguished French variations in the Francis I, Henry II, and Louis XIII styles, which we will discuss separately. Some writers and decorators offered variations in the Italian, German, and Dutch Renaissance modes, but for the most part, the Renaissance was an undifferentiated look that was massive and solid.

The Renaissance followed the patterns of other contemporary styles, and manufacturers produced wallpapers, textiles, porcelain, silver, iron, and brass in typical Renaissance designs. But often Renaissance decor was confined to furniture, curtains, walls, and ceilings. The Renaissance was an adaptive style, mixing relatively well with other styles. Very few Renaissance interiors were done with the comprehensive historical accuracy of the Louis XV room shown in Figure 119 on page 232.

Renaissance revival ewer and stand

Figure 101. Eastman Johnson. *The Hatch Family*. 1871. Oil on canvas, 48 in. ×
73⅜ in. (1.22 m × 1.86 m). The Metropolitan Museum of Art, New York
City. (Gift of Frederick H. Hatch, 1926).

Living on the northeast corner of Park Avenue and 37th Street in New York City,
the family of Alfrederick Smith Hatch had Renaissance motifs on their mantel, bookcases, monogrammed valance, reading table, and sofa. The canvas well illustrates why
the 1870s and 1880s have been called the "brown decades," for in the dark walnut
furniture, dark trim, and swagged curtains, reds and brownish blacks dominated. The
lampshade and table top were red, while the carpet was yellow and red with an
occasional touch of green. Note that the rounded door frames are reflected in the
design of the wallpaper.

Renaissance bookcase and writing table

FURNITURE

Renaissance revival furniture is characterized by massive form, deeply carved
ornament, cabochon decoration, portrait medallions, and caryatids. At times,
strap work decoration, from sixteenth-century design, appears in both furniture
and wall decoration. Tall sideboards or bookcases often had a rounded crest
surmounted by a cartouche or carved head. Walnut and mahogany were the
standard woods.

A variation of the Renaissance style was the neo-Grec, which involved the
application of Greek decorations to Renaissance shapes. Most characteristic of
this work was gilt decoration contrasting sharply with the surrounding dark
wood surfaces. Typical embellishments were palmettes, egg and dart designs,
fans, or urns with a solid gilt line surrounding the area decorated. Other neo-
Grec decorations were bronze or porcelain medallions placed on the central
panels of credenzas or chests. Figure 177 shows a neo-Grec table.

Urban centers produced spectacular examples of Renaissance furniture from the shops of Alexander Roux, Herter Brothers, and Leon Marcotte of New York City, and John Jelliff of Newark. By 1876, the Berkey & Gay Company of Grand Rapids, Michigan, was mass producing rather good Renaissance designs.

FLOOR COVERINGS

Renaissance revival floors were covered with fashionable carpets of the era, and no particular Renaissance designs were obvious.

Figure 102. *Library, Residence of LeGrand Lockwood, Norwalk, Connecticut. C.* 1870. Lockwood-Mathews Mansion Museum of Norwalk, Inc., Norwalk.

LeGrand Lockwood made a fortune in securities and railroads during the Civil War, and in 1868 he began construction of a sixty-room, fourteen-bath mansion of extraordinary expense ($1.5 million). The architect Detlef Lienau provided a Renaissance library that was designed by Leon Marcotte, and the furniture was manufactured by Herter Brothers. Before an embossed wallpaper imitating moroccan leather tooled with silver, Lockwood received his properly awed visitors from a thronelike canopied sofa, similar to the Renaissance beds appearing in Flemish and Dutch prints of the sixteenth and seventeenth centuries.

PICTURES AND MIRRORS

Pictures played an important role in the decor of a room, but very few are real Renaissance pictures or even of Renaissance themes. The round picture in the Beebe parlor is a notable exception (Fig. 103).

Mirrors were prominent as overmantels capped by massive architectural frames of the sort seen in Figure 103. Figure 106 shows a fine example of a tall pier mirror in a typical Renaissance frame.

TEXTILES

Upholstery and curtain fabrics often had little to do with specifically Renaissance themes, but the arrangement of curtains was one of the hallmarks of the style. Heavy fabrics hung from elaborate painted and gilt valances with fringed lambrequins made the draperies as monumentally impressive as some of the furniture. Johnson's portrait of the Hatch Family shows double lambrequins (Fig. 101). Such hangings were limited to families with considerable wealth. Note that in a country interior (Plate 22), only roller shades with a simple Renaissance border appear.

above: Figure 104. *Dining Room, Residence of James M. Beebe. 30 Beacon Street, Boston. C.* 1885. Society for the Preservation of New England Antiquities, Boston, Mass.

A massive Renaissance sideboard dominates the Beebes' dining room. The lion heads on the sideboard are repeated in the cresting of each of the chairs, which are upholstered in fabrics with lions and fleurs-de-lis. The heavy architectural valance and swagged curtains are typical designs recommended for the Renaissance revival, and the material of the curtains matches the upholstery fabric. The upper two shades on the sideboard are reminiscent of the home handicrafts suggested in many books or the shades advertised by the Denison Crepe Paper Company about 1895. Such repoussé silver was manufactured by Steiff of Baltimore and Tiffany of New York City, and later copied by other makers as its popularity spread.

opposite: Figure 103. *Parlor, Residence of James M. Beebe. 30 Beacon Street, Boston. C.* 1875–1880. Society for the Preservation of New England Antiquities, Boston, Mass.

James M. Beebe earned millionaire status in dry goods and real estate. Although the furniture in his room was notably eclectic, the Renaissance architectural detail dominated through the overmantel with its flanking Hermes, the cupboard door at the left, and the bookcases. The heavy egg and dart moldings appear in many Renaissance revival rooms, and the ceiling was painted in the designs decorators suggested for those who could afford them. Among the many pictures, only one— Botticelli's *Madonna of the Magnificat* framed in a Della Robbia wreath—is faithful to the Renaissance decor.

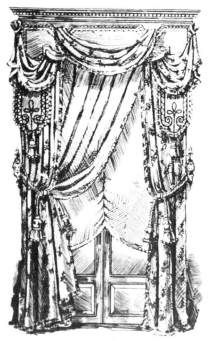

Renaissance window drapery

Renaissance wall decoration

WALL TREATMENT

Walls tended to be painted or papered in a solid color, the general fashion in the 1860s and 1870s when the Renaissance style gained great popularity. The Hatch Family (Fig. 101) had the wall divided into panels by the addition of moldings, and these panels were papered in a light diapered pattern. LeGrand Lockwood had a strongly figured paper in his library, but it was not a distinct Renaissance design of the sort that appeared later in Arcadia Bandini de Baker's apartment and in the Honolulu design (Figs. 105 and 110).

opposite, top: Figure 105. *Parlor, Residence of Arcadia Bandini de Baker. Los Angeles, California. C.* 1890. Los Angeles County Museum, Los Angeles, Calif.

Arcadia Bandini, the daughter of Don Juan Bandini, married Colonel R. S. Baker, who had become a millionaire in land, cattle, and grain ranching. In 1877, the Bakers demolished an old adobe and on the site built the new Baker Block seen here. The furniture, frieze, and ceiling put the room in the Renaissance category, and a fine Renaissance valance and drapery appeared in the far room as well. But the Victorian Classical piano stool, Turkish chair, and metal piano lamp add a note of eclecticism.

Figure 106. John B. Whittaker. *The Lesson.* 1871. Oil on canvas, 31 in. × 42 in. (79 cm × 107 cm). Collection of Elizabeth Ann Foster.

The family of John E. Tousey appear in 1871 in their home at 250 Henry Street, Brooklyn, New York. The Touseys were well-to-do, and Mr. Tousey's father, Sinclair Tousey, whose picture hangs over the mantel, had become a millionaire from his American News Company. Renaissance furniture provides the basic style of the room. Mr. Tousey was seated on a chair that matches the Renaissance sofa in the corner. The tall, narrow mirror combines several Renaissance motifs, while the piano (like several pieces of the period) mixes Renaissance with the sinuous curves of the rococo. The plain walls and marble mantel are typical of the 1860s and early 1870s, as is the large patterned rug with its realistic floral sprays.

Figure 107. Artist unknown. *Bedroom, Residence of H. A. W. Tabor. Denver, Colorado. C.* 1885. Library, The State Historical Society of Colorado, Denver.

Gold and silver mines made Tabor a millionaire, and his wife, Baby Doe, was soon to become the subject of the operetta *The Ballad of Baby Doe*. The Tabors later lost their fortune, but here they were living in high style in this Colorado interpretation of the Renaissance style. The squared wall pattern appears almost doubled in size in the ceiling border, while the center of the ceiling is a dizzying pattern of small circles.

ARCHITECTURAL DETAILS AND CEILINGS

Architectural details were vital in creating the formal Renaissance interior. Figure 103 shows the use of brackets at the ceiling, while Figure 104 shows a combination of dentil and egg-and-dart moldings. The Hatch interior (Fig. 101) is notable in that the door frames reinforced the rounded tops of the wall panels and bookcases. The spool work in Figure 105 was common toward the end of the century, but was not a Renaissance feature.

The Beebe parlor (Fig. 103) shows a typical, expensive Renaissance fireplace and overmantel.

Ceilings often carried considerable decoration. One fashionable ceiling had expensive, intricate moldings (Fig. 103), while others had papered or painted designs (Fig. 105).

Renaissance ceiling design in fireproof stereo relief

Figure 108. *Parlor and Music Room, Residence of Judge Augustus Macon, Canon City, Colorado. C. 1890.* Library, The State Historical Society of Colorado, Denver.

Judge Macon furnished his parlor with rather expensive Renaissance furniture with carved heads on each arm. The tufted upholstery of the sofa was protected by antimacassars arranged asymmetrically. Wicker furniture filled the music room. The same swirling acanthus paper influenced by the Aesthetic Movement covered the walls of both rooms, but the carpets were different. Note the great length of the floral portière.

LIGHTING

Distinctly Renaissance lighting fixtures were not so common as those with Gothic or rococo detail, but the chandelier in the Beebe parlor (Fig. 103) is an example of ornate work. The frosted globes were engraved with classical scenes. One of the matching wall sconces was guarded by a gryphon, and on the mantel were candelabra supported by Renaissance-style bronze figures.

COLOR

While there were no universal rules, heavy, warm colors often accompanied the Renaissance style. The Bullard parlor (Plate 23) was typical of many in its basic reliance on reds, long the standard shade for formal draperies. Note that contrasting panels of blue appear in the ceiling, and gilt is a unifying element on picture frames, walls, and ceilings.

opposite: Figure 109. *Model House Interior, Waterbury, Vermont.*
C. 1875. Society for the Preservation of New England Antiquities,
Boston, Mass.

George J. Colby was the architect of this model house, Number 7
in a Waterbury, Vermont, development. Although not yet fully
furnished, the architectural trim and furniture suggest the basic
Renaissance style, though the balloon back chair is rococo. The
double doors leading into the front rooms were common. The same
carpeting, based on Oriental designs, appeared in both rooms with a
different pattern in the hall. Kerosene provided the lighting, and the
hall lamp had a colored globe. The walls of the model house were
perhaps kept bare, awaiting an owner's selection of papers, but the
plain look seen here was fashionable in the 1860s and early 1870s.

above: Figure 110. C. B. Ripley and Arthur Reynolds. *Design for
a Dining Room. California Architect and Building News*
(December 1891).

C. B. Ripley and Arthur Reynolds were Honolulu architects, and
their design shows that the Renaissance style made an impact as far
west as Hawaii. The fans and arches together with the Corinthian
capitals were typical of some variants of the Renaissance revival. The
frieze at the left was either paper, Lincrusta Walton, or the stereo
relief panels generally available by the 1890s. Behind the columns
is a niche for a window seat, and there is a transom of stained glass
above the windows. The two built-in cupboards do not match, for
one has a curtain over open shelves. Though the table has some claim
to being Renaissance, the mass-produced chairs do not.

right: Figure 111. *Josephine Kingsley, Brooklyn, Connecticut.*
C. 1880. Lyman Allyn Museum, New London, Conn.

Josephine Kingsley (1859–1887) may have posed in a photographer's studio near her home in Brooklyn, Connecticut, but such
furniture was found in many houses. A collection of pictures was a
sign of culture, and a Renaissance portfolio stand was the perfect
place to keep them. Both the stand and chair have incised, gilt lines,
and the stand is further decorated with a painting draped by a scarf
with a Greek key border.

Figure 112. George Senyard. *Mrs. H. N. Whitbeck. C.* 1880. Oil on canvas, 63 in. × 48½ in. (1.60 m × 1.24 m). Western Reserve Historical Society, Cleveland, Ohio.

Frances C. Perry Whitbeck was the wife of a Berea, Ohio, merchant. The canvas provides a close look at a bureau top with a highly decorated cologne bottle, a vase of flowers, and a brush and mirror set in its case. The marble-top Renaissance bureau itself was probably from Grand Rapids, Michigan. Unlike many bedrooms of the 1870s and 1880s, the walls are plain.

English Revival

In the last three decades of the nineteenth century many revivals were proposed, but, surprisingly, English restorations were not as widespread as the French styles.

The Elizabethan style remained moderately popular (Figs. 91, 92), and Mrs. Spofford devoted a whole chapter of her *Art Decoration Applied to Furniture* to it. She treated it as the basic English Renaissance style, containing a strong mix of Gothic: "All the Renaissance that came into England through the Elizabethan gate had still to pay tribute to the Gothic on its way."[10] *The Decorator and Furnisher* offered very few designs in what it called the English Renaissance style.

In the twentieth century the Jacobean style would become much more prominent, but in the 1870s Mrs. Spofford described it as a "freak, and possibly a debasement, of the less pretentious and more pleasing Elizabethan."[11] Freak or not, a few Jacobean designs appeared in *The Decorator and Furnisher* and *Artistic Houses* illustrated several Jacobean rooms and described others. Rooms in the style had heavy carved furniture, often with dark, paneled walls and brass studs (Fig. 113). Architectural decorations were often based on the same motifs that adorned furniture: mermaids, rosettes, and scrolls. Although Mrs. Spofford commented that recent versions of the Jacobean had avoided the heavy look of the original period furniture, the massive built-in furniture like

Figure 113. *Dining Room, Residence of Herbert Sears, Commonwealth Avenue, Boston.* 1893. Society for the Preservation of New England Antiquities, Boston, Mass.

The Sears dining room was probably considered Jacobean, though all of the furniture was obviously created by applying revival motifs to modern forms. Note the use of embroidery to upholster the chairs. The wall paneling was dark, with a broad frieze above covered in a flocked paper reproducing an early textile design. The sideboard provides ample opportunity for an impressive display of silver. There is nothing Jacobean about the silver or portières.

Figure 114. *Library, Residence of T. Quincy Brown, 98 Beacon Street, Boston. C.* 1900. Society for the Preservation of New England Antiquities, Boston, Mass.

Two-tiered libraries were popular at the end of the century. The stair to the gallery began at the right of the fireplace, which had decorative tile, fleur-de-lis back, and matching andirons. The paneled wall, turned gallery rail, and the arabesque and shell carving above the curtain and seat at the right all present a mix of detail, but the armorial bearings atop the carved chair and its matching table give the room a Jacobean flavor. Neither fabrics nor wallpaper attempted a period look.

that seen in Figure 113 looks anything but light. Such solidity made the style most appropriate for libraries and dining rooms.

Hudson Holly illustrated a bookcase he labeled "Neo-Jacobean." It owed a strong debt to Eastlake, but the turned balusters and feet gave it what seventeenth-century flavor it had. The Jacobean style was undoubtedly what Charles Wyllys Elliott had in mind in describing the "Old English" dining room of Dr. James Chadwick of Boston. Wood tones (oak furniture with spiral turned legs, ash woodwork) dominated the color scheme with its light gray wall and wallpaper frieze of squirrels. No chandelier hung from the cross-timbered ceiling, for the decorator had chosen wall sconces for lighting. Further decoration included an old German picture dating from 1525 and a few pieces of armor on the mantel wall.

Mrs. Spofford ignored Charles I, who reigned from 1625 to 1649, but she did illustrate furniture from the reigns of Charles II (1660–1685) and James II (1685–1688). Curiously, decorators were quick to produce the niceties of the styles associated with the seventeenth-century French monarchs, but we have found not one American room of the eclectic period labeled Charles I, Charles II, or James II.

Revivals of the English William and Mary, Queen Anne, and Chippendale styles were swallowed up in the Colonial Revivals; and writers of the 1870s and 1880s seemed unconscious of the stylistic distinctions between American and English furniture in the Queen Anne and Chippendale styles. *The Decorator and Furnisher*, however, did present several Adam or "Adams" designs, one of which appears in Figure 115. The look was Federal, but the image explicitly evoked was English. Refer to the section on the Colonial Revival for details of the Federal-Adam style.

Figure 115. James Thomson. *An Adams Library. The Decorator and Furnisher* (June 1891), p. 85.

James Thomson won a prize for this "Adams" library. It is almost indistinguishable from the work he and his colleagues were turning out in the Colonial style.[40] In both, similar ceiling moldings and swag, shell, or urn decorative motifs dominated. Probably considered the most distinctively "Adam" was the detail of the fireplace with its side pilasters and arched grate.

Figure 116. Eastman Johnson. *Drawing Room of James and Eliza Brown.* 1869.
Oil on canvas. Private collection.

Prominent, millionaire New York City banker James Brown and his wife sit in their drawing room at 21 University Place as it appeared after expensive remodeling by Leon Marcotte in 1864. Marcotte introduced an extravagant statement of the Francis I style, with its flat strapwork and heavy moldings interspersed with brackets and diamond points. The stone color of the trim reinforces the architectural feeling of the decoration. A slightly neoclassical emphasis emerges from the accessories, the black compote and the plaster casts of the Temple of Saturn on the mantel. The empty bell jar perhaps once contained a pedestal clock.

French Revivals

French styles remained very fashionable throughout the eclectic period. The Louis XVI was probably the most continually popular variation between 1860 and the end of the century. The American reader could develop a keen eye for French revival styles from careful study of Harriet Spofford's *Art Decoration*

Applied to Furniture. She distinguished separate styles for Francis I, Henry II, Louis XIII, Louis XIV, Louis XV, Louis XVI, and Empire. With varying frequency, all of these styles were found in nineteenth-century American homes.

EARLY FRENCH

Early French revival furniture (Francis I and Henry II) was tall and narrow, with vaselike legs and decorations of scrolls and conventional and natural foliage and fruit. Mrs. Spofford said nothing of appropriate wall treatment, curtains, and ceilings, but she did call the overall effect one of "lovely, gay frippery."

In the literature of the late nineteenth century, references to Francis I and Henry II styles in American houses can be found, although these styles were never among the most prominent. Descriptions of such rooms sound like anything but frippery: Victor Newcomb's Henry II dining room was one of "somber stateliness," and John Martin's Francis I library was cited as rich and quiet.[12]

Francis I–style sofa

LOUIS XIII

The Louis XIII style was varied but always expensive. Some interpretations emphasized the union of late Renaissance and Italian styles, noting that Louis XIII's mother was Marie de Medici. Walls were generally covered with tapestries or expensive fabrics, and the paneled ceilings were painted in elaborate designs; there was a profusion of gilt on ceilings and walls. Moldings and fireplaces sometimes had heavy gadrooning, and portières often had elaborate embroideries. Bradley Martin of New York City used the style for his salon, where he installed a specially made crystal chandelier modeled on the one in the room in which Louis XIII died. Mrs. Spofford gave the following comparison of Henry IV and Louis XIII furniture with that of Francis I and Henry II: "The people were occupied with weightier matters; and the furniture of the reigns of Henri Quatre and Louis Treize is heavy and sad in comparison, the gayeties and

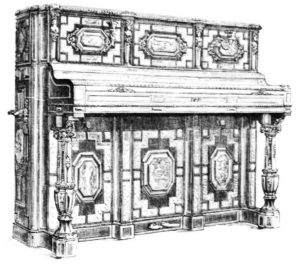

A Louis XIII–style piano, 1878

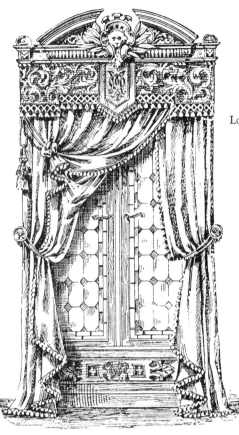

Louis XIII window drapery

Figure 117. *Drawing Room, Residence of Mr. H. Victor New-comb, 683 Fifth Avenue, New York City. C. 1883. Artistic Houses*, I, 180; see Bibliography.

As president of the Louisville and Nashville Railroad and of the United States National Bank of New York, H. Victor Newcomb (1844–1911) had ample wealth to afford this Louis XIII drawing room. The walls were treated with a dark paneled dado, salmon satin, and a frieze surmounted by stylized floral designs. The specially woven English carpet was a deeper shade of salmon than the walls. The portières were old pink plush, the bay window was hung with a pale blue plush, and the same fabric seems to have been used on some of the furniture.

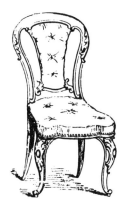

Louis XIV–style sofa and chair

fripperies usually wanting, but with the material adornments of rich inlay of ebony, lapis lazuli, pearl and other costly variegated substances."[13] Even though she held a Louis XIII room generally "so dismally dreary and formal as to be almost funereal," several prominent people in the 1880s adopted it for dining rooms or drawing rooms. It was little mentioned in the 1890s.

LOUIS XIV

Mrs. Spofford devoted a whole chapter to the Louis Quatorze style, describing it as bright and magnificent. It required the treatment of a room as a harmonious whole, and covered almost every surface with curves and flourishes. Both she and A. J. Davis emphasized the late Louis XIV-style furniture, illustrating pieces that the modern student would call Louis XV. As she describes the style, rooms were basically white with gilt decoration, and the hues in the carpets and curtains were soft and rich.

She recommended the style as "radiant and imposing," but it seems to have been little used except in the most spectacular settings. In the 1890s, *The Decorator and Furnisher* offered a few Louis XIV designs, but Louis XV designs were much more common.

Louis XIV spoon

Mrs. Spofford called this room Louis XIV, but the furniture today would be called Louis XV

231

Louis XV pier table (Downing called it Louis XIV)

LOUIS XV

The Louis XV style was one of the more popular French revivals, especially among the very wealthy.

To Mrs. Spofford's eye, the Louis XV was simply Louis XIV exaggerated—the Louis XV room presented a look of light, fantastic luxury, and dazzle. Yet she held that its furniture was the most comfortable ever developed. Louis XV furniture had inspired the rococo style, but in the Louis XV revival of the 1860s and 1870s, there was an emphasis on painting and gilding absent from the rococo. Louis XV furniture designs included some adaptations to nineteenth-century shapes, but generally, chairs and sofas were historically accurate. More lavish interiors in the style were furnished with real antiques.

Walls were covered with elaborate moldings and panels, enframing inserted oil paintings, frescoes, or tapestries. Rococo themes were often carried up from the walls to ceiling designs. Cross-hatched asymmetrical panels were characteristic wall decorations. Light colors and gilt predominate in these interiors.

opposite, top: Figure 118. G. Capaldo. *Prize Design for Louis XV Boudoir.* 1891. *The Decorator and Furnisher* (September 1891), p. 205.

Capaldo's design loses no opportunity to apply the rococo curve to every conceivable surface, from the decoration of the ceiling to the planter in front of the pier mirror. The painted wall panels added to the expense as well as the luxuriousness. Note that the drapery over the double doors is asymmetrical.

Figure 119. *Music Room, Residence of A. R. Peacock, Pittsburgh, Pennsylvania.* C. 1903. Croly, *Stately Homes in America*, p. 419; see Bibliography.

Peacock was an official in one of Andrew Carnegie's Pittsburgh steel operations. His music room shows a thorough Louis XV treatment in every detail. The same curves are found in the legs of the gilt furniture, in the design of the carpet, and in the rococo decorations at the top of each arch. The cross-hatched or diapered pattern in each arch is carried over into the wide ceiling molding, and rococo cherubs flank each of the arches and appear on the fireplace. The only modern adaptation is the gilt Louis XV piano.

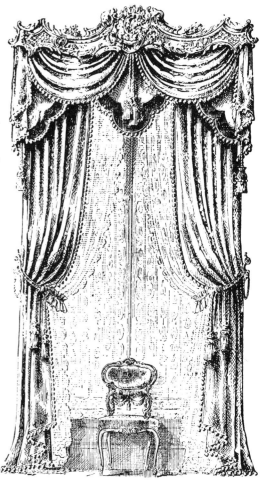

Louis XV window drapery

Figure 120. *Drawing Room, Residence of William C. Whitney, New York City.*
Croly, *Stately Homes in America*, p. 485; see Bibliography.

William C. Whitney (1841–1904), lawyer, Secretary of the Navy (1881–1885),
and financial organizer, left a fortune of $21,243,000. The splendor of Peacock's
music room (Fig. 119) pales by comparison with the grandeur of Whitney's drawing room with its Louis XIV and Louis XV furniture, paintings, and tapestries. Gilt
predominates on furniture, walls, and the painted ceiling. The cornice shows the
same diapering seen in Peacock's room, but the wall panels show less of the sinuous
rococo. A parquet floor is covered by Orientals at either end of the room. A mixture
of upholstery fabrics accentuates the moderate diversity of furniture styles.

Haviland vegetable dish

Numerous designs published in the press and many photographs document
the real impact the Louis XV revival had on the American interior. In its fullest
development, it was limited to wealthy families who could afford the decorative
investment comparable to that which had created the eighteenth-century original.

LOUIS XVI

The Louis XVI style was perhaps the most popular of the French revival
styles in America. Mrs. Spofford summarized it as more severe than the Louis
XV but still sumptuous and splendid. She commented, "It is well suited to the

frivolities of the life too frequently led nowadays by the extraordinarily wealthy."[14]

In virtually every element of an interior, the curve of the Louis XV rococo was replaced by the more severe, classic straight line. Although chairs and tables gained straighter legs, cabinetmakers continued to depend upon carving, inlay, gilding, and ormolu for decoration. Some Louis XVI was made abroad, but Mrs. Spofford wrote that "at present Louis Seize furniture is made in America with a nicety and purity quite equal to that which characterizes the best examples, and its wonderfully beautiful carving is unrivaled by any that comes from abroad."[15] Notable examples of the style came from the shops of Leon Marcotte and Herter Brothers, both of New York City.

In architectural details, wall panels became rectangular, with classical motifs introduced into carved or painted decoration. Classical pilasters might be fluted, and gilt with highlights in a copper red or silver green was common. Tapestries and silks were used for hangings, upholsteries, and draperies.

Louis XVI ceiling design

Figure 121. J. W. Bliss. *Prize Design for a Louis XVI Drawing Room.* 1981. *The Decorator and Furnisher* (February 1891), p. 161.

Bliss was a regular contributor to *The Decorator and Furnisher.* A profusion of neoclassic ornament has been showered on every detail, but the caryatids on the fireplace add a touch of the Empire. Symmetry reigns throughout the room, whose arrangement is clearly recognizable as late Victorian by the octagonal table with its two chairs.

Figure 122. *Drawing Room, Residence of LeGrand Lockwood, Norwalk, Connecticut.* 1868–1870. Lockwood-Mathews Mansion Museum of Norwalk, Inc., Norwalk, Conn.

Lockwood's drawing room was basically Louis XVI with a few Renaissance additions. Compared with later versions of the Louis XVI style, the walls were extraordinarily plain and the ceilings had rather heavy moldings. The ceiling painting, *Venus at Play with Her Cupids*, was done in Paris especially for the room. Ornate draperies cascade under carved cornices that might be labeled Renaissance rather than Louis XVI, and other photographs indicate that the chairs with oval backs had special upholstery incorporating Lockwood's initials.

The rooms were light, with white often the dominant color. Mrs. Spofford held that "the Louis Seize is now made with a perfection that gives it a right of existence until the spirit of the age shall develop something superior."[16] The wealthy agreed, and adopted the style for the most impressive rooms in their expensive houses. The LeGrand Lockwood house is but one of several examples

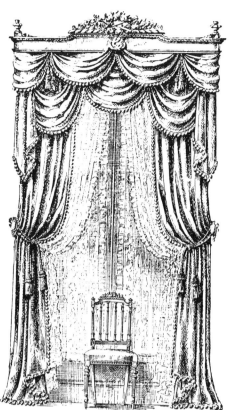

Louis XVI window drapery

Figure 123. Eastman Johnson. *Frederick Wells Gale*. 1876. Oil on board, 20¾ in. × 18½ in. (53 cm × 48 cm). Albany Institute of History and Art, Albany, N.Y.

Frederick Wells Gale is shown here in the house of his father E. Thompson Gale, president of a Troy, New York, bank and gas company. The door molding and corner block reveal that the house was a late Federal structure stylishly redecorated with a mixture of the Louis XVI and neo-Grec styles. The two pieces of crimson-upholstered Louis XVI furniture match a parlor set made by Marcotte in 1860,[41] while the piano with its gilt-incised lines is in the neo-Grec taste. The muted gold fleur-de-lis pattern of the pearl gray wallpaper provided an appropriate background for French revival furniture.

(Fig. 122). Unlike some of the other French revivals, the Louis XVI style found its way into less expensive furniture and other decorative materials. In the 1890s, *The Decorator and Furnisher* illustrated a great many Louis Seize and Empire designs, indicating that in the editors' view the style still had a right to exist.

Figure 124. *Parlor, Residence of Mrs. George Frederic Jones, West 23rd Street, New York City. C.* 1885. Wharton Papers, Collection of American Literature, Beinecke Library, Yale University, New Haven, Conn.

Mrs. Jones was the mother of Edith Wharton, the novelist and writer on interiors. Her parlor shows a profusion of chintz in a triple use rare in the late nineteenth century—upholstery, drapery, and wall covering. The woodwork is a solid color ornamented only by minimal gilded carving, probably in the Louis XVI style, as was the sofa at the right. The chairs are upholstered in the Turkish style, and the floor has a squared parquet design.

Figure 125. Charles P. Roos. *Modern Empire Interior.*
1893. *The Decorator and Furnisher* (November 1893),
p. 63.

In 1893, *The Decorator and Furnisher* published this suggestion for an Empire interior. The wreath motif of the
vertical striped paper is carried over into the valance, the
panel above the door, the garlanded frieze, and the painted
furniture. The swirled decoration of the heavy portières
does not adopt the wreath theme, and the curtains are
astonishingly simple. The picture hung from a picture rail
has nothing to do with the Empire style. Unfortunately,
the magazine provided no indication as to colors.

Empire window drapery

Figure 126. *Flat interior, New York City.* 1898. Johnson, *Inside of One Hundred Homes*, p. 40.

William Martin Johnson's *Inside of One Hundred Homes*, issued by the Ladies' Home Journal Library in 1898, dealt with smaller houses and apartments, like this flat in New York City. The room shows strong elements of the Empire revival in the fleur-de-lis wallpaper, the sofa, and the curtains. Yet the quasi-Windsor chair and the Morris chair introduce an eclecticism. The unused fireplace was draped over with red, figured China silk and filled with a Hepplewhite card table. As for the piano, Johnson wrote: "those who have attempted to sing against a wall while accompanying themselves on this instrument will appreciate the advantage of facing out into the room." (An embroidered curtain covered the back.)

The Exotics: Oriental, Egyptian, Pompeian, Byzantine, Aztec Renaissance, and Moorish

ORIENTAL—JAPANESE

Japanese motifs made a strong appearance in the 1870s and continued for the rest of the century. Japan opened to the West in 1854, but it was not until the London Exposition of 1862 that Westerners saw Japanese accessories and furnishings first hand. American interest in the arts of Japan and China grew after the displays at the Centennial Exposition in 1876. As Mrs. Spofford observed, Americans would have found authentic Japanese interiors with mats for beds and seats "prodigiously uncomfortable," and the authentic style was thus applied rather than adopted in American interiors.

Homes of the well-to-do occasionally had rooms done throughout in a Japanese style, but the style had an impact in even modest houses with the addition of bamboo furniture or accessories as simple and inexpensive as fans or parasols. Mrs. Spofford observed the style to be right for "the young and gay, and for those cosmopolitan people who are able to feel at home anywhere."[17]

FURNITURE

Some householders, like Dr. Williams (Fig. 127), furnished rooms with real Japanese furniture, but much of the style depended upon pieces made in this

Figure 127. *Japanese Library, Residence of Dr. Edward H. Williams, 101 N. 33rd Street, Philadelphia. The Decorator and Furnisher* (December 1884), pp. 78–79.

Dr. Williams, a millionaire, was inspired by the Centennial Exposition to visit Japan and furnish his library in the Japanese style. Beneath the deep blue ceiling with its flying storks was a frieze of bronze panels depicting the sacred dragon, and a wall painting by George Herzog of Japanese flowers in their natural colors with a poem in Japanese calligraphy. The poem spoke of the grasshoppers that appear in festive procession on the mantel tiles. The woodwork was of ebonized cherry and ebony, and based on Oriental designs. Schneider, Campbell, and Company of New York City made the chandeliers. Additional light came from gas burners above the skylight. Decorated in 1882, Williams's library is the most consistent and elaborate Japanese room we have found.[42]

country. Cook, in *The House Beautiful,* stressed the charm of bamboo furniture, both real and false. Real bamboo might sometimes be used where pieces were of the right size and strength, but turned wood could provide a false bamboo to continue the decorative scheme where necessary. Most often used in conjunction with real and false bamboo was bird's-eye maple. Nimura and Sato of Brooklyn and J. E. Wall of Boston were major manufacturers of real bamboo, while George Hunzinger, Kilian Brothers, and C. A. Aimone, all of New

Figure 128. *Parlor, Residence of George Walter Vincent Smith, Springfield, Massachusetts. C.* 1890. George Walter Vincent Smith Museum, Springfield, Mass.

George Walter Vincent Smith (1832–1923), who retired at the age of thirty-five after a New York career in carriage manufacture and importing, filled his house with his art collection. The photograph shows how porcelains and cloisonné alone could give a room a strong Oriental flavor, even amid an eclectic assemblage of furniture and painting. In 1893, Smith decided to give his whole collection to the city, and became the donor and first director of the Springfield Museum.

York City, produced large quantities of false bamboo. Bamboo and rattan chairs were very popular.

Following Edward Godwin's lead in England, American manufacturers, like Herter Brothers of New York, produced Anglo-Japanese furniture with light-hued wood, rectilinear lines, and Japanese tile decoration.

FLOOR COVERINGS

Many writers recommended Japanese straw matting as floor covering. Cook called it India matting, but whatever its source, most agreed it went well with Oriental decor. Photographs show that it was often used in rooms that had no other Oriental themes, especially in bedrooms (Fig. 147). The use of matting as an alternate floor covering when heavy rugs were removed in the summer continued into the twentieth century.

PICTURES AND MIRRORS

Dr. Hammond's bedroom (Fig. 129) shows the use of textiles and prints as wall decoration and a frieze. The American Bamboo Company of Boston advertised in 1887 that they produced bamboo easels and picture frames, but framed Japanese prints (regardless of frame) are uncommon in the photographs we have studied.

Japanese banner screen

TEXTILES

Japanese textiles, often with embroidered designs, appear draped on mantels or over tables or bedposts. Such fabrics were an obvious and accessible source for curtains and upholstery.

WALL TREATMENT

Walls in the Japanese style are rare, but Dr. Williams and Dr. Hammond (Figs. 127, 129) both showed what could be done. Williams's room, the more expensive of the two, had a frieze of bronze panels and a wall painted with a Japanese scene ornamented with calligraphy. Hammond had a frieze of prints with a wall covered with prints, textiles, and fans. Unfortunately, the authors of *Artistic Houses* do not say whether the wall was painted or covered with straw matting or paper.

LIGHTING

Dr. Williams had special chandeliers designed, while Dr. Hammond added a Japanese element (small parasols) to his chandelier.

Figure 129. *Japanese Bedroom, Dr. William A. Hammond, 54th Street near Fifth Avenue, New York City. Artistic Houses*, I, 88; see Bibliography. Yale University Library, New Haven, Conn.

Dr. Hammond's house was decorated primarily in the Egyptian style, but his spare bedroom was Japanese. The ceiling had a foo dog and dragon in addition to geometric design; the frieze was composed of colorful Japanese prints, while the walls were decorated with silk hangings, lacquer panels, and fans. A shelf over the mantelpiece displayed Oriental ceramics, a Japanese fabric was draped over the foot of the bed, and parasols disguised the chandelier.

244

COLORS

No special color schemes are associated with the Japanese style. Williams had a blue ceiling with wall designs painted in natural colors.

ACCESSORIES

Mrs. Spofford approved of Japanese accessories and admired the careful handiwork given to the most mundane objects. She exclaimed about the beauty of an iron tea kettle, the crackle of Satsuma ware, and the coral and creamy tints of Kyoto ware, and she added that fans, prints, and small bronzes did much for a room. Japanese fans found a place in the decor of many rooms—even those done in the Colonial Revival (Fig. 143, page 262).

About 1875, Japanese motifs appeared in silverware, characterized by bamboo handles and engravings of plants, flowers, and exotic birds. In the 1880s, Wood and Hughes introduced flatware patterns named "Celestial" and "Japanese," and Whiting offered "Bamboo" and "Honeysuckle." The "Chrysanthemum" pattern that Tiffany and Co. introduced in the 1870s is still popular today.

Quantities of Japanese ceramics entered the American market, and Japanese designs were readily adaptable to Western ceramics. Pinder Bourne & Co. in England produced a pitcher in 1877 with cherry blossom sprays and bamboo strips. In the 1880s, ladies were urged to paint china; many of them did so using Japanese designs of the sort the Rookwood Pottery in Cincinnati produced in great number, perhaps not surprisingly since Kataro Shirayamadani was one of their chief artists. Mason's Ironstone, under the probable influence of Imari ware, offered a "Japan" pattern that sold well in America.

An Oriental dragon was the motif of an uncommon pressed glass pattern produced in the Midwest. "Oriental" was a more common pattern. Also common was "Peachblow," a type of glass inspired by Chinese Peachblow porcelains that, like the glass, shaded gradually from deep red to pale peach green.

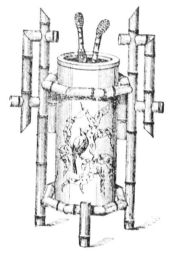

Bamboo umbrella stand, 1891

Rookwood vase decorated by
Shira-yamadani

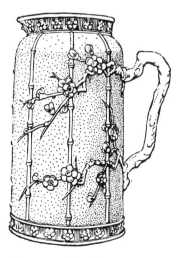

Japanese-style pitcher

Figure 130. *Chinese Room, Residence of T. A. Havemeyer, Madison Avenue,*
New York City. Photograph by Byron. The Byron Collection, Museum of the
City of New York.

In 1892, the list of millionaires included seven Havemeyers whose fortunes were
based on the Havemeyer Sugar Refining Company and Havemeyers and Elder Sugar
Refining Company. T. A. Havemeyer was among them. This is a rare example of a
room done completely in the Chinese manner. The furniture of carved ebony is dark
and heavy, obviously produced in China for the export trade. There is an abundance of Chinese bibelots, including snuff bottles, porcelains, small bronzes, and
cloisonné. Two embroideries in teak frames appear, one of which shows a peacock,
a favorite Oriental motif. A temple lantern with its painted scenes and tassels hangs
in the center of the room.

ORIENTAL—CHINESE

The Japanese was the most common Oriental style, but there were a few
Chinese rooms as well. Mrs. Spofford described deeply carved teak tables and
arm chairs specifically designed for export. Compared to the Japanese, she
judged these chairs heavier and less hospitable, and urged American buyers to
avoid any lacquered furniture, whether Japanese or Chinese. Being "dried and
shrunken by the alien air," it would not survive steam heat.

The Havemeyer residence (Fig. 130) was one of the few examples of a
consistently Chinese room. The furniture was heavy imported teak, and Chinese
motifs dominated. The walls, decorated with silks, were divided into panels in
the Chinese style, while hangings and tablecovers were of Chinese fabrics. The
tasselated Chinese lantern appears in other less thoroughly Chinese rooms.

EGYPTIAN

Designers promoted an Egyptian revival, but householders were not generally enthusiastic. The opening of the Suez Canal in 1869 rekindled popular interest in Egypt, an interest furthered even more by the presentation of Verdi's *Aida* in New York City in 1873. Americans saw another facet of Egypt with the erection of the obelisk in Central Park, New York City, in 1881.

The primary impact of the Egyptian style was in the bright additions of occasional motifs or accessories to rooms preponderantly decorated in other styles. Egyptian furniture of the sort proposed in *The Decorator and Furnisher* in September 1885 was rare. The set illustrated there could be bought for $300.

Figure 131. *Library, Residence of Chauncy M. Depew, 27 West 54th Street.* 1899. Photograph by Byron. The Byron Collection, Museum of the City of New York.

Chauncy M. Depew (1834–1928) was president of the New York Central Railroad, United States Senator, and a millionaire associate of the Vanderbilts. With its Elizabethan chair, Renaissance desk, and massive Turkish chandelier, this room is at best eclectic. Around the frieze and on the ceiling is a fine Egyptian scene. The decoration is faithful to ancient Egyptian art, especially the molding and ceiling decoration and the winged scarab. The small spaces of zigzag decoration above the bookcases, yet below the frieze, present a characteristic Egyptian motif. Note also the long lotus blossom at the right of the mantel and the sphinx heads carved in the mantel itself.

Tiffany synthesis of Egyptian and classical decoration, 1876

The table, much like tomb furniture, is an accurate reproduction with monoped legs with dog feet and heads. The angular dresser carries the same canine motif although the mirror and side bracket shelves are suggestive of a pylon temple entrance. The sleigh bed shows masklike heads derived from mummy cases. Probably very few readers ordered this set, but some wealthy households did have Egyptian motifs in one or two rooms.[18]

The parian ware bust of Cleopatra produced by the Etruria Pottery in Trenton, New Jersey, was a natural complement to the style.

POMPEIAN

The least evident of the styles to which Mrs. Spofford devoted whole chapters was the Pompeian, perhaps with good reason. She described it as a style of "great magnificence" costing a "vast amount of money," but for some it might be perfect: "If a millionaire is going to live a sybaritic, self-indulgent life of pleasure, he could not express his determination better than by furnishing his villa in the Pompeian."[19]

She analyzed the Pompeian style as a mixture of Roman and Greek art with

Figure 132. A. Moorman. *Pompeian Library. The Decorator and Furnisher* (January 1893), p. 136.

The same A. Moorman who produced the Aztec Renaissance library (Fig. 134) also contributed this version of a Pompeian library. As historical furniture was "too uncomfortable and inconvenient for use," he designed new pieces based on Pompeian motifs. Griffins are prominent. The 1890s more than Pompeii were the inspiration for the inglenook by the fireplace, but that area, walls, and ceiling were decorated with Pompeian designs. The floor was to be a Roman mosaic, and dark mahogany or walnut carving was to be edged in copper bronze. On the wall were painted tapestries depicting Fame, Justice, Literature, and Science. Modern electroliers in a Pompeian style were complemented by the reproduction oil lamp on the table. Moorman did not stipulate specific colors for the room.

POMPEIAN LIBRARY

A. MOOR

Figure 133. *Drawing Room, Residence of J. Pierpont Morgan, 36th Street at Madison Avenue, New York City. C. 1883. Artistic Houses*, I, 77; see Bibliography. Yale University Library, New Haven, Conn.

One of the richest men in America, J. Pierpont Morgan left $78 million in 1913, the kind of wealth that had easily supported Christian Herter's decoration of his New York house thirty years earlier. Herter produced an almost identical room with the same elliptical mantelpiece for Lieutenant Governor Oliver Ames of Boston. That room has recently been called an Aesthetic interior,[43] but *Artistic Houses* termed Morgan's of "Pompeian inspiration."[44] The woodwork was ivory with gilt, while the ceiling carried a "suggestion (not an imitation) of light colored mosaic." The frieze and walls were Pompeian red with gilt, and the furniture was upholstered in old Persian embroidery or cherry plush with gold embroidery. Edison invented the lightbulb in 1879, and by 1883 Morgan had this room lit by bare bulbs powered by a steam generator in his stable. For *Artistic Houses*, the room had a "mild gayety of expression amid the aroma of perfect taste."[45]

additional elements of Persia and Egypt. Walls received the most elaborate treatment, with their painted panels of nymphs or dancing girls, arabesques of flowers, sphinxes, and urns. Furniture included bronze tripods for braziers, flowers or candelabra, and tables decorated with leopards or sphinxes. Floors were mosaics. She held to her dictum that the same style should prevail throughout a house, but if one could not afford a complete Pompeian interior (she offered a bathroom design), other rooms in early Renaissance or Louis XVI were acceptable. The Louis XVI, she noted, was itself a "feeble echo" of the Pompeian.

By the early 1890s, the Pompeian style was more evident in the pages of *The Decorator and Furnisher* than it was in American houses. As elaborated in such drawings as Moorman's (Fig. 133), the style was certainly as expensive as Mrs. Spofford had claimed, with its emphasis on elaborate carving, mosaic floors, specially designed furniture, and appropriate lighting fixtures and plant stands. In 1897, the magazine commented wistfully: "This style seems to have but little favor with modern designers," but there were a few Pompeian rooms, all in houses of great wealth. In New York City, William H. Vanderbilt had a Pompeian vestibule and a dressing room decorated with a frieze of "women and mischievous Cupids."[20]

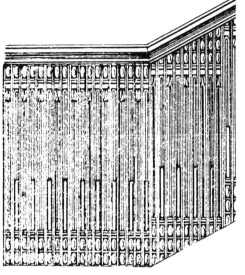

Pompeian-style wall decoration, 1892

BYZANTINE

Another style more proposed than adopted was the Byzantine. The suggestion for a dining room or library (as shown in the linecut below) emphasized high ceilings, heavy beams, generally massive architectural features, and swirling acanthus ornamentation. The tall fireplace jutting out from the wall was the focal point of the style in creating the interior. The wall and clerestory windows were of stained glass. Designer Edward Dewson was a proponent of the style, offering a Byzantine drapery design in *The Decorator and Furnisher* for August 1893. In November 1892, he had pointed out that the Byzantine made exciting hybrids with other styles. Byzantine ornament added to a Louis XV table produced "Franco-Byzantine." On a "modern Italian" dining table, the same ornamentation became "Italo-Byzantine." Inevitably, casual treatment of Byzantine motifs led to "neo-Byzantine."

A modern Byzantine dining room or library, 1897

Figure 134. A. Moorman. *Aztec Renaissance Library. The Decorator and Furnisher* (September 1894), p. 212.

Moorman's essay and graphic rendering was one of many attempts late in the century to use previously unexploited motifs to create new styles. Most of these ideas were of greater appeal to the artist than they were to the householder.

AZTEC RENAISSANCE

A further contribution to the 1890s search for "a distinctive American style" was the Aztec Renaissance library (Fig. 132) proposed by A. Moorman, writing in *The Decorator and Furnisher* for September 1894. He urged designers to follow ancient American as opposed to ancient European designs. If the Greeks had griffins and dolphins, he included the Aztec symbol of wisdom, the serpent, as a principal motif in the pilasters flanking the bookcases in his drawing. And rather than use the Greek acanthus leaf, his carvings are decorated with "the lactus (the national floral emblem of the Aztecs) in conventional form." The image of the Aztec god Tezcatlipoca was treated as a Renaissance grotesque in the overmantel, while the table and chairs were modeled on native stones and columns. The walls were yellow tan, the frieze a tan with blue and bronze reliefs, and the ceiling a light yellow tan. The furniture was upholstered in a deep blue leather, and the draperies were a dark tan. This drawing seems to have been the only appearance of the Aztec Renaissance in *The Decorator and Furnisher* or in any American house.

MOORISH

In the late 1860s and 1870s, Americans found a new exoticism in the Moorish style. Mrs. Spofford thought it "more in accord with the summer places of wealth than with the homes of people whose income is restricted," but she still believed that small houses might have at least one room, a conservatory, where "some features of the style may always be indulged." [21]

America had long kept up a distant, romantic fascination with the Near East. Washington Irving had excited the imagination of the country with his *Alhambra* (1832), and enthusiasm was created by E. W. Lane's translation of the *Thousand and One Nights* in 1840. Richard Burton's fuller translation in the 1880s engendered further interest. P. T. Barnum, master of the exotic, had built his Iranistan in Bridgeport in 1848, and just after the Civil War, artist Frederick Church scrapped his plans for a French villa in favor of a Moorish mansion he saw as "the Center of the World." As is evident from the photographs (Figs. 135–140), rooms began to take on the appearance of an Oriental bazaar with a profusion of hanging lamps, inlaid furniture, armor, and Persian tiles and plates.

FURNITURE

Quick to react to fads, the American furniture industry was soon supplying "Turkish"-style furniture—frames with springs, heavily upholstered and deeply tufted. A fringe usually fell from the upholstery to the floor. One characteristic piece was the circular sofa with a round, tufted back, capped by either a potted palm or a piece of exotic sculpture (Fig. 138). Small octagonal or hexagonal tables, many of them imported from the Near East, were very popular.

opposite, top: Figure 135. *Oriental Room, New York City.* 1904. Photograph by Byron. The Byron Collection, Museum of the City of New York.

This room is an extreme example of the full Moorish decor. The anonymous owner has acquired every possible Oriental accessory, including the expected small tables and folding chairs with Moorish inlay. The fireplace is faced with Persian tiles, and even the valance on the drapery has cusps to reinforce the Moorish theme. Hanging lamps are supplemented by the tall kerosene lamp on an iron frame at the left of the picture. Innumerable brass accessories are scattered throughout the room, and a hookah is on the tabourette in the foreground. At the right is a cozy corner with swagged tenting and a chair upholstered in a Turkish style.

Figure 136. *Hall with a View into the Parlor, Residence of Mr. and Mrs. Durante Da Ponte, 3512 St. Charles Avenue, New Orleans.* 1883. Thomas Sully Collection, Special Collections Division, Tulane University Library, New Orleans, La.

Da Ponte was the owner and editor of two newspapers, but not in the millionaire class. In his hall, designed by Thomas Sully, Moorish decor dominated walls, floor, and ceiling. Note the partition of the ceiling by pierced grill work and the wallpaper that imitated Persian tiles. The fur tufts in the doorways were foot wipers. *The Decorator and Furnisher* for October 1888 observed that the decorative effect of a floor could be "heightened . . . with a foxskin thrown on it." Animals were thus doubly right here, for household pets were "part" of the Moorish style.

Olana, Church's house in the Moorish style.

The cozy corner in an Outing version

opposite: Figure 137. Douglas Volk. *Interior with Portrait of John S. Bradstreet. C.* 1890, Oil on canvas, 17 in. × 22¼ in. (43 cm × 56 cm). Minneapolis Institute of Arts, Minneapolis, Minn.

Bradstreet has surrounded himself with Oriental memorabilia. Two mosque lights hang from the ceiling, and behind him is a mirhab, a screen of carved Indian pierced work. The mantel, apparently of brass, supports a brass tray, a bottle, and a realistic figure of an Arab on a camel. On the upper part of the wall is an Arabic inscription. A popular Moorish feature was the small hexagonal tabourette. Simple versions of such tables cost about $1.00, and they often found a place in rooms where they were the only Moorish feature. A kilim carpet is draped across a niche that holds a Japanese mikado chest.

By the 1890s, the Turkish cozy corner had become a popular craze. Naturally, one would prefer to have an entire Turkish room, but if that were not financially possible, it was easy to create a cozy corner with a low sofa, many cushions, and, if possible, a pair of long spears from which hangings could be draped. Initially Turkish, the cozy corner was soon adapted to a variety of other styles.

FLOOR COVERINGS

Oriental rugs were the logical floor coverings for the Moorish style, and they appear in profusion.

PICTURES AND MIRRORS

The most elaborate Moorish style includes virtually no pictures—no accident either, for Mrs. Spofford stipulates "neither pictures or statues can accompany it."[22] (Human images are forbidden by Muslim law.) Less literal interpreta-

tions of the style might include paintings that have nothing to do with the Moorish taste (Fig. 138).

TEXTILES

Kilim rugs and other Eastern textiles were draped over screens, tables, mantels, or strung over poles for a cozy corner. "Baghdad" portières were sometimes used in rooms that had no other Moorish features. Mrs. Spofford thought "sumptuous gold threaded material" most apt for upholstery, but even striped satin had an exotic look on Turkish tufted furniture. In the true Moorish style, upholstery or fringe reached the floor and no woodwork was seen on furniture. The New York Oriental room (Fig. 135) shows a drapery in the Moorish style. Obviously, the style demanded no careful coordination of textile designs, yet the combination of Oriental materials had a clear unity in itself.

opposite: Figure 138. *Parlor, Residence of Carolyn Whitney Suydam, Whitney Avenue at Cliff Street, New Haven, Connecticut.* 1890. Collection of Mrs. Helen Husted.

A circular Turkish sofa with an upholstered back dominates the room, but rather than a potted palm, a figure supporting a nautilus shell emerges from the center. There are matching corner sofas in the back of the room and four side chairs with peacock backs. Further evidence of the Moorish style is the small square table with light inlay and a Turkish flag draped in front of the fireplace. The parquet floor is covered with a large Oriental rug. The ceiling design is not necessarily Moorish, and the gas chandelier surely is not. The furniture and some of the accessories give the room a basic Moorish look, but the style is far from complete.

above: Figure 139. *Oriental Music Room, Everleigh Club, Chicago.* 1902. Courtesy, Chicago Historical Society, Chicago, Ill.

This illustration was taken from a flyer issued by the Everleigh sisters to promote their fashionable house of pleasure. The customer found the Oriental Music Room furnished with a complete set of Turkish tufted furniture and hanging brass lights, and the beauty of the residents was reflected in the mirrors that lined the walls. Moorish arch decorations encase the mirrors and extend to a deep ceiling cornice. The design is repeated in the plaster work of the ceiling.

WALL TREATMENT, ARCHITECTURAL DETAILS, AND CEILINGS

In the most elaborate interiors, like the Da Ponte house (Fig. 136), architectural details and wall decoration were closely tied together. Pointed onion and horseshoe arches were typically surrounded by wall designs in Moorish motifs.

Ceilings were likewise covered in Near Eastern designs, or, in the case of the Everleigh Club (Fig. 139), the textured wall decoration was carried onto the ceiling. *The Decorator and Furnisher* published appropriate ceiling designs during the 1880s.

LIGHTING

Mosque lights, often in several varieties, were a standard adjunct to the elaborate Moorish interior, but the Da Pontes had chandeliers with no obvious Moorish motifs (Fig. 136).

COLOR

Persian designs emphasized blue, green, gold, yellow, red, and black, but many intermediate shades found a place in their ornament. In general, strong, vibrant colors dominated the Moorish-style room.

ACCESSORIES

Moorish interiors reveal a wealth of Arabian and Persian accessories from ceramics to hookah pipes to armor hung on the walls. The peacock, favorite bird of the Orientals, offered many decorative motifs, and Church had a stuffed one in his front hall. So did other householders of the 1880s and 1890s. In the absence of a stuffed peacock, one could have a vase of peacock feathers near one's cozy corner—a Moorish touch readily adaptable to many other styles.

East Indian–style candlestick

The Colonial Revival

The American Colonial Revival began about the time of the Philadelphia Centennial Exposition of 1876 and reached full development in the 1880s. Although several individuals had collected American furniture and decorative arts since the beginning of the 1800s, popular interest in the seventeenth and eighteenth centuries had remained dormant. At the Centennial Exposition, visitors could see the New England Kitchen or "Log Cabin in 'Ye Olden Times.'" The exhibit, showing progress in kitchens and cooking over the past century, was furnished with a mix of old tables, cradles, Windsor chairs, and a spinning wheel. Hostesses in colonial costume served a boiled dinner with beans, brown bread, and old-fashioned pudding. Thousands saw it, just as they saw the exhibit of George J. Henkels of Philadelphia, who showed what guidebooks called "a set of chamber furniture in the style of 1776" made from an old maple from the grounds of Independence Hall. [23]

In the same year as the Centennial Exposition, Rhoda and Agnes Garrett published their *Suggestions for House Decoration* in London. In 1877, a Philadelphia publisher reprinted the book. The Garretts followed Charles Eastlake's general principle of honesty in furniture, but for some rooms they found eighteenth-century antiques most appropriate. Windsors in the hall were just as correct as a dining room furnished with old Chippendale chairs, strong and simply made with comfortable, wide seats. An entire drawing room with authentic walnut Queen Anne furniture was a delight. This furniture, they wrote, was "to be found in many of those old country houses from which the good old fashioned furniture has not yet been driven out by the 'grins and grimaces' of modern upholstery." A four-post bedstead complete with hanging, a large mahogany wardrobe, and an "old fashioned double chest of drawers" furnished a bedroom stylishly.

Clarence Cook likewise recommmended good early furniture that he mixed with modern pieces: "This mania . . . for old furniture is one of the best signs of returning good taste in a community that has long been the victim to the whims and impositions of foreign fashions. The furniture which was in use in this century in the time of our grandfathers . . . was almost always well designed and perfectly fitted for the uses it was to be put to." [24] Not everyone could find antiques, and by the 1880s, the Paine Furniture Company of Boston

New England kitchen at the 1876 Centennial Exposition

above: Figure 140. *Dining Room, Mount Vernon. C.* 1900. Colored postcard issued by Washington, Alexandria, & Mount Vernon Railway.

Although an attempt to restore Washington's eighteenth-century room, this scene is a late nineteenth-century interior. Typical of the period was the placement of extra pictures on the floor as their regular place of display. The chairs and center table date from long after Washington's death, as does the lavender and blue rug. Contemporary research finds a tan putty color most correct with a white cornice and ceiling, but at the turn of the century the walls were rose, the woodwork white, and the mantel a light green with a light blue mantel-shelf.

left: Figure 141. *Hall, Monticello.* 1899. Thomas Allen Glenn, *Some Colonial Mansions,* 2nd Ser., p. 212.

Only the architecture and the busts of Jefferson and Franklin would give the uninformed reader any clue that this is Jefferson's Monticello. The furniture and the lighting were exclusively late nineteenth century. Although Glenn commented that the house was "rejuvenated as in the days of its former owner," it would be many years before painstaking research and careful collection of original pieces restored the house with accuracy.

was producing what it called "colonial" furniture. At the end of the century, the large furniture companies were offering a wide variety of pieces in the style.

Further information for those interested in Colonial Revival came from Arthur Little of Swampscott, Massachusetts. His *Early New England Interiors,* published in 1878, was the first of many books showing colonial architecture and interior detail. Frank E. Wallis followed with *Old Colonial Architecture and Furniture* (1887) and *American Architecture, Decoration, and Furniture of the Eighteenth Century* (1896). Both were folios of drawings rather than detailed analyses.

The Decorator and Furnisher ran many designs in what by 1889 it called the "revived colonial style."[25] Generally, in the nineteenth century, the style was limited to more modest houses, never really gaining popularity in the villas of great magnificence. However, with the refinement of the interior around the turn of the century, the simplicity and elegance of the Colonial Revival brought it new favor in homes of wealth and simplicity alike. Later developments are described in Chapter 13.

FURNITURE

At first, most writers lumped the basic styles of the seventeenth and eighteenth centuries together under the general label "Colonial." By the 1890s, distinctions were made between Chippendale and William and Mary, but from the time of the Exposition of 1876, interiors often showed a mix of styles. A suite of dining room furniture might be basically Chippendale or Federal, but the pictures do not reveal conscious efforts to make rooms stylistically uniform. The dining

Figure 142. *Drawing Room.* 1877. Rhoda and Agnes Garrett, *Suggestions for House Decoration*; see Bibliography.

This English room undoubtedly inspired many American readers. The chairs, settee, table, and tall clock are in the Queen Anne style. The wall, divided into vertical panels, is papered with a floral pattern up to the level of the plain frieze. The floral motif is carried over into the design of the screen. A small Oriental rug lies atop a plain wall-to-wall carpet. The corner cupboard has some Hepplewhite features, but it is somewhat similar to a piece illustrated by Clarence Cook who describes it as made by Cottier and Co.[46]

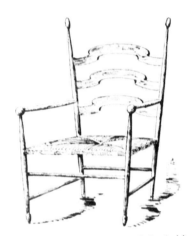

Colonial Revival version of the ladder-back chair with some Art Nouveau influence

Chippendale Colonial Revival arm chair

room at Mount Vernon and the hall at Monticello, both ostensibly restorations, are surprising cases in point (Figs. 140, 141).

Some furniture produced by Barnard and Simonds of Rochester, New York, or by the Bishop Company of Grand Rapids, Michigan, was faithful to the originals,[26] but mass producers often made "improvements" and adaptations.

In the Ladd dining room (Fig. 145), Hepplewhite lines have been added to a late nineteenth-century dining table and chairs. The china cupboard has no Federal prototype. In the Twichell dining room (Fig. 146), the glass-enclosed china closet became a standard piece by 1900. The claw-and-ball feet on that cupboard and the dining table also show the heavy-handed manner in which colonial details could be added to contemporary furniture. During this period, some genuine antiques were improved with additional carvings or extra parts; but original or reproduction, customers and cabinetmakers of the period favored heavy purple mahogany finishes, with virtually no regard for the wood to which they were applied.

Possibly the most grotesque of the new "creations" was the Old Flax Spinning Wheel Chair advertised by William B. Savage of Boston in 1887. Ever since the Centennial Exposition, spinning wheels had appeared in "colonial" settings, although the colonists themselves generally banished wheels and looms to the attic, chambers, or workrooms. Figure 147 shows a spinning wheel placed as an obstacle to anyone hurrying in or out of the period four-poster bed.

FLOOR COVERINGS

No particular carpets were recommended for the Colonial Revival. Photographs do show Oriental carpets and wall-to-wall carpeting with a great variety of patterns. The Washington dining room has a large hooked rug, a floor covering that would not have been known to the general himself.

PICTURES AND MIRRORS

Pictures were important in the Colonial Revival interiors, but were not necessarily of colonial themes. They were displayed in a manner consistent with other late nineteenth-century styles, even to the extreme of setting them on the floor (Fig. 140). As with other styles, symmetry governed the placement of pictures.

Illustrations of the 1880s and 1890s show no concern for choosing authentic styles in mirrors.

Figure 143. *Dining Room Chimney Piece.* 1877. Rhoda and Agnes Garrett, *Suggestions for House Decoration*; see Bibliography.

Through this illustration the Garretts showed the decorative value of early woodwork. The Adamesque mantel with its many urns typifies late eighteenth-century woodcarving, and the urns on the mantel shelf repeat the theme. Against the wallpaper with its strong pattern, inspired by the Aesthetic Movement, there is only one picture. The gas lamp next to the urn on the right is balanced by the Japanese fan and Oriental jar on the left.

TEXTILES

We have found no evidence that manufacturers or decorators used appropriate eighteenth-century fabrics or fabric designs as part of the early Colonial Revival. Nor was there a conscious effort to emulate eighteenth-century draperies.

Bed Curtains.   As bed curtains had gone out of style, inevitably one had to depart from current fashion for a fully curtained bed, and the lace tester (Fig. 147) only remotely suggests its colonial forebears.

WALL TREATMENT

In most illustrations, the three-part division of the wall popular in the Eastlake style is absent. Many show a two-part division—a lower part of the wall and a frieze—but a wall covered entirely in one paper was equally common. There seem to have been relatively few colonial wallpapers. A surprising number of photographs of Colonial Revival show floral rather than the few appropriate designs.

Late in the period, walls were painted solid colors with the woodwork in white or light colors.

CEILINGS AND ARCHITECTURAL DETAILS

The Colonial Revival often found a place in houses built in the late nineteenth century, but it also appeared in several eighteenth-century houses, which, of course, had period architectural details. Typical details for later construction included dentil moldings, swag carving, and fluted columns by fireplaces. Revival architects tended to favor Federal details. The mantel of the Twichell dining room (Fig. 146) owes as much to the late nineteenth century as it does to the eighteenth. One new architectural detail also seen in the Twichell room was the plate rail for the display of a china collection. Ceilings were generally white or light-colored and plain.

opposite, top: Figure 144. *Hall, Residence of Arthur Little. Swampscott, Massachusetts. C.* 1895. Society for the Preservation of New England Antiquities, Boston, Mass.

Little was a Massachusetts architect and proponent of the Colonial Revival, but in his own hall the Colonial style was transformed by a strong dose of the Aesthetic Movement. Two Morris-type papers, one light, one dark, cover the wall and frieze, and the stair carpet and pillows in the window seat have typical Aesthetic designs. White-painted woodwork, which in previous decades would have been stained dark, brightened the room. Two chairs and a late Federal mirror were also painted white.

Figure 145. *Dining Room, Residence of J. Wesley Ladd, West Park and Market Street, Portland, Oregon.* Oregon Historical Society, Portland.

Ladd was among the *World Almanac*'s 1902 list of millionaires. He made his money in real estate and banking. The dining room shows the look of the Colonial Revival in the late 1890s, but basically only the Hepplewhite furniture stems from the revival. There is nothing Colonial about the electric chandelier, the wallpaper of floral arabesques, the plates and brass on the walls, the Indian wastebasket, or the Oriental ceramics atop the breakfront. The drapes in a light floral design are straight hung and decorated only with a ball fringe. The wall-to-wall carpet presents a light diapered pattern.

LIGHTING

Styles in lighting fixtures were often unrelated to the rest of the room. Chandeliers in the photographs range from Eastlake to Art Glass. The Twichell dining room (Fig. 146) shows a popular fixture that reproduces no period at all. Such fixtures typically had marbled glass in a patinaed bronze frame with a deep beaded fringe.

COLOR

Writing in *The Decorator and Furnisher* for May 1891, James Carruthers noted that the prevalent colors for colonial decoration and hangings had been "orange, pale pink, a purplish red, warm drabs, blue, and ivory white." Walls had been invariably finished in "delicate tones of color." The Washington dining room (Fig. 140) about the year 1900 had pink walls with white woodwork and a green ceiling molding and curtains. The rug was lavender and light blue.

ACCESSORIES

The overabundance of accessories common to other styles abated somewhat in the Colonial Revival, but such objects are nonetheless evident and not necessarily related to the eighteenth century. An Indian basket, a fancy pin cushion, and the Venus de Milo make strange partners on a late Empire bureau (Fig. 147). A tinge of the Orient seems desired even in the colonial room, and practically every house displays Japanese bottles, platters, vases, or fans. The Garretts depicted a parlor cabinet filled with appropriate Oriental export china.

opposite, top: Figure 146. *Dining Room, Twichell Residence, Bryn Mawr, Pennsylvania. C.* 1900. Lyman Allyn Museum, New London, Conn.

Although the dining room chairs remained faithful to the originals, the table in this Pennsylvanian interior is a Chippendale adaptation rendered by the huge ball-and-claw feet and the gadrooned border of the table top. The same feet appear on the china cabinet with its diminutive swan neck cresting in the top. The sideboard is an Empire-style piece. The dark woodwork of the room was in keeping with the mahogany furniture. The lamp over the table is a typical product of the 1890s; barely evident is an electric cord from the left side of the table to the floor—undoubtedly an early electric buzzer to the kitchen.

Figure 147. *Bedroom, Lucy Abbot Throop. Furnishing the Home of Good Taste.* 1913; see Bibliography.

Here is a fine mix of Chippendale and Sheraton furniture, combined with an incongruous rustic spinning wheel. The bedroom's walls are a plain color and the ceiling is a lighter shade. Note that one picture is hung above the mirror of the Sheraton chest, while another larger picture is not hung, but set, on the Chippendale card table. Straw matting covers the floor, and a shield, possibly also of straw matting, protects the wall behind the pitcher and bowl.

Figure 148. *Dining Room, Lucy Abbot Throop. Furnishing the Home of Good Taste*, 1913; see Bibliography.

Miss Throop, like Candace Wheeler, argued for uniformity of decorative style within a room, and to a degree, this room followed her principles. The woodwork and the mantel were in the Federal period and the plate rail displayed a collection of blue Staffordshire pottery. The Spanish foot variation of the Queen Anne style was carried through the chairs, sideboard, and dining table, the latter two pieces obvious adaptations of the original style. Rustic andirons, fireplace tools, and the large Oriental rug on the board floor added to the Colonial effect, but the "decorative frieze in low tones above" was a product of the Aesthetic Movement.

The Aesthetic Movement: Tiffany, Eastlake, and Romanesque

In England in the 1860s, the efforts of William Morris, Bruce Talbert, and Lewis F. Day resulted in what was called the Aesthetic Movement. It was a reaction to the heavy furniture, gilt, and bright colors of the mid-Victorian interior. The partisans of the new movement introduced subdued colors and fewer pieces of simpler furniture. Walls were covered with papers bearing a profusion of stylized or realistic plants and flowers, with appropriate textiles to match the room. Japanese art blended easily into the style, providing wall hanging, tiles to decorate furniture, ceramics for display, or motifs for new English designs.

The style spread to America in the 1870s. The Eastlake variant was undoubtedly the most popular here, but it was by no means the only version. Tiffany and Associated Artists produced interiors that owed much to the Aesthetic Movement and almost nothing to Eastlake. Christian Herter likewise drew from the Aesthetic Movement for many of his interiors: two Herter rooms show the distinction between the Eastlake style and the English Aesthetic Movement (Figs. 134, 154). The Morgan and Vanderbilt rooms both show thin, simple furniture associated with the English movement, a style far from Eastlake. The heavy, neo-Gothic, honest furniture praised by Eastlake was produced in America to fill the demand created by the popularity of Eastlake's book.[27]

Harriet Spofford's *Art Decoration Applied to Furniture* (1878) synthesized elements of English decoration with Eastlake's own variant, as did Hudson Holly's *Modern Dwellings in Town and Country* (1878). As Spofford and Holly contributed to what was generally considered one basic style, we have discussed them under the rubric Eastlake. Tiffany and Associated Artists we treat separately, adding one interior by Christian Herter.

Figure 149. *Salon, Residence of George Kemp, 720 Fifth Avenue, New York City. C. 1883. Artistic Houses*, I, 53; see Bibliography. Yale University Library, New Haven, Conn.

In 1879 George Kemp, a millionaire drug manufacturer, commissioned Tiffany and Associated Artists to do their first domestic interior. *Artistic Houses* described the room as Arabic with an inclination to Persian. The ceiling shimmered in iridescent silver; the frieze, painted by Tiffany, had alternating squares and circles; and the mantel and wainscotting had eighteen different woods. Panels of Japanese brocade surmounted the mirror with blue glass lanterns in front, and old Arabic tiles and new opalescent glass tiles by Tiffany decorated the fireplace. Blue was the predominant color in walls, chandeliers, tiles, and plush portières. The many intricate strong patterns were unified by the blue and silver color scheme.

Figure 150. *Dining Room, Residence of Louis C. Tiffany, Top Floor, Bella Apartment House, 48 East 26th Street, New York City. Artistic Houses*, I, 4; see Bibliography. Yale University Library, New Haven, Conn.

Tiffany's own dining room combined eighteenth-century, Japanese, and Aesthetic traditions. The overmantel painting of turkey, pumpkin, and corn has little to do with the Japanese mushroom paper that covers the wall. The blue textile frieze also has a Japanese design of birds and clouds, and Japanese and Moorish ceramics are found on the shelves and walls. The influence of the Aesthetic Movement is evident in the tiles surrounding the fireplace, the floral arabesque paper above the mantel shelf, the repeated blue design on the ceiling, and the ivy leaves on the glass of the transom. Here as in the Kemp room (Fig. 149), Tiffany mixed strong patterns in close proximity.

TIFFANY AND ASSOCIATED ARTISTS

In 1879, Louis Comfort Tiffany, son of the New York jeweler, gave up painting for interior decorating. He found ready allies for a new venture in Candace Wheeler, who was interested in textile design; Samuel Colman, an artist, designer, and collector of textiles and china; and Lockwood de Forest, a painter and devotee of East Indian carving and fabrics. The group became known as Louis C. Tiffany and Associated Artists. The four collaborated, but Tiffany was the leading figure, and when *Artistic Houses* described some of their interiors, it was "Louis C. Tiffany and Co." who had done the work.

Figure 151. *Drawing Room, Residence of Hon. Hamilton Fish, 251 East 17th Street, New York City.* 1883. *Artistic Houses,* II, 94; see Bibliography. Yale University Library, New Haven, Conn.

Real estate made Hamilton Fish (1808–1893) a millionaire and public office brought him national fame. In his drawing room, Moorish and Indian motifs were prominent and blue was the unifying color, becoming lighter as it approached the ceiling. The dado was a peacock blue plush, paneled with wood of an old ivory color. The portières were blue silk, and the curtains, old blue plush and chocolate. The frieze, in bronze and "delicate colors," repeated the general pattern of the dado, and the stenciled ceiling was likewise squared. The fireplace was an obvious product of the Aesthetic Movement, and the mahogany desk had exposed wrought copper hardware.

The good social connections of all four soon brought numerous commissions from millionaires, the Seventh Regiment (for their Armory), and President Chester A. Arthur (for the White House). George Kemp's house (Fig. 149), their first private commission, was undertaken in 1879, and Tiffany's own apartment was done about the same time. Both show a fusion of the Moorish, East Indian, and Aesthetic.

The group continued until after the completion of the White House work in 1883. Then Tiffany turned his attention toward glass, while Candace Wheeler kept the name Associated Artists and devoted that firm to the design of textiles

Figure 152. *Hall, Residence of William S. Kimball, Rochester, New York.* 1883.
Artistic Houses, II, 159; see Bibliography. Yale University Library, New Haven,
Conn.

A millionaire cigarette manufacturer and bank president, William S. Kimball had a
house in the "colonial style, freely adapted." Only the tall clock gives a hint of that
style here. The furniture is of the same pattern as the desk in Hamilton Fish's drawing room (Fig. 151). The mantel is Siena marble, but the most prominent feature
of the hall is a great Moorish screen imported from India. Through the screen, the
visitor saw the staircase and its balusters, and past the screen and balusters, the pipes
of a great organ and the darkness beyond them. The calculated effect was "an impression of great distance and of mystery." The Moorish decoration of the organ pipes
reinforced the Oriental motifs of the hall.

and papers, doing occasional interiors for such people as Andrew Carnegie, Lily
Langtry, and Mrs. Potter Palmer. In their four years together, the group had
created an influential synthesis of several styles. The status of their clients made
the style fashionable, and publication of many of their rooms in *Artistic Houses*
spread this synthesis nationwide.

The Associated Artists' style received further publicity in Constance Cary
Harrison's *Woman's Handiwork in Modern Homes* (1881). Like Candace
Wheeler, she was particularly interested in the education of women in the decorative arts, and her book was devoted to embroidery and painting on china,
textiles, and mirrors. Offering several designs by Tiffany, Colman, and Mrs.
Wheeler, she summarized the work of the Associated Artists: "Their work is
as yet little known to the general public, and has been executed chiefly for

luxurious interiors intended to show every detail harmonized according to the highest standard of decorative art. It is marked by daring fancies in color and design; by the free use and combination of rich materials; by the adaptation of native American forms of flowers and plants to conventionalized ornament; and by the introduction, wherever possible, of American glass, woods, metals and textiles."[28]

FURNITURE

The Associated Artists put little emphasis on furniture. They provided designs and suggestions, as evidenced by the same style's appearance in two rooms (Figs. 151, 152); but seldom do descriptions of rooms emphasize the furniture, and we can see no distinct style as characteristic of their work.

Figure 153. *Library, Residence of Samuel Colman, Newport, Rhode Island. C.* 1883. *Artistic Houses*, II, Part 1, facing page 71; see Bibliography. Yale University Library, New Haven, Conn.

Tiffany and Associated Artists may have collaborated on this interior, but the design was basically Colman's. Most notable in this room is the ceiling, a lattice of Moorish design with a lustrous background of Japanese silks. The same pattern appears in the ceiling border and frieze and on the fireplace with its Moorish arches. The prevailing tone is blue-black, with the woodwork in ebony. The hanging over the fireplace carries a round motif similar to the one on Tiffany's dining room ceiling (Fig. 150).

Figure 154. *Drawing Room, Residence of William H. Vanderbilt, 51st Street and Fifth Avenue, New York City. C. 1883. Artistic Houses*, I, 114; see Bibliography. Yale University Library, New Haven, Conn.

Another variant of the Aesthetic interior was created by Christian Herter. Carnation red velvet with gilt appliqué covered the walls, and mother of pearl appeared in profusion on the furniture. Lighting was no less stunning: atop pedestals were round globes of colored glass containing gas jets, and the silver statues of young women in the corners held additional gas jets. The gilt, red, and pearl splendor was enormously expensive, but then Vanderbilt spent over $800,000 decorating this house, a sum a man who had $194 million could well afford.[47]

FLOOR COVERINGS

Oriental rugs appear in any pictures showing floor coverings.

PICTURES AND MIRRORS

The Associated Artists held that all parts of a room must fit into the whole, and pictures were no exception. Strong, assertive pictures would be out of place in some of their rooms, but for the useful canvas the frame determined whether a contemporary picture offended its environment or blended into it. Basically, a frame was to be nothing more than a molding holding the picture to the wall. A landscape was never to be surrounded with what looked like a window frame, for such would be a disappointing deception. Pictures should not tilt forward but be hung flat as part of the wall. The group saw fabrics as art, and in George Kemp's rooms, a Persian embroidery was framed as a pendant to a still life.[29]

TEXTILES

With a textile specialist like Candace Wheeler in the firm, it is not surprising that textiles were vital to the group's decorative schemes. Wall hangings and portières were the most prominent uses of textile decoration, with Japanese fabrics the most common.

WALL TREATMENT

Walls and color were the most memorable aspects of the Associated Artists interiors. In general, they followed the three-part division of the wall surface promoted by the Aesthetic Movement. Although the Associated Artists used a number of Aesthetic papers and designed their own in the Aesthetic tradition,[30] Tiffany's own preferences were for Japanese papers. He held that they were decorative yet always had the honest virtue of never looking like anything but paper.

Friezes were stunning features of these rooms, whether Japanese textiles, painted geometric designs, or realistic depictions of nature. Walls or fillings were covered with panels, brocades, stencils, or papers with an overall design. Aesthetic papers were frequent, and fillings were almost never left a plain solid color. Dadoes are often less distinct in photographs, but they usually are darker, with strong patterns repeated elsewhere in the room.

ARCHITECTURAL DETAILS AND CEILINGS

The Associated Artists handled architectural details in a notable way. Often moldings, like picture frames, were reduced to a bare minimum. Most obvious among the wood decorations of the room were the carvings that Lockwood de Forest imported after hiring 100 men to produce them in Ahmadabad. Moorish motifs are often found in mantels, and the fireplace and mantel were likely places to employ the iridescent glass tiles that increasingly absorbed Tiffany's attention. He found a place for his stained and opalescent glass in transoms over windows and doors.

Ceilings invariably carry strong designs, either in Indian woodwork, textiles, papers, or painting. They are seldom left plain and never white. Clarence Cook's *What Shall We Do With Our Walls?* (1881) illustrated a gilt ceiling paper with a Moorish-snowflake design by Tiffany.

The Associated Artists had a penchant for low wide shapes as opposed to wide vertical ones, and in one redecorated interior a vertical overmantel mirror was put on its side.[31]

top: Wall treatment by Walter Crane
right: The Peacock paper

LIGHTING

Lighting fixtures were in keeping with the rest of an interior, but the Associated Artists adopted no discernible style of lighting or placement of lights.

COLOR

Perhaps the most spectacular feature of these rooms was the iridescent silver, gilt, or bronze used with one predominant color, often blue. Tiffany probably

Figure 155. *Library, Residence of John A. Burnham, Commonwealth Avenue, Boston, Massachusetts.* 1876. Elliott, *The Book of American Interiors,* p. 115; see Bibliography.

Burnham's was one of many rooms with a large hood over the mantel. Not seen in the picture, but just below the presiding owl, was a motto "A GOOD FIRE, GOOD FRIENDS, GOOD BOOKS." Such mottos over the hearth became a basic part of the late nineteenth-century interior and great care went into their selection. Like the mantel, the bookcases are in basic Eastlake style. The color scheme is based on crimson and green. The silk curtains covering the bookshelves are green with crimson borders, and the wall or filling was in neutral green with a crimson band at base and top. The Indian carpet was red, green, and white, and the heavy wool window curtains were crimson with blue, green, and brown. The furniture was upholstered in the same fabric.

knew of Whistler's Peacock Room, completed in 1877, and something of the same vibrancy shows up in his own work. Cook's little book on walls also reproduces two wall designs and one ceiling by Samuel Colman, all of them printed in gleaming gilt and black. Not all rooms glittered thus. John Taylor Johnston had a room in warm colors—salmon, red, yellow, and brown—while Mark Twain of Hartford had a hall done in red, black, and silver.

ACCESSORIES

Accessories were an integral part of the room's decor, for Moorish or Japanese ceramics carried on motifs found in walls or fabrics. Shelves were carefully designed for particular items, a point specially evident in the Kemp music room. Tiffany favrile glass is, of course, about a decade in the future.

The Associated Artists had a split personality on the subject of symmetry. The mantels in Kemp's, Tiffany's, and Fish's rooms (Figs. 149, 150, 151) were arranged with meticulous symmetry, but the designs on the far wall in Kemp's room are anything but symmetrical. Likewise in W. S. Kimball's parlor (not illustrated), the Associated Artists put nonmatching windows on either side of a mantel. Perhaps such is what Tiffany meant by "irregular balance," a phrase *Artistic Houses* drew from his description of his own work.[32]

EASTLAKE

The most popular variant of the Aesthetic Movement was the Eastlake style. Charles Lock Eastlake (1836–1906) led the English vanguard in the call for honest furniture. Born of a wealthy family, he was an architect who turned his attention to interiors with the publication of *Hints on Household Taste* (1868), a book that became "extraordinarily influential in furniture design."[33] He sought models for furniture and decoration in the medieval styles, but his designs were purely secular.

An instant success in England, Eastlake's book soon found American publishers for five printings between 1872 and 1881. He quickly found American allies; like Eastlake himself, Charles Wyllys Elliott, a Boston architect, admired medieval life and furniture. Even though he comments on a likely table in his *Book of American Interiors* (1876) that it is "not Eastlake, a most vague and badly used term," his selection of plates numbers him among the publicists of the Eastlake style. Harriet P. Spofford's articles for *Harper's Bazar* were summarized in her important *Art Decoration Applied to Furniture*. Eastlake's advice, she wrote, was founded on "simplicity, honesty, and propriety." In 1877, Clarence Cook in his *House Beautiful* seconded Mrs. Spofford's approval of what they both called the Modern Gothic. Robert W. Edis also showed strong Eastlake influence in some of the suggestions in his *Decoration and Furniture of Town Houses*, an English book reprinted in America in 1881.

Eastlake brought America to a new consciousness of construction and design. Not so emphatically in favor of expensive hand-crafted items as William Morris, Eastlake's advice offered a broader appeal that American decorators followed throughout the century, most evidently in furniture, but also in wall

Figure 156. *Dining Room, Residence of J. H. Schoenberger, 43 West 57th Street, New York City. C. 1883. Artistic Houses*, II, 104; see Bibliography. Yale University Library, New Haven, Conn.

J. H. Schoenberger was a millionaire who had made his money in Pittsburgh iron. Although Eastlake was a proponent of oak, the Schoenberger dining room included an Eastlake-style mantel and wainscotting in mahogany. The walls were covered with an Aesthetic paper, and the ceiling combined brown and gold tones with a border of vines, grapes, and leaves. The portières were dark olive, and the chairs were probably inspired by the Charles II models illustrated and praised by Eastlake. The interior was the work of D. S. Hess and Company of New York City.

treatment, floor coverings, and the use of fabrics. A few decades later, Eastlake's style was still being distantly echoed in the mass-produced Mission furniture that gained popularity in the first decades of this century.

The Eastlake style gained wide use throughout the country. The relative scarcity of pure Eastlake rooms in *Artistic Houses* (1883) might lead one to conclude that it was not an influence favored by the wealthy. Certainly, its emphasis on honest simplicity did not allow the spectacular capital outlay available to the eager purchasers of the Louis XV style; but in 1882, Jay Gould—whose estate in 1892 was probably undervalued at $77 million—paid Herter Brothers $550 for one desk in an elaborate Eastlake style, and he had other Eastlake pieces among the furnishings of Lyndhurst.[34] William Carter, a

Philadelphia coal millionaire, likewise ordered Eastlake furniture from Herter Brothers; and in the 1870s and 1880s, Theodore Roosevelt's house on 57th Street in New York City had a considerable number of Eastlake pieces. Eastlake furniture and many elements of his style were common in middle-class houses, and mass production brought his taste into the most frugal homes.

FURNITURE

Eastlake called for "moral" or "honest" furniture—furniture that really was what it appeared to be. Veneers were deceiving, angular joints covered the true end grain of the wood, carving should be real and not pressed, and one should not hide hinges and other hardware but rather stress their utility. He offered suggestions for furniture for virtually every room of the house.

In the entrance hall should stand a substantial hall table, a pair of oak chairs, and a hat and umbrella stand. Turning to the dining room, Eastlake advocated a large sideboard, somewhat similar to a Welsh cupboard. The lower part of the sideboard contained cupboards with doors supported on heavy iron strap hinges, while on the shelves above one could display a tasteful collection of majolica, a selection of English pottery, and Venetian glass. Cut glass was to be avoided, as were pieces of modern Oriental ceramic. Eastlake was most adamant on one point: a telescoping extension table should not be found in the dining room or anywhere else. "When it is extended it looks weak and untidy at the sides; when it is reduced to its shortest length, the legs appear heavy and ill proportioned. . . . Why should such a table be made at all?" If one needed more places, one simply added another table.

For the drawing room, one could again turn safely to Tudor or Jacobean models. A sofa at Knole, the English estate in Kent, appealed for rectangular design and comfort: "After 250 years, this sofa is still *comfortable*." He illustrated chairs of his own design based on dignified Jacobean and Tudor models. The graining of tables and cabinets in the drawing room should "not be obscured and clogged by artificial varnish."

In the bedroom, Eastlake offered two options. One could choose a high-backed panel bed, a form with decorative panels and carving on a tall headboard and a low footboard. Or one might have a panel bed with the headboard continued up to a shallow canopy. Eastlake stipulated that such a bed should be curtained, with the curtains coming no closer than 3 inches to the floor. "When

Eastlake's design for a sideboard

An Eastlake bed

of greater length they trail upon the carpet and get soiled at their edges, or when drawn back they have to be looped up and pulled over the cord which confines them to their place." Such canopied beds could be made of iron or brass as well as solid wood, and one might support the canopy of an iron bed with heavy iron rods from the ceiling. In America the panel bed was common, but there were a few canopied ones. The American buyer, used to acquiring Gothic, Elizabethan, and rococo bedroom furniture in sets, found manufacturers of the Eastlake style no less obliging, and sets of panel beds with matching bureaus, wash stands, and shaving stands quickly brought the American bedroom up to date. The ultimate refinement for the bedroom was an icebox to provide a supply of cold water.

One piece of furniture often associated with Eastlake was the hanging shelf. It embodied his style of construction and design, offered an opportunity to display tiles with medieval scenes, and provided space to display a collection.

Figure 157. *Modern Gothic Library.* Spofford, *Art Decoration Applied to Furniture*, p. 213; see Bibliography.

Mrs. Spofford illustrated a very elaborate library, but, nonetheless, one that met her criteria. Books and things pertaining to books produced the chief decoration, and pictures and mirrors were generally absent. Admitting that glass doors might protect books better, Mrs. Spofford still preferred the warmth of the "invitingly open and handy" shelf. Her one concession to preventing dusty books was the addition of a scalloped leather valance at the top of each shelf. Curtains of decorated and tooled leather also covered some shelves for the same reason. The leather was to be stained the color of the bookshelves and have a tiny thread of gilding along the margin. Motifs of medieval scholarship dominate the frieze and cupboard doors.

FLOOR COVERINGS

Eastlake had definite ideas about floors. He held wall-to-wall carpets extremely wasteful, since they could not be reversed or moved elsewhere. And such carpets left no evidence of the type of floor beneath, "contrary to the first principles of decorative art, which require that the nature of construction, so far as is possible, should always be revealed, or at least indicated, by the ornament which it bears." Far better was a removable carpet surrounded by 2 to 3 feet of bare parquet floor border as a finish to the room. Eastlake offered several designs for parquetry, all geometric shapes. Mrs. Spofford advocated the square carpet with a border of bare wood as particularly apt for a dining room. In the absence of a fine carpet, a drugget covered a dining room floor well in winter. She left its removal in summer to the householder's option.

Both Mrs. Spofford and Eastlake recommended Oriental rugs, especially of dull India red, or manufactured carpets (Kidderminsters or ingrains) of simple diaper designs with no obvious repeat. The carpet should contrast with the wallpaper, and Mrs. Spofford suggested that the carpet be darker in tone than the walls.

For halls, Eastlake favored encaustic tiles. He offered several designs and a color plate to illustrate their decorative effect. Typical colors were terra cotta, cream, black, and dark blue.

PICTURES AND MIRRORS

Eastlake advised careful hanging of pictures. Oil paintings should be kept in a room by themselves, since their strong colors made water colors look feeble. Some rooms could have many water colors or drawings, but they should not be crowded. They should be hung "in one row only"—otherwise the house looks like an "annual public exhibition," and in order to avoid monotony, a single row should be broken up occasionally with a mirror or wall bracket holding a statuette or vase. Pictures should never be hung from one nail, nor should the cord be so long that the picture might tip forward at the top. He suggested simple oak frames on all pictures, but the look of oak grain as seen through gold leaf was acceptable. Very small prints could be grouped together, two or three in a frame at eye level. Woodcuts were the most desirable examples of modern art, but chromolithographs did "more harm than good."

Mrs. Spofford offered specific suggestions for pictures appropriate to particular rooms. In the dining room, she was wary of the contemporary practice of hanging still lifes of game, fish, and fruit: "the perpetual reminder of dead flesh and murderous propensities is not agreeable at table." Eastlake had suggested that the dining room be hung with family portraits, and although Mrs. Spofford preferred such portraits in the hall, she would accept the "last generation" hanging in the dining room within the daily gaze of their children and grandchildren. By far the best pictures for the dining room, she held, were "pictures of a curious nature, and those involving memorabilia," subjects that would stimulate conversation and give guests with little in common something to talk about. The library should have very few pictures, and mirrors were most out of place there.

Figure 158. *Drawing Room Design, A. Kimbel and J. Cabus, New York City.*
1876. Illustrated in Spofford, *Art Decoration Applied to Furniture*; see
Bibliography.

The overall appearance of this room, prepared for the Philadelphia Centennial Exposition of 1876 by prominent New York City decorators, was very busy with its multiplicity of designs. Right angles dominate the wallpaper, the rug, dado, and ceiling border. Mrs. Spofford was a strong advocate of Eastlake's honest furniture, and the "Modern Gothic" style—which she illustrated with this photograph—followed his principle of revealing the details of construction. A general tone of medievalism is reinforced by the scene on the frieze. The room also displays the proper placement and use of a hanging shelf.

TEXTILES

Mrs. Spofford stipulated that the well-decorated room should indicate careful planning of different fabrics and colors. Long gone was the Federal scheme of the same fabric for all purposes in the room. Contrast was vital to her decorative schemes, but it should not be harsh, nor should the colors. The imaginative decorator nonetheless could devise hundreds of unusual combinations, all pleasing.

Usual upholstery fabrics were rep and velvet in deep green and deep crimson. Eastlake praised cretonne, a heavy printed cotton, for its washability, but he was critical of available patterns. Mrs. Spofford suggested that dining chairs were best upholstered in morocco or, if one could not afford real leather, in enameled cloth. Much of the factory-produced Eastlake furniture appeared with horsehair upholstery. Plush was sometimes used for chairs, but it also gained a general decorative use for covering table tops, mantelboards, and picture frames.

Eastlake's and Mrs. Spofford's illustrations show that tight upholstery without tufting was the most fashionable style. Eastlake advised that tufted upholstery should be avoided, as should fringed furniture of any sort. Fringe was originally the ragged edge of wool tied to prevent unraveling and was not honestly meant as a decoration where not necessary.

The dominant style of draperies advocated by both Spofford and Eastlake was the straight drapery hung from rings on a very evident rod. Both disliked curtains excessively long, heavy, or intricately draped—at best they merely collected dust. Valances were out: Eastlake thought them "contemptible" and "worse than useless." Those made out of pressed metal, he thought, were inclined to cut and fray the curtains.

For curtains, Eastlake suggested another new fabric, cotelan, a mixture of silk, wool, and cotton, ribbed or worked into a diaper pattern. Another possibility was algerine, a cotton fabric designed with horizontal stripes of color on an unbleached white ground; it was washable and inexpensive. But the best curtain fabric, in Eastlake's estimation, was cretonne. He held that any striping in curtains must run vertically, for otherwise one might "confuse the eye." He recommended Swiss lace for summer curtains.

Where one wanted to shut out an exterior scene and still have a translucent effect of great light, Mrs. Spofford held that lace curtains with shades of fluted silk underneath were appropriate to the drawing room. Otherwise, silk curtains were acceptable. For a bedroom, chintz was still desirable, or one could hang delicate white or dotted muslin with a ribbon inserted in the hem. Under these curtains, she suggested white linen shades. (Eastlake disliked muslin.)

For the rare canopied bed, Eastlake prescribed crisp box plaits and fringe with box plaits in the dust ruffles as well.

Mrs. Spofford accepted only white linens at the dining table. She advocated dyed leather curtains for one's bookcase shelves. Green was the best color, though many chose red, which she thought too bright. Eastlake limited himself to suggesting a leather scalloping along the tops of library shelves to prevent dust from gathering on the books.

WALL TREATMENT

Eastlake and his followers were advocates of a three-part wall decoration: a dado, of which "either paper or distemper should rise to a height of three or four feet from the floor"; a frieze just below the ceiling (a feature without which a wall was unrelieved and monotonous); and a papered or painted wall or filling. Mrs. Spofford sought to vary the walls and their decoration with the room, their placement, and their spirit. The drawing room was one in which she thought Eastlake's scheme of dado, paper, and frieze was most appropriate. The paper should be rather indistinct in design, with conventionalized or idealized floral arabesques or vague geometric patterns. The frieze must be planned carefully. One should avoid a frieze with obvious themes from medieval or classical legends, for such would detract from one's paintings. The historical motif would find a useful place in the frieze of the library, a room in which paintings are not important.[35] Again in the dining room, a leather dado and rich elegant papers are to be surmounted by a simple frieze. The dining room is the only one in which she allowed gilt papers, but even there the gilt should be toned down. A somber version of the three-part treatment is to be applied to the hall.

The three-part division of the wall is not so important in Mrs. Spofford's treatment of other rooms. In bedrooms and boudoirs, papers with idealized arabesques or boughs or diaper patterns are best. Bedrooms receiving a lot of sun need light-colored papers, but those with northern exposures may well be papered in deep blue, reds, or violets. The frieze in a bedroom should be of leaves, wheat, or flowers, or perhaps hawks or hounds.

Both Eastlake and Mrs. Spofford held that wallpapers should be selected with the greatest care. He even advised bringing home several lengths and suspending them in the room for which they were being considered. He offered a few patterns for stencils, but held that papered walls were generally more satisfactory. Mrs. Spofford thought that, compared with color, the pattern of a paper was "an affair of merely secondary difficulty." She recommended, however, papers with close and small designs for any but very large rooms; in large rooms, large designs were appropriate. Diapered, damasked, or calendered

Figure 159. *Dining Room, Residence of George James, Nahant, Massachusetts. C. 1876.* Elliott, *The Book of American Interiors,* p. 118; see Bibliography.

This dining room, designed by Sturgis and Brigham of Boston, is a textbook example of the American Eastlake style. The mantel, walls, architectural details, and furniture incorporate the basic elements, and the same motifs are found in the door and window frames and moldings. The ceiling with its simple squaring was a lighter brownish gray, and the "lines of the cornices and above the dado" were strong reds, browns, and blues. Furniture and woodwork were unvarnished ash, making the room "bright" and "cheerful." Moorish curtains were hung from brass rods, and the Persian carpet was blue, gray, and brown.

papers were always in good taste, but she was critical of stripes, especially when used to give the appearance of height to a room. Leaf or floral decoration was useful only if conventionalized, and she held the wallpapers of William Morris to be specially successful.

ARCHITECTURAL DETAILS AND CEILINGS

The Eastlake style was very conscious of architectural details. Throughout, wood is more evident than in previous styles and architectural members are often not disguised. Wood trim, often dark in tone (sometimes black for Mrs. Spofford), was seen in dadoes, exposed timbered ceilings, paneling, and linen fold carving. The mantel was usually a massive achievement. Eastlake mantels typically have one or two high shelves in addition to the mantel shelf itself, thus offering more area to display rare glass and china. Typical treatment of paneling used molded boards placed diagonally in a variety of patterns.

Window frames were relatively simple. Stained glass made a strong appearance, especially in halls. A similar but cheaper effect came through the application of a diamond and fleur-de-lis decal, which could cover an entire window pane.

Mrs. Spofford offers few suggestions about ceilings, and one would suppose her advice for the hall to be characteristic of her treatment throughout the house. There the ceiling, if frescoed, should be done with some formality. If plain, it should be tinted harmoniously; if one has dark rafters, the result will be "very noble." Ceilings apparently never were to be pure white. Eastlake offers no elaborate ceiling designs, but a few of his cuts and many of those of Mrs. Spofford show ceilings of beams and rafters or of coffering. A plain flat ceiling did not catch the right spirit.

LIGHTING

Neither Spofford nor Eastlake spent much time discussing lighting. Eastlake advised that although "our forefathers managed to dispense" with gas chandeliers, these relatively recent developments could be treated "quite consistently with mediaeval principles." Mrs. Spofford preferred chandeliers with candles. Whatever the illumination, she was aware of fire hazards, and treatment of textile decoration should be handled with an eye toward the dangers of fire.

Eastlake illustrated a "design" (right) any village blacksmith could adapt in making an iron candlestick. He notes that this Swiss candlestick is "suggestive" —he does not say of what.

Medieval-type candlestick advocated by Eastlake

COLOR

Mrs. Spofford analyzed color in terms of harmonies and contrasts. Never should one use the same color unmodified throughout a room. Often, the trim should be two or three degrees darker than the paper. The choice of dominant colors depended upon the purpose and location of a room. The serious hospitality of the hall is reflected in dark wood tones, tints in darker shades, and a deep red Bukhara. In the solid comfort of the dining room, one wants colors that suggest permanence: rich crimson, dark blue, dull Pompeian red, and olivine. The carpet color should be chosen with an eye toward dirt as well as elegance. She quoted an old saying: "Green eats grease, drab eats dirt, but red eats a hole in the pocket." Crimson is thus the essence of warmth and luxury, but it will cost "one's good name as a house-keeper." Other dining room color combinations for carpets and papers were a royal purple carpet with a paper in citrine or bluish-slaty gray with pale red patterns; a rich peach green carpet with a pale azure and delicate lemon paper; or a Turkish or Bukhara carpet with the fatal crimson and blue together with red papers.

The drawing room was the place for light, airy, feminine elegance. Suggested colors for the room were peach bloom, tender blue, and ethereal green. Gold-colored satin would supply a happy sunshine when clouds were gray. Curiously, Mrs. Spofford offers an unusual variable to consider in choosing drawing room colors: the complexion of the family. Pale and sallow people should avoid green, and a "very rosy lady" is unwise to surround herself with "the ruddier colors."

The library is another sober room with little ornament. Purple and violet and strong emerald green are appropriate.

The bedroom's colors are selected according to the sunlight they receive. Rooms with a sunny southern view are best done in cool gray greens and sea blues, but never bright apple greens, bad colors for any room for medical reasons. (A friend had found a dead rat that had nibbled the border of her rich green velvet paper whose arsenic base had obviously proven fatal.) Dark bedrooms with northern exposures merit violets, deep blues, and reds—colors that absorb heat.

ACCESSORIES

For Mrs. Spofford, decorative accessories assumed a new theoretical importance, for they revealed the culture of the family. The family that had a clutter of poor and tasteless items told as much about itself as those who had bare shelves and tabletops. One should have a collection of pieces of quality, items that were not necessarily very expensive. "The mere shape of a lamp shows whether people buy what their neighbors buy, or have any individual taste of their own to exercise, or give a thought to the matter of educating what we may call the aesthetic senses." Eastlake did not attach such great significance to accessories, but he shared Mrs. Spofford's preference for those items that added culture and taste to one's house.

Both Eastlake and Mrs. Spofford spoke highly of old Oriental porcelain, Italian majolica plates, and Venetian glass. Eastlake had a special fondness for Moorish lustre ware plates, ginger jars, Minton or Wedgwood china (regilded china was to be strictly avoided), and "delf" ware. Only the Delft and ginger jars were inexpensive, but all were worthy of attention. Mrs. Spofford was more elevated in her taste: genuine old bronzes, a Wedgwood copy of the Portland vase, Sèvres and Dresden china, Palissy mugs, and Henry II pitchers all were expensive and all added greatly to the decor and taste of a house. To have such

An Aesthetic faïence vase

pieces, one might have to forego other luxuries; but in the end, "it is better to strive to reach such things by imitation than not to care for them at all."

ROMANESQUE

The Romanesque was one of the greatest architectural developments of the nineteenth century, but as an interior style it was relatively uncommon. The whole style was more or less the creation of Henry Hobson Richardson (1838–

Figure 160. *Parlor, Residence of Ralph H. White, Boston. C. 1883. Artistic Houses*, II, 125; see Bibliography. Yale University Library, New Haven, Conn.

Ralph H. White was a millionaire dry goods merchant in Boston. Architects Peabody and Stearns, who also did the decoration, adapted a stunning version of the Romanesque, perhaps influenced by the iridescent effects Tiffany was producing in New York. The arch and walls above the paneling were plaster painted many times to resemble old gold. Swirling Romanesque acanthus decorated the molding and frieze. With their spool turnings, the low chairs bear similarity to chairs designed by H. H. Richardson about the same time, and the chairs with the splayed backs were a further adaptation of an architectural style to furniture. Note the deeply coffered ceiling.

1886), the Boston architect, but it had a following among other architects and decorators, several of them also in Boston. *The Decorator and Furnisher* carried sporadic essays in the style between 1887, the year after Richardson's death, and 1894. It is probably revealing that there were more suggestions and plans than there were descriptions of rooms actually done in Romanesque. In the hands of a gifted architect working for a wealthy client, it could be very impressive (Fig. 160), and like many other styles, it had an impact on simpler houses and furniture, too (Fig. 162).

Figure 161. Jasper Cropsey. *Studio Interior at Warwick, New York.* 1883. Pen and ink drawing. George Walter Vincent Smith Museum, Springfield, Mass.

Two pieces in Cropsey's studio are indicative of his taste. To the side of the fireplace is a large Eastlake bookcase with iron hinges, and in the foreground is an arm chair designed by H. H. Richardson, who first used the style for the Woburn Public Library in 1878. The exposed chimney and open rafters were both characteristic of Eastlake honesty.

Figure 162. *Library, Residence of the Reverend E. B. McGinley, Chula Vista, California.* 1898. Lyman Allyn Museum, New London, Conn.

McGinley was a Congregational minister who later moved from Chula Vista to Shrewsbury, Massachusetts. His library showed Romanesque details added to a basic Eastlake bookcase. (Richardson had added a similar broad curve to a fireplace in the rectory of Trinity Church, Boston.) The same radiating spool effect unified the overmantel and the Romanesque chair. Note the curtains over the bookshelves, and the Mideastern portières, which undoubtedly added considerable color.

One senses a considerable affinity with certain elements of the Aesthetic Movement. Richardson designed some of his furniture in honest oak, and he seems to have drawn some of his ideas from Eastlake. The architects Robert Peabody and John G. Stearns may have been influenced by Tiffany's gilt walls, and they certainly found a place for Aesthetic textiles in their rooms (Fig. 160).

Richardson and his associate Francis Bacon designed much of the furniture for his interiors. His best-known design was that produced for the Woburn Public Library, Woburn, Massachusetts, in 1878. Other architects created their own translations of Romanesque architecture into furniture, with an arch often prominent.

No distinctive textiles are evident in the photographs, but the style readily

A Malden Public Library chair, 1885

289

incorporated popular fabrics of the time. Expensive Romanesque walls were seldom plain. Richardson used the same square paneling found in Fig. 160, but Peabody and Stearns produced a florid treatment with molded plaster and glass mosaic.

The style was basically architectural, and the rounded arch was its most characteristic detail. Such arches were evident in fireplaces, mantels, and windows. Thin twisted columns with acanthus (but not Corinthian) capitals, or simple long thin Romanesque columns were also common in expensive work. Richardson planned large fireplaces projecting from the wall and supported by columns. The architectural details of simpler versions of the style show strong affinity to Eastlake.

Figure 163. Henry Walton. *A Miner at Rough and Ready.* 1853. Water color, pen, and ink. Oakland Museum History Department, Oakland, Calif.

William D. Peck, pictured here, was a miner who had furnished his cabin with no thought to decorative style. Utility governed all. Walton documented a normal stock of utensils in the iron pots, griddle, tin canisters, coffee grinder, and wooden boxes. Peterson suggested that Peck probably made his arm chair himself as the legs do not match.[48] The scale under his finger and the weights in his hand were invaluable to a miner. All the woodwork is unpainted wood, and only the blue and white coverlet and the tan and white hide trunk add color to the room.[49]

Figure 164. Eastman Johnson. *Dressing the Doll. C.* 1860. Oil on canvas, 13½ in. × 17½ in. (36 cm × 46 cm). The Thomas Gilcrease Institute of American History and Art, Tulsa, Okla.

This pioneer cabin again illustrates minimal furnishing. The rafters were exposed and the walls were not plastered. Heat, fortunately, was provided by a small iron stove at the left. Storage chests offered seating and the bed was supported on simple, square posts. Other boxes were stored on the shelf at the upper right.

The Frontier or Rustic Style

The frontier or rustic style, unlike all the others in this book, began of necessity in the country and then spread to the urban wealthy. For decades, settlers had used such decor because they had no alternative; but the romantic view of the West in newspapers, magazines, and novels led many wealthy Easterners to find charm in such primitivism.

A home on the Tennessee from Mrs. Lamb's *Houses of America.*

above: Figure 165. Peter P. Tofft. *My Cabin, Elk Creek, Montana Territory.* 1866. Water color. Courtesy, Museum of Fine Arts, Boston, Mass. (M. and M. Karolik Collection).

Tofft's cabin in Montana was quite comfortably set up. The artist is seated in a folding chair, smoking his pipe and wearing his Turkish slippers. His cabin is not entirely primitive, considering the two paintings hanging on the rough wall. A coffee grinder was on the left wall, and the suspended cloth pouch probably held foodstuffs. The house was of log construction, with small four-paned windows providing the interior with a minimum of light.

left: Figure 166. W. H. Jackson. *Sawtell's Ranch House, Fremont County, Idaho Territory.* 1872. Montana Historical Society, Helena.

Photographer W. H. Jackson recorded a ranch house, primitive at best, but a decorative concern was evident in the symmetrical arrangement of guns on the wall. The crude Windsor chair is elegant in comparison to the rest of the furniture, walls, and floor. If the mantel shelf is indicative, these ranchers depended on candles for lighting.

Figure 167. Edward Graham Hayes. *Z A Ranch*. 1886–1890. Drawing. Library,
The State Historical Society of Colorado, Denver.

Edward Graham Hayes worked at the Z A Ranch near Colorado Springs from 1886
to 1889. His well-constructed log cabin was attractively and comfortably furnished.
The room boasted a pair of captain's chairs, a flip-top desk, and a good-sized iron
stove. Illumination was provided by a student lamp on the table. There was even
the additional touch of frontier elegance in the pull curtains at the windows.

Furniture on the nineteenth-century frontier was limited to those pieces
brought with the settlers or that could be made locally. The contents of a cabin
or room were limited to practical items of daily necessity, and there were
virtually no decorative objects. But Sawtell's Ranch House (Fig. 166) shows
that by the 1870s, bare necessities could be arranged in decorative patterns. The
rifles and pistols are placed with the same symmetry that governed the arrangement of rarities in a Beacon Hill parlor. As soon as possible, residents of
frontier areas plastered and papered their rooms, making them almost indistinguishable from those in New York, Charleston, Chicago, or Bangor.[36]

Rope portières

This rifle table cost $8.75
in walnut or cherry

293

The Decorator and Furnisher chronicled the growing popularity of the rustic style in fashionable houses during the 1880s. One article even offered a philosophy behind this "Occidental" style (Fig. 169), suggesting that the motivating influence might be the search for a distinctive American look, which would offer decorators freedom from copying European styles. Never really called the Occidental, the style had a limited impact in many houses (Fig. 171). Rustic, unbarked woodwork found a regular place in summer homes (Fig. 189), as did horn furniture in the 1890s.[37]

The Wigwam style, however, never made a substantial impact. Gariboldi's

Figure 168. *Interior of a Log Cabin in Eastern Oklahoma. C.* 1900. Western History Collections, University of Oklahoma Library, Norman.

Not all frontier houses were plastered and papered by the turn of the century. As in earlier centuries, the hearth continued to be the center of food preparation, and the photograph documents a considerable inventory of iron utensils as well as a wooden potato masher on the mantel. The brick floor was partially covered with a rag carpet, and a patchwork quilt was on the low bed. As in earlier Eastern houses, residents were cooking, eating, and sleeping in the same room.

above: Figure 169. *C. W. Clark. An Occidental Interior. The Decorator and Furnisher* (November 1888), p. 53; see Bibliography.

Clark's study for *An Occidental Interior* was an escape from Renaissance and Moorish styles. The walls were Lincrusta Walton, and the floors bare boards with animal skins or Oriental rugs. Indian blankets (which cost $5–150) or Mexican serapes draped the windows, and animal horns and heads ornamented the walls. Furniture included the crude table, a horn stool, and chairs made from barrels. The owner (not shown here), dressed in buckskins and moccasins, completed the interior.

left: Figure 170. Gariboldi. *A Wigwam Interior. The Decorator and Furnisher* (May 1894), p. 59; see Bibliography.

Gariboldi's design was offered with no explanation, but it was typical of attempts to create a distinct American style. Indian motifs were used to create a novel look. The dado was covered with a geometric pattern of either sticks or incised work, and the same texture appears in the floor and woven look of the stool. The wallpaper carried a tall grass or palm design (supplemented with a live palm behind the curtain), and the draperies (with appropriate Indian prints and fringes) were hung by rope from a spear.

A
PADDLE
BACK
CHAIR

design (Fig. 170) appeared in *The Decorator and Furnisher* in 1894, followed the next year by R. Davis Benn's article, "Why Not a Wigwam Style?" Benn sought indigenous sources of ornament, finding them in "primitive" motifs like tomahawks, canoes, and paddles. (The linecut at left shows how a canoe paddle could be transformed into a chair.) Fortunately, the style had no "strict or harrassing rules," and it was thus adaptable to many forms, even though he admitted it was not apt for upholstered furniture. Sensing he might not be making a persuasive case, he concluded that the style was "not outside the bounds of reason."[38]

Figure 171. *Smoking Room, Residence of Frank Furness, 711 Locust Street, Philadelphia.* 1883. *Artistic Houses*, II, 169; see Bibliography. Yale University Library, New Haven, Conn.

Frank Furness was no cowboy. He was an important Philadelphia architect, who designed the Pennsylvania Academy of Fine Arts; he spent his summers in the Rockies, bringing back trophies—skins and antlers—every fall. Furness built a one-story addition to his house to create the atmosphere he loved. The walls were cedar slabs with a dado of unbarked cedar saplings. Inside, the wall was virtually papered with steel engravings of the West. The draped skins created a color scheme that *Artistic Houses* called "artistic to a high degree."[50]

Figure 172. *Veranda, Lodge at Lake Wilbert, Franklin County, New York.* 1911.
Saylor, *Bungalows*, p. 100; see Bibliography.

By the turn of the century, the West had become extremely popular, due in part to
William Cody and his Wild West Show, and to Theodore Roosevelt's stress on the
healthy, out-of-door life. Consequently, log cabins imitating real ones began to
appear as summer homes. This one in New York State may be considered typical.
The logs had been carefully scraped free of bark to avoid danger from borers, and
the chinking was very solid. The furniture on the porch (often used both inside and
out) frequently had bark and splint seats to produce a rough-hewn effect.

The Eclectic Look

A new age of pluralism hit American interiors. There was no longer one correct
style, and the writer who urged the householder to use a single style—any
style—throughout the house was a voice unheeded. At best, many ordered a
room or two in one consistent style, and then finished the others in a variety of
tastes.[39] Mrs. Spofford noted that people had Moorish conservatories, Pompeian parlors, and Chinese boudoirs. But eclecticism soon invaded rooms as
well as houses, and from the surviving pictures one senses that householders
vied with one another as to how many styles they could incorporate in one
room. Often the "something of everything" philosophy prevailed, and, after all,
many guidebooks stressed that a rich assortment of diverse objects was not only
educational but also revealing of the culture and taste of those who dwelt
within.

above: Figure 173. *Main Gallery, Residence of Mr. and Mrs. Potter Palmer, 1366 Lake Shore Drive, Chicago.* 1892. Courtesy, Chicago Historical Society, Chicago, Ill.

Dry goods, a hotel, and real estate built Potter Palmer a fortune of $8 million by his death in 1902. In 1882, Mrs. Palmer began a house intended to cost $90,000. Mr. Palmer told his accountant to stop informing him of costs after the expenses had mounted to near $700,000.[51] The grandiose gallery demonstrated the same eclecticism found in more modest settings, with its Louis XIV table, Louis XV and Louis XVI side chairs, gilt Empire seats, and brass-studded sofa covered with a leopard skin.

right: Figure 174. *Parlor, Residence of Mr. and Mrs. Josiah Quincy, Jr., 4 Park Street, Boston. C. 1865–1870.* Society for the Preservation of New England Antiquities, Boston, Mass.

Seen here are Mr. and Mrs. Josiah Quincy, Jr., and their son Samuel Quincy. Both men were lawyers, wealthy and socially prominent. The house dated from the Federal period (Stuart's portrait of Josiah Quincy, 1824, had probably hung in that spot since it was painted), but mid-Victorian eclecticism dominates the room. Mrs. Quincy sits on a Turkish tufted sofa and Samuel on a rococo chair that matches the style of the fireplace. An Elizabethan chair appears at the right. Early evidence of Oriental influence is the Japanese silk tacked on the door.

One might assume that C. W. Clark's "Study of an Interior," published in the April 1888 *Decorator and Furnisher*, was a satirical sketch, were there any reinforcing clues in the text of the magazine. However, Clark's accompanying illustration (Fig. 169) makes it rather clear that the "Study" was a suggestion, not a criticism. What a dizzying amalgamation it is! Beneath a coffered Renaissance ceiling, one finds a frieze inspired by the Renaissance or the Aesthetic Movement, and on the inaccessible shelf above the mantel is an accumulation of pottery and two Oriental fans. The pictures range from the owl to the buxom portrait in the French manner. On the mantel itself are a stuffed peacock (Moorish), a French clock, four Japanese fans, and vases filled with plants arranged in a manner reminiscent of Aesthetic designs. The small nude on the mantel is but another of the statues ranging in subject from classical enthusiasm to what could be General Sherman riding through Georgia.

C. W. Clark. *Study of an Interior.* 1888.

above: Figure 175. *Drawing Room, Residence of Dr. William A. Hammond,*
54th Street near Fifth Avenue, New York City. C. 1883. Artistic Houses, I, 88;
see Bibliography. Yale University Library, New Haven, Conn.

Dr. Hammond had eclectic tastes, noted earlier in his Egyptian library and Japanese
bedroom (Fig. 129). A frieze copying the Bayeux tapestry set the tone for this room,
but the full decor was hardly "Early English and Celtic" as the writers of *Artistic
Houses* claimed. True, the turquoise ceiling was covered with Celtic ornaments, but
the Persian, Moorish, Egyptian, Chinese, and Japanese ceramics caught the visitor's
eye, too, as did the marble Venus de Milo. The architectural details were Renaissance.
The raw silk that covered the wall took on a "rich and soft" tone in the light from
predominantly ruby-stained glass windows.

opposite: Figure 176. *Drawing Room, Residence of Governor Marcus L. Ward,*
49 Washington Street, Newark, New Jersey. C. 1890. Collection of The Newark
Museum, Newark, N.J.

Marcus L. Ward, a former Governor of New Jersey and real estate millionaire, had
a veritable chair museum in his late Empire parlor. Both Chippendale chairs were
antiques, and the ball-and-claw chair was typical of New York work, as was the
Hepplewhite chair.[52] The tall Gothic chair (see Fig. 82), the variety of Renaissance
chairs, the Japanese chair, and the Gothic desk, neo-Grec corner cupboard, Renaissance–Louis XVI cabinet, statuary, paintings, and chandelier guaranteed that no one
style would predominate.

The furniture is no more uniform. The eye passes quickly from the Hepplewhite china cabinet to the Dante chair, posed invitingly with a drape across and a book on the seat, to a Turkish-style arm chair upholstered in a fleur-de-lis fabric. The central table with its claw-and-ball feet might best be described as tortured Chippendale. As will be seen, many American interiors resembled the model Clark presented.

It is almost impossible to reduce the rooms that follow to analytic patterns, for they were deliberate attempts to accumulate stray elements of a diversity of styles. Some are more hectic than others, some are relatively successful, but all show the many currents of the era.

above: Figure 177. *Front Parlor, Residence of James Lancaster Morgan, 7 Pierpont Street, Brooklyn, New York.* 1887. Museum of the City of New York.

Morgan's Elizabethan hall appears in Figure 92, but his parlor was a rich eclectic assemblage. Much of the furniture was Renaissance, but other pieces were Renaissance–neo-Grec or Chinese, and the large table with a lamp gave a strong hint of Art Nouveau. Eastlake and Aesthetic design influenced the cabinet with tile doors along the left wall. The walls were plain with a very light frieze decoration, but much richer were the cornice and Renaissance ceiling with a design like those that often appeared in *The Decorator and Furnisher.*

opposite, top: Figure 178. *Parlor, Residence of Victor Lawson, 317 (933) LaSalle Street, Chicago. C.* 1890. Courtesy, Chicago Historical Society, Chicago, Ill.

The Lawson parlor documents the eclecticism of a well-to-do house, for he was the millionaire editor and publisher of the *Chicago Daily News.* A Turkish chair was seen through the arch, the small stool before the fireplace was Japanese, the low-backed chair at the left was a Grand Rapids product, and the stand at the right with its three carved heads might be called Pompeian. The center table is perhaps best called simply eclectic. Note the painting, *Bridge of Sighs,* filling the fireplace. The walls were plain, with decoration reserved for cornice and ceiling.

Figure 179. *Hall, Residence of C. H. Lewis, Portland, Oregon. C.* 1900. Oregon Historical Society, Portland.

C. H. Lewis earned millionaire status from investments in wharf property, merchandising, and the storage business. His walls were covered with one of the textured materials—Anaglypta or Lincrusta Walton—available at the end of the century. The dado of the stair wall presents a Moorish pattern, while the wall itself was Aesthetic. Note the radiator in the lower right-hand corner. Although Lewis was able to afford spectacular decor, this hall is relatively simple when compared with those of *Artistic Houses* or *Stately Homes.*

above: Figure 180. *Stair landing, Residence of James Campbell, 2 West Moreland Place, St. Louis, Missouri.* 1916. The Missouri Historical Society, St. Louis.

James Campbell was a millionaire broker who had William Albert Swasey design his house. In addition to the placement of a circle of electric light bulbs around the opening of the landing, the varied wall treatment is the most notable feature of this setting. Arabesque ornament on the walls and ceiling provided a strong decorative unity. The landing curtains had gilt cornices atop a lambrequin, but the fabric with its large floral design was incongruously informal. This is our only photograph showing a phonograph, seen here surrounded by chairs.

opposite: Figure 181. *Parlor, Residence of George Gray, Stockton, California.* C. 1890. Collection of Pioneer Museum and Haggin Galleries, Stockton, Calif.

The pier mirror, side chair, and gilt valances were in the Renaissance style, as were the ceiling and molding decorations. But the whatnot was influenced by the Art Nouveau. The statue in the niche reinforces the Renaissance theme, but those on the painted stand and on the shelf of the mirror are more in the nineteenth-century taste. The stand in the window is Eastlake, and the upholstered chairs have fringes typical of the Turkish style. Note the picture displayed on the floor.

below: Figure 182. *Drawing Room, Residence of James Joseph Brown, 1340 Pennsylvania Street, Denver, Colorado. C. 1895.* Library, The State Historical Society of Colorado, Denver.

Restraint was not necessarily part of striking decor, especially in the hands of the Unsinkable Molly Brown (Mrs. James Joseph Brown), so called because she survived the *Titanic.* At one glance the eye beheld a Renaissance piano and window seat, a French revival table, a wicker easy chair, and an arm chair with Turkish fringe. It is an understatement to say that the polar bear rug dominated the room. Like everything else in the room, the statues by the door were a bit larger, a bit more bold than the average treatment in *Artistic Houses.* The swagged draperies were an appropriate finish to the room, especially when decorated with feathers. Note, too, the foliage on the mantel and the fireboard.

opposite, top: Figure 183. *Drawing Room, The Sweat Mansion, Portland, Maine.* Before 1908. Portland Museum of Art, Portland, Maine.

"How could all this have happened?" Mrs. Sweat seems to ask. Seated in a wicker chair, she contemplates her collection of a Gothic chair and screen, a Louis XV wing chair, and a Renaissance table and piano. To these pieces she added an Oriental screen, a rococo mirror, and Turkish portières. The large embroidered lambrequin on the mantel contributes to the general eclecticism of the room. Note that the Renaissance table was *in* the fireplace, a usage that appears in several other period pictures (Fig. 126). Note, too, that an authentic interior need not have an upright piano placed against a wall.

Figure 184. *Parlor, Residence of Dr. J. W. Robinson, Jacksonville, Oregon. C.* 1896. Southern Oregon Historical Society, Jacksonville.

Dr. Robinson assembled an eclectic houseful of mass-produced furniture unified by no design or theme. The mantel and the sideboard were basic Eastlake designs with Renaissance details, while the table in the foreground and its matching chair by the fireplace were influenced by the Art Nouveau. The firescreen was strongly Oriental and the low plant stand was Renaissance. The combination of dark throw rugs on a light carpet was unusual. The modillion wallpaper had a peacock border paper and a nonmatching ceiling paper and border. The large cheval glass is an unusual living room item, but often present in middle-class pictures of the era were portrait cushions of the sort seen on the sofa.

below: Figure 185. *Parlor, Residence of Mr. and Mrs. J. Edwin Wesson, 7 Linden Street, Worcester, Massachusetts. C.* 1875. Collection of Miss Orie Wesson Sherer.

The parlor of the Wesson house contained an eclectic assemblage of furniture. Perhaps most interesting is the profuse use of shawls. The detail of the photograph provides a good look at the sewn carpeting popular during the period. Note the late use of a fireboard. The decorative objects on the mantel included a French clock, a peachblow vase, a horn drinking cup, and a barely draped nude. Although the walls were plain, the ceiling received elaborate decoration.

opposite, top: Figure 186. George Newell Bowers (1849–1909). *The Newsboy.* 1889. Oil on canvas, 18 in. × 14¼ in. (46 cm × 36 cm). The Springfield Museum of Fine Arts, Springfield, Mass. (Horace P. Wright Collection).

Bowers' *Newsboy* offers a rare glimpse into the interior of what is either an apartment or office building. The walls of the hall are light and plain except for the simple frieze at the ceiling. The columns are likewise almost without ornament. The interior of the artist's studio is equally simple, with a hardwood floor and painted walls. The glass panel in the door is covered by fabric.

Figure 187. *Sitting Room, Residence of Zebulon Hancox, Stonington, Connecticut. C.* 1885. Collection of Mr. and Mrs. Minor Myers, jr.

Zebulon Hancox (1809–1899) was eccentric, not poor. Once a schoolteacher and store clerk, he became a frugal fisherman-recluse. His room was furnished with no sense of decoration, and nothing that could be called a style is evident. However, one sees an early nineteenth-century fireplace adapted to a later iron stove, and the working interior of a fisherman's house. Note the fresh fish in the basket, and the latch on the shutter seen through the door, a remnant from the early nineteenth century. Hancox perhaps made the chair in which he sat. In spite of appearances, Hancox built, owned, and rented fifteen houses.

Figure 188. *Slum Interior, New York.* 1896. Photograph by Byron. The Byron Collection, Museum of the City of New York.

Joseph Byron recorded an unidentified interior of the sort inhabited by thousands in New York and other cities. The Elizabethan spool bed was one of those mass produced in the mid-nineteenth century. The arabesque design of the wallpaper and the two-tone paint on the door date from mid-century, when the room was a more elegant habitation. These people had at least one more room, seen through the doorway leading to the window, but it is clear that this room was used for both cooking and sleeping. The floors are worn, bare boards; the shelves hold a miscellaneous collection of glass, tin, and wooden implements.

12

Mission and Art Nouveau

1895–1915

THE Aesthetic Movement of the 1870s continued, splitting in the 1890s into two variants of interior decor: the very popular Mission style and the surprisingly less common Art Nouveau. Mission emphasized angles, sharp lines, and plain surfaces, while the Art Nouveau relied on sinuous lines, curves, iridescent and irregular surfaces. As will be seen, the two styles might blend together in the furniture designs of Will Bradley or the furniture produced by Charles Rohlfs, Edward Colonna, and the anonymous craftsmen of the Grand Rapids factories. Pottery, too, sometimes defies easy classification into one style or the other.

Standing between the old aestheticism and the new Mission style was Candace Wheeler (d. 1923), who had collaborated with Louis C. Tiffany between 1879 and 1883. After Tiffany turned to glass, she continued to produce interior designs. Her *Principles of Home Decoration* (1903) offered basic rules that might be applied (and were, given the illustrations) to grandly furnished rooms in the English Renaissance style or to those decorated in the simpler Mission style. Her comments have been incorporated into discussions of the Mission style, but one should remember that they were equally applicable to other styles, even to the Colonial Revival (Fig. 192).

Three qualities governed the furnishing of her interiors: absolute fitness, actual goodness, and real beauty. Fitness or use was primary. For her, "the use to which a room is put must always govern its furnishing and in a measure its color." Goodnesss required fine craftsmanship. Far better to have old wall panels and first-rate rush-bottomed chairs than shaky chairs with more expensive leather seats. Beauty, of course, required aesthetic qualities for each element of a room, but beauty was not to be considered apart from the other two criteria.[1]

Rejecting the eclecticism of previous decades, she criticized the practice of doing rooms in different styles. The more exotic styles—presumably the Moorish and Oriental—were objectionable because they represented "the fashion of nations and peoples whose lives are totally dissimilar." Preferable were any

styles whose origin was "not too far removed from the interests and ways of our own time." Thus, for the average small house a simple style was best, but exoticism might still find a place in "grand houses, which are always exceptions to the purely domestic idea." However, true decorative beauty was by no means limited to wealth. Like earlier proponents of the Aesthetic principles, the honesty she demanded in later work was not necessarily expensive, and "the man of moderate means expects beauty in his home as confidently as if he were a world ruler."[2]

Mission

The Mission style had strong beginnings in upper New York State, but very comparable designs were soon evident in the Midwest and California, especially in Pasadena and San Francisco. Two origins for the name have been suggested: one draws the name from the similarity of Mission furniture to that of the Spanish missions in the West, while the other suggests that the style had a mission to perform—the transformation of earlier mistakes in decoration.

American arts and crafts organizations in the late nineteenth century were spurred into action by the arts and crafts movement in England. A strong Arts and Crafts Exhibition Society was founded in London in 1888, and one followed in Boston in 1897, as many Americans began following the lead of Morris, Eastlake, and Ruskin in stressing honest furniture and craftsmanship.

Gustave Stickley was one of the early great American leaders of the movement. In 1898, he founded the Gustave Stickley Company in Eastwood, a suburb of Syracuse, New York, to be distinguished from his brothers' rival firm, L. and J. G. Stickley Company. Gustave used the trade name Craftsman for his

opposite, top: Figure 189. *Sitting Room, Country House of Washington E. Connor, Onteora, New York. C.* 1903. Wheeler, *Principles of Home Decoration,* p. 92; see Bibliography.

Washington E. Connor, New York millionaire, made his money in railroads and communications and more or less retired in 1887 at the age of thirty-eight. With its diverse furniture, his sitting room presents an early twentieth-century version of the eclectic look. The inlaid Renaissance chair was a far cry from wickerwork, further still from the rustic birch that railed the balcony. Mrs. Wheeler, unfortunately, did not describe this room, but illustrated it in a chapter dealing with the way in which tapestries, papers, and textiles could introduce color and beauty into a room. Note the draped rugs across the balcony, undoubtedly coordinated for their color. Note, too, the Aesthetic needlework designs on the portières and curtains. The same heavy fireplace in the dining room with its rounded opening reappears here.

Figure 190. *Dining Room, Country House of Washington E. Connor, Onteora, New York. C.* 1903. Wheeler, *Principles of Home Decoration,* p. 198; see Bibliography.

Mrs. Wheeler described this room as "the prettiest country dining room I know." Blue china plates brought color and contrast to the wall and set the color scheme. The carpet was an India cotton of dark and light blues and white. Blue and white reappeared in the blue denim draperies (not seen here) with their white outline designs of leaping fish. Had this room a northern exposure, Mrs. Wheeler would have used a red color scheme.

Stickley's device

products—furniture and work in metal, leather, and linen—and in 1901, he started a monthly magazine to promote the new look. *The Craftsman* featured writings of the current art movement and showed ideal interiors adapted to either large homes or bungalows. Stickley's motives were financial as well as aesthetic, for the magazine carried yearly price lists of his products. His symbol was a joiner's compass with the words ALS IK KAN ("If I can"), a motto borrowed from a painting by Jan van Eyck.

Perhaps too enthusiastically Stickley expanded operations, moving his executive offices to New York City while the manufacturing continued in Eastwood. Bankruptcy followed in April 1915, and *The Craftsman* died the following year. His two brothers bought the business and continued production of his designs, but their later furniture was not so well made.

Stickley's main rival as leader of the movement was Elbert Hubbard, the publicist founder of the Roycroft Shops in East Aurora, New York, which produced a great variety of decorative items. Inspired by William Morris and his Kelmscott Press, Hubbard began printing similar volumes with elaborate sinuous designs and limp chamois covers in 1895. Hubbard, a charismatic figure, organized an apprentice system in East Aurora, attracting workers from near and far. He too had his small magazine, *The Philistine*, and he too had identifying symbols, marking his pieces with the orb and cross or boldly emblazoning the name Roycroft. The Hubbards went down with the *Lusitania*, but the Roycroft shops continued until 1938 when they failed in the depression.

The new style quickly moved westward. Frank Lloyd Wright was a leader in the Midwest. He saw furniture as part of the whole scheme of a house, and he favored built-in seats and bookcases with movable pieces matching them in spirit. He urged that people should "strip the wood of varnish and let it alone, stain it." Wright's designs appeared in the D. R. Martin House in Buffalo (1904) and, in Chicago, in the Ray Evans House (1908) and the well-known Frederick Robie House (1908). In California, the firm of Greene and Greene designed furniture for the David B. Gamble House in Pasadena (1908), much of which remains intact. Lucia and Arthur F. Mathews, both painters, had a studio in San Francisco active from 1906 to 1920. Their version of Mission furniture had Oriental overtones, especially in chairs with wide center splats and simple turned top rails and sides. Mrs. Mathews made liberal use of floral motifs, and her boxes and screens were scattered with poppies and rhododendrons, often in bright green and orange.

If Mission was popular with the wealthy, it was either in the expensive, thorough work of Frank Lloyd Wright and the Greenes or in the simpler furnishings of the country houses. It was not suited to the townhouse. The middle and lower classes, who had no country or summer houses but who lived in the newly popular bungalows year round, took to the style readily, for much of it could be produced at home. In 1909, the Popular Mechanics Library published the first of three volumes (50¢ each) entitled *Mission Furniture: How to Make It. Arts-Crafts Lamps* (1911) and *Metal Work and Etching* (1911), both by John D. Adams, enabled the home craftsman to complete his interior. Charles Frank Warner's *Home Decoration* (1911) was another practical text on how to create the Mission look yourself in furniture, textiles, pottery, leather, and iron.

There was little regional variation in the Mission style as it swept across

America. It came as a relief from the richly ornate styles of previous decades, but was quickly lost in the chaos of World War I. It was perhaps symbolic that Hubbard went down on the *Lusitania*.

FURNITURE

Mrs. Wheeler's basic demands for furniture were strong construction and good design. Colonial furniture met these needs well, and so did Mission or "Morris" furniture, but some pieces of the latter she found too heavy or blocky for

Figure 191. *Dining Room, Cottage of Mrs. Boudinot Keith, Onteora, New York. C.* 1903. Wheeler, *Principles of Home Decoration*, frontispiece; see Bibliography.

The Boudinot Keiths were not on the roster of millionaires, but they did appear in the *Social Register*. Mrs. Wheeler chose an illustration of their cottage as the frontispiece to her book. This is an example of a late version of aestheticism applied to the Colonial style. A Colonial serving maid surrounded by swirling borders decorated the door, and the frieze carried a motto on a scroll, a popular motif with the Aesthetic Movement. The overmantel shelves held a collection of polished pewter and the dresser displayed the china. A very coarse material covered the wall.

Figure 192. *Sitting Room, Residence of Candace Wheeler. C.* 1903. Wheeler, *Principles of Home Decoration,* p. 168; see Bibliography.

A similar eclectic mixture appeared in Candace Wheeler's own sitting room. A painted rocker is combined with a Colonial mantel, an old English hob grate, a day bed covered with Aesthetic fabrics, and an Aesthetic frieze. Mrs. Wheeler urged readers to find old furniture and interior woodwork that might bring them extraordinary craftsmanship at very reasonable prices. A miscellany of plates, abalone shells, the hanging pot, and the picture displayed over the day bed remind us that the nineteenth century was not long past, but the simplicity of the walls and the rug point toward the twentieth-century interior.

cottage furnishing. One had to choose with care. She illustrated a Mission sofa that she had designed, upholstered with a simply worked textile and ornamented with brass-headed nails and Aesthetic carving.

Mission furniture was basically heavy and square, of simple, angular construction. In many cases the pegging showed, and the stretchers of tables or the shelves under desks clearly penetrated the leg—thus the construction was "honest." Circular tables were common, frequently covered with a natural leather skin, and square chairs usually had leather seats featuring heavy circular studs.

Rockers were not favored, though they did appear; characteristic of the style was the Morris chair with its adjustable back. Small portable tables to hold ash trays, boxes, or flowers were sometimes decorated with flowing Art Nouveau patterns, either painted or done in pyrography, a popular craft of the day. Most Mission pieces were of chestnut or fumed oak, though Stickley also used willow. Willow was available in two color schemes—muted wood tones of greenish silver or golden brown. Neither color was far removed from the honest, natural, rubbed willow tone. Furniture from any of the various makers blended well together. Without examining the labels, it is almost impossible to tell one maker's style from the other.

FLOOR COVERINGS

Mrs. Wheeler admired wood floors casually covered with scatter rugs, but Orientals were desirable if one could afford them. If carpeting was selected, it should be monochrome, preferably in green. Carpets should not be so large that they could not be taken out and cleaned. Tile was best for the kitchen, but a floor tiled with squares of "oilcloth" was acceptable if the budget was limited.

Illustrations show varying floor coverings in Mission interiors, with Navajo rugs highly favored. Druggets in beige and brown with similar, stylized Indian motifs were often found, too. Orientals were used, but they did not complement the consistent style so well as carpets with Mission or Art Nouveau designs (Plate 30).

PICTURES AND MIRRORS

Mrs. Wheeler held that pictures could have a greater influence on an interior "than all other things put together." She gave little advice on selection and placement, as she assumed that "any one who loves pictures well enough to buy them, can hardly help placing them not only where they are at their best, but where they will also have the greatest influence."[3]

Illustrations show a relative lack of pictures, but where they did appear landscapes were preferred. Paintings of bibulous monks were also popular, at times used as mantel decorations (Fig. 193). Pictures, often small, were sometimes displayed on plate rails interspersed with vases and steins. (Fig. 190).

Mirrors were seldom used as decorative items. They seem to have been generally confined to a utilitarian role in bedrooms and halls.

TEXTILES

Mrs. Wheeler devoted a whole chapter to textiles. Curtains were to be hung straight and never looped or elaborately draped. For curtains, portières, or screens she recommended cotton, linen, or woolens, which were easily washable. If the walls were plain, she advised figured draperies, and vice versa. Damask could serve for both draperies and wall covering, and transparent china

Table scarf design

silk made excellent glass curtains, though thin cotton or linen was also permissible. If chintz was selected for curtaining, it should be lined with a plain color, both to give body and contrast. She preferred a "good" chintz or cotton to flimsy silk or brocade, and she admired blue denim for cottages, noting that it improved with washing.

The illustrations show that textiles, although simple, were an important aspect of the Mission interior. Muslin, linen, monk's cloth, or denim, just the sort of fabrics Mrs. Wheeler recommended, were popular. Chintz or cretonne appeared frequently in bedrooms, as crossed scarves of linen did in dining

Figure 193. *Living Room, Residence of Martin Hawley, 1801 Eutaw Place, Baltimore, Maryland. C. 1900.* Maryland Historical Society, Baltimore.

Hawley's living room presented a model Mission interior. Most notable was the fireplace with large hood and tile facing. The same straight lines are seen in the ceiling beams, the lattice of the room divider at the left, and the leather-upholstered chairs. Steins and other ceramic decoration on the mantel and shelf are typical, as are the rugs with Indian design. A hint of Art Nouveau appears in the curved design of the chandelier and the foliage around the heraldic design on the stool.

Figure 194. *Living Room, Residence of Judge McGowan, Alaska. C.* 1900.
Seattle Historical Society, Seattle, Wash.

Judge McGowan's Alaskan living room, decorated for a reception, showed a mixture of Mission and Art Nouveau with the earlier Moorish style. The sinuous floral design on the Moorish tabourette is in the same spirit as the Morris-type fabrics used with Persian fabrics in the cozy corner. The four-legged tabourette is at once reminiscent of both Moorish and Mission. Wall treatment is very simple, with white trim. The elongated pictures were typical of the Mission style, as were the steins. Log rafters (one of them suspended by a chain) went well with the vines and greenery in the hothouse noticeable through the arch. The rugs were commercial manufactures in imitation of Orientals.

rooms. Simple drawn work was featured on the borders of such scarves and curtains; many articles in *The Craftsman* and period books taught the householder how to create such decoration. Handwoven fabrics made fine pillow covers, and Morris design fabrics on the walls were natural parts of the style.

WALL TREATMENT

For Candace Wheeler, walls were fundamental in creating an interior, and "the true principle of wall treatment is to make the boundary stand for colour and

beauty, and not alone for division of space." Wallpaper, she held, was the "chief means of wall-covering" because it was cheap and practical. Modest interiors required papers of "inconspicuous design . . . good and nearly uniform color." Tapestries excited her greatest interest. They might be used effectively in some grand settings, yet they were rare and costly and more fitted "to the period of windy palaces." Modern reproductions were anathema to her, but damasked cloths, painted burlap, Japanese papers, and coarsely woven linens could be quite successful. Tooled Spanish leathers made expensive and elegant wall coverings, but Japanese paper imitations were cheaper and no less attractive. Whether painted or kept in natural wood tones, paneling had a "richness and sober dignity."[4]

Generally, if many pictures were to be used, the wall treatment should be relatively plain. Even though she gave up the earlier Aesthetic division of the wall into three parts, walls still needed variation. Large plain surfaces could be monotonous or fatiguing, and thus where a line of pictures or a molding atop paneling left a plain upper space on a wall, "a broad line of flat decoration should occur." Stencils were a fine means of frieze decoration, especially if the stenciling repeated designs found in the carpet (Fig. 191).

The illustrations show that paneling was common, usually finished off with a plate rail. A plain oatmeal paper often appeared above, but householders

opposite, top: Figure 195. *Craftsman Living Room.* Throop, *Furnishing the Home of Good Taste,* p. 160; see Bibliography.

Lucy Abbot Throop illustrated a typical Mission room with appropriate architectural detail and furniture, but almost lacking in characteristic textiles or carpets. The untrimmed skin on the table contributes to the honest look of the furniture.

Figure 196. *Living Room, Residence of George F. Cottrell, 233 Taylor Avenue, Seattle, Washington. C. 1900.* Seattle Historical Society, Seattle, Wash.

Cottrell, a surveyor and engineer who had migrated to America from England at the age of twenty, was a professional man of solid means. The simple lines of architectural detail might qualify this room as Mission, but the paneling, fireplace, ceiling beams, and wall treatment so evident in Figures 193 and 195 are totally lacking. The heavy table is clearly Mission, while the far rocker is typical of Grand Rapids work. The closer chair was a Mission design, possibly by Charles Rohlfs. The chandelier lacks the consistent straight lines of pure Mission work but nonetheless bears its influence.

Wall stencil designs by
Candace Wheeler

frequently added the stencils Mrs. Wheeler recommended. Wallpapers in Morris-type designs were also frequently used.

ARCHITECTURAL DETAILS AND CEILINGS

The Mission style was one largely created by architectural detail as well as by furniture and textiles; such detail showed the same angularity evident in the furniture. Straight, long, vertical, and horizontal lines gave even empty rooms a distinctive flavor. The style excluded curves, and one almost looks in vain for a rounded molding. Typical overmantels had hoods, large and small (Fig. 193), with the fireplace surrounded by tile or brick. Common in country houses were massive fieldstone fireplaces.

Plain, light ceilings were common with the style, but beamed ceilings were frequent. Natural logs might be used as ceiling rafters in vacation lodges.

LIGHTING

The highly elaborate chandeliers of the 1870s and 1880s gave way to simpler, less conspicuous fixtures, with straight angular lines typical of the Mission style.

Figure 197. *Mission Bedroom. C. 1910. Your Home and Its Decoration*, p. 143; see Bibliography.

Architectural detail was at a minimum in this upstairs room, but the same simple, straight lines were evident in doors and picture molding. The bed with its attached seat, the dresser, and side table all exhibit the same angularity. The four small rugs have geometric patterns rather than Art Nouveau motifs, and the chintz curtains with their simple valance are in a different fabric from the bedspread. Note the typical Mission lamp above the bed. The candle on the side table is for decoration only.

Figure 198. *Dining Room. C.* 1910. Wilson, *The Bungalow Book*, p. 150.

Henry L. Wilson's model dining room was rigorously Mission in both furniture and chandeliers. The wall treatment was unusual with its cutout designs at the joints of the vertical wainscotting. Stylized deer fill the frieze that surmounts the plate rail with its collection of similar but unmatched china. Once occupied, the model room would probably have had a carpet. Note the simple curtain on the door.

Iron, copper, and brass were shaped into lantern designs, which hung from the center of the room, and the home craftsman might make himself matching table lamps. Electricity was now standard, but *Mission Furniture: How to Make It* did include a plan for an "Artistic Mission Style Oil Lamp."

COLOR

Mrs. Wheeler adopted the popular dictum of using warm colors for rooms with northern exposure and cooler blues and greens for rooms with windows facing south. The color scheme of a room began with the walls; well decorated, a wall would "stand for colour and beauty, and not alone for division of space." Color could be light or dark in tone, but the "quality of it must be soft and charitable, instead of harsh and uncompromising."

Since a dining room should be decorated with china rather than pictures, blue was especially appropriate there. Libraries should have warm colors, such as red, gold, or orange. Entrance halls were best in Damascus or Pompeian red, colors that were just complements to the yellows of oiled wood paneling.[5]

Strong color schemes were variably important in a Mission room. Stickley favored wainscotting of rubbed or fumed oak or chestnut. The exposed walls, he wrote, should carry natural rough plaster or a rough-textured oatmeal paper, and tiles should be a yellow brown with a matte finish, harmonizing with the copper hood of the fireplace. Stickley's color schemes were rich but quiet. Other Mission rooms showed bright colors, especially greens, usually in textiles or in the frieze.

ACCESSORIES

Some Mission rooms were notably spare in accessories, but others were fully furnished with items exhibiting appropriate motifs. Hammered copper and brass items were common, as were beer steins. Plants and hanging baskets were popular, often in Mission-style planters. Appropriate pottery was often hard to distinguish from the Art Nouveau style. The products of the Rookwood Pottery factory in Cincinnati possibly led in popularity, followed by Dedham and Greubey. The Van Briggle Pottery Company in Colorado Springs, still active today, also produced considerable quantities, as indeed did many home craftsmen and craftswomen. Typical pottery had a matte finish overflowing with splash glazes. Floral designs were popular.

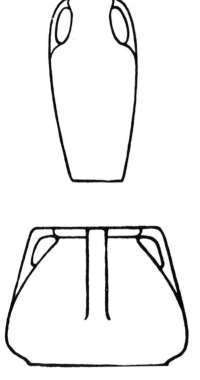

Typical Art Nouveau pottery shapes

Art Nouveau

The Art Nouveau style is historical paradox, for it was widely publicized, yet its best-known variation seems to have produced very few interiors.

As the Art Nouveau evolved out of the earlier Aesthetic Movement in the 1890s, two principal variants emerged. In the hands of Victor Horta of Brussels, Henry Van de Velde in Germany, Antoni Gaudi in Barcelona, or Hector Guimard of Paris, Art Nouveau design was a profusion of sinuous curves. It is this sinuous version that is popularly associated with Art Nouveau as a whole. But the work of Charles Rennie Mackintosh of Scotland, Adolph Loos and Joseph Hoffmann of Vienna, gave the style a more rectilinear form.

Americans had many opportunities to know both variants. *The International Studio* appeared in 1897. It was a publication devoted to illustrating new developments in world art, and for many years Art Nouveau, sinuous and rectilinear, filled its pages. Americans attending the St. Louis Exposition of 1904 saw a full, sinuous interior in the French pavilion.[6] Yet American interiors in the sinuous variant, like those in Figures 204 to 206, are extremely rare. They occurred sporadically, scattered throughout the country. Unlike

Figure 199. *Dining Room Design. The Craftsman* (November 1905), p. 237.

Although appearing in *The Craftsman*, primary advocate of the Mission style, this design bears the strong influence of the sinuous Art Nouveau in the stained glass window above the built-in sideboard. Note the embroidered table scarves and the rug that matched them in spirit. The floor was buff, and the carpet dull green in the center with yellow, blue, red, and gray in the border decoration. The curtains were red and white, and the top row of glass in the side windows was tinted the same blue found in the top of the stained glass window.

many other styles, the best and most consistent examples were not found in the townhouses of New York City, Boston, and other urban centers.

The rectilinear version of the style was more prominent. The early work of Frank Lloyd Wright in the Midwest, the California houses of the brothers Henry Mather and Charles Sumner Greene, and the designs Will Bradley produced for the *Ladies Home Journal* in 1901 and 1902, all show highly individual forms of the rectilinear style. Some of the creators of the rectilinear style had earlier associations with the sinuous variant. Bradley, for example, had done

Figure 200. *Studio of Louis C. Tiffany, 72nd Street at Madison Avenue, New York City. C.* 1903. Croly, *Stately Homes in America*, p. 445; see Bibliography.

Louis C. Tiffany's father, Charles L. Tiffany, had become a millionaire in the jewelry business in New York City, and in 1885 built a mansion for his family at a cost of $100,000. The father never in fact moved in, but Louis Tiffany maintained the top floor as his studio for the rest of his life. The four-sided fireplace, designed by Tiffany himself about 1883, was an early declaration of the sinuous Art Nouveau; so, too, was the swirling iron bracket that sprang from it. Hanging lamps showed the deep impression Tiffany's travels in the Middle East had made upon him.

graphics in the sinuous variant, an influence clearly evident in the decoration of his rooms. In some ways, both the rectilinear variant and the Mission style were revolts against the earlier sinuous version, and several illustrations defy easy classification as Art Nouveau or Mission.

The rectilinear variant was much more common, but it was not a style favored by the very rich. It was more at home in the bungalows of the middle class in the Midwest and far West. George W. Maher, a Chicago architect, observed in *Architectural Record* in 1907 that Eastern work was stultified by tired copying of historical European models. "New art" had made little progress there. An editor responded that Eastern architects built what clients wanted, houses that were "big and bold and stunning and redundant." In the Midwest, he continued, "the state of mind which is too big and overflowing for anything but a baronial hall is not so frequent as in the East," and "the successful Western business man is usually satisfied with something simpler and more genuinely domestic, but it is not anything less traditional." Even in the West, the editor held, the client's basic preference was for the Colonial, Jacobean, or Elizabethan styles, and only a persuasive architect could bring about anything else.[7]

FURNITURE

Furniture in both variants of the style was produced domestically. Edward Colonna— a naturalized German who worked in Dayton, Ohio, in the 1880s and 1890s, before going to Paris where he gained international fame— designed furniture with gently sinuous legs and a cresting suggesting waterlilies, a favorite Art Nouveau motif. Charles Rohlfs and eight assistants had a shop in Buffalo. He exhibited there in 1901, in Turin in 1902, and in St. Louis in 1904, showing such pieces as a fumed oak chest carved with a swirling pattern inspired by smoke curling into the air, or a fancy chair with a high back and whipping lacertine ornament. Neither Colonna nor Rohlfs had a wide American audience. About 1909, the New York firm of George Flint produced a few commerical pieces in the sinuous variant, usually copying designs of Louis Majorelle of Nancy.

Bric-à-brac table with Art Nouveau influence, 1888

Figure 201. *Center Court, Residence of Louis C. Tiffany, Cold Spring Harbor, Long Island, New York. C.* 1907. *Catalogue . . . Architectural League of New York* (1907).

Tiffany built Laurelton Hall at Cold Spring Harbor in 1905 at a cost of nearly $200,000. The center court was sometimes described as Persian, but its elements were arranged in the Art Nouveau style. Its interior was organized around a fountain that flowed down the sides of a tall, clear vase, reflecting the green colors of the flowers and plants. The pierced decorations on the far wall were green at the base and light bronze in the upper tiers, taking their colors from the copper pieces in front. The hanging lanterns were an iridescent bronze.[10]

Art Nouveau-influenced chair

Grand Rapids furniture produced from 1895 to 1905 often exhibits faint traces of the Art Nouveau style: cabriole legs that were not quite Louis XV and chair backs decorated with sinuous lines. Grand Rapids-made furniture was within the reach of all—an Art Nouveau rocker could be bought for $6.89, a buffet for $24.50, and a whole parlor set for as little as $25.

Furniture in the rectilinear style was often the creation of the architect who designed the house, as in the example of Wright's Robie House, the Greenes' Gamble House, or George W. Maher's house for James A. Patten (Fig. 202). In its simpler forms, the rectilinear style is virtually indistinguishable from Mission.

Usually, Art Nouveau furniture was finished in natural wood tones, just as Mission furniture was so treated. The sinuous version was more likely to be mahogany or other dark woods. Figure 206 illustrates painted furniture in the sinuous style. Bradley's designs incorporated both natural wood tones and painted surfaces, and pieces of either sort were decorated with painted Art Nouveau designs.

opposite, top: Figure 202. *Dining Room, Residence of James A. Patten, Evanston, Illinois.* 1907. *Architectural Record* (June 1907), p. 440.

James A. Patten (1852–1928) had prospered as a grain commission merchant, but his name did not appear on the roster of millionaires. Architect George W. Maher of Chicago designed both the house and its interior. Maher was known to prefer the rectilinear Art Nouveau bordering on Mission, but in this dining room the simple honesty of the Mission look was given up for elegance. The room almost anticipates the Art Deco look of the 1920s. Maher supported "the movement for a new art," free from the binding precedents of past styles. The Patten dining room was based on the thistle theme. Thistle carvings are on the table and crested rolls of the chairs, while an abstract thistle design appears in the overmantel mirror, the frieze, and the portières. Unfortunately, no details of color were given.

Figure 203. *Study, Residence of Felix Peano, Santa Monica, California.* 1909. *Architectural Record* (July 1909), p. 35.

Felix Peano, an Italian sculptor, settled on the West Coast about 1904 and designed a house incorporating features of the sinuous and rectilinear Art Nouveau. The bench and table were built as one piece, the leather hangings were reminiscent of Mackintosh, and polished stones were inserted in plaster walls "to give effect to the color scheme," a scheme unfortunately never described. The corner post in the arch was probably an example of his exotic lighting, for the trefoils seem to be filled with the translucent shells behind which he placed electric lights. On the table was a bronze model of the house.[11]

Will H. Bradley. *Furniture designs.* The Metropolitan Museum of Art (Gift of Fern Bradley Dufner, 1952).

Figure 204. *Living Room, Fischer Residence, Germantown, Pennsylvania.*
C. 1912. American Country Houses of Today, p. 124; see Bibliography.

Milton B. Medary, Jr. (1874–1929), of Philadelphia, architect of the Fischer House, created one of the few American interiors close to the sinuous Art Nouveau. The style was most clear in the rounded corners of the glass doors and the transom. The table at the left and the matching piano stool at the right are reminiscent of furniture by Hector Guimard, and the upholstery of the chairs in the corner is equally inspired by the new art. The walls in the corner were decorated with an Art Nouveau border, while the shelf held a collection of art pottery and glass.

FLOOR COVERINGS

Art Nouveau designs usually extended to the creation of floor coverings as well. The Greenes created an olive green rug with a conventionalized Tree of Life pattern in blue, rose, and ochre, and Louis Tiffany designed a rug for his dining room at Laurelton Hall with a deep blue field and three large circular arabesque medallions in grayish gold, with flying cranes woven into the design. All the Bradley designs had appropriate carpeting with Art Nouveau motifs, as did many of the interiors actually created (Fig. 207). In some rooms, carpets were of solid colors with simple borders reinforcing the unity of the room's design but not carrying its primary decoration (Fig. 202). Designers occasionally used Orientals with the Art Nouveau (Fig. 203), and rooms furnished with Grand Rapids-Art Nouveau often had carpeting that bore no relation to the style (Fig. 208).

PICTURES AND MIRRORS

Art Nouveau was essentially pictorial, so it is not surprising that the most elaborate interiors include almost no pictures. In Will Bradley's nursery design and in the Greenes' Freeman A. Ford House (1907), pictures or prints were framed into the wall construction.

Mirrors were restricted to utilitarian uses in bedrooms and bath. Even in

Figure 205. *Dining Room, Fischer Residence, Germantown, Pennsylvania. C.* 1912. *American Country Houses of Today*, p. 125; see Bibliography.

The most obvious Art Nouveau feature of the Fischer dining room was the favrile glass chandelier, but the curved wall, leaded glass in the china case, and the rounded corners of the doors and buffet were consistent with the rectilinear version of the style. The table was anything but Art Nouveau, yet despite their turned legs, the chairs' backs showed a pattern of restrained curves. The molded border in the ceiling is too indistinct in the picture to discern whether it has Art Nouveau motifs.

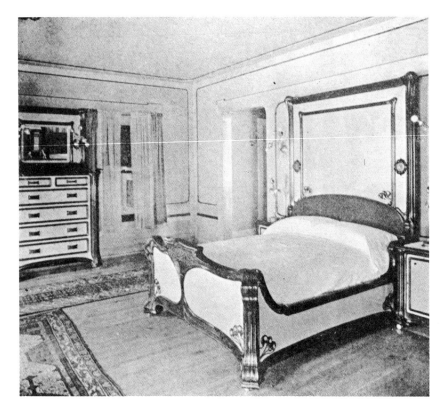

Figure 206. *Bedroom. C.* 1907. Croly, *Houses for Town or Country*, p. 182; see Bibliography.

Croly did not specify that this was an American room, but presumably it was since the book was a collection of American interiors. The bed and dresser display the sinuous curves of the Art Nouveau, forms rare in America. The bed was painted the same tone as the wall, and the wall and ceiling had simple, painted line borders. The curtain was very plain, but the lighting—four sconces and two bedside lamps—was spectacular. The door had rounded corners, a characteristic feature of the Art Nouveau.

Figure 207. *Bedroom. C.* 1907. Croly, *Houses for Town or Country*, p. 183; see Bibliography.

This second Art Nouveau bedroom shows simpler treatment. The bed has simple Mission lines, but the sinuous elements of the footboard and the textile decoration of the headboard indicate Art Nouveau. The chair similarly has Art Nouveau lines, and both the strip sewn carpet and the frieze carry out the decorative scheme.

Bradley's bedroom design, no mirror is seen. Maher's dining room (Fig. 202), however, does use an overmantel mirror.

TEXTILES

Textiles played a variable role. Curtains and portières were relatively plain, hung in straight lines without a valance. Upholstery and cushions, on the other hand, could be quite vibrant in color and design. Table scarves, usually white, had embroidered or block-printed decoration of stylized flowers, and two such scarves might be hung at right angles on a table (Fig. 199).

Most favored for needlework were coarse cotton or linen; printed chintz or cretonne appeared in some interiors.

Figure 208. *Bedroom, Residence on East 122nd Street, New York City. C. 1895.* Lyman Allyn Museum, New London, Conn.

At first glance, this room is anything but Art Nouveau. However, the mirrored dressing table and the tall cheval glass are good examples of the mass-produced furniture influenced by the Art Nouveau. The brass beds exhibit sinuous S curves in head- and footboards, but there is no other evidence of the Art Nouveau. Other notable features are the quarter canopy, the intricate picture frame, and the subtle but lavishly painted ceiling. The embroidered glass curtains and the juxtaposition of wicker and mahogany are also of interest.

Stencil design

Art Nouveau hardware, 1906

WALL TREATMENT

Walls were an important element in creating the Art Nouveau look. In the Bradley drawings, plastered walls were richly loaded with Art Nouveau papers and painting. Every inch of the nursery wall was decorated; only in the bedroom was there a tall frieze simply painted a plain white.[8] The Aesthetic tripartite division of the wall was gone, but in its most ornate form Art Nouveau continued to emphasize the frieze, sometimes 4 feet tall. Walls and fabrics were often coordinated in terms of design. In Laurelton Hall, Tiffany chose white walls decorated with stylized cypress trees (Fig. 201), yet many walls were surprisingly plain (Fig. 204).

Wallpaper was important. The M. H. Berge Company of Buffalo introduced embossed paper with swirling Art Nouveau patterns available in silver, blue, or red on an olive ground. They also exhibited a paper with a "Half-bronze" effect, reflecting the iridescence favored in Art Nouveau glass.

Greene and Greene used rich wood paneling with vertical moldings in many of their commissions; contrasting horizontal boards created a frieze effect in some rooms. Frank Lloyd Wright similarly included relatively plain plastered or paneled walls in his houses.

A costly element in wall decoration was the stained glass window in dazzling Art Nouveau patterns of the sort Tiffany was producing. In the Gamble House (1908), the Greenes decorated the front hall with a broad expanse of such glass.

ARCHITECTURAL DETAILS AND CEILINGS

No American interior decorators present the sinuous line of railings, woodwork, and ceilings found in the interiors of Horta or Guimard. Milton B. Medary's Fischer House perhaps comes the closest, with the rounded corners of the doors and the moderately sinuous transom (Fig. 204).

The rectilinear style varied in its use of architectural details. Bradley's drawings depended very little on such details for their effect. Where decoration was less dependent on color, paint, and wallpaper, however, architectural details were naturally more important. The Greenes and Maher used intricate angular patterns in stair and balcony railings and fireplaces to gain their effect. Wide expanses of windows were popular in the avant garde houses, and window and door frames were predictably simple. Angular fretwork dividers separating rooms or areas added interest.

The P. & F. Corbin Company of New Britain, Connecticut, advertised sinuous Art Nouveau hardware in 1906, but we have been unable to find illustrations of any interior using them.

LIGHTING

Art Nouveau artists put great effort into electric lighting fixtures, but kerosene continued in use.

Chandeliers and ceiling lamps in a variety of shapes were popular. Some were made of stained glass, while others, round or square, had frosted glass and an obvious Oriental influence.

The sinuous Art Nouveau had a strong impact on lighting. Chandeliers, hanging lamps, sconces, table lamps, and floor lamps all received elaborate treatment in the hands of Louis C. Tiffany and those who followed his lead in favrile and stained glass. Tiffany's hanging and standing lamps sold at over $100 each, and his Wisteria lamp of 1904, designed by Mrs. Curtis Freschel, sold for $750 in its largest version. It is thus not surprising that these fixtures are missing from more modest interiors. His famous lily cluster design with Morning Glory shades (Fig. 205) won a grand prize at Turin in 1902.

COLOR

Color was important in the Art Nouveau interior. Bradley's designs were rich with color in warm reds, browns, and tans. A basic harmony of colors rather

Figure 209. *Dining Room, Residence of Martin Ausley. Portland, Oregon. C. 1900.* Oregon Historical Society, Portland.

Little is indicated of the Art Nouveau in this room except the mass-produced furniture that carries a faint echo of the sinuous variant in the chairs' backs and legs. Tiffany, too, used fluted, turned legs on some of his furniture designs,[12] but created an effect of light gracefulness rather than ponderous weight. The portières display a swirling floral pattern, possibly Art Nouveau. The walls have the plain look that became fashionable in turn-of-the-century decor.

than even muted contrasts was fundamental to his color schemes. However, the plates in the Sherwin-Williams Company's *Your Home and Its Decoration* emphasized greens, and Tiffany's work at Laurelton Hall, like his glass, emphasized blues and greens. Both Tiffany and Bradley juxtaposed bright colors in a manner other decorators would have found unsettling.

In the work of Frank Lloyd Wright and the Greenes, warm wood tones predominated, harmonizing well with the Orientals often seen in their interiors.

ACCESSORIES

Accessories in the sinuous variant of the style were widely produced, but beyond a few vases in characteristic shape, many interiors are notably sparse in their use of accessories. Art Nouveau designers put away many of those items whose continual display earlier generations had held necessary.

Floral designs flowed over the squat or tall elongated shapes of the ceramics produced at the time. Similar shapes were seen in glass, a form in which Art Nouveau reached great heights in the iridescent and favrile glass of Louis Tiffany. After many experiments, he was able to imitate the iridescence Roman glass had acquired through centuries of partial decomposition. "Favrile" was his term for glasses of various colors worked together while hot. Favrile glass was not cheap. In 1911, decanters cost $10 each, 10-inch vases $30, and wine glasses $30 to $85 a dozen.[9]

Several silver companies produced Art Nouveau pieces with swirling designs. Unger Brothers and Gorham created ash trays, desk trays, tea services, and jewel chests, all with flowing water lilies, irises, and lilies. Typical was a hand mirror the back of which was decorated with a mermaid whose whiplike, Botticelli hair flowed into a handle. Gorham produced what was called Martelé silver, in which the workman's hammer marks show clearly, proving that it was honest and handmade.

Art Nouveau silver
hand mirror, 1902

13

The Twentieth-century Look

Purity, Simplicity, and Grandeur

BY the end of the century, eclecticism had almost cluttered itself out; new trends were on the way as writers, many of them women, demanded greater simplicity in the American interior, however grand, and a more accurate understanding of historical styles.

An early indication of these new trends came in *The Decoration of Houses* (1897) by Edith Wharton and Ogden Codman, Jr. Young and intellectual, Edith Wharton had toured Europe with a critical eye and a somewhat disinterested husband. Her novels were still in the future when she joined Codman, an architect and fellow listee in the *Social Register*, in a critique of "the piling up of heterogeneous ornament" and "the multiplication of incongruous effects. . . . Rooms may be decorated in two ways; by a superficial application of ornament totally independent of structure, or by means of those architectural features which are part of the organism of every house, inside as well as out."[1]

The authors urged that interiors be planned to present a harmonious unity with the architectural background. There should be no strong contrast, and rooms should blend easily into one another. Each room should be homogeneous, for the eye is offended when "delicate old marquetry tables are covered with trashy china ornaments." Discard the poor pieces and let a few good ones show to advantage. Rather than have inferior trash, one should live with "willow chairs and stained deal tables until it is possible to buy something better." A willow chair done up in corduroy or denim was better than a "parlor suit." They admitted, begrudgingly, that taste was expensive, but the masses copied the rich, and every tasteful improvement made "by those who can afford to indulge their taste, will in time find its way to the carpenter-built cottage."[2]

The Wharton-Codman book, with its fifty-six plates of European furniture and architecture, anticipated by a decade the publishers' bonanza of surveys of authentic historical styles. Lucy Abbot Throop's *Furnishing the Home of Good Taste* (1912) began with the Greeks but spent most of its time on English and French historical styles. Frank Alvah Parsons, president of the New York

School of Fine and Applied Arts, published his *Interior Decoration* in 1916. He drew lessons from historic styles for modern decoration, as did Harold D. Eberlein, Abbot McClure, and Edward S. Holloway in *The Practical Book of Interior Decoration* (1919). Eberlein and McClure had also produced *The Practical Book of Period Furniture* (1914).

If authenticity of ornament and furniture was the emphasis of some, simplicity was the not incompatible focal point of others. After five decades of eclecticism, a time when there was no one "right" look, the American interior took on a new uniformity. Themes of specific styles still predominated—Colonial, Louis XV, Jacobean—but rooms came to look much alike. They were light, uncluttered, and spacious, emphasizing solid colors rather than patterns for carpets, walls, and upholstery.

One of the foremost exponents and practitioners of this new look was Elsie de Wolfe (1866–1950), who had turned to interior decorating in 1905 after a not-too-successful career on the stage. Her move to decorating was strongly supported by Miss Elisabeth Marbury, with whom she shared a charming townhouse at 122 East 17th Street in New York City. Miss de Wolfe was well born, moved in the correct social circles in New York (as did Edith Wharton), and much of her success lay in her social contacts with people of substance in New York and elsewhere.

She summarized her ideas in *The House in Good Taste* (1913), a practical and precise definition of what a house should look like. Her stylistic trademarks were light-toned walls, Louis XVI furniture (either real or reproduction), and a great deal of chintz. Chintz flowed by the yard on her beds, curtains, slipcovers,

Figure 210. *Dining Table Setting.* 1901. Holt, *Encyclopaedia of Etiquette*, p. 84.

This type of table arrangement continued in fashion throughout the first decades of the century. In the 1920s, such a setting was termed "English."

Figure 211. *Library, Land's End, Residence of Mrs. Edith Wharton. Newport, Rhode Island. C.* 1900. Wharton Papers, Collection of American Literature, Beinecke Library, Yale University, New Haven, Conn.

Mrs. Wharton's library is an outstanding example of a Louis XV room. The library table in the foreground, the commode, lamp stand, and bookcase, have rococo gilt decoration, while the upholstered chairs are either in natural wood or painted. The rococo theme carries over into the three-armed wall sconce, the picture frames, the andirons, and the fireback. The same decor governs the top of the overmantel mirror and the cast plaster decoration of the ceiling. The fabric covering the walls is used again in the portières, and even the art fits with the period decor. An Oriental rug on the hardwood floor is the most notable departure from an otherwise comprehensive Louis XV style.

and dressing tables. She, too, stressed suitability, proportion, and simplicity.

The book was partly autobiographical, for she told the story of the consecutive redecorations of her house on 17th Street, the former home of Washington Irving, and then of the townhouse on 55th Street that she acquired some years later. Since she believed that the first really comfortable houses had been the small French townhouses of the eighteenth century, she may have been automatically predisposed to French styles, especially Louis XVI, for her own townhouse commissions. But she held that Hepplewhite, Sheraton, and Adam were also acceptable.

Figure 212. *Library, The Mount, Residence of Mrs. Edith Wharton. C.* 1905.
Lenox, Massachusetts. Wharton Papers, Collection of American Literature,
Beinecke Library, Yale University, New Haven, Conn.

Mrs. Wharton found great charm in a wall of books, and created these walls in her
own library in Lenox, Massachusetts. Like the room at Land's End (Fig. 211), the
basic decor is Louis XV. The chaise longue and cane back chairs are all unpainted,
as are the bookcases with their ornamental carvings. The coved ceiling is plain, but
the cornice has three courses of molding decoration. The curtains are plain dark
plush, hung on rings from a simple rod. Not all is in the Louis XV style, but the
library table, the lamps, and the two settees do not clash with the basic look of the
room and, indeed, add to its appearance of comfort. The Oriental rug covers the
central portion of a parquet floor.

A room-by-room survey of each house offered many practical suggestions,
as well as her philosophies of individual rooms. The hall should be considered
merely an entrance, furnished sparsely with a bench, a pair of urns, or an
imported porcelain stove. A hall might even appear cold with its squared marble
floor so that the warmth of the drawing room was even more appealing by
contrast. The drawing room was to have intimate groupings of furniture, with
comfortable chairs, but the fireplace was to be the focal point. Small tables with
lamps should be well placed, with flowers and plants used in profusion. A piano
was proper only if someone in the house played and played well. A dining room
might be small, but mirrors would give the illusion of double the space. Rich

displays of silver characteristic of the nineteenth century were to be omitted. Marble console shelves were better than large sideboards, for they took up less space.

Her ideal bedroom would be heavily draped in chintz, and would contain a small table by the bed, a dressing table, and a small desk. She much preferred a simple French day bed or chaise longue, and noted three great American errors in taste: rocking chairs, lace curtains, and brass beds.

The book was a publishing success, but to the average reader it must have seemed written (as it was) for the millionaire class, many of whose houses she had decorated. Her commissions took her not only to the townhouses of New York City and the Colony Club (perhaps her most famous commission), but also to Chicago to work for J. Ogden Armour, to Burlingame, California, for William Crocker, and to Galveston, Texas, for Mrs. George Sealy.

The translation of her ideas into terms affordable by the great middle class fell to others, many of whom published books with titles similar to hers. As mentioned, Lucy Abbot Throop had produced *Furnishing the Home of Good Taste* in 1912, and Richardson Wright followed in 1915 with *Inside the House of Good Taste*. Corporations, sensing the potential of the new look, published manuals too, and thus the Sherwin Williams Company produced *Your Home and Its Decoration* in 1910. That book is naturally very useful in documenting colors, as any paint company would be meticulous in specifying the colors of everything.

Ekin Wallick produced three guides promoting the new simplicity, with a clear emphasis on economics as well as taste: *Inexpensive Furnishings in Good Taste* (1915), *The Small House for a Moderate Income* (1915), and *The Attractive Home* (1916). Wallick's plates show the same light woodwork, solid pastel colors, painted furniture, and even some of the same chintzes found in Elsie de Wolfe's book. But totally lacking was her Louis XVI furniture. Instead, Wallick and others tended to emphasize the Colonial style that had gained increasingly in popularity since the 1880s.

As with the European styles, several studies had led the way to a more accurate understanding of the Colonial look. In 1891, Dr. Irving Whitall Lyon published his *Colonial Furniture of New England*, the first serious study of early American furniture styles. Esther Singleton followed in 1901 with *The Furniture of Our Forefathers*, a still useful study of "who had owned what" throughout the thirteen colonies. Architecture received new and careful examination. Norman Isham and Albert Brown, both architects, collaborated on books on Rhode Island (1895) and Connecticut (1900). Harold Donaldson Eberlein surveyed all the colonies in his *Architecture of Colonial America* (1915).

Mary H. Northend published a careful study of Colonial interiors in her *Colonial Homes and Their Furnishings* (1912). She considered clocks, lighting, silver, and pewter, as well as furniture and architecture. Her *Remodeled Farm Houses* (1915) was an early guide to the restoration of period interiors for contemporary domestic life, as was *Reclaiming the Old House* (1913) by Charles Edward Hooper.

The simple lines of the Colonial style went well with the new simplicity, and as in the eighteenth century, it was suited to a variety of economic tastes. The smaller-income householder might buy more inexpensive original pieces or new

Colonial Revival house, 1917

Dutch colonial house, 1913

Bungalow costing $3,300

authentic reproductions, but those of wealth might buy original American furniture of the same stature as the Louis XVI originals purchased by some of Miss de Wolfe's clients.

George S. Palmer of New London, Connecticut, was a typical wealthy enthusiast of the Colonial Revival. With a fortune made in the family quilt mills, he spent thirty years traveling New England to find the best examples of early American furniture. In 1906, to house his collections, he had the architect Charles A. Platt design a house based on William Byrd's Virginia mansion, Westover. Authentic colonial detail governed the furnishing throughout, and one of the bedrooms provided its occupant with the use of three block and shell pieces (Fig. 225). The household was served by a staff of seventeen. After World War I, Mr. Palmer sold forty-one pieces of early American furniture to the Metropolitan Museum of Art, where they may be seen today.

Few were as meticulous as Palmer in copying the architecture of one colonial house, but many of the rich and middle class built in the Colonial style. The wealthy favored the Georgian look of eighteenth-century Virginia, while the less well-to-do found models in Amyar Embury II's *The Dutch Colonial House* (1913). These Dutch colonials with their green shutters and white clapboards were built by the thousands.

There were other styles for exteriors. The very wealthy continued to build on a grand scale, but perhaps not quite so grandly as in the late nineteenth century, and the Renaissance and French styles continued to serve them well. But for the middle-class and lower-income families, there were new options. Highly popular was the half-timbered house, described in a book by Allen Jackson in 1912. *Concrete and Stucco Houses* (1912) by Oswald C. Hering outlined another alternative.

In his *Small House for a Moderate Income*, Wallick offered Colonial, Dutch Colonial, "American," and "English"-style plans, which he estimated would cost between $4,000 and $7,000 to build. His "economical" house figured at $3,800. None of these plans included a servant's room.

By far the most important new house plan was the California Bungalow, which soon spread from coast to coast. *The Bungalow Book* by Henry L. Wilson, known as "The Bungalow Man," had reached a fifth edition by 1910. For $10, Wilson would send out plans for houses costing from $800 to $10,000, with most plans estimated between $1,500 and $3,000. Maids' rooms appeared in plans estimated at as little as $3,300. Bungalows were most often furnished in the Mission or Art Nouveau styles, a few used as vacation lodges had rustic interiors, but some were given interiors not much different from those described by Wallick. Henry Saylor's *Bungalows* (1911) offered plans for entire housing developments, and they were built by the thousands.

The most elaborate interiors remained the preserve of the very wealthy. Statistics on incomes for 1910 are illuminating. Scholars classified the 65 percent of the families who had incomes under $1,000 per year as poor. The next 15 percent, labeled lower middle class, had incomes ranging between $1,000 and $1,200; while the next 18 percent, the upper middle class, received between $1,200 and $3,600. The top 2 percent, the rich, had incomes above $3,600. Out of 27,945,190 American families, 3,560 had incomes of over $100,000 per year, but only 154 had annual incomes of over $1 million.[3]

In 1916, Mrs. Frederick, author of *The New Housekeeping*, assumed that

Figure 213. *Bedroom, Residence of Elsie de Wolfe and Elisabeth Marbury.*
Irving Place at 17th Street, New York City. Before 1910. De Wolfe, *The House*
in Good Taste, p. 38; see Bibliography.

Miss Marbury's bedroom in the old Washington Irving house had white enamel
furniture, ivory white walls, and a rug in a soft dull blue. The same Bird of Paradise
chintz covered the couch, bed, and screen at the head of the bed. The photograph is a
useful document on de Wolfe's method of hanging pictures. She wrote: "Be wary of
hanging many pictures in your bedroom. I give this advice cheerfully, because I
know you will hang them anyway (I do) but I warn you you will spoil your room
if you aren't very stern with yourself." Note that the uppermost pictures are hung
from a rail.

the average live-in maid or cook would make $5 a week or roughly 8¢ an
hour.[4]

Householders received no end of decorative advice from books and magazines. *The Decorator and Furnisher* was dead, but other magazines kept one
informed of the latest changes. *Woman's Home Companion* (begun in 1873),
Ladies Home Journal (1883), *Good Housekeeping* (1885), *House Beautiful*
(1896), *House and Garden* (1901), and *American House and Garden* (1905),
in varying degrees, all provided practical decorative suggestions. *Country Life in
America* (1901) (Fig. 225) showed the middle classes what the wealthy were
doing, while *Architectural Record* (1891) (Figs. 202, 203), *Arts and Decoration*
(1910), and *Good Furniture and Decoration* (1913) had a more-or-less professional appeal to architects and well-to-do householders. Not technically a periodi-

cal, *American Country Houses of Today* nonetheless appeared sporadically (in 1912, 1915, 1917, 1922, 1930, 1935), each time offering a portfolio of fashionable, expensive interiors and exteriors (Figs. 204, 205). *Stately Homes in America* by Harry Desmond and Herbert Croly was D. Appleton and Company's effort to duplicate in 1903 what it had done twenty years earlier with *Artistic Houses*. The book provided a general history of American decoration, showing that the true principles of interior decor had really only been mastered in the late nineteenth century. Its pictures were surely studied with some envy by those who were just barely within the millionaire class.

Figure 214. *Dining Room, Residence of Elsie de Wolfe, 122 East 17th Street, New York City.* 1896. Photograph by Byron. The Byron Collection, Museum of the City of New York.

The first of four pictures to show the transformation of Elsie de Wolfe's dining room over seventeen years, this was taken before Miss de Wolfe began her career as a professional decorator. The room was a basic statement of the eclectic–Colonial Revival, with Chippendale-style chair and clock, and a Hepplewhite sideboard massed with silver. Twenty-nine plates decorated the wall, a vaguely Aesthetic tapestry was behind the sideboard, and a Renaissance chair stood at the head of the table. Striped wallpaper was surmounted by a lightly figured frieze with a light design over the entire ceiling.

Amid the diversity of sources, there was a surprising agreement. Basically, writers discussed the simplified and purified revival styles or turned toward the Mission or Art Nouveau styles.

We have approached the revivals through the eyes of Elsie de Wolfe, who assumed that her readers of "good taste" could afford considerable elegance, and of Ekin Wallick, who wrote deliberately for those of moderate and lesser means. Though agreeing on many decorative principles, the economic variation in their outlook becomes evident as they discuss the rooms of their "average" house.

Only Miss de Wolfe speaks of a drawing room. It was to be a room of elegant formality. Her living room, on the other hand, was big, restful, comfortable, "the jolliest place in the world," and even "a little shabby."[5] Wallick saw his living room similarly, emphasizing comfort and convenience.

Miss de Wolfe wanted a light, gay dining room done with "simplicity," a

Figure 215. *Dining Room, Residence of Elsie de Wolfe, 122 East 17th Street, New York City.* 1898. Photograph by Byron. The Byron Collection, Museum of the City of New York.

By 1898 Miss de Wolfe had redone her dining room significantly in a style that began to anticipate the look of the early twentieth century. The Chippendale chairs are gone, replaced by painted cane back chairs in a simple Louis XVI style. The light color of the chairs is carried over to the dado, frieze, ceiling, and woodwork. A simple, solid carpet has succeeded the Orientals. The plates, portrait, and clock are supplanted by mirrors with candle sconces and the large overmantel mirror with its eighteenth-century bust.

word Wallick himself used for the room. Miss de Wolfe, writing of nonmillionaires, held that in a small house a combined living room-dining room was quite fine, but one should keep dining equipment out of sight between meals. Both likewise held that the bedroom should be a restful expression of the individuality of the occupant.

Wallick's list of rooms stopped at this point, but Miss de Wolfe went on to discuss the boudoir (the luxurious and comfortable, small personal sitting room of a woman of many interests), library, tea room, breakfast room, and trellis room. These rooms were lacking in the $800 bungalow. Bungalows had their own specialized rooms, but they had more utilitarian and "honest" names like "den" or "sewing room." A literally exterior room built with many bungalows was the sleeping porch, a second-floor porch that allowed the ooccupants the healthful opportunity to sleep in the open air without camping out.

In asides Miss de Wolfe refers to her interiors as showing "elegant simplicity and aristocratic reserve" and "expensive simplicity."[6] Wallick simply sought good taste and harmony at moderate cost.

FURNITURE

Miss de Wolfe urged her fashionable readers to buy furniture of good traditional design, particularly in the Louis XV and Louis XVI styles. Antiques were fine if one could afford them and if one could be sure of buying the genuine article, but there was nothing wrong with reproductions, indeed, they were sometimes to be preferred. She admitted: "There is a graceful Louis XV sofa in the Petit Trianon that I have copied many times," and added: "I fancy the furniture of the mid-Victorian era will never be coveted by collectors, unless someone should build a museum for the freakish objects of house furnishing."[7]

Wallick agreed. Reproductions or adaptations of Jacobean, William and Mary, Queen Anne, Chippendale, or Sheraton all made very fashionable rooms, and both writers noted that reproductions offered the possibility of adapting old styles to modern forms. Both writers described rooms with the same basic furniture style throughout, but both were wary of matched sets that introduced the aura of manufactured uniformity. There was more charm and elegance in near matches.

Wallick showed how earlier furniture could be cut, painted, and transformed into modern styles

De Wolfe, Wallick, and many a cabinetmaker were all ready to improve earlier pieces. Miss de Wolfe was the more restrained, but she herself had a former bookcase that had been converted to a display space for china. Wallick devoted an entire section to cutting and painting earlier pieces into the simpler enameled furniture both authors admired. Wallick disliked golden oak as much as Miss de Wolfe did brass beds. Mahogany, walnut, and dark oak were correct, as were enameled pieces decorated by painting or stenciling.

FLOOR COVERINGS

Many of Miss de Wolfe's illustrations show Oriental carpets, and Chinese or Aubusson rugs were equally preferred by her. But plain carpets in a solid color, particularly soft blue or taupe, were also fashionable. Wallick thought plain

Figure 216. *Dining Room, Residence of Elsie de Wolfe, 122 East 17th Street, New York City.* 1910. *Your Home and Its Decoration*, Figure 106; see Bibliography.

Fortunately, the Sherwin-Williams Company, publishers of *Your Home*, provided detailed notes on the colors of Miss de Wolfe's room as it appeared some twelve years after she became an interior decorator. The dining chairs had been repainted gray, as were those on the side, and the earlier table had been replaced with one more ornate. The walls were painted a pearl gray, the woodwork a gray enamel, and varying shades of gray made up the design of the Superbus Wilton carpet. The bust was the only remnant of the old mantel. Not pictured here were English chintz curtains with a floral design of pink, rose, and blue on a ground of gray.[14]

carpets were "more effective" in bedrooms than were Orientals, since the latter might interfere with the color scheme. In almost any room, he thought wall-to-wall carpeting "more charming." The vacuum cleaner refuted objections that wall-to-wall carpets could not be kept clean.

For a hall, Miss de Wolfe thought a squared marble floor most elegant if one could afford it. Wood floors should be dark, well buffed or polished.

PICTURES AND MIRRORS

Both Miss de Wolfe and Wallick exercised restraint in the use of pictures, for clutter was to be avoided on walls as well as on tables. De Wolfe used prints and oils, large and small, to achieve her "expensive simplicity." Wallick, on the other hand, advised less expensive but still "quaint" prints. One should not hang too many pictures in a room. Wallick thought two or three were enough for a bedroom, and all should have similar frames rather than present the eclectic look of earlier decades. Miss de Wolfe was more liberal in her use of pictures and in her acceptance of a variety of frames (Figs. 213, 218). Wallick advised hanging pictures with the bottom edge of the frame 5 feet from the floor.

Miss de Wolfe used mirrors to create the illusion of larger space, and in one room she introduced virtual floor-to-ceiling mirrors around windows. Overmantel mirrors taller than they were wide were common but not universal in

Figure 217. *Dining Room, Residence of Elsie de Wolfe. 123 East 55th Street, New York City. C.* 1913. De Wolfe, *The House in Good Taste*, p. 57; see Bibliography.

In its fourth form, the dining room was in a different house. The room was planned around a new Chinese rug and the Monnoyer paintings, one of which was framed in a center wall panel. Transplanted from the old house were the console table, wall sconces, and marble mantel with its bust, but the mantel is no longer surmounted by a painting, and the gilt clock is not balanced by another item on the other side of the mirror. The same color scheme continued, with the walls "the same tone of gray —darker than silver gray and lighter than pewter," but the blue and yellow Chinese rug determined the colors for the rest of the room. The old dining table was repainted cream pointed with blue, as were the new Louis XVI dining chairs with blue and yellow striped upholstery. The top of the table was painted with urns and sprays of flowers, all protected by a glass plate.

Figure 218. *Drawing Room, Residence of Elsie de Wolfe, 123 East 55th Street, New York City. C.* 1913. De Wolfe, *The House in Good Taste*, p. 138; see Bibliography.

The caption to this picture of Miss de Wolfe's own drawing room read: "The drawing-room should be intimate in spirit." By intimate she did not mean informal, but a room organized into many small conversational centers, such as the one seen here around the fireplace. It was relatively small, and Miss de Wolfe used pier mirrors between the windows to give a greater sense of space. The walls were a deep cream color. Many of the chairs were antiques, with upholstery in Aubusson tapestry and the rose brocade of the sofa.

her decorative schemes. These and other decorative mirrors were often enclosed in moldings and thus treated more as part of the wall. However, old mirrors hung like pictures also appear, and occasionally, she had large oils framed like wall panels. The oils or prints Miss de Wolfe chose for her commissions were invariably eighteenth-century or earlier.

TEXTILES

Both Miss de Wolfe and Wallick depended more on textiles than wallpaper to create the decorative effect of their rooms. In contrast to simple walls and floors, textiles offered strong patterns and bright colors. Miss de Wolfe drew from a wide variety of fabrics, ranging from silks to chintz, while Wallick emphasized less expensive fabrics.

Upholstery in damask or needlepoint was a fitting complement to Louis XV furniture, but Miss de Wolfe illustrated with equal enthusiasm a Chippendale sofa covered in chintz. She wrote of chintzes: "It seems to me there are no more charming stuffs for bedroom hangings that these simple fabrics, with their enchantingly fanciful designs. Think of the changes one could have with several sets of curtains to be changed at will, as Marie Antoinette used to do at the Petit Trianon. How amusing it would be in our own modern houses to change the bed coverings, window curtains, and so forth, twice or three times a year!"[8] Wallick likewise used chintz for upholstery in both hard seats and slipcovers, but many of his illustrations show side chairs with solid-color seats and sofas and other large pieces upholstered in less pronounced patterns. Wallick favored stripes for upholstery and cushions as he did for wallpaper.

The drapery patterns presented by both writers were remarkably similar. Both often used simple, straight-hung curtains, with no valance, in lengths

Figure 219. *Bedroom, Residence of Elsie de Wolfe and Elisabeth Marbury, 123 East 55th Street, New York City. C.* 1913. De Wolfe, *The House in Good Taste,* p. 231; see Bibliography.

In the new house, Miss Marbury used the same blue and cream Persian rug seen in Figure 213. The print at the left also appeared in her old bedroom. Blue was the dominant color. The walls were blue-gray, with the furniture painted a cream color and upholstered in the same rose and cream chintz that skirts her dressing table. The curtains were a plain light blue linen, with blue and white fringe borders and no valance.

extending to the floor or just below the window frame. Both offered simple valances for floor-length curtains. These valances might be scalloped or shaped and decorated with lace and fringe, but they were never as intricate as the productions of thirty years before. On some windows, Miss de Wolfe used only muslin glass curtains. Wallick held that with a figured paper, curtain fabrics must be plain.

Miss de Wolfe had a penchant for early styles, and bed curtains were therefore natural in her work. Color and effect were more important than historical accuracy in designing such curtains. For a Louis XVI bed, she chose chintz with the curtains suspended from a frame attached to the wall. For four-poster beds, however, simplified valances without a full set of bed curtains were adequate to the decor. Other beds had chintz quarter canopies. Studying the fabrics in her commissions, one sees clearly why she was called "the chintz lady."

WALL TREATMENT

Simplicity reigned in wall treatment. Miss de Wolfe and Wallick both avoided the strongly patterned papers of earlier decades. The wall papered or painted a solid color was right for almost every room. Miss de Wolfe wrote that only in the dining room were bold decorative papers appropriate. Chinese rice papers with birds and flowers were just as proper for some dining rooms as "quaint landscape papers" were for New England colonial dining rooms. Paneling painted a light color was another desirable effect in many rooms. Miss de Wolfe illustrated elaborate panels with contrasting moldings, but both authors wrote that if paneling was too expensive, strips of wood or molding applied to the wall and painted would do nicely. In one design, Miss de Wolfe chose a floral figured wallpaper—an "Elizabethan" pattern she thought an apt complement to Elizabethan oak furniture. Wallick believed French striped paper in white or cream to be both "dignified and refined," and always proper with mahogany or painted furniture. He rejected the Aesthetic division of the wall into three parts. According to Wallick, if the ceiling were low, a wall should be papered all over; but if the ceiling were high, the picture molding should be dropped to 2 to 3 feet below the ceiling with paper below it. The frieze created should be painted white or cream; to cover that frieze, as the Aesthetics had, with a different paper would be both ugly and confusing. Decorative wallpaper borders should be used only with care and only on plain walls or with simple striped papers. Otherwise, Wallick thought, there would be "too much decoration."

Faced with difficult problems in decorating a room with no windows at the Colony Club in New York, Miss de Wolfe resorted to a wall treatment seldom seen in her other rooms. The wall was divided into her usual panels, and the wall painted a yellow-tan. But the panels themselves were gray, and decorated with classical designs in "pinky-yellow" and browns. This unusual use of eighteenth-century French classical wall decoration shows how much she had simplified the style, or at least the late nineteenth century's version of the style.

The wall treatment for which Miss de Wolfe was best known was "trelliage" —a device she drew from garden architecture. With the great success of the Trellis Room at the Colony Club (Fig. 220), she received many requests to produce similar rooms for houses, and trellis rooms became relatively common

Figure 220. *Trellis Room, The Colony Club, 546 Park Avenue, New York City.*
C. 1907. De Wolfe, *The House in Good Taste,* p. 270; see Bibliography.

This room created the genre of the trellis room in American houses, clubs, and department stores. Miss de Wolfe covered the entire gray wall with green trellis work,
except for the ovals from which the sconces emerged. Real ivy grew on the trellis,
and an indoor fountain—a feature she recommended for houses and apartments—
stood at the far end of the room. The design of the furniture complements the trellis
work. The floors were red tile. She described the chandelier as "an enchanting lantern
made up of green wires and ivy leaves and little white flames of electric light."

among the wealthy. In the Colony Club, she used a green trellis work applied to
gray plaster walls and ceilings; there, ivy actually grew on the trellis, but many
of her trellis rooms lacked vines.

LIGHTING

By this time, electric lights were standard although kerosene remained common
in unelectrified areas for many years.

Three forms of lighting were available: chandeliers, wall sconces, and table
lamps. Miss de Wolfe favored sconces used in combination with chandeliers or
lamps. Rarely did all three forms appear in one room. Wallick concurred in
favoring sconces and lamps, but labeled chandeliers "abominable."

Miss de Wolfe used expensive crystal or glass chandeliers, and wall sconces

Figure 221. *Trellis Room, Summer Residence of Mr. and Mrs. Ormond G. Smith, Centre Island, New York. C.* 1913. De Wolfe, *The House in Good Taste,* p. 275; see Bibliography.

Ormond G. Smith, a Harvard graduate of 1883, managed Street and Smith, New York publishers of six magazines. The 1913 *Social Register* listed the Smiths as members of nine clubs, none of them the Colony Club, the obvious inspiration of their trellis room.[15] Miss de Wolfe designed this room to harmonize with their gardens. Four long sofas were arranged parallel and back to back in pairs, separated by a long narrow table with a built-in planter. Painted and wicker furniture completed the garden effect. Miss de Wolfe summarized her work modestly: "The room is classic in its fine balance and its architectural formality, and modern in its luxurious comfort and its refreshing color."

that were either antiques or reproductions of eighteenth-century pieces. Lamps were more varied; some were electrified candlesticks, large and small, with plain paper shades, while others were larger Oriental jars with large pleated shades. Wallick, as might be expected, presented simpler, cheaper, less formal designs. His sconces were not precise antique reproductions, and his lamps were based on modern vases rather than classic porcelains. Appearing in his designs, but absent from Miss de Wolfe's rooms, was the floor lamp.

COLOR

Color was a primary consideration in the conception of a room. Miss de Wolfe reduced the question to psychological principles. One with a hasty temper would be upset in a red room, but rich red Italian damask hangings might give courage to the timid. In the simpler Middle Ages, "people worked hard, and they got downright blues and reds and greens—primitive colors, all. Nowadays, we must consider the effect of color on our nerves, our eyes, our moods, everything."[9] She did her best to suit a color scheme to an individual's personality and the house's setting, and sometimes even to treasured possessions that went into the room.

She began the color scheme by considering what was seen through the windows and from what direction natural light came: "Rooms facing south may be very light gray, cream, or even white, but northern rooms should be rich in color, and should suggest warmth and just a little mystery." Blues, grays, cool greens, and "all the dainty gay colors" were "charming" for southern rooms, but northern rooms required rich effects readily available from wood paneling in pine, cherry, chestnut, cypress, or California redwood.[10] Despite the warm endorsement, these natural wood panels are lacking in illustrations of her designs.

Figure 222. *Dining Room, Residence of Ogden Goelet, Ochre Court, Newport, Rhode Island. C.* 1895. Croly, *Stately Homes in America*, p. 143; see Bibliography.

When Ogden Goelet died in 1897, his fortune was estimated at $80 million. No expense was spared in furnishing Ochre Court, his mansion designed by Richard M. Hunt and built between 1888 and 1891. Hunt's late Gothic architecture was evident in the massive double fireplace. The room's details mix Renaissance and rococo. For example, the tapestry was basically Renaissance, yet the furniture and florid decoration beneath the eighteenth-century portrait were rococo–Louis XV.

Having stated these principles, she then ignored them in explaining how a unified color scheme could grow out of a single favorite object—in the case given, a pair of Chinese jars destined for the mantel of the room. On a cream ground they had a design of blue, green, mauve, and mulberry with flecks of black. She describes how she went to work: "First I found a wee Oriental rug that repeated the color of the jugs. This was to go before the hearth. Then I worked out the shell of the room: the woodwork white, the walls bluish green, the plain carpet a soft green." A chest and day bed were painted a soft green, and the bed upholstered in the same mauve chintz used for chairs and curtains."[11]

She favored soft colors, simply presented—another example of her "elegant simplicity and aristocratic reserve."[12] Two basic colors, usually pastels or tertiary shades, provided the color scheme for most of Miss de Wolfe's rooms. A "red and blue" bedroom was more accurately "old fashioned rose" or lavender and a "cool dull blue," but such a room she held was still "full of color." Mauve and dull green provided the scheme for the room inspired by the Chinese jars, and a hall was tastefully and formally done in green and white. Her

Figure 223. *Gallery, Residence of William C. Whitney, Westbury, Long Island.*
C. 1903. Croly, *Stately Homes in America*, p. 475; see Bibliography.

In 1904, William C. Whitney left an estate valued at $21,243,000. In addition to this house on Long Island, he had another, even more grand, residence in New York City (Fig. 120). The gallery attempted to create a reasonably authentic Jacobean style in walls, ceiling, paintings, and some of the furniture.

Figure 224. *Drawing Room, Residence of George M. Pullman, 1912 Prairie Avenue, Chicago.* 1900–1906. Courtesy, Chicago Historical Society, Chicago, Ill.

The sleeping car business and real estate investments had made Pullman a multi-millionaire. In his drawing room, the Louis XVI style reigned consistently in walls, furniture, and draperies. The bust, too, went with the style, but the plant stand was Elizabethan and the polar bear rug pure late nineteenth century. The walls were covered with moiréed fabric.

sitting room had pale "egg shell blue-green" walls, with a jade green rug and an upholstery with gray-green figures. She described enthusiastically a music room in "soft shimmering green" and cream, a room that was "incomplete and cold" when empty, but which came alive when the bright colors of women's gowns were added. Rose or "ashes of roses" was one of her favorite colors, especially when fabrics of that color were used with gray walls. Soft dove gray was another favorite. "Soft," "light," "neutral" were the words she continually used to describe her colors. Woodwork was to be gray, ivory, cream, white, or some soft tone of the wall color. Only in the living room did she offer the option of stained and waxed rather than painted woodwork. Ceilings were white.

Wallick's colors, by comparison, were more vivid. Like Miss de Wolfe, he demanded unity in a color scheme, rejecting earlier styles that used one color on

Figure 225. *Guest Bedroom, Residence of George S. Palmer, New London, Connecticut. C.* 1910. *Country Life in America* (January 1916), p. 28.

Mr. Palmer was a wealthy quilt manufacturer and collector who built his house in 1906. The guest room was furnished with some of his most important pieces of Americana. The highboy was by William Savery of Philadelphia. (Together with the two Newport blockfront chests, it later went to the Metropolitan Museum of Art.) Both window curtains and bed valances were attempts to reproduce eighteenth-century originals. Note that the plain walls were dark in comparison with the light woodwork.

the wall, another in draperies, and still a third in upholstery. He wrote that it was safe to let a room reflect one color, and many of his designs were organized around varying intensities of one basic color. His general principle was the larger the area, the lighter the color. Thus, walls and woodwork were to be light, with contrasts in hangings, rugs, and upholstery, and brilliant colors in small objects. In several designs, he used a plain-colored rug with a wide border in a deeper shade of the field. Ideal wall colors were tan, ivory, putty, and gray.

Some of his suggestions on color are close to Miss de Wolfe's. He agreed that rooms with northern exposures needed golden browns, yellows, and soft reds, while southern, sunny rooms were proper settings for blues and greens. But many of his designs, especially in the 1916 book, show stronger, darker blues and greens than Miss de Wolfe might have used. One could generalize that, as in the Federal period a century before, the high style houses of Miss de Wolfe were decorated in more subtle colors than the more moderate houses to which Wallick's work applied.

Woodwork for Wallick was generally painted, and white woodwork was more or less mandatory with the Colonial style. Whether to paint or stain woodwork depended in part on one's furniture. Mahogany or walnut furniture (William and Mary, Queen Anne, Chippendale, or Adam) required ivory or white woodwork. Mahogany doors and white woodwork were also a good combination. Oak furniture (Jacobean or Charles II) called for stained wood.

Only two of the many color illustrations in his 1916 book show white ceilings. Even in rooms where there was white woodwork or a white frieze, Wallick's ceiling was usually the same color, but in a lighter shade, as either the carpet or textiles, or (less often) the wall.

Figure 226. *Drawing Room, Struve Residence.* 1905. Seattle Historical Society, Seattle, Wash.

A consistent Louis XV style governed the furnishing of the Struve drawing room. Much of the furniture was either antique or costly reproduction. The rococo architectural detail and light, swagged ceiling painting reinforce the style. Mirrors filled the wall panels, and, as Miss de Wolfe advised, photographs were confined to the desk top. The portières and window draperies are consistent with the style, but much simpler than the Louis XV look of twenty years before. Note the planter that filled the fireplace in summer.

TABLE-SETTING ARRANGEMENT

Several books offered instruction on proper arrangement of the dinner table. The arrangement in Figure 210, taken from Emily Holt's *Encyclopaedia of Etiquette* (1901), was still being endorsed in the 1920s as a proper "English" setting.

Each place was set with a plate and a napkin, folded to show the monogram, and "with a dinner roll or a square of bread laid between the folds." To the left were three silver forks, prongs up (a fourth fish fork was optional), and to the right, two large knives (silver handles, steel blades) and a small silver knife, all with edges toward the plate. Next to the knives was a soup spoon (bowl up) and an oyster fork laid at an angle to the spoon.

"Nearly touching the tips of the knife blades" were four glasses: a water goblet or tumbler, a small, tapering sherry glass, a conventional claret glass, and a champagne glass, very tall or very flaring.

The tablecloth was placed with meticulous care, its four corners almost touching the floor. At the center, a square or circular piece of nappery lay beneath a silver or crystal bowl of flowers. (Mirrors, once acceptable under the flowers, were passé.) The lamp shades were the same color as the principal flowers. Four single candlesticks with shades stood equidistant from each other, and the flowers were augmented at times by candelabra springing from the middle of the basket. Decanters, saltcellars, pepper boxes, compotiers of bonbons, and salted nuts were then placed. For a "ceremonious" dinner, butter never appeared on the table, and celery, radishes, olives, and mustard were passed by servants. "Carafes and menus, favors, individual bouquets of flowers, and groups of handsome but useless spoons have wisely been banished as clumsy and meaningless."[13]

Appendix A

American Kitchens, Bathrooms, and Heating Systems

Kitchens

During the early seventeenth century, the kitchen was generally not a separate room.[1] In the small, two-room house, all living took place in the hall or common room where the family worked, cooked, and slept. By the second half of the century, in larger New England houses the kitchen was usually a separate room at the rear of the salt box house. Adjacent to the kitchen was a small room called the larder, buttery, or pantry, where foods were stored. Other utensils were kept in a small bedroom also at the rear of the house and usually on the south and warmer side.

The typical seventeenth-century kitchen had a wide, deep fireplace with a bake oven at the rear. The chimney contained a lugpole from which trammels were suspended, and trammels in turn supported the cooking pots. The lugpole was later replaced by a swinging crane that was much easier and safer to handle, for iron pots full of stew could often weigh as much as 40 pounds. Utensils vary in number and quality in the many inventories that survive from the seventeenth century. Typical kitchen furnishings and utensils included: basins, box irons and heaters, candlesticks, chafing dishes, cheese presses, cobirons, dripping pans, fender, flagon, flesh fork, fire shovel, firepan, frying pan, gridiron, jack and spit, keeler (a low tub), kettles, ladles, mortar and pestle, peel, plates, porringers, pot hangers, pots, saltcellars, skillets, skimmer, slice, still (alembic or limbeck), toaster, tongs, trammel, trivet, warming pan, and sometimes andirons (or dog irons) and fireback. In most cases, the utensils were of iron, though brass kettles and mortars and pestles also were often listed.

In the North during the eighteenth century, the kitchen remained a separate room, and, in the South, a separate building. A one-room "kitchen house" might be found in New England, but such buildings were never common there. In the South, the kitchen was usually built of brick in order to fireproof this vulnerable area. As in the seventeenth century, the large fireplace dominated the room, the hearth was built of brick, occasionally of stone, and the fire was kept going continuously. Iron firebacks with raised designs helped to reflect the heat and to prevent the crumbling of the brick and mortar at the rear. Some of the fireplaces were deep enough for seats to be built in at the sides, a good warm spot during a New England winter. The floor of the kitchen was usually of random-width boards or stone. In the South, the floor was frequently brick. Walls were usually wood-paneled or plastered, or a combination of the two.

The eighteenth-century fireplace was altered from the seventeenth-century design, with the bake oven moved to one side of the fireplace (Fig. 227). The bake oven became more accessible, and by having its ashpit beneath, it was more easily cleaned. The ashpit was closed with a tin or iron door. Smaller, shallower fireplaces reflected more heat into the room. The kitchen furniture was still simple: a few chairs, stools, and a stretcher table.

Kitchen equipment was quite similar to that found in seventeenth-century inventories. A few items did occur that were not commonly listed before, most notably, copper molds, skewers, triangular trivets, and tin items such as candlesticks,

Figure 227. Edward Hill. *Waiting for the Kettle to Boil.* 1885. Oil on canvas,
14 in. × 20 in. (36 cm × 51 cm). Collection of Nina Fletcher Little.

Although this picture dates from 1885, it clearly shows an unchanged eighteenth-
century kitchen. Note the crane in the fireplace, the bake oven flush with the fireplace, and the ashpit underneath. Two poles were hung from the ceiling, from which
drying herbs and food were suspended. A lantern provided general illumination and
candlesticks were grouped on a fireplace shelf.

lanterns, graters, coffee bean roasters, and reflecting ovens. Wooden bowls, plates, spoons, and cookie boards continued to be popular. Horn spoons and scoops also appeared. Well-to-do houses contained greater quantities of pewter, more brass and copper (which did not break as easily as iron but was more expensive), and more expensive ceramics, although the best tea wares were often kept in the parlor with earthenware confined to the kitchen. Silver was usually stored in the parlor, but an occasional piece was kept in the kitchen. Guns were placed on ceiling pegs (not over the mantel), and candlesticks were grouped on a shelf. For a detailed inventory of a well-to-do Philadelphia merchant's kitchen in 1762, consult Frances Phipps, *Colonial Kitchens.*

As early as 1803, Americans were hearing about "newly invented" refrigerators,[2] but refrigerators were far from common until mid-century. By the 1860s, both upright and chest types were widespread. Usually made of wood with insulated walls, the average refrig moor held about 100 pounds of ice.

The nineteenth-century kitchen was more comfortable.

The cooking range, which evolved during the 1830s and 1840s, burned hard or soft coal or wood and heated the kitchen during the winter. Peterson noted that Millard Fillmore was the first President to install a cookstove in the White House, only to find that the cook refused to use it.[3] The kitchen sink, now standard, was of soapstone, wood, granite, or iron, and water was provided either from a pump or from spigots. Linoleum, patented in 1860 and 1863, became common in American kitchens by the end of the century.

In her *Domestic Receipt Book,* Miss Beecher supplied a full inventory (see page 364) of the properly furnished kitchen of the mid-nineteenth century. Requisite furniture included two tables, one for meals and the other for cooking. Above the cooking table should hang a wall shelf.

Another useful kitchen piece was a settee that could be folded over into an ironing table; a bunk settee was also helpful if servants slept in the kitchen. A tin safe was valuable to preserve food in hot weather and protect it from mice under all conditions. A clock was indispensable in the kitchen; so, too, was an oilcloth on the floor. A carpet would only accumulate grease and filth, and a painted floor could not be removed and cleaned. Miss Beecher recommended a refrigerator for keeping meat and dairy products in hot weather.

She also advised that a closet be made for the kitchen. The list on page 364 includes the articles that should, by rights, be in it.

In 1869, in *The American Woman's Home*, Miss Beecher and Mrs. Stowe offered a plan for arranging shelves and implements around a kitchen sink; and as standard equipment they recommended an improved stove, which they said would pay for itself in the fuel economy achieved in one year. It burned either coal or wood, and baked, roasted, and heated water.[5]

The early twentieth-century kitchen seemed to be bare as the all-white look began to dominate. Walls were frequently covered with white ceramic tiles or glossy enamel paint, and furniture and woodwork were painted white, too. Sinks were usually made of whiteware—white porcelain enameled on iron. Both coal stoves and gas ranges were popular, and combination ranges, using coal and gas, were now available (Fig. 235). Pots and pans were frequently made of granite ware and aluminum rather than brass or cast iron. In 1886, new production techniques made previously expensive aluminum much cheaper, and by the 1890s aluminum ware was common but still not inexpensive. In 1897, Sears, Roebuck and Company offered aluminum 2-quart coffee pots for $1.50. In gray-enameled granite ware, the same size pot was 40¢, and in tin it was 9¢.

Mrs. Christine Frederick, a consulting editor of the *Ladies Home Journal*, documented the arrangement of the ideal kitchen of 1913 just as Miss Beecher had in 1869.

Figure 228. Artist unknown. *Primitive Interior. C.* 1840. Oil on wood, 20¼ in. × 28⅛ in. (51 cm × 71 cm). Collection of Hirschl and Adler Galleries, New York City.

The charm of this primitive painting is in its lack of proportion, though it is quite informative as to kitchen furnishings. The deep fireplace had a bake oven at the rear, a storage box at the left, and a stool for the small child at the right. A dough box on a stand was placed under the window, and the Welsh dresser contained a few pieces of china. The simple pull curtains were probably on iron or brass wire; a gun was stored for safety almost totally inaccessible on two wooden slats between the beams. Notable were the vertical wainscot wall and batten doors.

Miss Beecher's Recommended Contents for Kitchen Table, Hanging Shelf, and Kitchen Closet[4]

HANGING SHELF

Attached to sides:
   coffee mill
   salt box
   soap dish

Left side:
   large canisters for sugar and starch
   medium canisters for tea, coffee, table salt, ginger
   small canisters for cream of Tartar, indigo, mustard,
      sweet herbs, spices
   junk bottles for vinegar, molasses, ketchup
   wide-mouth jar for soda or saleratus

Right side:
   dredging box
   kitchen pepper box
   2 graters
   2 sieves
   bottle brush
   phial tunnel (vial funnel)
   larger tunnel (funnel)
   quart, pint, gill measures
   gravy strainer
   corkscrew
   6 bowls
   6 cups and saucers
   2 small pitchers
   spice mill
   a balance

In the drawers of the shelf:
1. needles
   thread
   twine
   wax
   cotton
   linen
2. recipe book
   paper
   pencil
   account book
   pen and ink

DRAWERS OF THE WORK TABLE

Left, undivided drawer:
   rolling pin   chopping knife
   griddle spad   egg and cake beaters
   iron meat fork   potato beetle
   coffee stick   apple corers
   mush stick   meat hammer
   gridiron scraper   butter spad
   skewers   whetstone
   saw knife

Middle drawer:
   front section   rear
      kitchen knives and forks   bags
      carver   pudding cloth
      spoons   jelly strainer
   center   starch strainer
      kitchen tablecloths

Right drawer:
   front section
      clean dishcloths and towels
      roller and tumbler towels
   back
      clean lamp towels
         and holders
      dust cloths

THE KITCHEN CLOSET

clothes frames, large and small
skirt board
bosom board
press board
yard stick
3 or 4 brooms
floor brush for sweeping oilcloths and painted floors
cobweb brush
long brush to wash windows outside
carpet stretcher
whitewash brush
long-handled upright dustpan
common dustpan
rag bag
scrubbing brush
shoe brushes and blacking
brass and silver cleaning supplies
lamps and candlesticks (on one of the closet shelves)
tools
clothes broom and clothes brush
table rug

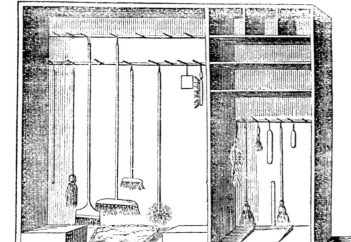
Beecher and Stowe's well-stocked broom closet

Figure 229. Attributed to August Kollner. *Country Life, Pennsylvania, 1840.* Water color. Courtesy, Chicago Historical Society, Chicago, Ill.

This water color represents a simple country kitchen before breakfast. The fireplace lacked andirons or a crane, though the coffee was warming in a pot before the fire. A simple storage cupboard appeared at the left, and a gun and powder horn were stored at the right. The furniture was simple and probably homemade.

Beecher and Stowe's efficient storage and food preparation areas

above: Figure 230. J. H. Matteson. *Now or Never. C.* 1850. Oil on canvas, 26⅝ in. × 33¾ in. (69 cm × 86 cm). Clark Collection, Parrish Art Museum, Southampton, N.Y.

This painting shows the introduction of an iron stove placed in an earlier fireplace. Iron stoves became common with the advent of the Industrial Revolution. The kitchen furnishings were still simple, indicating wooden bowls, earthenware crocks, and a copper pan in use. Herbs are seen drying on suspended ceiling racks. The window at the left seems to be the main source of light and the window sill displayed growing herbs and plants. Note the mirror at the right of the window, probably tilted to provide good light for shaving. An inaccessible shelf held valuables and perhaps poisons. A country Empire secretary had been relegated to the kitchen.

opposite, top: Figure 231. F. W. Edmonds. *The Windmill. C.* 1850. Oil on canvas, 30 in. × 24 in. (76 cm × 61 cm). Courtesy of The New-York Historical Society, New York City.

In this painting, an iron stove has been placed in an earlier fireplace, but seen for the first time is the copper water heater at the side. Copper was thus important in the nineteenth century in heaters as well as pots. Miscellaneous candlesticks and earthenware appear on top of the mantel and the typical storage cupboard. The chair and stool are very simple, and in an era that generally plastered ceilings, the kitchen beams still showed.

Figure 232. Jarves G. Clonney. *The Story. C.* 1845. Courtesy, The Frick Art Reference Library, New York City.

Clonney lived in New Rochelle, New York, when he painted this interior of a laundry, probably located in a building separate from the main house. Laundry tubs and a washboard appear at the left, a kettle of hot water rested on the hearth, and three irons were on the mantel along with a coffee grinder. The simple chairs had rush seats, and wicker baskets and hampers were stored on the chimney and above the chest at the right. The andirons, tongs, and crane perhaps date from the eighteenth century. On the mantel is evidence of the value of mirrors in an earlier period, for a small fragment of looking glass has been carefully framed after the larger mirror broke.

Fuel-efficient stove

Applying her husband's interest in industrial efficiency to the management of her own kitchen, she published *The New Housekeeping: Efficiency Studies in Home Management* (1913). Mrs. Frederick asked not merely what should be in the well-furnished kitchen but how it should be arranged for maximum efficiency. Dividing kitchen functions into those connected with preparing meals and those associated with serving meals, she arranged her kitchen accordingly. For efficiency, a small kitchen well arranged was often better than an ill-sorted large one.

Mrs. Frederick included, among her new devices for the kitchen of 1913: for cooking—fireless cooker, electric toaster and grill, electric percolator, Thermos bottles, triplicate or double pots for one burner, manual cake and bread mixers, meat chopper, and potato ricer; for cleaning—electric vacuum cleaner, long-handled dust-pan, dustless mop, dish dryer; and for laundry—self-heating mangle, electric washing machine, self-heating iron (electric, alcohol, or gasoline), and electric sewing machine.

above: Figure 234. Lewis Cass Lutz. *Interior in Cambridge, Indiana.* 1880. Oil on canvas, 24 in. × 29 in. (61 cm × 74 cm). Cincinnati Art Museum, Cincinnati, Ohio.

One might assume this to be a New England kitchen of the eighteenth century were it not known otherwise. In fact, the painting documents the persistence of architectural styles as Eastern settlers moved west. Many items in this kitchen would have been in an eighteenth-century kitchen, most notably a pierced lantern on the mantel, a Betty lamp, a tin roasting oven, and a candle mold. At the left is an iron coffee grinder and a corn popper. The turkey wing at the right is a hearth brush. Serving pieces on the wall at the right included a gourd dipper and a board with a blade for slicing cabbage. A dough trough and rolling pin rest on the simple table.

opposite: Figure 233. *Kitchen in a Model House, Waterbury, Vermont. C.* 1875. Society for the Preservation of New England Antiquities, Boston, Mass.

In model house Number 10 in George J. Colby's development in Waterbury, Vermont, stood this kitchen with all the modern conveniences of the 1870s. The iron stove was placed on a metal protective pad, and the sink boasted taps for running hot and cold water (though well water could also be pumped by hand). The plastered walls were plain, with simple, dark wooden moldings around the doors and windows. Note the painted window shade, and the folding towel rack near the stove.

Electric range, 1907

opposite: Figure 235. *Kitchen, House in St. Louis. C.* 1905. Missouri Historical Society, St. Louis.

The elaborate kitchen range in this Midwestern house used coal on the left side and gas on the right. Both gas and electricity by the turn of the century helped the cook considerably. The white sink should be noted, for white and light colors were becoming more prominent in turn-of-the-century kitchens. The wood and wicker furniture appear to be inexpensive Grand Rapids pieces. The cover on the table, the birdcage, and letter rack add a homey touch lacking in many kitchen illustrations. The walls were papered in a simple abstract pattern that conflicted with the tile pattern of the linoleum on the floor. Rugs protected the floor in front of the stove and sink.

above: Figure 236. *Kitchen, Residence of Mrs. Helen Terry Potter, New Rochelle, New York.* 1909. Photograph by Byron. The Byron Collection, Museum of the City of New York.

Typical of many late nineteenth- and early twentieth-century kitchens, Mrs. Potter's kitchen showed the transition from one technology to another. She had a large coal stove next to a gas stove, and although the room was illuminated by electricity, it may once have used gas. A dish pan, tray, and other implements were hung beside the cast iron sink. Both the linoleum floor and oilcloth table covers were recommended for their cleanliness, and the two chairs painted white reflected trends toward sanitary kitchens and painted furniture.

Electric coffee percolator, 1907

371

The earth closet

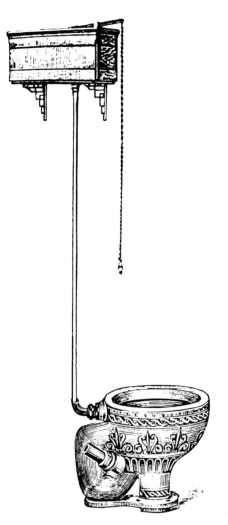

Renaissance revival water closet, 1891

Her list of new items for the kitchen indicates that gas and electricity as well as a host of mechanical gadgets had come to the aid of the homemaker, but that the electric mixer had not yet appeared. So numerous were the new devices that she cautioned again a clutter of too many seldom-used specialty items—bean slicers, for example.

New efficiency in serving became possible with the wheel tray, or tea wagon, and it remained a regular part of kitchen decor for the next few decades. Summers were made more comfortable with the addition of the electric fan.

Bathrooms

Indoor plumbing existed in homes of the wealthy by the 1830s.

Alexander Cummings had secured the first patent for a water closet in England in 1775, but the progress of his invention in America is difficult to trace.[6] Charles Bulfinch in 1808 finished his third house for Harrison Gray Otis of Boston. The building was soon assessed for $20,000, and its plans included an indoor four-seat privy adjacent to the stable, but no water closet.[7] By 1833, however, James Gallier's *American Builders' General Price Book and Estimator* treated water closets as nothing out of the ordinary. The notably unsuccessful but enduring pan closet cost $50, while an improved variety with a patented valve cost $60.[8]

By 1850, Downing's plans in *Country Houses* show that the W.C. had become a regular fixture only in grand houses. He included one water closet, usually on the second floor, in houses costing between $6,000 and $14,000. The W.C. in the design costing $4,600 seems to be an exception, and Downing himself says that the water closet in the basement of a $3,000 cottage gave that building "a villa-like completeness."[9] In the same decade, A. Bryant Clough's *Contractor's Manual and Builder's Price Book* (1855) priced water closets at between $10 and $70. Clough commented that within the past fifteen or twenty years, plumbing had become "more fashionable in our habitations."[10]

By mid-century, new inventions had improved the water closet, and it found a not-very-serious rival in the earth closet discussed by Mrs. Stowe and Miss Beecher in *The American Woman's Home.* The apparatus, invented by an English priest and manufactured in the 1860s in Hartford, Connecticut, stored a reservoir of dry earth for use much as water was contained in a water closet. Unlike the water closet, it had to be emptied about once a week.

In the 1870s, Holly's *Modern Dwellings* regularly included a "lavatory" in the plans for some houses of fashion, but the water closet was still missing from his simpler designs.

Most fixtures were imported from England until Thomas Maddock began successful American production in New Jersey in 1873. Other companies followed quickly, and the householder soon found many kinds from which to choose.

Figure 237. *Bathroom, Residence of H. A. W. Tabor, Denver, Colorado. C.* 1890.
Library, The State Historical Society of Colorado, Denver.

The Tabors' bathroom was decorated with the same enthusiasm displayed in their
bedroom decor (Fig. 107). Judging an Aesthetic wallpaper incapable of remaining
unadorned, they added a landscape in a heavy gold frame. The straw mat protected
the wallpaper from splashing water. The wicker corner basket was embellished with
ribbons, and the lambrequin on the Eastlake shelf and towel rack was the kind of
ladies' work recommended by many books. The arrangement of bath tub and water
closet side by side was common mid-century practice; so, too, was the wainscotted
front of each. The water closet was probably new to some in Denver when this
photograph was taken, for framed above the pillow were directions for using it.

Earlier English water closets had carried transfer designs of
flowers and fruit or landscapes. Later toilets appeared with
embossed and transfer printed exteriors suitable for the
Renaissance or rococo style, and English makers produced
versions with Colonial, Aesthetic, or Art Nouveau decoration.
In 1891, Joseph Buddé of San Francisco advertised a transfer
printed toilet in a "Pioneer of '49" design that was certainly
fitting for the frontier-style bathroom.

By the 1890s, the American bathroom had developed the
general equipment and arrangement that characterize it
today. Standard fixtures included a bath or shower, a toilet,
a wash basin, and, rarely, a bidet. A room so furnished had
appeared in George Vanderbilt's house in New York City;

Joseph Buddé's "Pioneer of '49," 1891

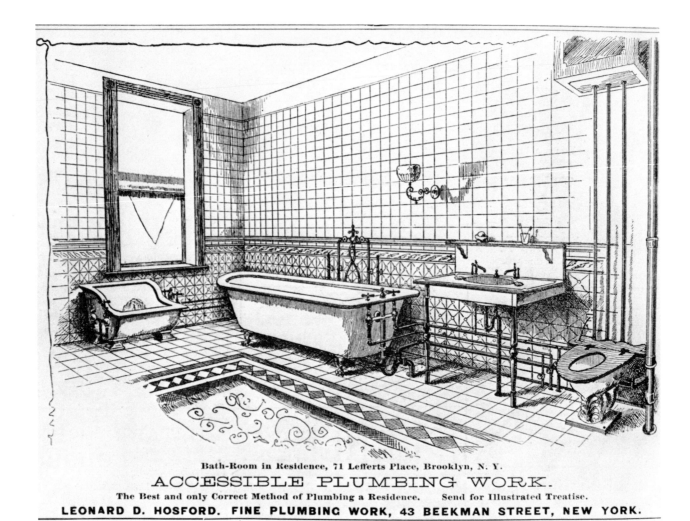

above: Figure 238. *Bathroom, 71 Lefferts Place, Brooklyn, New York.* 1891. *The Decorator and Furnisher* (June 1891), p. 118.

Leonard D. Hosford presumably did the plumbing in this Brooklyn bathroom that appeared in his advertisement. The floor and possibly the wall were tiled, but the tiling made no effort to conceal the water pipes, although the gas pipe was hidden in the wall. Bidets were somewhat unusual in American bathrooms, though they occurred in several advertisements. The squared and diapered pattern on the wall, the tile pattern and rug on the floor, and the acanthus decoration on the toilet provide considerable decoration in a utilitarian room. Note the toothbrushes in the glass and the ball of soap in its bowl on the shelf of the basin. Although there was a light, there was no shaving mirror above the basin.

opposite: Figure 239. *Bathroom, Residence of George A. Kessler, Fifth Avenue, New York City. The Decorator and Furnisher* (March 1895), p. 211.

George A. Kessler made a fortune as head of the firm importing Moet & Chandon champagne. About 1895, he had his bachelor apartment redecorated. With no obvious economies, each room was redone in a fantasy of different styles. The bathroom was outstanding. Above a marble dado was a wall of soft pink tiles augmented by a garland of solid silver connecting each incandescent bulb. The whole room glowed pink. The bath tub was decorated in pink and gold Linspar relief, and the cheval glass was silvered bronze. All the fixtures were silver-plated. The toilet was discreetly covered by the mirror, and at the other end of the room was a shower. The "center of attraction" in the room was *The Surprise* by Italian sculptor A. Frille. An Oriental rug adorned the floor.

but, though Gallier's price list of 1833 had included all the components, such rooms remained far from common in American houses. In 1864, LeGrand Lockwood began building his house (at a cost of $1.5 million) and included an astounding fourteen bathrooms.

Gallier's price list of 1833 includes a bath tub at $23, lined with lead, but the first reference we found to an American bath tub appeared as part of an original design in Shaw's *Rural Architecture* (1843), in which the second floor of the Grecian Doric House included a "bathing room." Webster and Parkes (1845) had illustrated a simple bath tub, as well as a more elaborate shower bath, that appeared in a Boston advertisement of 1847. Both showers and bath tubs obviously persisted, whether built separately or in conjunction with each other. Clough's list of 1855 priced showers from $7 to $30, but bath tubs, depending upon their lining, ranged from $16 (lead) to $27 (tinned copper). Showers mounted over bath tubs were advertised in the 1850s, and both tubs and showers appeared in great variety during the rest of the century. Many carried the motifs of particular decorative styles.

Some of Downing's designs put the water closet and bath in different rooms but, by the 1870s, both were generally built in the same room, though perhaps discreetly separated by a partition.

Basins with running water appeared in the 1830s. Gallier's price list quotes a plain basin at $8, but a blue transfer ware basin cost $10. By 1855, one could have a marbletop

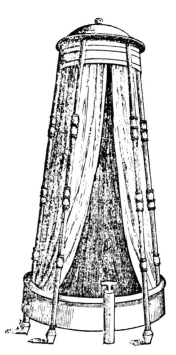

Shower of 1845

wash basin with silver-plated fixtures for $50. As silver fixtures imply, one could lavish great expense on a bathroom, like any other room, and several people did.

By the early twentieth century, specific styles were discarded and bathroom fixtures became a plain sanitary white, even though the walls might be as carefully decorated as those of any other room.

By 1910, only the least expensive house ($800) in Henry L. Wilson's *Bungalow Book* was without a full bath, but even it had a toilet room. The house costing $850 had a full, modern bath.

Heating Systems

Until the middle of the eighteenth century, the open fireplace was the only source of heat. Early chimneys of wood and clay gave way to safer brick construction as soon as possible. Iron firebacks appeared in the seventeenth century, supplementing the heat and protecting the brick or stone fireplace.

The six-plate stove of the eighteenth century offered new efficiency in heating throughout the colonies. A five-plate variant, fed through the kitchen fireplace wall, appeared only in Pennsylvania German areas.

Franklin's stove of 1742 was an attempt to produce great heat while lowering fuel consumption (Figs. 35, 36). The smoke from the open fire passed over an iron box that radiated heat into the room. It gained ready acceptance, advertised in Boston in 1745 as a "Philadelphia fireplace." One pleased observer noted that a room in winter heated by a Franklin stove rose to 56° F. These stoves were designed for installation in existing fireplaces, and both illustrations and architectural evidence indicate that fireplaces became smaller as the century progressed.

The Franklin stove was an improvement, but greater progress was still to be made. Register grates with straight bars were an attempt to improve heating efficiency and lessen smoke. In 1796, Sir Benjamin Thompson, Count Rumford, published designs for improved fireplaces with curved grates and specially designed firebacks. Even though Rumford had been a Tory during the Revolution, Americans reprinted his London essays promptly (1798). Whatever the improvements of the Rumford grate (Plate 4), the future of domestic heating lay with stoves and, more importantly, the furnace.

Box stoves, descended from the earlier six-plate stoves, were mass produced in the 1830s and remained in production until the end of the century.

Steam and hot air were soon to be used. The factories of the Harmony Society in Pennsylvania were heated by steam pipes from a boiler as early as 1825, and in 1835, William A. Wheeler of Worcester began the manufacture of hot air furnaces for domestic heating. By the 1840s, others had entered the business, and in 1848, anthracite was first used in a hot air furnace.[11]

Typical grate before Rumford's improvements

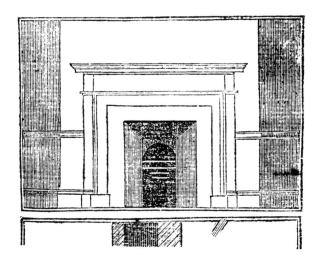

Rumford's plan for his new grate from the first American edition of his *Essays,* 1798.

opposite: Figure 240. *Bathroom, Brandus Residence, 16 West 88th Street, New York City.* 1902. Photograph by Byron. The Byron Collection, Museum of the City of New York.

Considerable decorative energy went into furnishing this bathroom. The doors of the Renaissance cabinet at the right had expensive veneered fronts, and the basin set in the marble top had a blue transfer print decoration. A border of relief tiles with shells topped the tiled dado, and a squared paper with classic wreaths covered the wall. Note the gas heater under the window, the wicker wastebasket, and the fringe on the window shade. In the corner was a fine example of Grand Rapids–Art Nouveau, complete with asymmetrical mirror. The mat in the enameled, cast iron tub was inscribed BATH MAT, and the rug adjacent to the tub bore a simple Mission-style motif.

By 1850, Downing preferred an open fireplace to even the improved varieties of stoves, but hot air furnaces, he held, had much to recommend them. Chilson's furnace he thought was the best, as it avoided the unwholesome air believed to come from the red-hot iron in other furnaces. But the best heating of all was hot water. Downing admitted that hot water heat was five times as expensive as hot air and that it was "confined to town houses of the first class, in our cities."[12] Clough's *Contractor's Manual* of 1855 noted that Chilson's furnace completely installed cost between $100 and $180, depending upon size.

By 1859, the householder had seven possibilities for heating. William C. Baker reviewed them all in his *Artificial Warmth and Ventilation and the Common Modes by Which They Are Produced*, published in New York City that year. Fireplaces and stoves both gave inferior heat, he held, while hot air furnaces injured the health as they leaked gases. There was also an unequal distribution of heat, with as much as a 15-degree difference between floor and ceiling. The remaining four choices were low-pressure hot water, high-pressure hot water, low-pressure steam, and high-pressure steam. Of the four, Baker considered low-pressure steam the best. High-pressure steam was good too, but it was dangerous. When James J. Lawler published *Modern Plumbing, Steam and Hot Water Heating* in 1899, the options, though not necessarily the judgments, were still basically the same.

Although furnaces were confined to the basements, these new heating systems brought intrusions into the interiors in the form of radiators, pipes, registers, and ventilators. Radiators became a basic item to be painted but not often disguised. Elsie de Wolfe did the best she could with a pair of radiators by "building two small cabinets with panels of iron framework gilded to suggest a graceful metal lattice . . . lined with rose-colored silk."[13]

Hot air registers, on the other hand, were normally given considerable style. By 1855, Clough's *Manual* listed prices for them in black, white enamel, fancy enamel, gold bronze, electro-plated, or leaf-plated, and they often carried the motifs of basic styles. Openings visible near the ceilings in some rooms were ventilators to ensure the circulation of fresh air throughout the interior. Architects and engineers worried greatly about the problem of stale air, and virtually every book on domestic architecture had at least a short section on the necessities of adequate ventilation.

Although a furnace could only be fired in the basement, by the 1890s it could be controlled from the first floor of the house. With temperatures under control, Emily Holt in 1901 recommended that dining rooms be kept between 70° and 75° F. A ballroom was likewise to be kept between 70° and 78° F.[14]

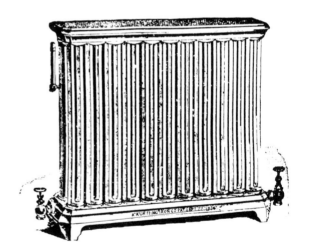

Radiator typical of the 1870s and 1880s

Appendix B

Museums, Societies, and Organizations Housing Major American Furniture Collections

Albany Institute of History and Art (N.Y.)
Baltimore Museum of Art (Md.)
Bayou Bend Collection (Houston, Tex.)
Brooklyn Museum (New York City, N.Y.)
Chatham Shaker Village (Chatham, N.Y.)
Chester County Historical Society (West Chester, Pa.)
Chicago Art Institute (Ill.)
City Art Museum (St. Louis, Mo.)
Colonial Williamsburg (Williamsburg, Va.)
Concord Antiquarian Society (Concord, Mass.)
Connecticut Historical Society (Hartford, Conn.)
Cooper-Hewitt Museum (New York City, N.Y.)
Currier Gallery of Art (Manchester, N.H.)
Detroit Institute of Arts (Mich.)
Diplomatic Reception Rooms, Department of State (Washington, D.C.)
Essex Institute (Salem, Mass.)
Grand Rapids Public Museum (Mich.)
Henry Ford Museum (Dearborn, Mich.)
Heritage Foundation (Old Deerfield, Mass.)
Hitchcock Museum (Riverton, Conn.)
Hudson River Museum (Yonkers, N.Y.)
Lyman Allyn Museum (New London, Conn.)
Metropolitan Museum of Art (New York City, N.Y.)
Mount Vernon (Fairfax County, Va.)
Munson-Williams-Proctor Institute (Utica, N.Y.)
Museum of the City of New York (New York City, N.Y.)

Museum of Early Southern Decorative Arts (Winston-Salem, N.C.)
Museum of Fine Arts (Boston, Mass.)
Museum of Modern Art (New York City, N.Y.)
National Museum of History and Technology, Smithsonian Institution (Washington, D.C.)
Newark Museum (N.J.)
New Hampshire Historical Society (Concord, N.H.)
New Haven Colony Historical Society (Conn.)
New-York Historical Society (New York City, N.Y.)
Old Sturbridge Village (Sturbridge, Mass.)
Philadelphia Museum of Art (Pa.)
Rhode Island Historical Society (Providence, R.I.)
Rhode Island School of Design Museum of Art (Providence, R.I.)
St. Louis Art Museum (Mo.)
Shelburne Museum, Inc. (Shelburne, Vt.)
Sleepy Hollow Restorations, Inc. (Tarrytown, N.Y.)
Society for the Preservation of New England Antiquities, Inc. (Boston, Mass.)
Stowe-Day Foundation (Hartford, Conn.)
Virginia Museum of Fine Arts (Richmond, Va.)
Wadsworth Atheneum (Hartford, Conn.)
Western Reserve Historical Society (Cleveland, Ohio)
White House (Washington, D.C.)
Winterthur Museum (Winterthur, Del.)
Yale University Art Gallery (New Haven, Conn.)

Notes

The notes include not only sources for the superscript numbers found within the text, but also for those superscript numbers within lists, tables, and, occasionally, captions to the halftones.

1 · The Early Seventeenth Century: 1607–1675

1. Esther Singleton, *The Furniture of Our Forefathers* (New York: Doubleday, Page, 1900; reissued New York: Blom, 1970), p. 158. Hereafter cited as Singleton.

2. Eaton's whole inventory is given in Norman M. Isham and Albert F. Brown, *Early Connecticut Houses* (Providence, R.I.: Preston & Rounds, 1900), pp. 287–295.

3. Singleton, p. 7; and Philip Alexander Bruce, *Economic History of Virginia in the Seventeenth Century* (New York: Macmillan, 1896), II, 148.

4. Bruce, II, 184, 184–185n.

5. Quoted in Singleton, p. 29.

6. *Virginia Historical Magazine*, II, 416–417.

7. Singleton, pp. 7–8, 157.

8. *Ibid.*, p. 165.

9. *Ibid.*, p. 170.

10. Saintsbury Calendar of State Papers, as quoted in Singleton, p. 43.

11. William M. Sargent, *Maine Wills, 1640–1760* (Portland, Me.: Brown Thurston, 1887); *The Probate Records of Essex County, Massachusetts*, edited by George Francis Dow (Salem, Mass.: Essex Institute, 1916); Charles W. Manwaring, *A Digest of the Early Connecticut Probate Records* (Hartford, Conn.: Peck, 1904); John Warner Barber, *History and Antiquities of New Haven* (New Haven, Conn.: Barber, 1834); *Calendar of New Jersey Wills*, I, edited by William Nelson (Paterson, N.J.: Press Printing, 1901); and *Probate Records of the State of New Hampshire*, edited by Albert Stillman Batchellor (Concord, Mass.: Rumford, 1907).

12. Harold R. Shurtleff, *The Log Cabin Myth: A Study of the Early Dwellings of the English Colonists in North America* (Gloucester, Mass.: Peter Smith, 1967), pp. 86, 136–142.

13. *Antiques* (February 1971), pp. 238–240.

14. See Mario Praz, *An Illustrated History of Furnishing* (New York: Braziller, 1964), pp. 104–133.

15. See Antonia Fraser, *King James, I of England, VI of Scotland* (New York: Knopf, 1975), pp. 171, 195, 207; and Margery Corbett and Michael Norton, *Engraving in England in the Sixteenth and Seventeenth Centuries* (Cambridge, Eng.: Cambridge University Press, 1964), Part III, Plate 56.

16. Dow, ed., *The Probate Records of Essex County, Massachusetts*, I, 105–106.

17. Praz, *An Illustrated History of Furnishing*, pp. 110, 111, 113.

18. As quoted in Marion Day Iverson, "Table Linen in Colonial America," *Antiques* (November 1959), p. 426.

19. Martin S. Briggs, *The Homes of the Pilgrim Fathers in England and America* (London: Oxford, 1932), p. 176 and Plate 87.

20. G. Malcolm Watkins, "Lighting Devices," *The Concise Encyclopedia of American Antiques*, edited by Helen Comstock (New York: Hawthorn, 1958), pp. 358–359.

21. Abbott Lowell Cummings, *Rural Household Inventories, 1675–1775* (Boston: Society for the Preservation of New England Antiquities, 1964), p. 25.

22. Linda R. Baumgarten, "The Textile Trade in Boston, 1650–1700," in *Arts of the Anglo-American Community in the Seventeenth Century*, edited by Ian M. G. Quimby (Charlottesville, Va.: University of Virginia Press for Winterthur, 1975), pp. 223–225; and Dean A. Fales, Jr., *American Painted Furniture, 1660–1880* (New York: Dutton, 1972), pp. 10–17.

23. Ivor Noel Hume, *Here Lies Virginia: An Archaeologist's View of Colonial Life and History* (New York: Knopf, 1963), pp. 274–277.

24. G. Bernard Hughes, *English, Scottish and Irish Table Glass* (New York: Bramhall House, 1956), pp. 44–45.

25. Richard B. Bailey, "Pilgrim Possessions, 1620–1640," *Antiques* (March 1952), pp. 236–239.

26. John Marshall Phillips, *American Silver* (New York: Chanticleer, 1949), p. 26.

27. Helen Sprackling, "Fruit Trenchers of the Sixteenth and Seventeenth Centuries," *Antiques* (July 1960), pp. 48–51.

28. Hughes, *English, Scottish and Irish Table Glass*, pp. 30–31, Plate 9.

2 · *The Late Seventeenth Century: 1675–1715*

1. Singleton, pp. 30–32.

2. Mary Newton Stanard, *Colonial Virginia, Its People and Customs* (Philadelphia: Lippincott, 1917), p. 100.

3. *The Correspondence of the Three William Byrds of Westover, Virginia, 1684–1776*, edited by Marion Tinling (Charlottesville, Va.: University Press of Virginia for the Virginia Historical Society, 1977), pp. 135, 155.

4. Quoted in Singleton, p. 229.

5. R. W. Symonds, "The English Export Trade in Furniture to Colonial America," *Antiques* (June 1935), p. 156.

6. Symonds, "English Export Trade," pp. 214–217; also *Antiques* (October 1935), pp. 156–159; and E. T. Joy, "English Furniture Exports to America, 1697–1830," *Antiques* (January 1964), pp. 92–98.

7. Phillips, *American Silver*, p. 30.

8. John J. McCusker, *Money and Exchange in Europe and America, 1600–1775: A Handbook* (Chapel Hill, N.C.: University of North Carolina Press, 1978), pp. 307–308; and Singleton, p. 238.

9. Data from Sargent, *Maine Wills*; Manwaring, *Early Connecticut Probate Records*; and *Calendar of New Jersey Wills*, I.

10. George Francis Dow, *The Arts and Crafts in New England, 1704–1775* (New York: Da Capo, 1967), p. 107.

11. John T. Kirk, *Connecticut Furniture, Seventeenth and Eighteenth Centuries* (Hartford, Conn.: Wadsworth Atheneum, 1967), pp. 116–123.

12. Singleton, p. 229.

13. Singleton, pp. 261–263.

14. Mildred B. Lanier, *English and Oriental Carpets at Williamsburg* (Williamsburg, Va.: Colonial Williamsburg Foundation, 1975), p. 8.

15. Singleton, p. 631.

16. Cummings, *Rural Household Inventories*, p. 55.

17. Singleton, pp. 52–54.

18. Antoinette F. Downing and Vincent J. Scully, Jr., *The Architectural Heritage of Newport, Rhode Island* (Cambridge, Mass.: Harvard University Press, 1952), p. 17; and Antoinette F. Downing, *Early Homes of Rhode Island* (Richmond, Va.: Garrett and Massie, 1937), p. 71.

19. Singleton, p. 31; and Stanard, *Colonial Virginia*, p. 73.

20. Janet Waring, *Early American Wall Stencils* (New York: Scott, 1937), p. 20; and William Salmon, *Polygraphice: or the Arts of Drawing, Engraving, Etching, Limning, etc.* (London, 1675), summarized in *Antiques* (September 1970), p. 360.

21. J. Frederick Kelly, *Early Domestic Architecture of Connecticut* (New York: Dover, 1963), p. 141; and Henry Chandlee Forman, *The Architecture of the Old South: The Medieval Style* (Cambridge, Mass.: Harvard University Press, 1948), p. 141.

22. Isham and Brown, *Early Connecticut Houses*, p. 100n.

23. Noel Hume, *Here Lies Virginia*, p. 278.

24. F. Gordon Roe, "Old Metal Fenders," *Antiques* (April 1939), pp. 178–181.

25. Fiske Kimball, *Domestic Architecture of the American Colonies and of the Early Republic* (New York: Scribners, 1922), pp. 62, 65; and Hugh Morrison, *Early American Architecture from the First Colonial Settlements to the National Period* (New York: Oxford, 1952), pp. 475–477.

3 · *The Queen Anne Style: 1715–1750*

1. Herbert Cescinsky, *English Furniture from Gothic to Sheraton* (New York: Bonanza, 1968), pp. 112, 169; Singleton, pp. 51, 65; and Dow, *The Arts and Crafts in New England*, p. 106.

2. Quoted in Singleton, p. 372.

3. Quoted in *ibid.*, p. 373.

4. W. T. Baxter, *The House of Hancock* (Cambridge, Mass.: Harvard University Press, 1945), pp. 68, 224; Singleton, pp. 374–377.

5. Symonds, "English Export Trade," pp. 214–217; also *Antiques* (October 1935), pp. 156–159; and Joy, "English Furniture Exports to America," pp. 92–98.

6. Alice R. Huger Smith and D. E. Huger Smith, *The Dwelling Houses of Charleston, South Carolina* (Philadelphia: Lippincott, 1917), pp. 368–369.

7. Singleton, p. 109.

8. A superb reference for sorting out rates of exchange for each colony month by month as well as year by year is McCusker, *Money and Exchange in Europe and America, 1600–1775: A Handbook*. On the currency itself, see Eric P. Newman, *The Early Paper Money of America* (Racine, Wis.: Whitman, 1967).

9. Data for table from Sargent, *Maine, Wills*; Manwaring, *Early Connecticut Probate Records*; and Metcalf, *Probate Records of . . . New Hampshire*.

10. Singleton, p. 109.

11. *Ibid.*, pp. 274–276.

12. Minor Myers, jr., and Edgar deN. Mayhew, *New London County Furniture, 1640–1840* (New London, Conn.: Lyman Allyn Museum, 1974), p. 118.

13. Dow, *Arts and Crafts in New England*, p. 17.

14. Benno M. Forman, "The Crown and York Chairs of Coastal Connecticut and the Work of the Durands of Milford," *Antiques* (May 1974), pp. 1147–1154.

15. Helen Comstock, *American Furniture* (New York: Bonanza, 1962), p. 74.

16. Isham and Brown, *Early Connecticut Houses*, p. 66.

17. P. K. Thornton, "Room Arrangements in the Mid-Eighteenth Century," *Antiques* (April 1971), pp. 556–561.

18. Dow, *Arts and Crafts in New England*, p. 110.

19. Nina Fletcher Little, *Floor Coverings in New England before 1850* (Sturbridge, Mass.: Old Sturbridge Village, 1967), p. 4.

20. Lanier, *English and Oriental Carpets*, pp. 33–34, 59.

21. *Antiques* (January 1965), pp. 48–49.

22. Singleton, p. 378.

23. *Ibid.*, pp. 91–93.

24. *Ibid.*, pp. 275–276.

25. Cummings, *Rural Household Inventories*, p. 147.

26. Dow, *Arts and Crafts in New England*, p. 14.

27. Singleton, p. 93.

28. Thomas Tileston Waterman, *The Mansions of Virginia, 1706–1776* (Chapel Hill, N.C.: University of North Carolina Press, 1946), pp. 118–119; Singleton, pp. 275, 377.

29. John Fowler and John Cornforth, *English Decoration in the Eighteenth Century* (Princeton, N.J.: Pyne, 1974), pp. 131–139.

30. *Ibid.*, pp. 137–138.

31. Singleton, pp. 374–375.

32. Edward B. Allen, *Early American Wall Painting* (New Haven: Yale University Press, 1926), pp. 4–7.

33. Morrison, *Early American Architecture*, p. 308.

34. Comstock, *American Furniture*, #191.

35. *Antiques* (August 1944), pp. 84–86; and George Francis Dow, ed., *The Holyoke Diaries* (Salem, Mass.: Essex Institute, 1911), pp. 7, 9, 15, 24.

36. *Antiques* (October 1932), pp. 139–142.

37. Alfred Coxe Prime, *The Arts and Crafts in Philadelphia, Maryland, and South Carolina, 1721–1785* (n.p.: The Walpole Society, 1929), p. 299.

38. Kimball, *Domestic Architecture*, p. 136.

39. *Antiques* (April 1945), p. 228.

40. Dow, *Arts and Crafts in New England*, p. 238; and Mrs. Rita Susswein Gottesman, *The Arts and Crafts in New York, 1726–1776* (New York: New-York Historical Society, 1938), pp. 350, 352.

41. Margaret B. Schiffer, *Chester County, Pennsylvania Inventories, 1684–1850* (Exton, Pa.: Schiffer, 1974), pp. 78–80.

42. Schiffer, *Chester County, Pennsylvania Inventories*, p. 176.

43. *Antiques* (July 1963), pp. 68–71.

44. *Antiques* (February 1934), pp. 60–63.

45. *Antiques* (May 1932), pp. 218f.; (May 1938), pp. 262–264.

46. *Virginia Historical Magazine*, II, 278–279.

47. Thomas Tileston Waterman, *The Colonial Dwellings of Colonial America* (Chapel Hill, N.C.: North Carolina University Press, 1950), p. 42; Dow, *Arts and Crafts in New England*, p. 110; Singleton, pp. 91–93; and Fowler and Cornforth, *English Decoration*, p. 138.

48. Geoffrey Wills, *English Looking-glasses* (New York: Barnes, 1965), pp. 106–110.

49. Jules David Prown, *John Singleton Copley in America, 1738–1774* (Cambridge, Mass.: Harvard University Press, 1966), p. 127; and *Antiques* (January 1976), p. 155.

50. Kirk, *Connecticut Furniture*, #234; cf. Joseph Downs, *American Furniture* (New York: Macmillan, 1952), #64.

51. John Gloag, *A Social History of Furniture Design* (London: Cassell, 1966), p. 156.

52. The estimate of weight is based upon Queen Anne and George I examples illustrated in Elizabeth B. Miles, *English Silver* (Hartford, Conn.: Wadsworth Atheneum, 1976).

53. Phillips, *American Silver*, p. 64.

54. Illustrated in Miles, *English Silver*, p. 46.

55. William Peirce Randel, *The American Revolution: Mirror of a People* (Maplewood, N.J.: Hammond, 1973), p. 35 (illustrated there in color).

56. Similar chairs appear in the Queen Anne drawings of Alexander Hamilton illustrated in the plates of Carl Bridenbaugh, ed., *Gentleman's Progress: The Itinerarium of Dr. Alexander Hamilton* (Chapel Hill, N.C.: North Carolina University Press, 1948). John T. Kirk, *American Chairs, Queen Anne and Chippendale* (New York: Knopf, 1972), illustrates somewhat similar chairs as Figures 203 and 204.

4·*The Chippendale Style: 1750–1810*

1. Singleton, p. 332.

2. *Ibid.*, pp. 492–493.

3. Benjamin Franklin to Deborah Franklin, February 19, 1758, *The Complete Works of Benjamin Franklin*, edited by John Bigelow (New York: Putnam, 1887), III, 6–9.

4. *The Writings of George Washington from the Original Manuscript Sources*, edited by John C. Fitzpatrick (Washington, D.C.: Government Printing Office, 1931), II, 161–162. Hereafter cited as *Writings of Washington*.

5. *Antiques* (October 1938), p. 199.

6. Prime, *Arts and Crafts in Philadelphia*, p. 277.

7. *Paul Revere's Boston, 1735–1818* (Boston: Museum of Fine Arts, 1975), p. 54.

8. Kimball, *Domestic Architecture*, pp. 122–124.

9. Prime, *Arts and Crafts in Philadelphia*, pp. 201–202.

10. Cummings, *Rural Household Inventories*, pp. 257–260.

11. *Antiques* (November 1925), p. 310; (September 1925), p. 141.

12. McCusker, *Money and Exchange in Europe and America, 1600–1775*, as the source for comparative value of currencies on a month-by-month basis. Also useful on the money itself and the comparative values of old, new, and middle tenors (as the revalued currencies were called) is Eric P. Newman, *The Early Paper Money of America.*

13. Data taken from *The Probate Records of Lincoln County, Maine*, edited by William D. Patterson (Portland: Maine Genealogical Society, 1895), and Manuscript Probate Records for Lyme, Groton, and Stonington, Connecticut; and *Calendar of New Jersey Wills*, IV, edited by A. Van Doren Honeyman (Somerville, N.J.: Unionist-Gazette, 1928); see also generally Jackson Turner Main, *The Social Structure of Revolutionary America* (Princeton, N.J.: Princeton University Press, 1965), especially Chapter 3.

14. Wendell Garrett, *Apthorp House* (Cambridge, Mass.: Harvard University Press, 1960).

15. Charles Carroll of Annapolis to Charles Carroll of Carrollton, June 1, 1772, *Antiques* (June 1973), p. 1188, citing *Maryland Historical Magazine* (June 1919), p. 146.

16. John Adams, *Diary and Autobiography*, edited by L. H. Butterfield (Cambridge, Mass.: Harvard University Press, 1961), I, 293–294.

17. Prown, *John Singleton Copley in America*, I, 125–126.

18. *Antiques* (October 1968), pp. 570–577.

19. Cummings, *Rural Household Inventories*, pp. 193, 235; Schiffer, *Chester County, Pennsylvania Inventories*, p. 193; and *Antiques* (June 1973), p. 1188.

20. Irving W. Lyon, *The Colonial Furniture of New England* (New York: Dutton, 1977), p. 163.

21. Comstock, *American Furniture*, pp. 118–119.

22. *Antiques* (June 1976), p. 1204.

23. *Antiques* (September 1929), p. 203.

24. John F. Watson, *Annals of Philadelphia* (Philadelphia: Hunt, 1830), p. 184.

25. *Ibid.*, p. 206.

26. *Ibid.* (1830 edn.), p. 184.

27. Quoted in Lanier, *English and Oriental Carpets*, p. 4.

28. *Antiques* (January 1976), p. 146.

29. *Antiques* (January 1976), pp. 155, 158.

30. Benjamin Franklin to Deborah Franklin, February 19, 1758, *The Complete Works of Benjamin Franklin*, III, 7.

31. Rodris Roth, *Floor Coverings in Eighteenth Century America* (Washington, D.C.: Smithsonian, 1967), p. 12.

32. Little, *Floor Coverings*, pp. 20–21.

33. Roth, *Floor Coverings*, p. 29.

34. *Antiques* (April 1931), pp. 296–301.

35. Prown, *John Singleton Copley in America*, I, 75–76.

36. Watson, *Annals of Philadelphia* (1830 edn.), p. 184.

37. *Writings of Washington*, II, 23.

38. *Antiques* (December 1971), p. 880.

39. Watson, *Annals of Philadelphia* (1830 edn.), p. 184; Schiffer, *Chester County, Pennsylvania Inventories*, p. 183; and Cummings, *Rural Household Inventories*, p. 200.

40. *Antiques* (June 1966), pp. 856–861; (November 1966), p. 693.

41. Cummings, *Rural Household Inventories*, pp. 151–154.

42. *Ibid.*, pp. 165–169, 245.

43. Seymour Howard, "Thomas Jefferson's Art Gallery for Monticello," *The Art Bulletin* (December 1977), pp. 583–600.

44. *Writings of Washington*, II, 332–334.

45. Florence Montgomery, *Printed Textiles* (New York: Viking Press, 1970), pp. 55–56; *Writings of Washington*, II, 320; and Dow, *The Arts and Crafts in New England*, pp. 124–125; and Franklin to Deborah Franklin, February 19, 1758, *Complete Works of Benjamin Franklin*, III, 7.

46. *Antiques* (October 1968), p. 536.

47. The whole price list is reproduced in Harrold E. Gillingham, "Benjamin Lehman, A Germantown Cabinetmaker," *The Pennsylvania Magazine of History and Biography* (October 1930), pp. 289–306.

48. *Writings of Washington*, II, 335, 433.

49. *Antiques* (October 1951), pp. 310–311.

50. *Antiques* (August 1964), pp. 184–187.

51. Schiffer, *Chester County, Pennsylvania Inventories*, p. 86.

52. *Antiques* (December 1964), pp. 722–727.

53. Prime, *Arts and Crafts in Philadelphia*, pp. 205, 214.

54. *Ibid.*, p. 219.

55. *Ibid.*, pp. 214–215; *Antiques* (February 1948), pp. 130–131.

56. Data from Fowler and Cornforth, *English Decoration in the Eighteenth Century*, pp. 131–136.

57. Benjamin Franklin, *Memoirs* (Philadelphia: M'Carty and Davis, 1837), II, 498–499.

58. Prime, *Arts and Crafts in Philadelphia*, p. 275.

59. Fowler and Cornforth, *English Decoration in the Eighteenth Century*, p. 139.

60. *Antiques* (September 1952), pp. 216–217.

61. Prime, *Arts and Crafts in Philadelphia*, p. 274.

62. *Ibid.*, p. 276; *Writings of Washington*, II, 23.

63. Waterman, *The Mansions of Virginia*, p. 280.

64. Dow, *Arts and Crafts in New England*, p. 259.

65. Philip Vickers Fithian, *Journal and Letters, 1767–1774*, edited by John Rogers Williams (Princeton, N.J.: University Library, 1900), p. 65.

66. *Antiques* (January 1960), p. 95.

67. Dow, ed., *The Holyoke Diaries*, p. 15.

68. Singleton, pp. 333–334.

69. *Writings of Washington*, II, 320.

70. Dow, *The Arts and Crafts in New England*, p. 215.

71. Schiffer, *Chester County, Pennsylvania Inventories*, pp. 78–80.

72. Based on Dow, *Arts and Crafts in New England*, p. 250;

and Prime, *Arts and Crafts in Philadelphia*, pp. 299–300, 301, 304, 306.

73. *Antiques* (October 1968), pp. 570–577.

74. Ledlie Irwin Laughlin, *Pewter in America: Its Makers and Their Marks* (Boston: Houghton Mifflin, 1940), I, 23.

75. Eric de Jonge, "Pewter," in *The Concise Encyclopedia of American Antiques*, edited by Helen Comstock (New York: Hawthorn, 1958), p. 158.

76. *Paul Revere's Boston*, p. 54.

77. *Antiques* (August 1925), pp. 79–84; (May 1978), pp. 1044–1051.

78. *Antiques* (March 1959), pp. 264–271.

79. Prown, *John Singleton Copley in America*, I, 127; *Antiques* (January 1976), pp. 142–167.

80. E. Alfred Jones, *American Members of the Inns of Court* (London: St. Catherine, 1924), pp. 153–154; and Parke Bernet Sale, Dec. 12, 1978, #247. Cf. Miles, *English Silver*, #154, for a pair of similar candelabra produced by Cafe in the same year. For a careful exploration and background of Roupell's picture and the people in it, see Anna Wells Rutledge, "After the Cloth Was Removed," *Winterthur Portfolio*, No. 4., edited by Richard K. Doub (Charlottesville, Va.: University of Virginia Press for Winterthur, 1968), pp. 47–62.

81. Nancy McClelland, *Historic Wall-Papers* (Philadelphia: Lippincott, 1924), pp. 324–329.

82. Illustrated in *Antiques* (February 1935), p. 73.

83. *Antiques* (April 1969), p. 565; and Charles F. Montgomery, *American Furniture: The Federal Period* (New York: Viking Press, 1966), p. 428.

84. For Latrobe's notes on the game depicted here (it is one of two possibilities, both in Hanover Town, Virginia, in November 1797), see *The Virginia Journals of Benjamin Henry Latrobe, 1795–1798*, edited by Edward C. Carter II (New Haven, Conn.: Yale University Press, 1977), II, 325.

85. Myers, jr., and Mayhew, *New London County Furniture*, illustrates an identical chair from either Lyme or Eldredge's native Groton, Plate 84. For a similar chair from North Bennington, Vermont, see Dean A. Fales, Jr., *The Furniture of Historic Deerfield* (New York: Dutton, 1976), p. 63.

86. Peterson, *Americans at Home*, illustrates three of her other pictures, Plates 149, 151, and 152.

5 · *The Federal Period: 1785–1815*

1. Washington to Samuel Vaughan, Feb. 5, 1785, *Writings of Washington*, XXVIII, 62–64.

2. *Paul Revere's Boston*, p. 187.

3. *Ibid.*, p. 161 (quoting R. B. Haas, "The Forgotten Courtship of David and Marcy Spear, 1785–1787," *Old Time New England* [Winter 1962], pp. 61–74).

4. *Ibid.*, p. 145.

5. Peter Whitney, *History of the County of Worcester* (Worcester, Mass.: Thomas, 1793), p. 224.

6. Figures are estate totals except for Ulster County, New York, for which administrative bonds for each estate have been used. *Ulster County Probate Records*; Patterson, ed., *The Probate Records of Lincoln County, Maine*; and Manuscript probate records for Groton, Stonington, and Lyme, Connecticut.

7. *Dilworth's Assistant*, edited by James Gibbons (New York: Kirk, 1805), pp. 48, 49, 58.

8. *Daboll's Almanack for 1791* (New London, Conn.: Green, 1790), unpaginated.

9. Harold Kirker, *The Architecture of Charles Bulfinch* (Cambridge, Mass.: Harvard University Press, 1969), passim.

10. Prime, *Arts and Crafts in Philadelphia*, p. 184.

11. Mabel M. Swan, "The Furniture of His Excellency, John Hancock," *Antiques* (March 1931), pp. 119–121.

12. See Sir Francis Watson, "Jefferson and French Eighteenth-Century Furniture," in *Jefferson and the Arts: An Extended View*, edited by William Howard Adams (Washington, D.C.: National Gallery of Art, 1976), pp. 271–293.

13. Montgomery, *American Furniture: The Federal Period*, illustrates spectacular Federal adaptations of Chippendale secretaries, one from Boston, the other from Connecticut or Rhode Island, #176, 177.

14. For an excellent survey of regional variations, see Montgomery, *American Furniture: The Federal Period*.

15. Price books appeared in Hartford (1792), Philadelphia (1794, 1796), New York (1796, 1802, 1810), Hatfield, Mass. (1796, 1797), and Baltimore (1817). For full bibliographic information, see Montgomery, *American Furniture: The Federal Period*, p. 488.

16. Roth, *Floor Coverings*, pp. 55–56.

17. *Ibid.*, p. 56.

18. *Antiques* (February 1947), pp. 118–119.

19. Roth, *Floor Coverings*, pp. 26–27.

20. *Ibid.*, p. 29.

21. Little, *Floor Coverings*, p. 33.

22. *Antiques* (December 1971), p. 880; (November 1971), p. 752; (August 1925), pp. 85–89; (October 1929), pp. 322–327.

23. *Antiques* (May 1949), p. 299.

24. Helen Comstock, *The Looking Glass in America, 1700–1825* (New York: Viking Press, 1968), pp. 66, 69.

25. Schiffer, *Chester County, Pennsylvania Inventories*, p. 119.

26. Montgomery, *American Furniture: The Federal Period*, p. 44.

27. Montgomery, *Printed Textiles*, p. 70.

28. *Antiques* (July 1929), p. 35.

29. *Antiques* (June 1931), p. 454.

30. *Antiques* (February 1929), p. 123.

31. Esther Stevens Fraser, "Excavating Old Wallpapers," *Antiques* (May 1923), pp. 216–221. The wallpapers are illustrated in the article.

32. Waring, *Early American Wall Stencils*, Plate 55.

33. Little, *American Decorative Wall Painting*, p. 98.
34. *Ibid.*, p. 84 and Fig. 108; Edward B. Allen, *Early American Wall Paintings* (New Haven, Conn.: Yale University Press, 1926), pp. 60–61.
35. Little, *American Decorative Wall Painting*, pp. 114, 116, 135, 148.
36. Joseph T. Butler, *Candleholders in America* (New York: Bonanza, 1967), p. 81.
37. Watson, *Annals of Philadelphia*, edited by Willis P. Hazard (Philadelphia: Stuart, 1887), III, 130–131; and Joseph T. Butler, *American Antiques, 1800–1900* (New York: Odyssey, 1965), p. 135.
38. *Antiques* (April 1929), pp. 293–294.
39. Singleton, p. 514.
40. Prime, *Arts and Crafts of Philadelphia*, p. 306.
41. *Antiques* (December 1929), p. 501.
42. Schiffer, *Chester County, Pennsylvania Inventories*, pp. 78–80.
43. H. Reynolds, *Directions for House and Ship Painting* (New Haven, Conn.: Hudson, 1812), reproduced in its entirety in *Antiques* (April 1978), pp. 849–853.
44. *Antiques* (December 1975), p. 1161.
45. *Antiques* (July 1951), pp. 46, 50.
46. Margaret Brown Klapthor, *Official White House China* (Washington, D.C.: Smithsonian, 1975), pp. 25–26.
47. *Antiques* (May 1941), pp. 238–241; (March 1959), pp. 282–285.
48. Prime, *Arts and Crafts of Philadelphia*, p. 96; Phillips, *American Silver*, pp. 101–102; and Schiffer, *Chester County, Pennsylvania Inventories*, pp. 337–338.
49. *Antiques* (July 1977), p. 121.

6 · *The Empire Style: 1810–1830*

1. Frances Trollope, *Domestic Manners of the Americans* (New York: Knopf, 1949), p. 338.
2. *Antiques* (January 1958), p. 69; (July 1968), pp. 101–103.
3. *Antiques* (April 1956), pp. 346–349.
4. Nina Fletcher Little, *American Decorative Wall Painting* (New York: Dutton, 1972), p. 101.
5. Robert Roberts, *The House Servant's Directory* (Boston: Monroe and Francis, 1827; reprinted Waltham, Mass.: Gore Place Society, 1977), pp. 46–53.
6. Jean McClure Mudge, *Chinese Export Porcelain for the American Market* (Wilmington, Del.: University of Delaware Press, 1962), pp. 179, 183–184.
7. Klapthor, *Official White House China*, pp. 40–41.
8. *Antiques* (July 1934), p. 17f.
9. Mudge, *Chinese Export Porcelain*, pp. 90, 184; and *Antiques* (January 1924), pp. 21–25; (November 1934), p. 196.
10. *19th-Century America: Furniture and Other Decorative Arts* (New York: Metropolitan Museum of Art, 1970), Plate 79.
11. Downing, *Early Homes of Rhode Island*, p. 401.

7 · *Victorian Classical: 1830–1850*

1. Minor Myers, jr., "Who Bought Webster and Parkes' *Encyclopaedia of Domestic Economy?*" *Antiques* (May 1979), pp. 1028–1031.
2. Gustavus Myers, *History of the Great American Fortunes* (New York: Modern Library, 1936), pp. 145–146.
3. A large Greek revival brick house was built in Kansas City, Missouri, in 1858 at a cost of $981—*Antiques* (March 1977), p. 530.
4. Quoted in *Classical America, 1815–1845* (Newark, N.J.: The Newark Museum, 1963), p. 23.
5. Pauline W. Inman, "House Furnishings of a Vermont Family," *Antiques* (August 1969), pp. 228–233.
6. Dean A. Fales, Jr., *American Painted Furniture, 1660–1880* (New York: Dutton, 1972), p. 203.
7. Peter C. Welsh, "Patents and the Decorative Arts: A Portent of a Changing Society," *Antiques* (July 1962), pp. 72–75.
8. A. J. Downing, *The Architecture of Country Houses* (New York: Dover, 1969), pp. 412–413.
9. *Antiques* (August 1975), pp. 278–279.
10. Nina Fletcher Little, *Floor Coverings in New England Before 1850* (Sturbridge, Mass.: Old Sturbridge Village, 1967), p. 11; and J. Leander Bishop, *A History of American Manufactures for 1608 to 1860* (Philadelphia: Young, 1868), II, 383.
11. *Antiques* (August 1963), pp. 454–457; Edward Biddle and Mantle Fielding, *The Life and Works of Thomas Sully* (Philadelphia: Wickersham, 1921); and Louis L. Noble, *The Course of Empire* (New York: Lamport, Blakeman & Law, 1853), pp. 176–179.
12. *Antiques* (April 1963), pp. 454–457.
13. Bishop, *History of American Manufactures*, II, 404.
14. See *Antiques* (December 1939), pp. 399–401.
15. Frances Byerly Parkes, *Domestic Duties or Instructions to Young Married Ladies* (London: Longman, Hurst, Rees, Brown, and Green, 1825), p. 194.
16. Catherine Lynn Frangimore, *Wallpapers in Historic Preservation* (Washington, D.C.: National Park Service, 1977), pp. 14, 30.
17. *Antiques* (September 1936), pp. 113–117.
18. Parkes, *Domestic Duties*, p. 195.
19. James Gallier, *The American Builders' General Price Book and Estimator* (New York: Stanley, 1833), pp. 117–121.
20. Schiffer, *Chester County, Pennsylvania Inventories*, p. 21.
21. *Antiques* (April 1930), pp. 332–337.
22. *Antiques* (January 1940), pp. 29–31.
23. Edwin A. Barber, *The Pottery and Porcelain of the United States* (New York: Putnam, 1893), pp. 149–151; and *Antiques* (December 1946), p. 410; (February 1930), p. 168.
24. Bishop, *History of American Manufactures*, II, 377.

8 · *The Spanish Southwest: 1560–1850*

1. Edwin Bryant (1846), as quoted in Harold Kirker, *California's Architectural Frontier* (San Marino, Calif.: The Huntington Library, 1960), p. 9.
2. See Kirker, *California's Architectural Frontier*, p. 17.
3. Richard Henry Dana, *Two Years Before the Mast* (New York: Collier, 1909), p. 86.
4. *Ibid.*, pp. 395, 408–409, 411.
5. *Antiques* (April 1922), pp. 167–168.
6. Alan C. Vedder, *Furniture of Spanish New Mexico* (Santa Fe, N.M.: Sunstone, 1977), p. 9.
7. *Antiques* (August 1943), p. 61.
8. San Diego Division of Beaches and Parks, "Furnishing an Early California Home," mimeographed, 1967, p. 3.
9. *Ibid.*, p. 4.
10. *Ibid.*, p. 5.
11. *Ibid.*, p. 7.
12. *Ibid.*, p. 19; and *Antiques* (September 1975), p. 472.
13. "Furnishing an Early California Home," p. 3.
14. *Antiques* (September 1975), pp. 472, 474n.
15. "Furnishing an Early California Home," p. 7.
16. *Ibid.*, p. 10.
17. *Antiques* (February 1933), p. 49.
18. *Antiques* (August 1943), p. 62.
19. "Furnishing an Early California Home," pp. 2–3.
20. *Antiques* (February 1978), p. 431.
21. *Antiques* (August 1959), pp. 155–156.
22. *Antiques* (July 1968), pp. 96–100.
23. "Furnishing an Early California Home," p. 11.
24. *Antiques* (May 1925), p. 251.
25. "Furnishing an Early California Home," p. 4.
26. *Antiques* (April 1978), p. 826.
27. "Furnishing an Early California Home," p. 3.
28. *Ibid.*, p. 17.
29. *Antiques* (May 1963), p. 566.
30. "Furnishing an Early California Home," p. 15.
31. Lottie Westcott, as quoted in "Furnishing an Early California Home," p. 7.
32. "Furnishing an Early California Home," p. 13.
33. *Ibid.*, p. 4.
34. *Antiques* (October 1937), pp. 182–183.

9 · *Gothic and Elizabethan Styles: 1836–1870*

1. Downing, *Country Houses*, pp. 257–258.
2. *Ibid.*, p. 40.
3. J. C. Loudon, *Encyclopaedia of Cottage, Farm, and Villa Architecture and Furniture* (London: Longman *et al.*, 1842), p. 1093.
4. Thomas Webster and Frances Byerly Parkes, *An Encyclopaedia of Domestic Economy* (New York: Harper, 1845), p. 277.
5. Katherine M. McClinton, "Furniture and Interiors Designed by A. J. Davis," *Connoisseur* (January 1969), p. 61.
6. Downing, *Country Houses*, p. 422.
7. Gervase Wheeler, *Rural Homes or Sketches of Houses Suited to American Country Life* (New York: Scribners, 1852), pp. 208–209.
8. Loudon, *Encyclopaedia*, p. 344.
9. *Ibid.*, p. 344.
10. *Ibid.*, p. 285.
11. *Ibid.*, p. 341.
12. Downing, *Country Houses*, p. 388.
13. *Ibid.*, p. 398.
14. *Ibid.*, p. 402.
15. *Ibid.*, pp. 403–405.
16. Wheeler, *Rural Homes*, p. 196.
17. Loudon, *Encyclopaedia*, p. 353.
18. *Ibid.*
19. Wheeler, *Rural Homes*, p. 216.
20. Downing, *Country Houses*, p. 391.
21. *Ibid.*, p. 451.
22. Wheeler, *Rural Homes*, pp. 213–214.

10 · *The Rococo Style: 1850–1870*

1. Downing, *Country Houses*, p. 286.
2. O. S. Fowler, *A Home for All*, as quoted by Russell Lynes in *The Tastemakers* (New York: Harper, 1954), p. 36.
3. Downing, *Country Houses*, p. 405.
4. Barbara Franco, "New York City Furniture Bought for Fountain Elms by James Watson Williams," *Antiques* (September 1973), p. 462.
5. Downing, *Country Houses*, p. 372.
6. Samuel Sloan, *Homestead Architecture* (Philadelphia: Lippincott, 1861), p. 323.

11 · *The Eclectic Decades: 1865–1895*

1. Catherine Beecher and Harriet Beecher Stowe, *The American Woman's Home* (New York: Ford, 1869), pp. 441–446.
2. Robert Hunter, *Poverty* (New York: Macmillan, 1906), p. 42.
3. *The Decorator and Furnisher* (June 1893), p. 91.
4. Clarence Cook, *What Shall We Do with Our Walls?* (New York: Fuller, 1881), pp. 12–13.
5. J. Pickering Putnam, *The Open Fireplace in All Ages* (Boston: Osgood, 1882), p. 1.
6. Cook, *What Shall We Do with Our Walls?*, p. 30.
7. Table reprinted from *The Decorator and Furnisher* (January 1895), pp. 144–145.
8. Harriet Spofford, *Art Decoration Applied to Furniture* (New York: Harper, 1878), p. 224.
9. Clarence Cook, *The House Beautiful* (New York: Scribner Armstrong, 1878), p. 236.
10. Spofford, *Art Decoration Applied to Furniture*, p. 101.
11. *Ibid.*, p. 112.
12. *Artistic Houses* (New York: D. Appleton, 1883), I, 142, 183.
13. Spofford, *Art Decoration Applied to Furniture*, p. 96.
14. *Ibid.*, p. 129.
15. *Ibid.*, p. 130.

16. *Ibid.*

17. Spofford, *Art Decoration Applied to Furniture*, p. 162.

18. *The Decorator and Furnisher* also ran a selection of typical Egyptian motifs in November 1894, pp. 58–60. Dr. Hammond, whose bedroom appears in Figure 129, also had an Egyptian library, described but not illustrated in *Artistic Houses*, I, 87–89.

19. Spofford, *Art Decoration Applied to Furniture*, p. 131.

20. *Artistic Houses*, I, 126.

21. Spofford, *Art Decoration Applied to Furniture*, p. 144.

22. *Ibid.*, pp. 145–146.

23. J. S. Ingram, *The Centennial Exposition Described and Illustrated* (Philadelphia: Hubbard, 1876), p. 382. The question of whether "Centennial" furniture was actually present at the Centennial Exposition has been much debated. Ingram's comment makes it clear that at least one manufacturer had tried to duplicate revolutionary styles.

24. Cook, *The House Beautiful*, p. 163.

25. *The Decorator and Furnisher*, June 1889, p. 53.

26. In the early 1880s, New York City cabinetmaker Ernest Hagen reproduced three Duncan Phyfe chairs for a customer, but fifty years later the owner's family could not tell which were the originals and which Hagen's reproductions. Few Colonial Revival pieces were so faithful to the originals—Ruth Ralston, "Ernest Hagen's Order Books," *Antiques* (December 1945), p. 356.

27. Elizabeth Aslin, *The Aesthetic Movement: Prelude to Art Nouveau* (New York: Praeger, 1969), p. 61.

28. Constance Cary Harrison, *Woman's Handiwork in Modern Homes* (New York: Scribners, 1881), p. 5.

29. *Artistic Houses*, I, 56.

30. Some of these papers are reproduced in stunning gilt in Cook, *What Shall We Do with Our Walls?*

31. See also *Artistic Houses*, I, 3.

32. *Ibid.*, II, 160; I, 6.

33. *Eastlake Influenced Furniture, 1870–1890* (Yonkers, N.Y.: Hudson River Museum, 1973), p. 1.

34. Myers, *History of the Great American Fortunes*, pp. 492–494; *Eastlake Influenced Furniture*, #24.

35. On historical friezes, see Holly, *Modern Dwellings in Town and Country*, pp. 151, 159, 170.

36. Several interiors in Seale, *The Tasteful Interlude* (New York: Praeger, 1975), show well-furnished rooms in frontier states: #71–73 (Idaho in 1888–90), #98–101 (New Mexico in 1891), #185–186 (Alaska in 1909).

37. Seale, *The Tasteful Interlude*, #107.

38. *The Decorator and Furnisher* (August 1895), p. 165.

39. For illustrations of a sequence of rooms in diverse styles within a single house, see Byron, *Photographs of New York Interiors*, #28–32. In 1899, Byron photographed the residence of Edward Lauterbach recording a Moorish hall, medieval dining room, more or less rococo drawing room, Japanese billiard room, and Empire revival bedroom.

40. Thomson illustrated his prize design for a Colonial Reception Room in *The Decorator and Furnisher* for October 1890, p. 9.

41. *19th-Century America*, #153.

42. For another thorough but not so pure Japanese room, see the billiard room in the Lauterbach House in New York City (1899), illustrated in Joseph Byron, *Photographs of New York Interiors at the Turn of the Century* (New York: Dover, 1976), #31; see also *Artistic Houses*, I, 121.

43. William Seale, *The Tasteful Interlude*, #49; see also Marilyn Johnson Bordes's review of Seale in *Decorative Arts Newsletter* (Winter 1976), pp. 13–14.

44. *Artistic Houses*, I, 76.

45. The identical illustration appeared in *Artistic Houses* and in Desmond and Croly, *Stately Homes in America*.

46. Cook, *The House Beautiful*, p. 105.

47. A chromolithograph of the Pearl Room, as this room was called, is reproduced in color in Marshall B. Davidson, *The American Heritage History of Antiques from the Civil War to World War I* (New York: American Heritage, 1969), p. 100.

48. Peterson, *Americans at Home*, #81.

49. For additional scenes of frontier life, see Seale, *The Tasteful Interlude*, #84 (Dakota), #86, 93 (Montana), #41, 85 (Colorado). Peterson, *Americans at Home*, illustrates the interior of a sod house, #155.

50. Seale, *The Tasteful Interlude*, #164, shows a very similar room in Alaska.

51. Aline B. Saarinen, *The Proud Possessors* (New York: Random House, 1958), pp. 4–5.

52. Kirk, *American Chairs*, Nos. 136–138.

12 · *Mission and Art Nouveau: 1895–1915*

1. Candace Wheeler, *Principles of Home Decoration* (New York: Doubleday, Page, 1903), pp. 160, 182.

2. *Ibid.*, pp. 96, 162, 163.

3. *Ibid.*, p. 225.

4. *Ibid.*, pp. 89, 95, 106–109, 112.

5. *Ibid.*, pp. 89, 107, 109, 192.

6. The room is illustrated in Robert Bishop, *How to Know American Antique Furniture* (New York: Dutton, 1973), p. 193; it also appears in Marshall B. Davidson, *The American Heritage History of Antiques*, pp. 256–257.

7. George W. Maher, "A Plea for an Indigenous Art," *Architectural Record* (June 1907), pp. 429–433; and H. D. C., "What Is Indigenous Architecture?" *Architectural Record* (June 1907), pp. 434–442.

8. Bradley's designs for five rooms are illustrated in color in Davidson, *American Heritage History of Antiques*, pp. 310–311.

9. Robert Koch, *Louis C. Tiffany: Rebel in Glass* (New York: Crown, 1964), p. 180.

10. For an early color view of this room, see Henry H. Saylor, "The Country Home of Mr. Louis C. Tiffany," *Country Life* (December 1908), pp. 157–162.

11. Peter B. Wright, "The Sculptor as His Own Architect and Builder," *Architectural Record* (July 1909), pp. 33–37.

12. See, for example, the table illustrated in Davidson, *American Heritage History of Antiques*, p. 261.

13 · *The Twentieth-century Look: Purity, Simplicity, and Grandeur*

1. Edith Wharton and Ogden Codman, Jr., *The Decoration of Houses* (New York: Scribners, 1897), pp. xix, xx.
2. *Ibid.*, p. xxii.
3. Willford Isbell King, *The Wealth and Income of the People of the United States* (New York: Macmillan, 1919), pp. 224–235.
4. Christine Frederick, *The New Housekeeping* (New York: Doubleday, Page, 1916), p. 165.
5. Elsie de Wolfe, *The House in Good Taste* (New York: Century, 1913), pp. 148, 153.
6. *Ibid.*, pp. 147, 179.
7. *Ibid.*, pp. 262, 263.
8. *Ibid.*, p. 197.
9. *Ibid.*, p. 71.
10. *Ibid.*, p. 77–78.
11. *Ibid.*, pp. 79–80.
12. *Ibid.*, p. 147.
13. Emily Holt, *Encyclopaedia of Etiquette* (New York: McClure Phillips, 1901), pp. 85–89.
14. *Your Home and Its Decoration* (n.p.: Sherwin Williams Company, 1910), p. 186.
15. For a trellis room in Louisville, Kentucky, see Seale, *Tasteful Interlude*, #226. James Ross Todd's architects, Carriere and Hastings, had hired a New York decorator, in all probability Elsie de Wolfe herself or someone influenced strongly by her. Seale attributes the furniture to John Helmsky of New York.

Appendix A · *American Kitchens, Bathrooms, and Heating*

1. Two books deserve careful consultation by anyone restoring or researching kitchens: Frances Phipps, *Colonial Kitchens, Their Furnishings, and Their Gardens* (New York: Hawthorn, 1972); and Louise K. Lantz, *Old American Kitchen Ware, 1725–1925* (Camden, N.J.: Nelson, 1970).
2. Thomas Moore, *An Essay in the Most Eligible Construction of Ice-Houses. Also, a Description of the Newly Invented Machine Called the Refrigerator* (Baltimore: Bonsel and Niles, 1803). Mrs. M. Randolph in *The Virginia Housewife* (Washington, D.C., 1825) also discussed the refrigerator and offered a cut of one.
3. Peterson, *Americans at Home*, Plate 85.
4. Reprinted from Catherine Beecher, *Domestic Receipt Book*, pp. 253–259.
5. Cuts of suggestions for arranging the kitchen in the 1870s can be found in Peterson, *Americans at Home*, Plates 117, 118.

6. Three books review English developments well but say little about America: Lawrence Wright, *Clean and Decent* (London: Routledge & Kegan Paul, 1960); Roy Palmer, *The Water Closet: A New History* (Newton Abbot, Devon: David & Charles, 1973); and Lucinda Lambton, *Temples of Convenience* (New York: St. Martin's, 1978).
7. Kirker, *The Architecture of Charles Bulfinch* (Cambridge, Mass.: Harvard University Press, 1969), pp. 226–229.
8. Gallier, *American Builders' General Price Book*, p. 115. Mary Cable wrote that George Vanderbilt had the first indoor bathroom in America, one added to his house in New York City in 1855. It is clear that his bathroom was not the first, but it was an early, luxuriously complete room of the sort only the rich could afford—Mary Cable, *American Manners and Morals* (New York: American Heritage, 1969), p. 236. The bathroom is illustrated in Wright, *Clean and Decent*, p. 224.
9. Downing, *Country Houses*, p. 126.
10. A. Bryant Clough, *The Contractor's Manual and Builder's Price Book* (New York: Hallet, 1855), p. 162.
11. Bishop, *History of American Manufactures*, II, 302 and 302n.
12. Downing, *Country Houses*, p. 478.
13. De Wolfe, *The House in Good Taste*, p. 186.
14. Holt, *Encyclopaedia of Etiquette*, pp. 83, 129.

Notes to Color Plates

4. Sir Benjamin Thompson, Count Rumford (1753–1814), born in Woburn, Massachusetts, was a Tory who in 1775 went to England, where he became a distinguished scientific and political figure. On leaving America he left behind a wife, who died in 1792, and his daughter Sarah Thompson, Countess Rumford (1774–1852). Rumford never returned to America after his service as a British officer during the Revolution, but the well-to-do count nonetheless left Harvard $50,000. His daughter later joined her father in Europe but eventually returned to America and lived in Concord, New Hampshire, from 1799 to 1811. The watercolor is probably by the countess, who was quite proud of her drawing.
5. Judge William Cooper, who built Otsego Hall, had a fortune in excess of $200,000. Mrs. Cooper was distressed at the rural location of the house and sought to introduce as much taste and polish as possible. The house itself was modeled on one of the Van Rensselaer houses in Albany. The chandelier was covered with netting for summer. In addition to the barometer and the painted Windsor chairs, perhaps the most noticeable feature was, as Mrs. Cooper's son James Fenimore Cooper wrote in *The Pioneers*, "an enormous settee, or sofa, covered in light chintz. . . ."
9. In 1854 a writer for *Putnam's Monthly* considered this house "the most elegant Grecian mansion" in New York City.

A Selective Bibliography

In addition to the numerous articles in *The Magazine Antiques*, an immense number of useful books have appeared in recent years. A short bibliography cannot even begin to present a comprehensive list of the studies available, and we have thus confined these listings to four basic categories: Additional Picture Sources and Guides to Period Use; Regional Studies (with a few books on specific styles); Price Books, Analyses of Probate Inventories, and Guides to Currency Values; and Late-nineteenth- and Early-twentieth-century Guides to Decoration. Museums, libraries, and historical societies can point to other studies of local interest toward seeking out further details about a given region; and guides to antiques and collectibles offer good bibliographies of silver, glass, ceramics, and the like.

A · *Additional Picture Sources and Guides to Period Use*

ALLEN, EDWARD B. *Early American Wall Paintings, 1710–1850.* New Haven, Conn.: Yale University, 1926.

BISHOP, ROBERT, and PATRICIA COBLENTZ. *The World of Antiques, Art, and Architecture in Victorian America.* New York: Dutton, 1979.

BOGER, LOUISE ADA. *The Complete Guide to Furniture Styles.* New York: Scribners, 1969.

BRIGGS, MARTIN S. *The Homes of the Pilgrim Fathers in England and America.* London: Oxford, 1932.

BUTLER, JOSEPH, JR. *Candleholders in America, 1650–1900.* New York: Bonanza, 1967.

CANDEE, HELEN CHURCHILL. *Decorative Styles and Periods in the Home.* New York: Stokes, 1906.

CLAIBORNE, HERBERT A. *Some Paint Colors from Four Eighteenth Century Virginia Houses.* Portland, Me.: Antheonsen Press, n.d.

COMSTOCK, HELEN. "Eighteenth Century Floorcloths," *Antiques,* January 1965, pp. 48–49.

———. *The Looking Glass in America, 1700–1825.* New York: Viking, 1964.

CORNFORTH, JOHN. *English Interiors, 1790–1848.* London: Barrie and Jenkins, 1978.

DUTTON, RALPH. *The Victorian Home.* London: Batsford, 1954.

ENTWISLE, E. A. *The Book of Wallpaper.* London: Barker, 1954.

FOWLER, JOHN, and JOHN CORNFORTH. *English Decoration in the Eighteenth Century.* Princeton, N.J.: Pyne, 1974.

FRANGIMORE, CATHERINE LYNN. *Wallpapers in Historic Preservation.* Washington: U.S. Department of Interior, 1977.

FRASER, ESTHER STEVENS. "Some Colonial and Early American Decorative Floors," *Antiques,* April 1931, pp. 296–301.

HAYWARD, ARTHUR. *Colonial Lighting.* Boston: Little, Brown, 1927.

LANDREAU, ANTHONY. *America Underfoot: A History of Floor Coverings from Colonial Times to the Present.* Washington: Smithsonian, 1976.

LANIER, MILDRED B. *English and Oriental Carpets at Williamsburg.* Williamsburg, Va.: Colonial Williamsburg, 1975.

LINCOLN, WALDO. *Bibliography of American Cookery Books, 1742–1860.* Worcester, Mass.: American Antiquarian Society, 1929.

LITTLE, NINA FLETCHER. *Floor Coverings in New England Before 1850.* Sturbridge, Mass.: Old Sturbridge Village, 1967.

MAAS, JOHN. *The Victorian Home in America.* New York: Hawthorn, 1972.

MCCLELAND, NANCY. *Historic Wall-papers.* Philadelphia: Lippincott, 1924.

MCGRATH, ROBERT L. *Early Vermont Wall Paintings, 1790–1850.* Hanover, N.H.: University Press of New England, 1972.

MONTGOMERY, FLORENCE M. *Printed Textiles: English and American Cottons and Linens, 1700–1850.* New York: Viking, 1970.

———. "Room Furnishings as Seen in British Prints from the Lewis Walpole Library," *Antiques,* June 1973, pp. 1068–75, and March 1974, pp. 522–53.

NYLANDER, JANE C. *Fabrics for Historic Buildings.* Washington: National Trust for Historic Preservation, 1977.

PETERSON, HAROLD L. *Americans at Home.* New York: Scribners, 1971.

PETTIT, FLORENCE H. *America's Printed and Painted Fabrics, 1600–1900.* New York: Hastings House, 1970.

PHIPPS, FRANCES. *Colonial Kitchens, Their Furnishings, and Their Gardens.* New York: Hawthorn, 1972.

PRAZ, MARIO. *Conversation Pieces.* University Park, Pa.: Pennsylvania State University, 1971.

———. *An Illustrated History of Furnishings.* New York: Braziller, 1964.

ROTH, RODRIS. *Floor Coverings in Eighteenth Century America.* Washington: Smithsonian, 1967.

SEALE, WILLIAM. *Recreating the Historic House Interior.* Nashville, Tenn.: American Association for State and Local History, 1979.

———. *The Tasteful Interlude.* New York: Praeger, 1975.

SHERRILL, SARAH B. "Oriental Carpets in Seventeenth- and Eighteenth-Century America," *Antiques,* January 1976, pp. 142–67.

TALBOT, GEORGE. *At Home: Domestic Life in the Post Centennial Era.* Madison: State Historical Society of Wisconsin, 1976.

THORNTON, P. K. "Room Arrangements in the Mid-Eighteenth Century," *Antiques,* April 1971, pp. 556–61.

———. *Seventeenth-Century Interior Decoration in England, France, and Holland.* New Haven, Conn.: Yale University, 1978.

VON ROSENSTIEL, HELENE. *American Rugs and Carpets.* London: Barrie and Jenkins, 1978.

WARING, JANET. *Early American Wall Stencils.* New York: Scott, 1937.

B · Regional Studies (*with a few books on specific styles*)

ANDREWS, WAYNE. *American Gothic.* New York: Vintage Books, 1975.

BISSELL, CHARLES S. *Antique Furniture in Suffield, Connecticut.* Hartford: Connecticut Historical Society, 1956.

Boston Furniture of the Eighteenth Century. Boston: Colonial Society of Massachusetts, 1974.

BRIGHTMAN, ANNA. "Woolen Window Curtains: Luxury in Colonial Boston and Salem," *Antiques,* December 1964, pp. 722–27.

CARPENTER, RALPH E., JR. *The Arts and Crafts of Newport, Rhode Island.* Newport: Preservation Society of Newport County, 1954.

COMSTOCK, HELEN. *American Furniture.* New York: Viking, 1962.

———. "Furniture of Virginia, North Carolina, Georgia, and Kentucky," *Antiques,* January 1952, pp. 58–99.

DAVIS, DEERING. *Annapolis Houses.* N.p.: Architectural Book Publishing Co., 1947.

DOWNING, ANTOINETTE FORRESTER. *Early Homes of Rhode Island.* Richmond, R.I.: Garrett and Massie, 1937.

DOWNING, ANTOINETTE, and VINCENT SCULLY, JR. *The Architectural Heritage of Newport, Rhode Island.* Cambridge, Mass.: Harvard University, 1952.

DOWNS, JOSEPH. *American Furniture, Queen Anne and Chippendale Periods.* New York: Macmillan, 1952.

Eastlake Influenced American Furniture, 1870–1890. Yonkers, N.Y.: Hudson River Museum, 1973.

FAILEY, DEAN F. *Long Island Is My Nation.* Setauket: Society for the Preservation of Long Island Antiquities, 1976.

FALES, DEAN A., JR. *American Painted Furniture.* New York: Dutton, 1972.

———. *Essex County Furniture.* Salem, Mass.: Essex Institute, 1965.

———. *The Furniture of Historic Deerfield.* New York: Dutton, 1976.

FENNELLY, CATHERINE. *Textiles in New England.* Sturbridge, Mass.: Old Sturbridge Village, 1961.

FORMAN, HENRY CHANDLEE. *The Architecture of the Old South.* Cambridge, Mass.: Harvard University, 1948.

———. *Early Manor and Plantation Houses of Maryland.* Easton, Md.: the author, 1934.

———. *Early Nantucket and Its Whale Houses.* New York: Hastings, 1966.

GREENLAW, BARRY. *New England Furniture at Williamsburg.* Williamsburg, Va.: Colonial Williamsburg, 1974.

HAMLIN, TALBOT. *Greek Revival Architecture in America.* New York: Dover, 1964.

HOWE, KATHERINE S., and DAVID B. WARREN. *The Gothic Revival Style in America.* Houston, Tex.: Museum of Fine Arts, 1976.

The John Brown House Loan Exhibition of Rhode Island Furniture. Providence: Rhode Island Historical Society, 1965.

JOHNSTON, FRANCES BENJAMIN, and THOMAS TILESTON WATERMAN. *The Early Architecture of North Carolina.* Chapel Hill: University of North Carolina, 1947.

KIRK, JOHN T. *American Chairs: Queen Anne and Chippendale.* New York: Knopf, 1972.

———. *Connecticut Furniture: Seventeenth and Eighteenth Centuries.* Hartford, Conn.: Wadsworth Atheneum, 1967.

———. *Early American Furniture.* New York: Knopf, 1977.

KIRKER, HAROLD. *California's Architectural Heritage.* San Marino, Calif.: Huntington Library, 1960.

LOTH, CALDER, and JULIUS T. SADLER, JR. *The Only Proper Style: Gothic Architecture in America.* Boston: New York Graphic Society, 1975.

MONTGOMERY, CHARLES F. *American Furniture: The Federal Period.* New York: Viking, 1966.

——. "Regional Preferences and Characteristics in American Decorative Arts: 1750–1800," *Antiques,* June 1976, pp. 1196–1211.

MYERS, MINOR, JR., and EDGAR DEN. MAYHEW. *New London County Furniture.* New London, Conn.: Lyman Allyn Museum, 1974.

NEWCOMB, REXFORD. *Architecture of the Old Northwest Territory.* Chicago: University of Chicago, 1950.

NICHOLS, FREDERICK D. *The Early Architecture of Georgia.* Chapel Hill: University of North Carolina, 1957.

19th Century America: Furniture and Other Decorative Arts. New York: Metropolitan Museum of Art, 1970.

NOEL HUME, IVOR. *Here Lies Virginia.* New York: Knopf, 1963.

RAYMOND, ELEANOR. *Early Domestic Architecture of Pennsylvania.* New York: Helburn, 1931.

STITT, SUSAN. *Museum of Early Southern Decorative Arts.* Winston-Salem, N.C.: Hunter, 1970.

TATUM, GEORGE B. *Philadelphia Georgian.* Middletown, Conn.: Wesleyan University, 1976.

TRACY, BERRY B. *Classical America, 1815–1845.* Newark, N.J.: The Newark Museum, 1963.

VAN RAVENSWAAY, CHARLES. *The Art and Architecture of German Settlements in Missouri.* Columbia: University of Missouri, 1977.

VEDDER, ALAN C. *Furniture of Spanish New Mexico.* Santa Fe: Sunstone, 1977.

WATERMAN, THOMAS TILESTON. *The Mansions of Virginia.* Chapel Hill: University of North Carolina, 1946.

WINTERS, ROBERT E., JR., ed. *North Carolina Furniture, 1700–1900.* Raleigh: North Carolina Museum of History, 1977.

C · *Price Books, Analyses of Probate Inventories, and Guides to Currency Values*

The Buffalo Book of Prices for Manufacturing Cherry and Black Walnut Cabinetwork. Supplementary to the New York Book of Prices of 1834. Buffalo, N.Y.: Steele, 1836.

The Cabinetmakers' Philadelphia and London Book of Prices. Philadelphia: Snowden and M'Corkle, 1796.

CLOUGH, A. BRYANT. *The Contractor's Manual and Builder's Price Book.* New York: Hallet, 1855.

CUMMINGS, ABBOTT LOWELL. *Rural Household Inventories, 1675–1775.* Boston: Society for the Preservation of New England Antiquities, 1964.

DOW, GEORGE FRANCIS. *The Arts and Crafts in New England, 1704–1775.* New York: Da Capo, 1967.

GALLIER, JAMES. *The American Builders' General Price Book and Estimator.* New York: Stanley, 1833.

GOTTESMAN, RITA S. *The Arts and Crafts in New York, 1726–1776.* New York, 1938.

——. *The Arts and Crafts in New York, 1777–1799.* New York, 1954.

——. *The Arts and Crafts in New York, 1800–1804.* New York, 1965.

The Journeymen Cabinetmaker & Chair Makers' New York Book of Prices. New York: Swords, 1796.

LYON, IRVING WHITALL. *The Colonial Furniture of New England.* New York: Dutton, 1977.

McCUSKER, JOHN J. *Money and Exchange in Europe and America, 1600–1775: A Handbook.* Chapel Hill: University of North Carolina, for the Institute of Early American History and Culture, 1978.

The New York Revised Prices for Manufacturing Cabinet and Chair Work. New York: Southwick and Pelsue, 1810.

"The Price Book of the District of Columbia Cabinetmakers, 1831," edited Wendell Garrett, *Antiques,* May 1975, pp. 888–97.

PRIME, ALFRED COXE. *The Arts & Crafts in Philadlephia, Maryland, and South Carolina, 1721–1785.* N.p.: Walpole Society, 1929.

——. *The Arts & Crafts in Philadelphia, Maryland, and South Carolina, 1786–1800,* Series Two. N.p.: Walpole Society, 1932.

SCHIFFER, MARGARET B. *Chester County, Pennsylvania Inventories, 1684–1850.* Exton, Pa.: Schiffer Publishing, 1974.

SINGLETON, ESTHER. *The Furniture of Our Forefathers.* New York: Doubleday, Page, 1900.

WRIGHT, JOHN. *The American Negotiator, or Various Currencies of the British Colonies in North America.* London: Smith, 1765.

D · *Late-nineteenth- and Early-twentieth-century Guides to Decoration*

American Country Houses of Today. New York: Architectural Book Publishing, 1912.

Artistic Houses. New York: Appleton, 1883–1884.

BEECHER, CATHERINE. *Miss Beecher's Domestic Receipt Book.* New York: Harper, 1868.

BEECHER, CATHERINE, and HARRIET BEECHER STOWE. *The American Woman's Home.* New York: Ford, 1869.

BRUNNER, ARNOLD W., and THOMAS TRYON. *Interior Decoration.* New York: Comstock, 1887.

COOK, CLARENCE. *What Shall We Do with Our Walls?* New York: Fuller, 1881.

CROLY, HERBERT. *Houses for Town or Country.* New York: Duffield, 1907.

DOWNING, ANDREW JACKSON. *The Architecture of Country Houses.* New York: Appleton, 1850.

DESMOND, HARRY W., and HERBERT CROLY. *Stately Homes in America.* New York: Appleton, 1903.

DE WOLFE, ELSIE. *The House in Good Taste.* New York: Century, 1913.

EASTLAKE, CHARLES L. *Hints on Household Taste.* London: Longmans, Green, 1872.

ELLET, MRS. E. F. *The New Cyclopaedia of Domestic Economy and Practical Housekeeper.* Norwich, Conn.: Bill, 1872.

ELLIOTT, CHARLES W. *The Book of American Interiors.* Boston: Osgood, 1876.

EMBURY, AYMAR, II. *The Dutch Colonial House.* New York: McBride, Nast, 1913.

GARRETT, RHODA, and AGNES GARRETT. *Suggestions for House Decoration.* Philadelphia: Porter and Coates, 1880.

HARRISON, CONSTANCE CARY. *Woman's Handiwork in Modern Houses.* New York: Scribners, 1881.

HOLLY, HENRY HUDSON. *Holly's Country Seats.* New York: Appleton, 1866.

————. *Modern Dwellings in Town and Country.* New York: Harper, 1878.

HOOPER, CHARLES EDWARD. *Reclaiming the Old House.* New York: McBride, Nast, 1913.

JACKSON, ALLEN W. *The Half Timber House.* New York: McBride, Nast, 1912.

LOUDON, J. C. *An Encyclopaedia of Cottage, Farm, and Villa Architecture and Furniture.* London: Longman, Brown, Green, and Longmans, 1842.

MASURY, JOHN W. *House Painting, Carriage Painting, and Graining: What to Do, and How to Do It.* New York: Appleton, 1891.

NORTHEND, MARY H. *Colonial Homes and Their Furnishings.* Boston: Little, Brown, 1912.

————. *Remodeled Farmhouses.* Boston: Little, Brown, 1915.

PARKES, FRANCES BYERLY. *Domestic Duties.* London: Longman, Hurst, Rees, Brown, and Green, 1825.

ROBERTS, ROBERT. *The House Servant's Directory.* Boston: Munroe and Francis, 1827; reissued Waltham, Mass.: Gore Place Society, 1977.

SAYLOR, HENRY. *Bungalows.* New York: McBride, Winston, 1911.

SHERWIN-WILLIAMS COMPANY. *Your Home and Its Decoration.* N.p.: Sherwin-Williams, 1910.

SPOFFORD, HARRIET PRESCOTT. *Art Decoration Applied to Furniture.* New York: Harper, 1878.

STICKLEY, GUSTAV. *Craftsman Homes.* New York: Craftsman Publishing, 1900.

STURGIS, RUSSELL, *et al. Homes in City and Country.* New York: Scribners, 1893.

THROOP, LUCY ABBOT. *Furnishing the Home of Good Taste.* New York: McBride, Nast, 1912.

VAUX, CALVERT. *Villas and Cottages.* New York: Harper, 1864.

WALLICK, EKIN. *The Attractive Home.* Boston: Carpenter, Morton, 1916.

————. *The Small House for a Moderate Income.* New York: Hearst's International Library, 1915.

WALLIS, FRANK E. *American Architecture, Decoration, and Furniture of the Eighteenth Century.* New York: Wenzel, 1896.

————. *Old Colonial Architecture and Furniture.* Boston: Polley, 1887.

WEBSTER, THOMAS, and FRANCES B. PARKES. *Encyclopaedia of Domestic Economy.* New York: Harper, 1845.

WHARTON, EDITH, and OGDEN CODMAN, JR. *The Decoration of Houses.* New York: Scribners, 1897.

WHEELER, CANDACE. *Principles of Home Decoration.* New York: Doubleday, 1903.

WHEELER, GERVASE. *Homes for the People.* New York: Woodward, 1867.

————. *Rural Homes.* New York: Scribners, 1852.

WILLIAMS, HENRY T., and MRS. C. S. JONES. *Beautiful Homes.* New York: Williams, 1878.

Index

Italicized entries indicate illustrations.